CASE CLOSED™

VOLUME 59

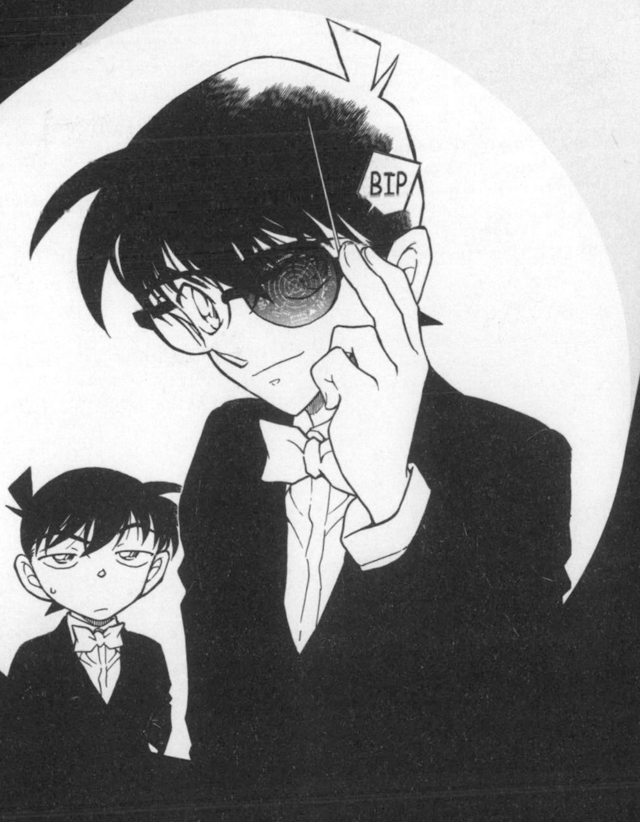
BIP

Gosho Aoyama

Case Briefing:

Subject:
Occupation:
Special Skills:
Equipment:

Jimmy Kudo, a.k.a. Conan Edogawa
High School Student/Detective
Analytical thinking and deductive reasoning, Soccer
Bow Tie Voice Transmitter, Super Sneakers,
Homing Glasses, Stretchy Suspenders

The subject is hot on the trail of a pair of suspicious men in black when he is attacked from behind and administered a strange substance which physically transforms him into a first grader. When the subject confides in the eccentric inventor Dr. Agasa, they decide to keep the subject's true identity a secret for the safety of everyone around him. Assuming the new identity of first-grader Conan Edogawa, the subject continues to assist the police force on their most baffling cases. The only problem is that most crime-solving professionals won't take a little kid's advice!

Table of Contents

CASE CLOSED!

CONFIDEN

CASE CLOSED
Volume 59
Shonen Sunday Edition

Story and Art by GOSHO AOYAMA

MEITANTEI CONAN Vol. 59
by Gosho AOYAMA
© 1994 Gosho AOYAMA
All rights reserved.
Original Japanese edition published by SHOGAKUKAN.
English translation rights in the United States of America, Canada,
the United Kingdom and Ireland arranged with SHOGAKUKAN.

Translation
Tetsuichiro Miyaki

Touch-up & Lettering
Freeman Wong

Cover & Graphic Design
Andrea Rice

Editor
Shaenon K. Garrity

Printed in the U.S.A.

Published by VIZ Media, LLC
P.O. Box 77010
San Francisco, CA 94107

10 9 8 7 6 5 4 3 2 1
First printing, July 2016

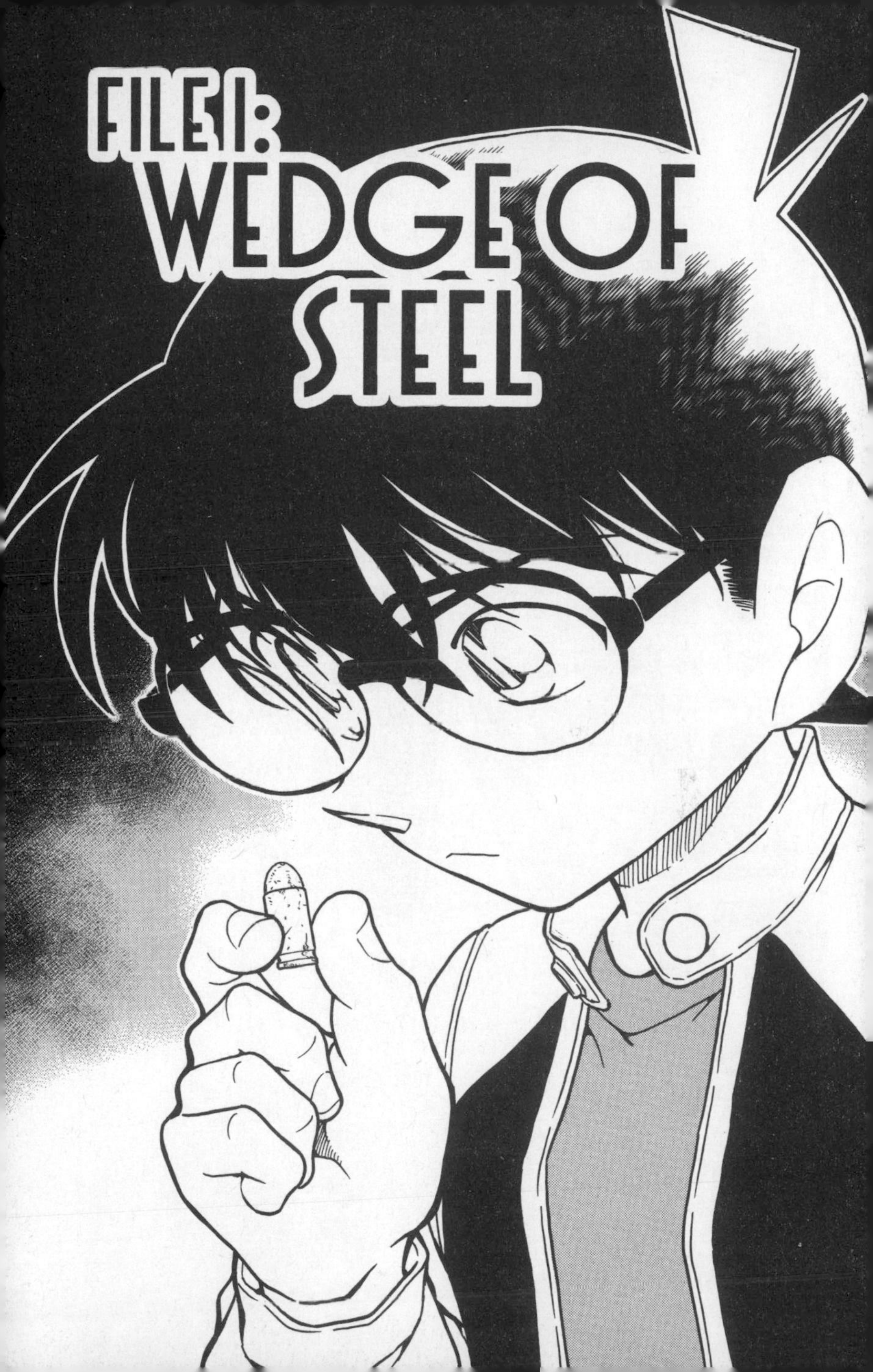
FILE 1:
WEDGE OF STEEL

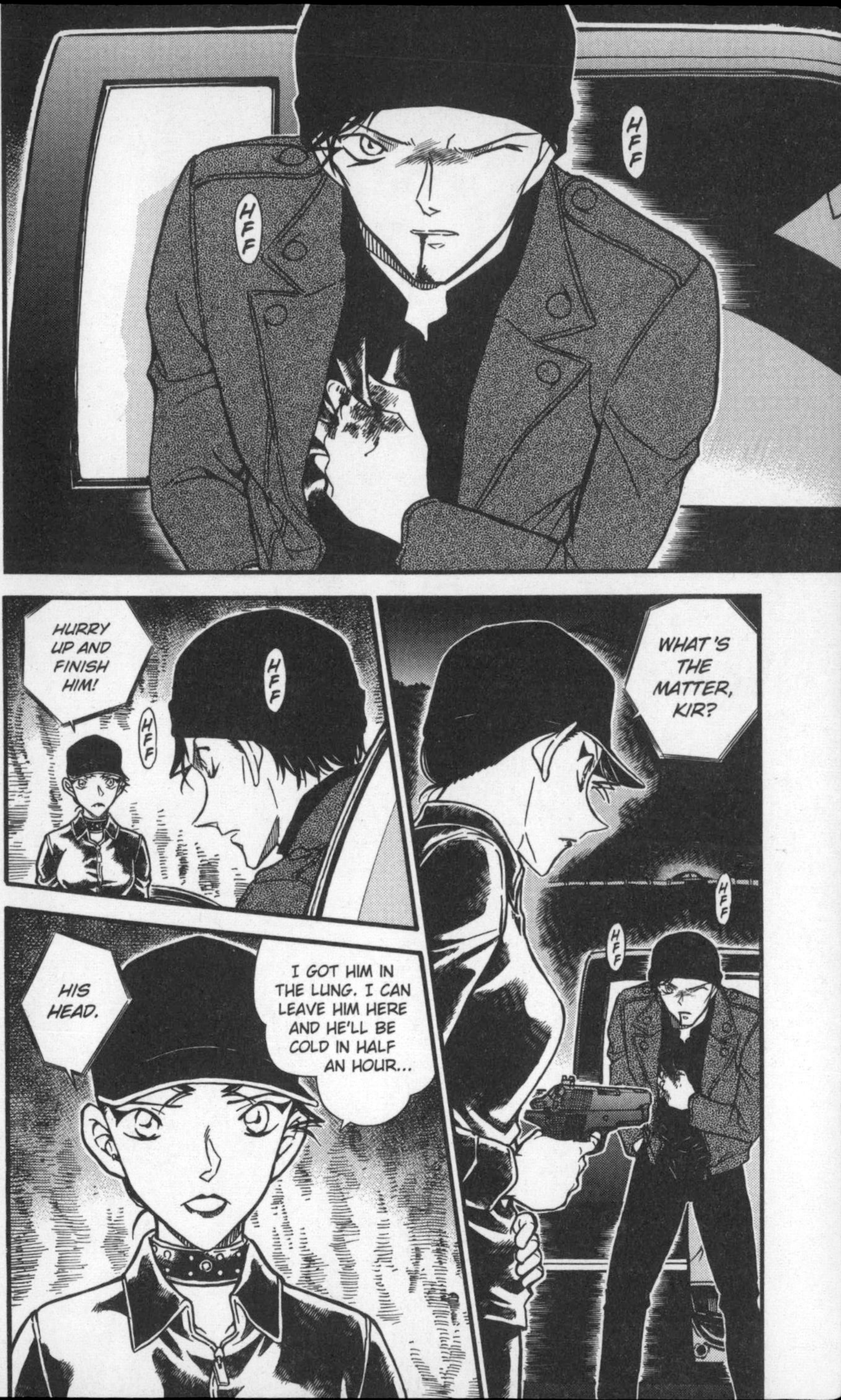
HFF
HFF
WHAT'S THE MATTER, KIR?
HFF
HFF
HFF
HFF
HURRY UP AND FINISH HIM!
I GOT HIM IN THE LUNG. I CAN LEAVE HIM HERE AND HE'LL BE COLD IN HALF AN HOUR...
HIS HEAD.

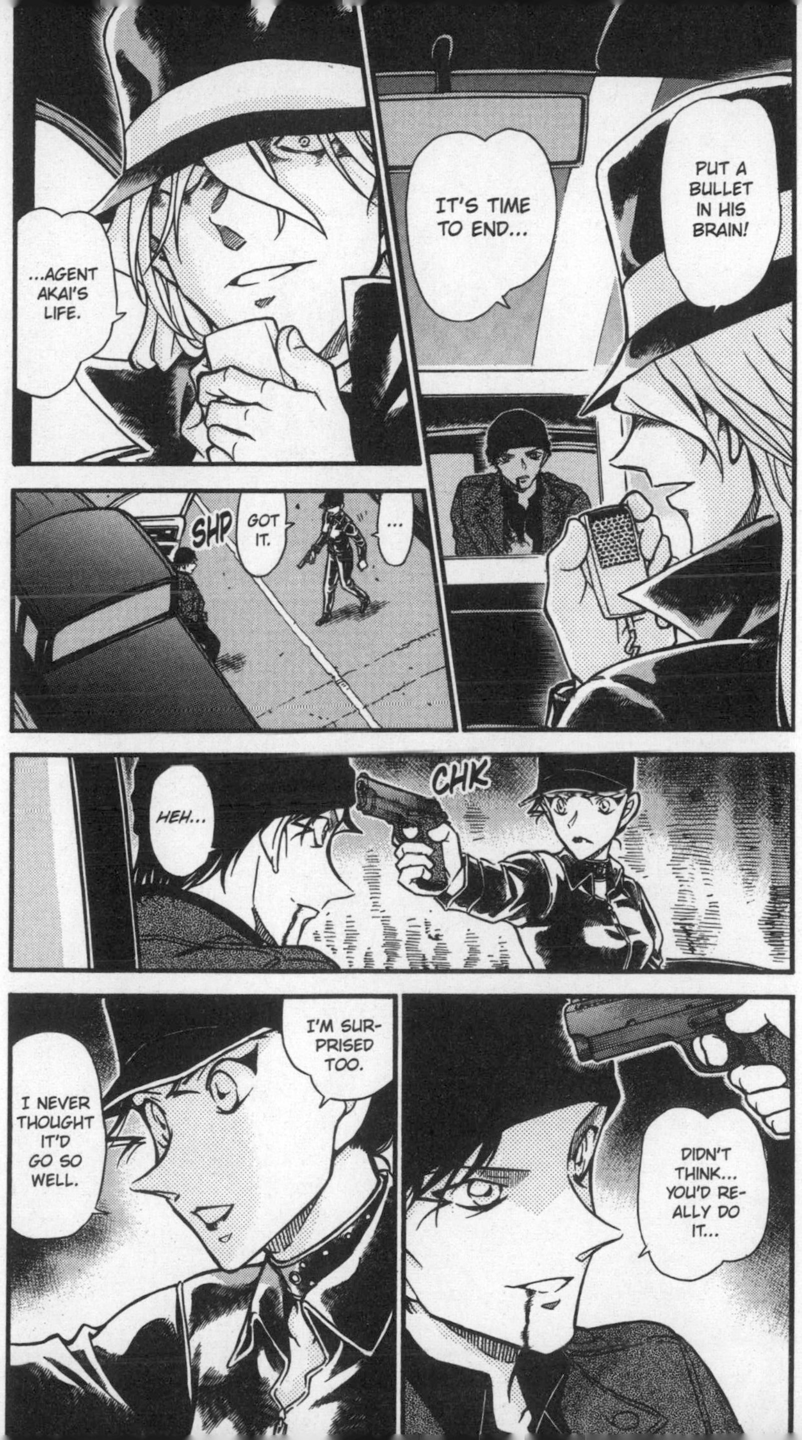
PUT A BULLET IN HIS BRAIN!
IT'S TIME TO END...
...AGENT AKAI'S LIFE.
...
GOT IT.
SHP
CHK
HEH...
DIDN'T THINK... YOU'D RE-ALLY DO IT...
I'M SUR-PRISED TOO.
I NEVER THOUGHT IT'D GO SO WELL.

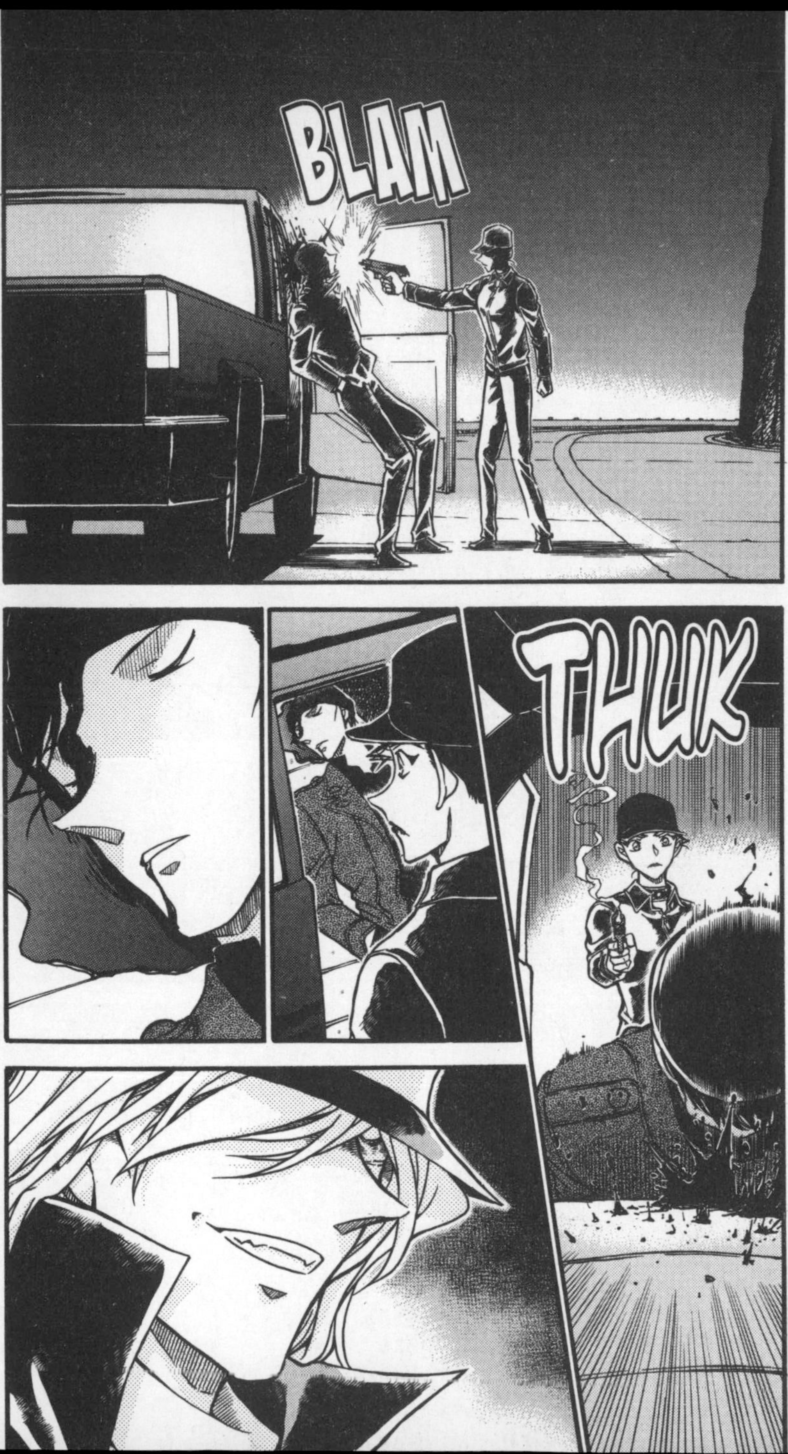
BLAM
THUK

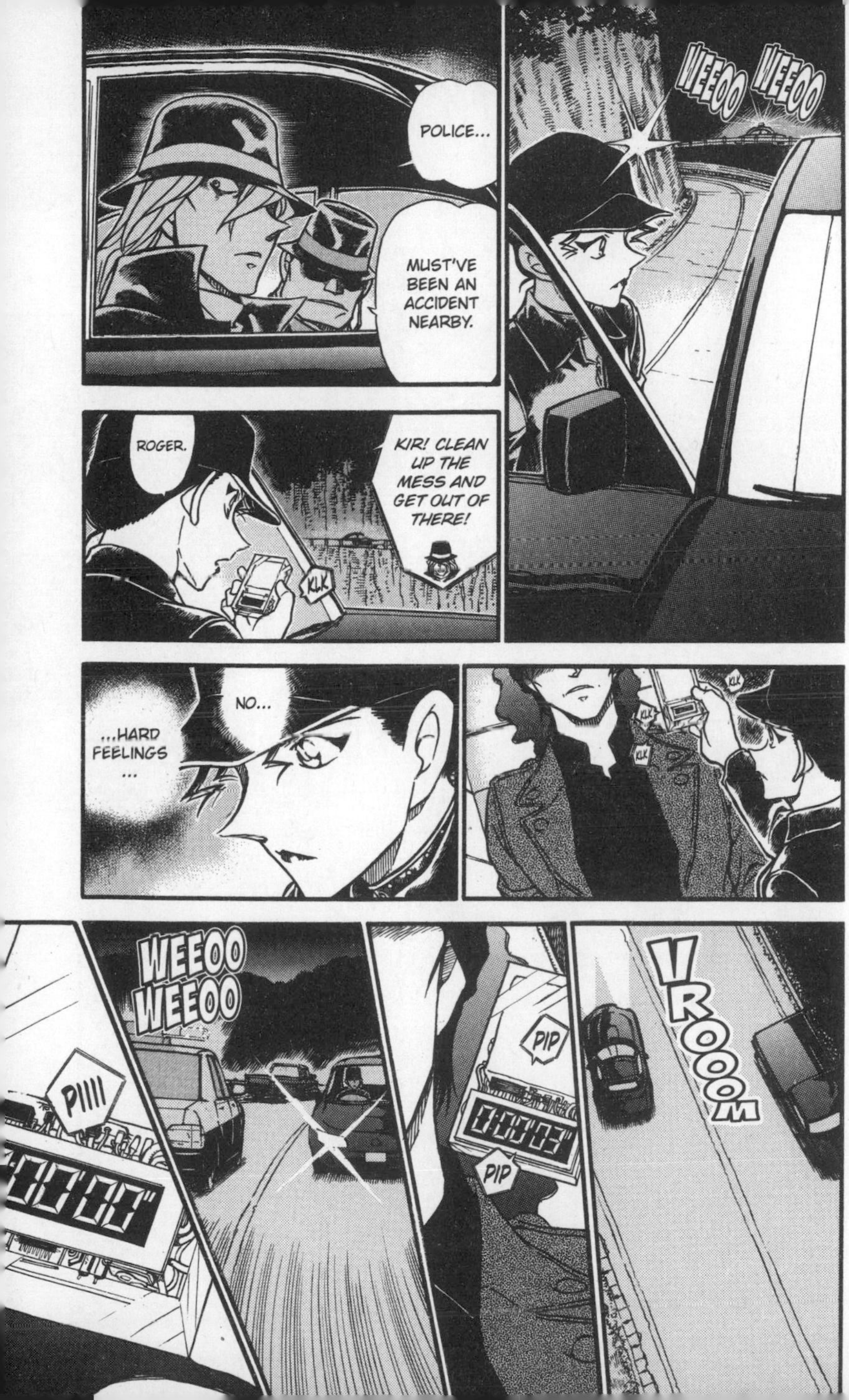
WEEOO WEEOO
POLICE...
MUST'VE BEEN AN ACCIDENT NEARBY.
KIR! CLEAN UP THE MESS AND GET OUT OF THERE!
ROGER.
KLK
KLK
KLK
KLK
NO...
...HARD FEELINGS ...
VROOOM
PIP
PIP
WEEOO WEEOO
PIIII

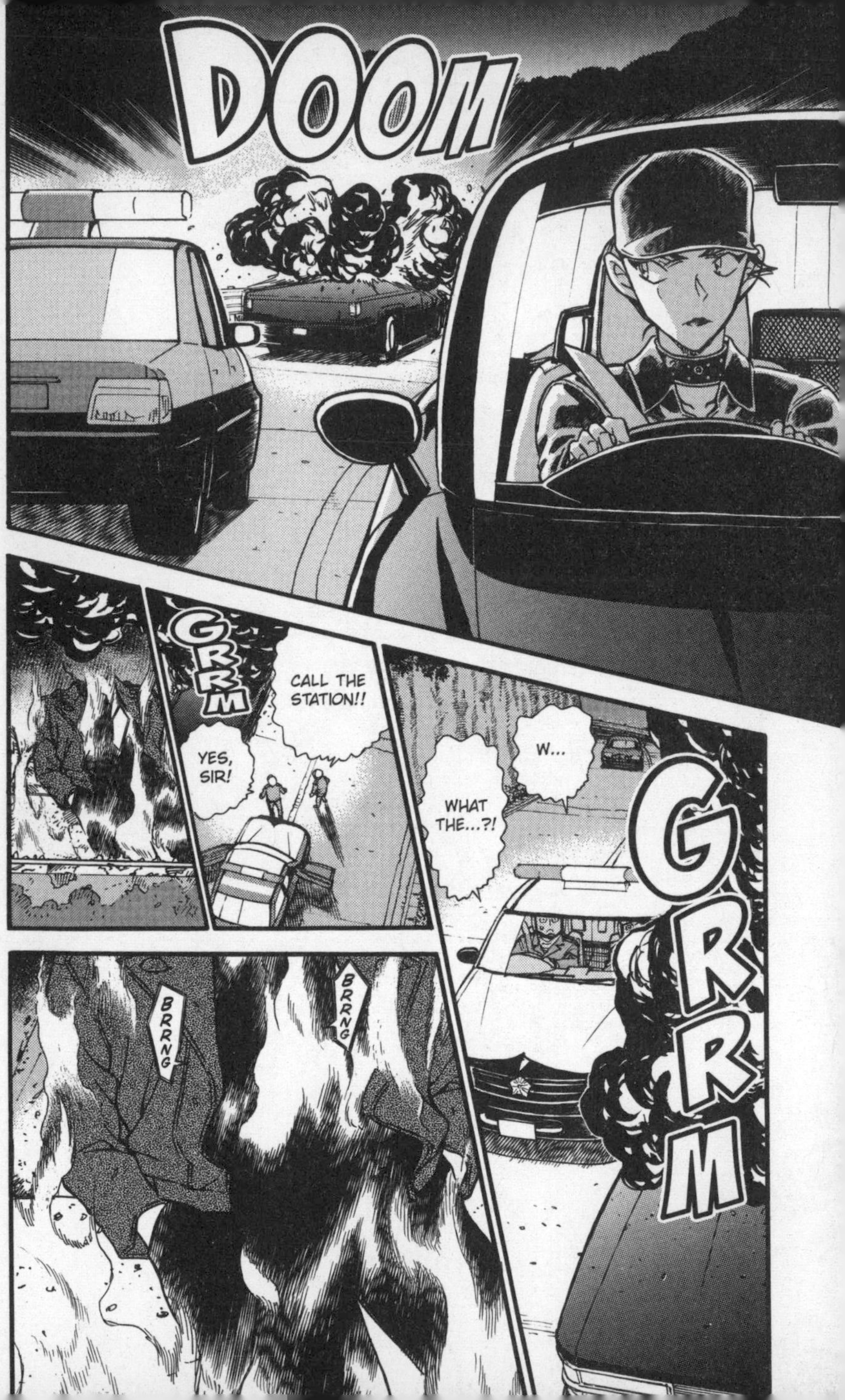
DOOM
W...
WHAT THE...?!
GRRRM
GRRM
CALL THE STATION!!
YES, SIR!
BRRNG
BRRNG

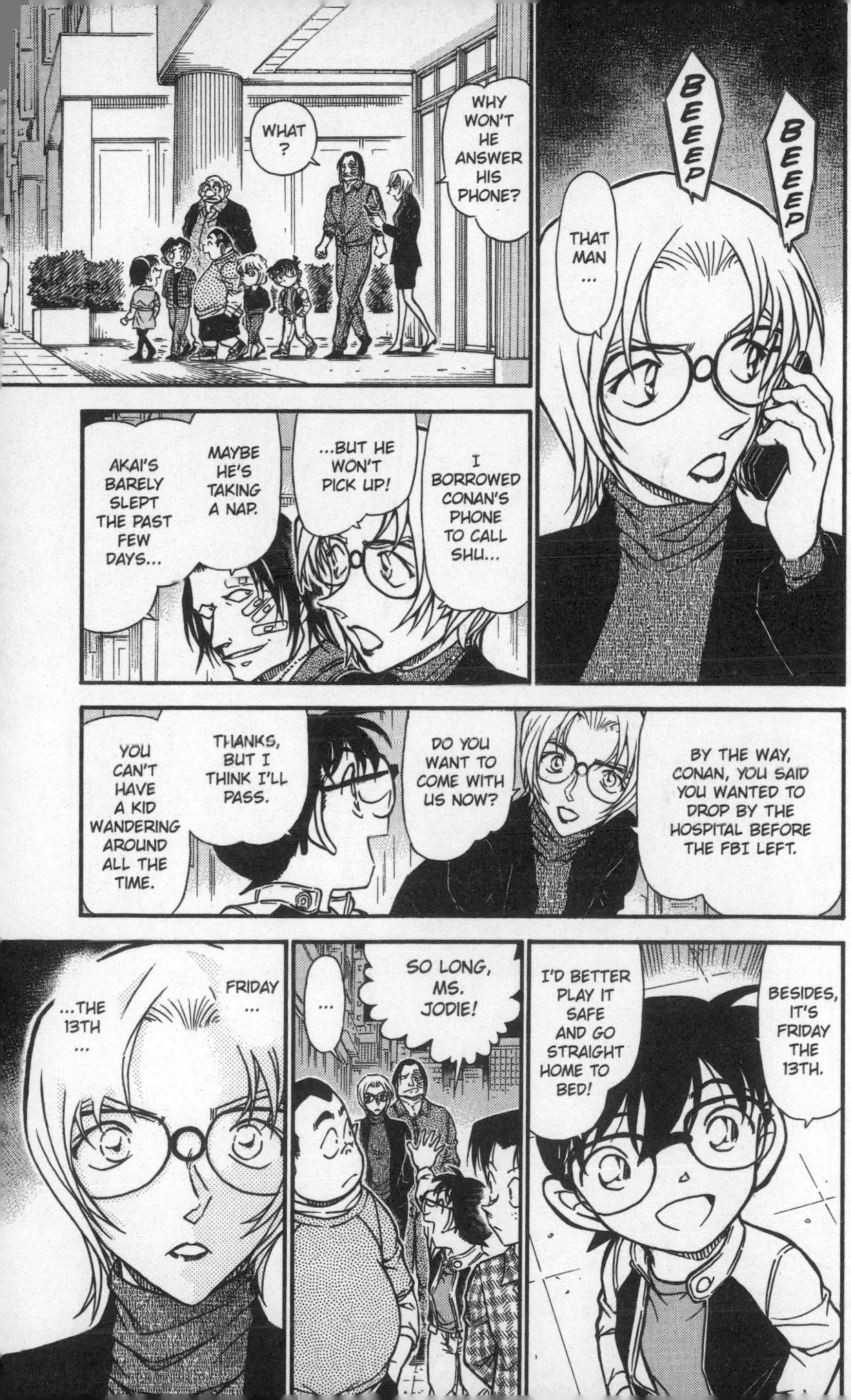
BEEEP
BEEEP
THAT MAN...
WHY WON'T HE ANSWER HIS PHONE?
WHAT?
I BORROWED CONAN'S PHONE TO CALL SHU...
...BUT HE WON'T PICK UP!
MAYBE HE'S TAKING A NAP.
AKAI'S BARELY SLEPT THE PAST FEW DAYS...
BY THE WAY, CONAN, YOU SAID YOU WANTED TO DROP BY THE HOSPITAL BEFORE THE FBI LEFT.
DO YOU WANT TO COME WITH US NOW?
THANKS, BUT I THINK I'LL PASS.
YOU CAN'T HAVE A KID WANDERING AROUND ALL THE TIME.
BESIDES, IT'S FRIDAY THE 13TH.
I'D BETTER PLAY IT SAFE AND GO STRAIGHT HOME TO BED!
SO LONG, MS. JODIE!
...
FRIDAY...
...THE 13TH...

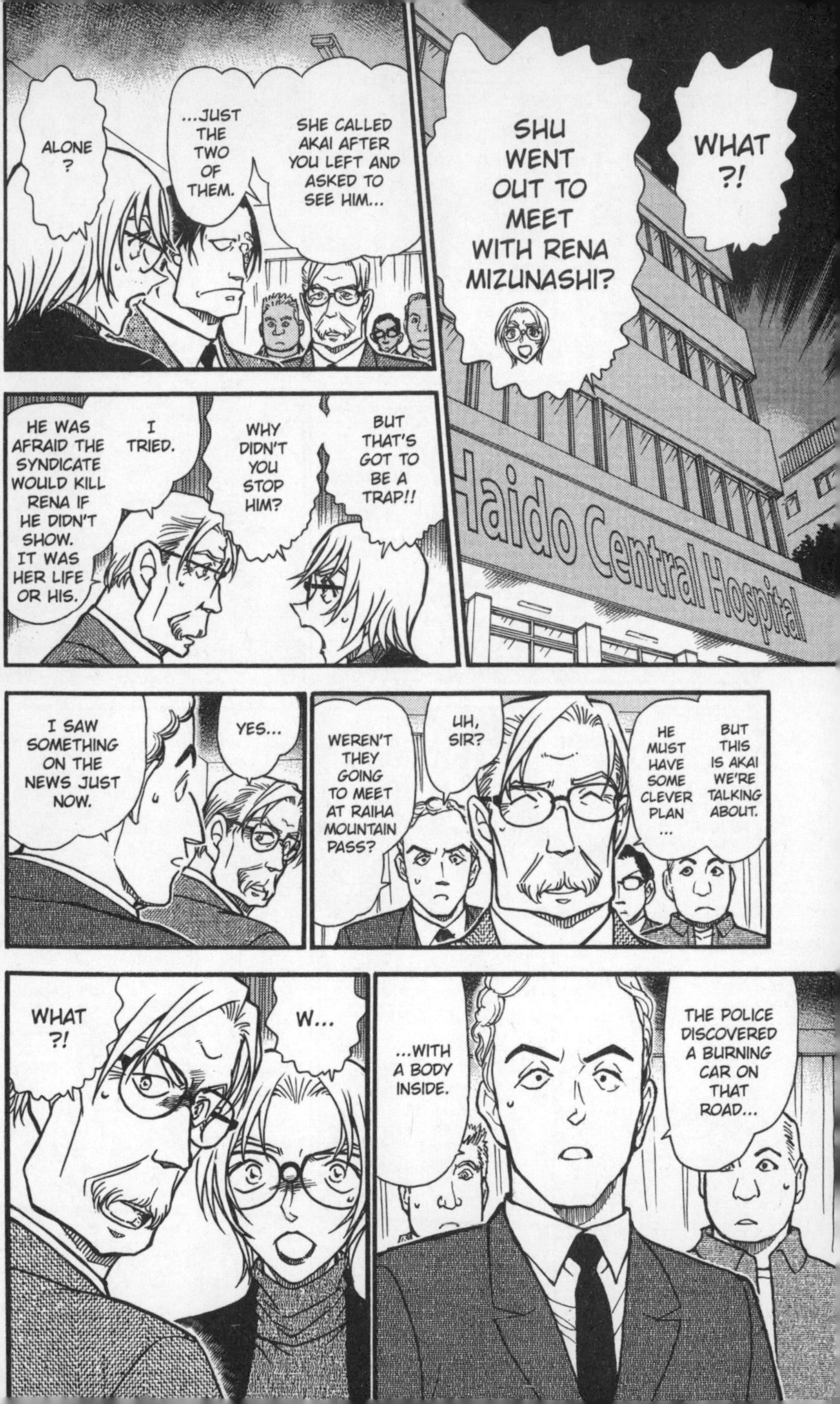
WHAT ?!
SHU WENT OUT TO MEET WITH RENA MIZUNASHI?
Haido Central Hospital
SHE CALLED AKAI AFTER YOU LEFT AND ASKED TO SEE HIM...
...JUST THE TWO OF THEM.
ALONE ?
BUT THAT'S GOT TO BE A TRAP!!
WHY DIDN'T YOU STOP HIM?
I TRIED.
HE WAS AFRAID THE SYNDICATE WOULD KILL RENA IF HE DIDN'T SHOW. IT WAS HER LIFE OR HIS.
BUT THIS IS AKAI WE'RE TALKING ABOUT.
HE MUST HAVE SOME CLEVER PLAN ...
UH, SIR?
WEREN'T THEY GOING TO MEET AT RAIHA MOUNTAIN PASS?
YES...
I SAW SOMETHING ON THE NEWS JUST NOW.
THE POLICE DISCOVERED A BURNING CAR ON THAT ROAD...
...WITH A BODY INSIDE.
W...
WHAT ?!

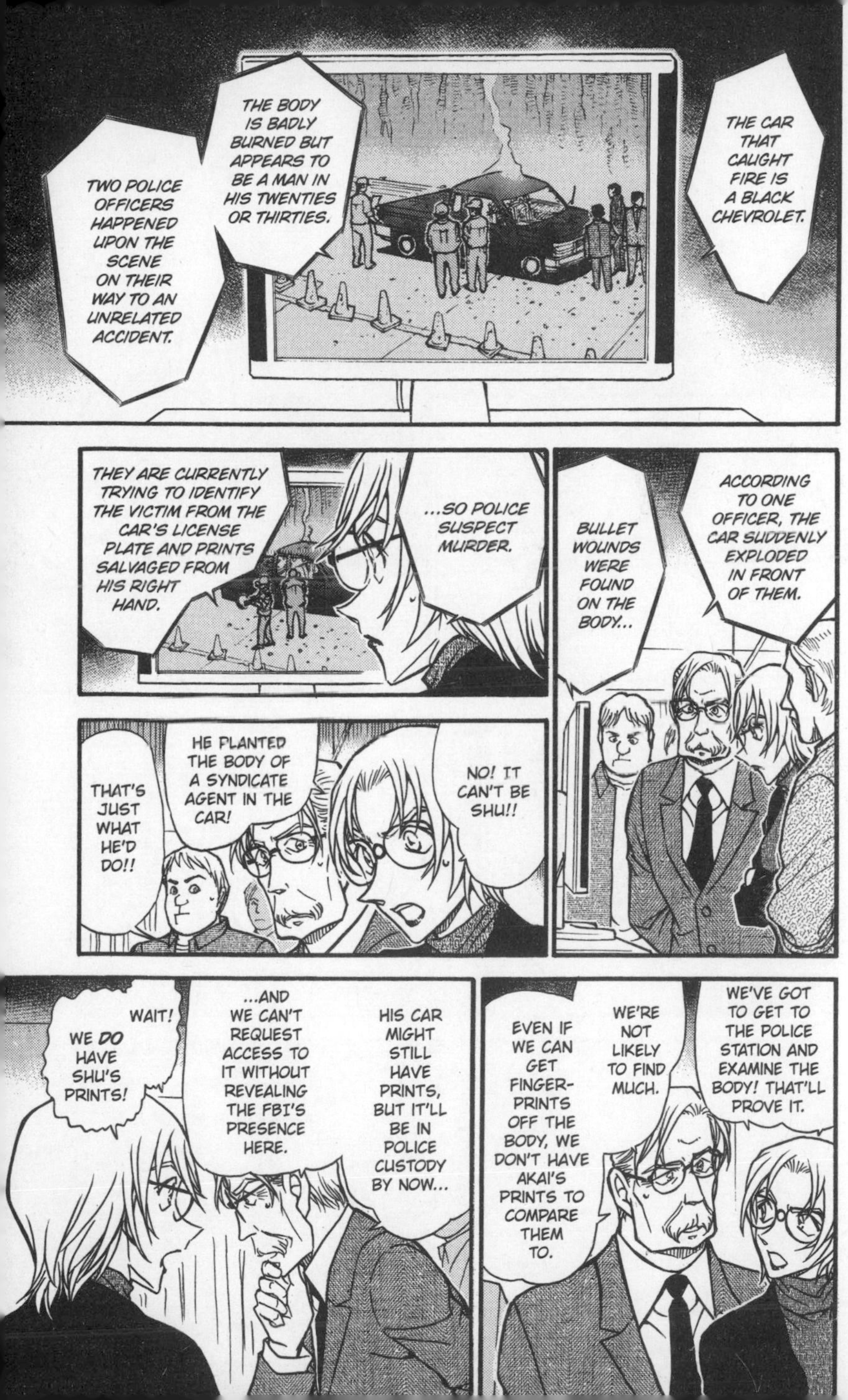
THE CAR THAT CAUGHT FIRE IS A BLACK CHEVROLET.
THE BODY IS BADLY BURNED BUT APPEARS TO BE A MAN IN HIS TWENTIES OR THIRTIES.
TWO POLICE OFFICERS HAPPENED UPON THE SCENE ON THEIR WAY TO AN UNRELATED ACCIDENT.
ACCORDING TO ONE OFFICER, THE CAR SUDDENLY EXPLODED IN FRONT OF THEM.
BULLET WOUNDS WERE FOUND ON THE BODY...
...SO POLICE SUSPECT MURDER.
THEY ARE CURRENTLY TRYING TO IDENTIFY THE VICTIM FROM THE CAR'S LICENSE PLATE AND PRINTS SALVAGED FROM HIS RIGHT HAND.
NO! IT CAN'T BE SHU!!
HE PLANTED THE BODY OF A SYNDICATE AGENT IN THE CAR!
THAT'S JUST WHAT HE'D DO!!
WE'VE GOT TO GET TO THE POLICE STATION AND EXAMINE THE BODY! THAT'LL PROVE IT.
WE'RE NOT LIKELY TO FIND MUCH.
EVEN IF WE CAN GET FINGER-PRINTS OFF THE BODY, WE DON'T HAVE AKAI'S PRINTS TO COMPARE THEM TO.
HIS CAR MIGHT STILL HAVE PRINTS, BUT IT'LL BE IN POLICE CUSTODY BY NOW...
...AND WE CAN'T REQUEST ACCESS TO IT WITHOUT REVEALING THE FBI'S PRESENCE HERE.
WAIT!
WE DO HAVE SHU'S PRINTS!

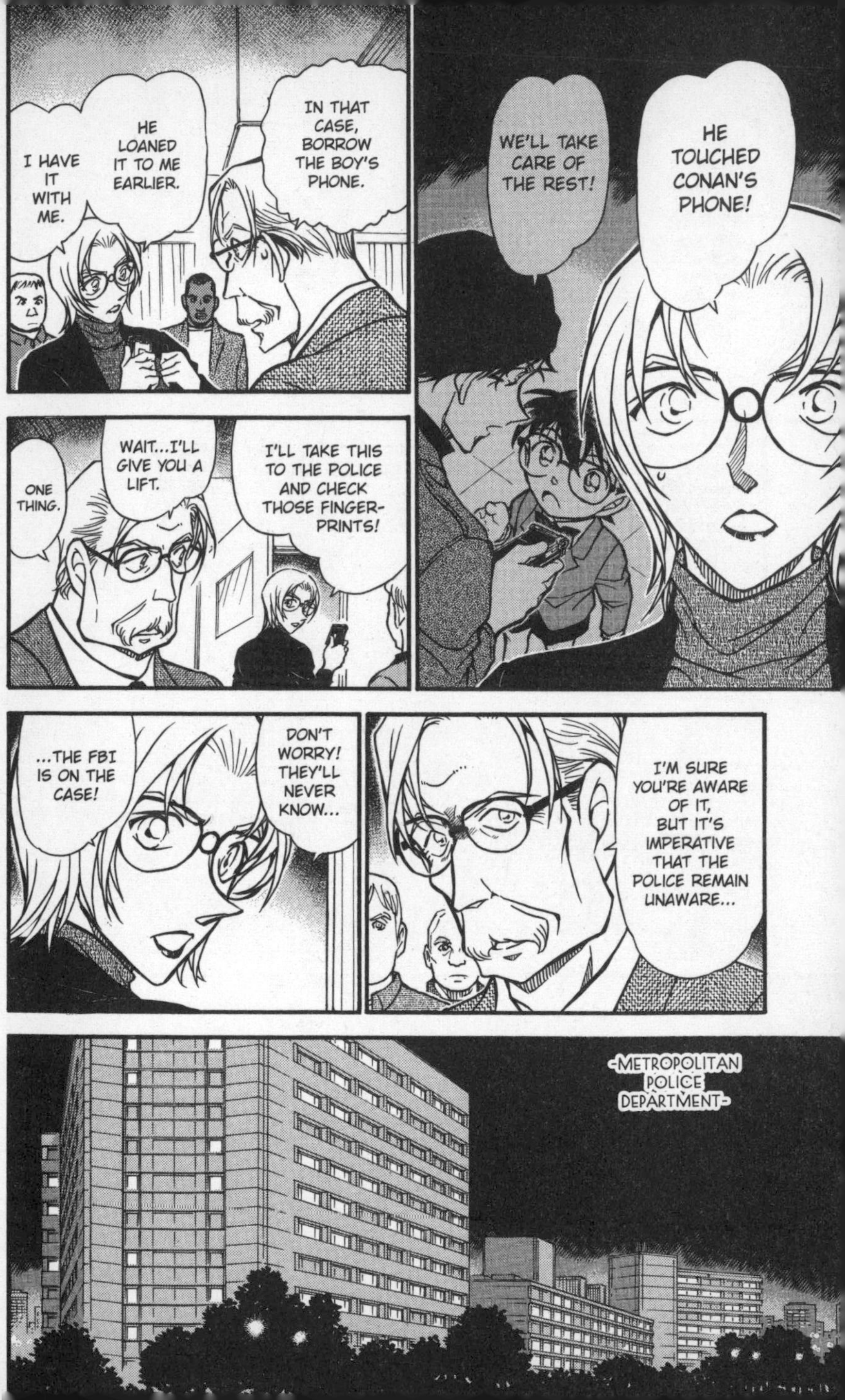
HE TOUCHED CONAN'S PHONE!
WE'LL TAKE CARE OF THE REST!
IN THAT CASE, BORROW THE BOY'S PHONE.
HE LOANED IT TO ME EARLIER.
I HAVE IT WITH ME.
I'LL TAKE THIS TO THE POLICE AND CHECK THOSE FINGER-PRINTS!
WAIT...I'LL GIVE YOU A LIFT.
ONE THING.
I'M SURE YOU'RE AWARE OF IT, BUT IT'S IMPERATIVE THAT THE POLICE REMAIN UNAWARE...
DON'T WORRY! THEY'LL NEVER KNOW...
...THE FBI IS ON THE CASE!
-METROPOLITAN POLICE DEPARTMENT-

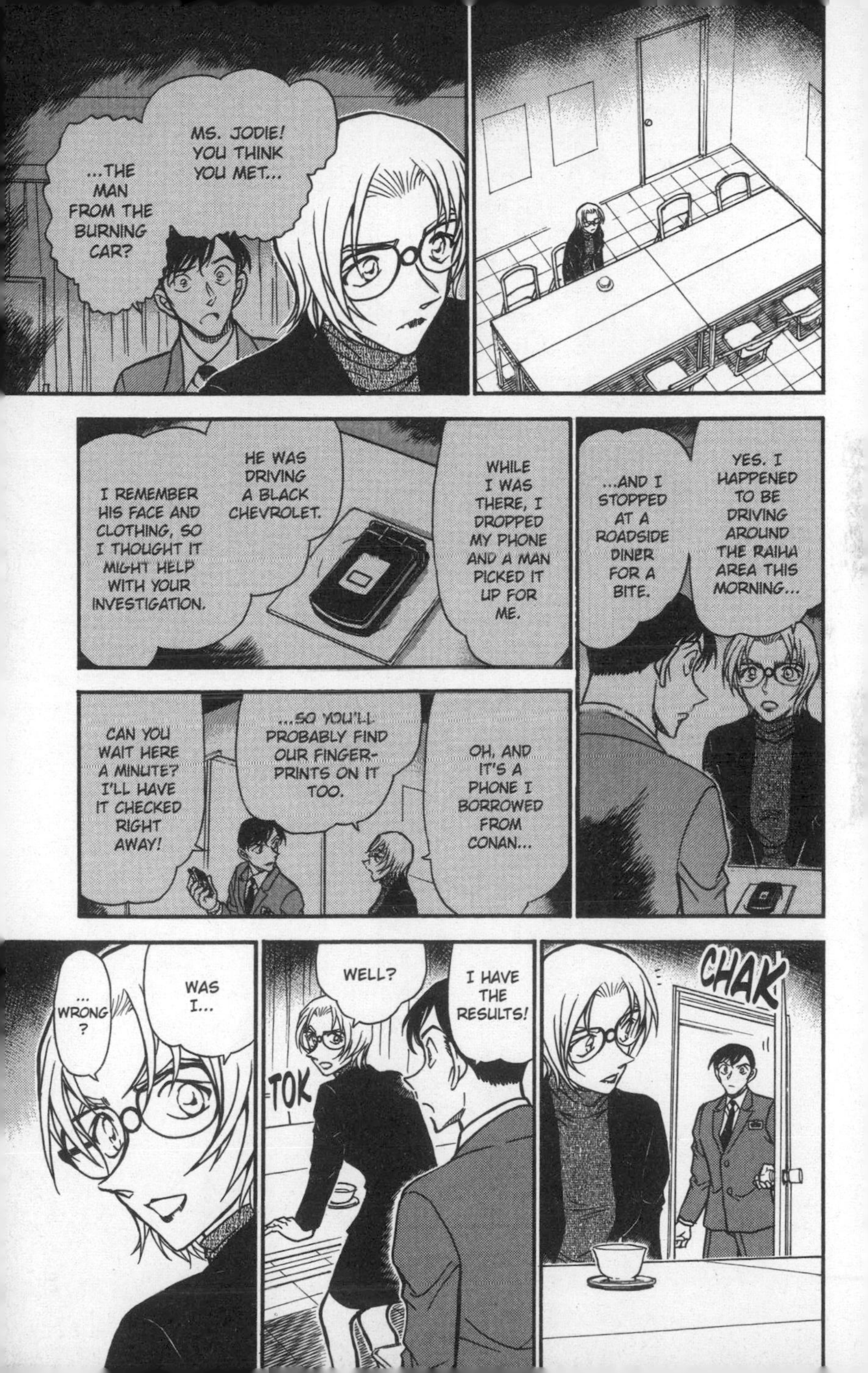
MS. JODIE! YOU THINK YOU MET...
...THE MAN FROM THE BURNING CAR?
YES. I HAPPENED TO BE DRIVING AROUND THE RAIHA AREA THIS MORNING...
...AND I STOPPED AT A ROADSIDE DINER FOR A BITE.
WHILE I WAS THERE, I DROPPED MY PHONE AND A MAN PICKED IT UP FOR ME.
HE WAS DRIVING A BLACK CHEVROLET.
I REMEMBER HIS FACE AND CLOTHING, SO I THOUGHT IT MIGHT HELP WITH YOUR INVESTIGATION.
OH, AND IT'S A PHONE I BORROWED FROM CONAN...
...SO YOU'LL PROBABLY FIND OUR FINGER-PRINTS ON IT TOO.
CAN YOU WAIT HERE A MINUTE? I'LL HAVE IT CHECKED RIGHT AWAY!
CHAK
I HAVE THE RESULTS!
WELL?
TOK
WAS I...
...WRONG?

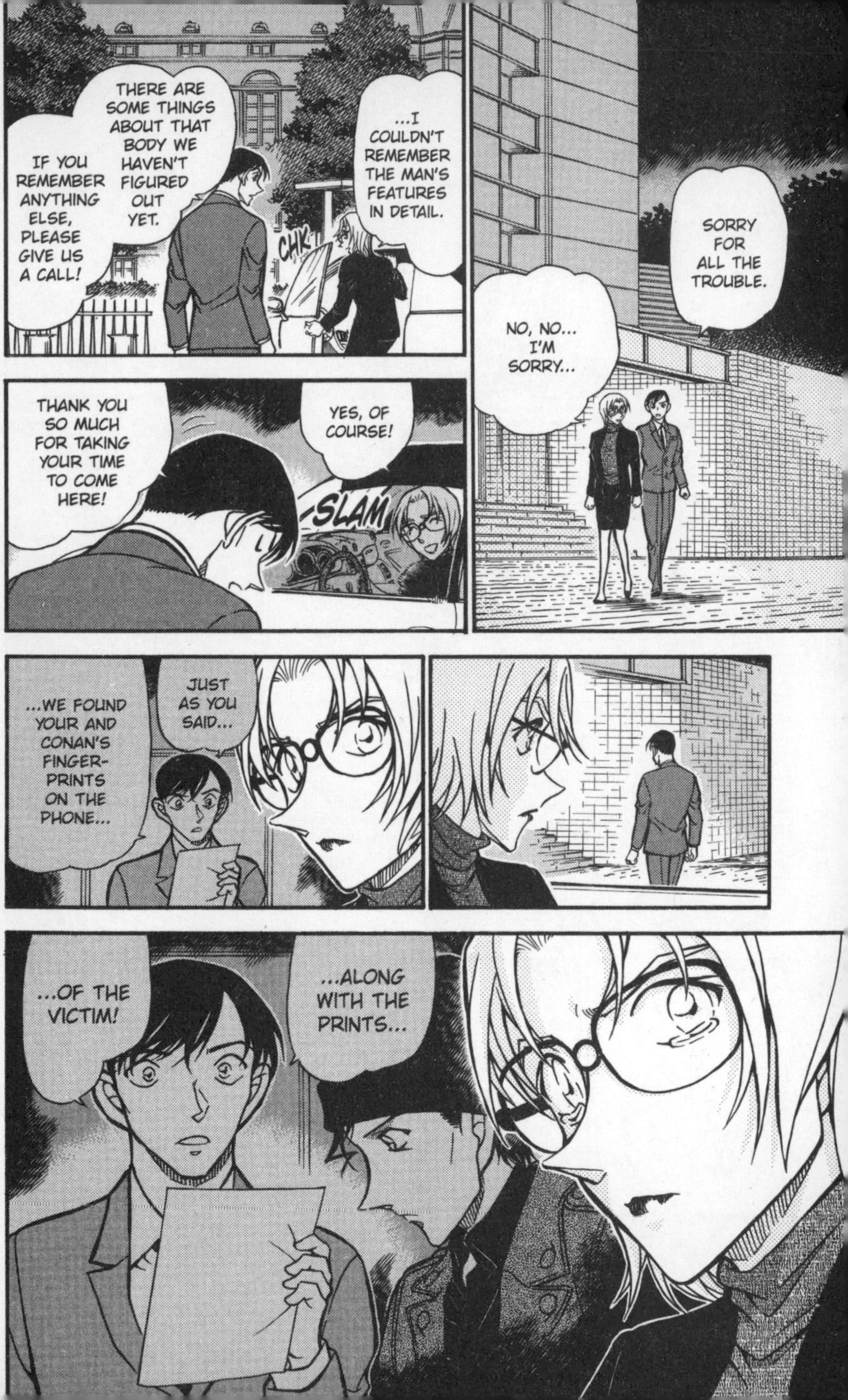
SORRY FOR ALL THE TROUBLE.
NO, NO... I'M SORRY...
...I COULDN'T REMEMBER THE MAN'S FEATURES IN DETAIL.
CHK
THERE ARE SOME THINGS ABOUT THAT BODY WE HAVEN'T FIGURED OUT YET.
IF YOU REMEMBER ANYTHING ELSE, PLEASE GIVE US A CALL!
YES, OF COURSE!
SLAM
THANK YOU SO MUCH FOR TAKING YOUR TIME TO COME HERE!
JUST AS YOU SAID...
...WE FOUND YOUR AND CONAN'S FINGER-PRINTS ON THE PHONE...
...ALONG WITH THE PRINTS...
...OF THE VICTIM!

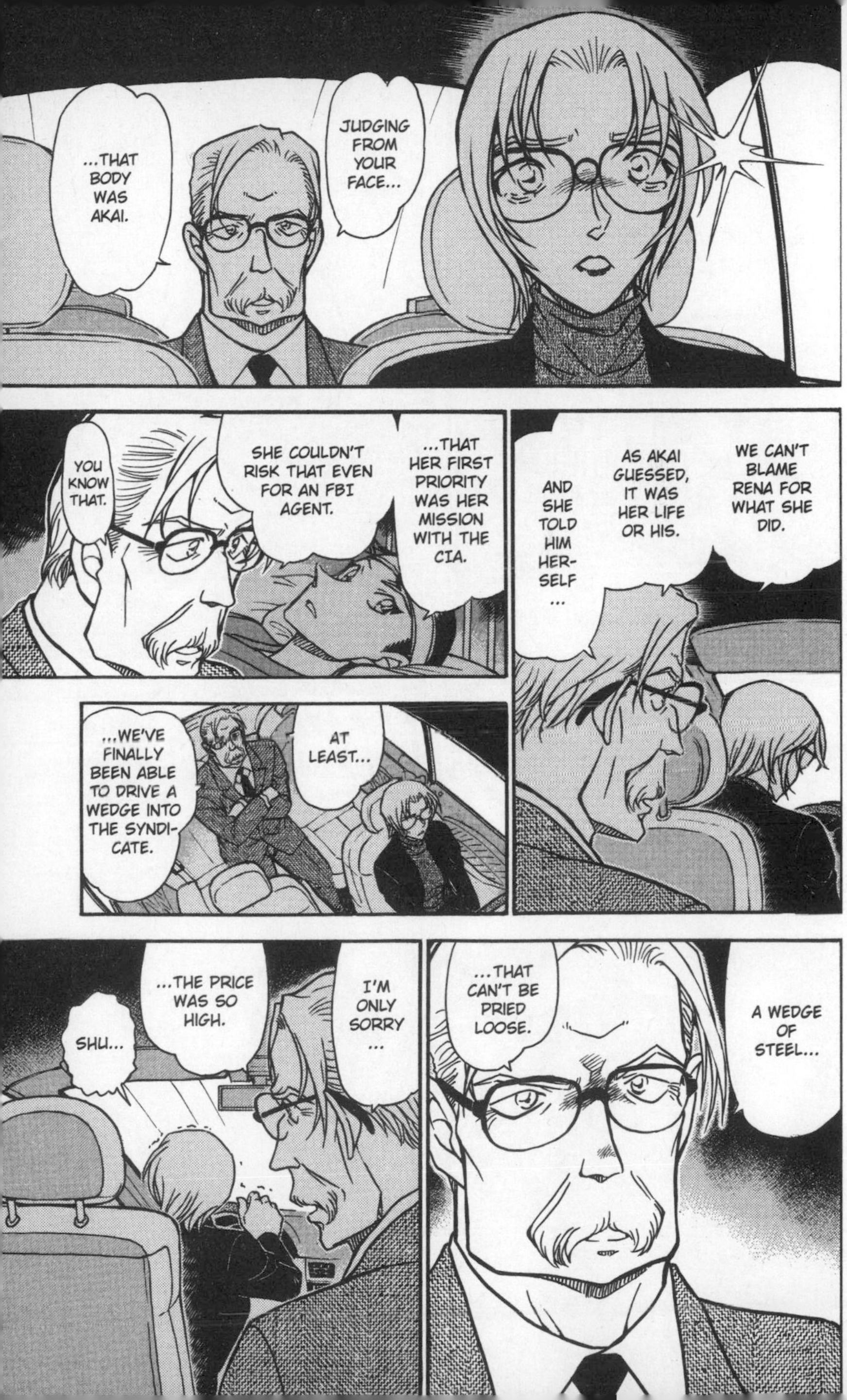
JUDGING FROM YOUR FACE...
...THAT BODY WAS AKAI.
WE CAN'T BLAME RENA FOR WHAT SHE DID.
AS AKAI GUESSED, IT WAS HER LIFE OR HIS.
AND SHE TOLD HIM HER-SELF...
...THAT HER FIRST PRIORITY WAS HER MISSION WITH THE CIA.
SHE COULDN'T RISK THAT EVEN FOR AN FBI AGENT.
YOU KNOW THAT.
AT LEAST...
...WE'VE FINALLY BEEN ABLE TO DRIVE A WEDGE INTO THE SYNDI-CATE.
A WEDGE OF STEEL...
...THAT CAN'T BE PRIED LOOSE.
I'M ONLY SORRY...
...THE PRICE WAS SO HIGH.
SHU...

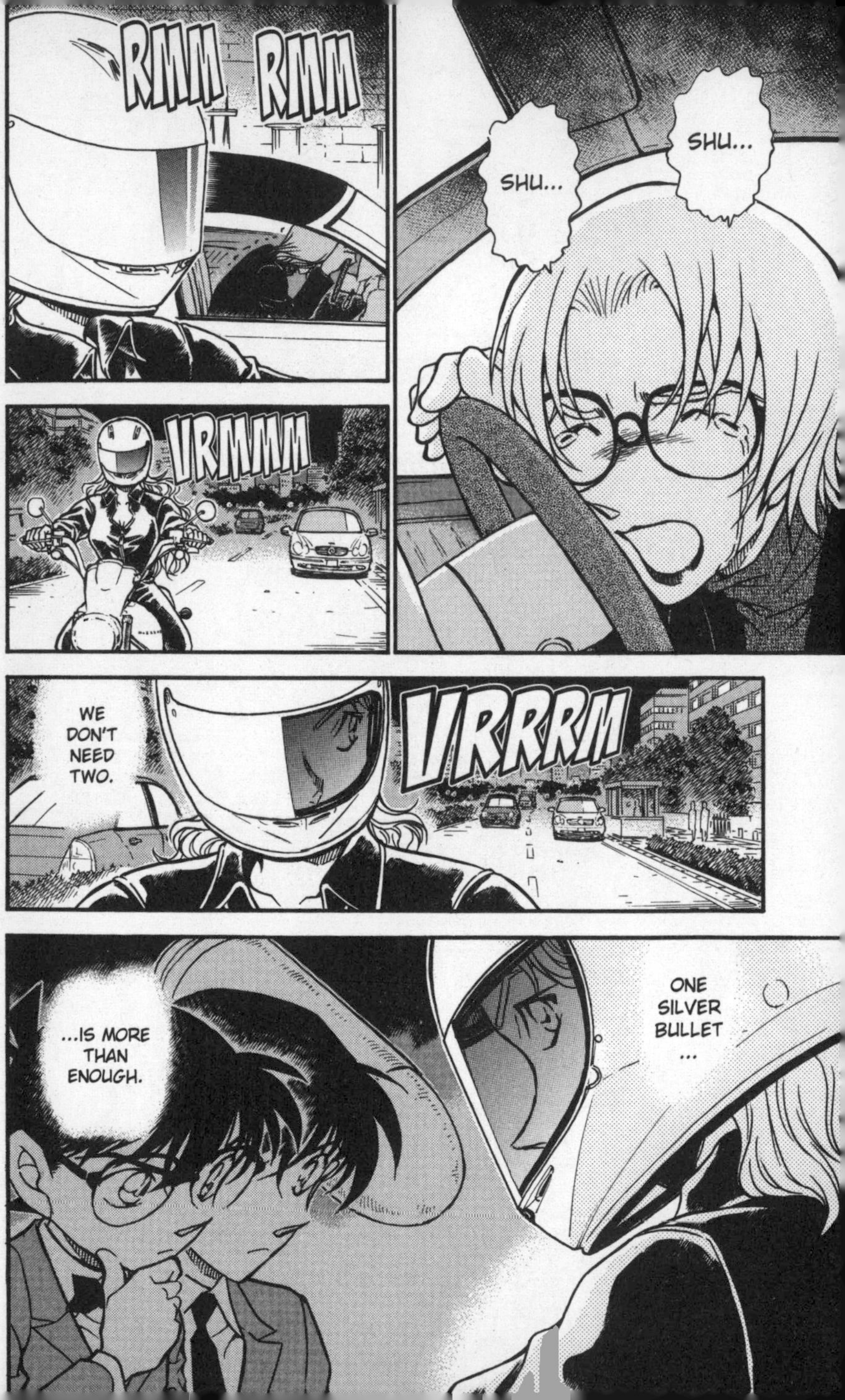
SHU...
SHU...
RMM RMM
VRMMM
VRRRM
WE DON'T NEED TWO.
ONE SILVER BULLET ...
...IS MORE THAN ENOUGH.

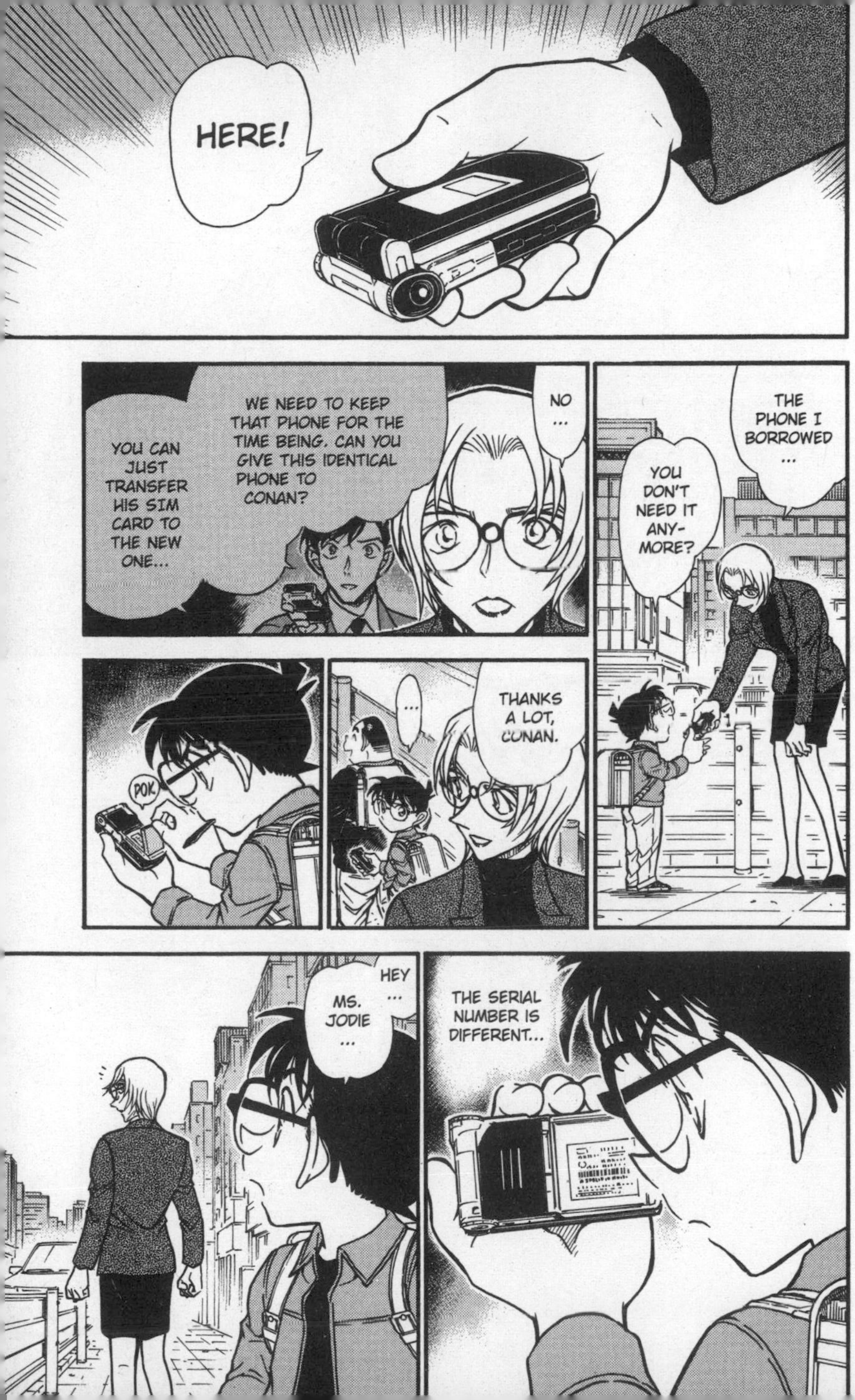
HERE!
THE PHONE I BORROWED ...
YOU DON'T NEED IT ANYMORE?
NO ...
WE NEED TO KEEP THAT PHONE FOR THE TIME BEING. CAN YOU GIVE THIS IDENTICAL PHONE TO CONAN?
YOU CAN JUST TRANSFER HIS SIM CARD TO THE NEW ONE...
THANKS A LOT, CONAN.
...
POK
THE SERIAL NUMBER IS DIFFERENT...
HEY ...
MS. JODIE ...

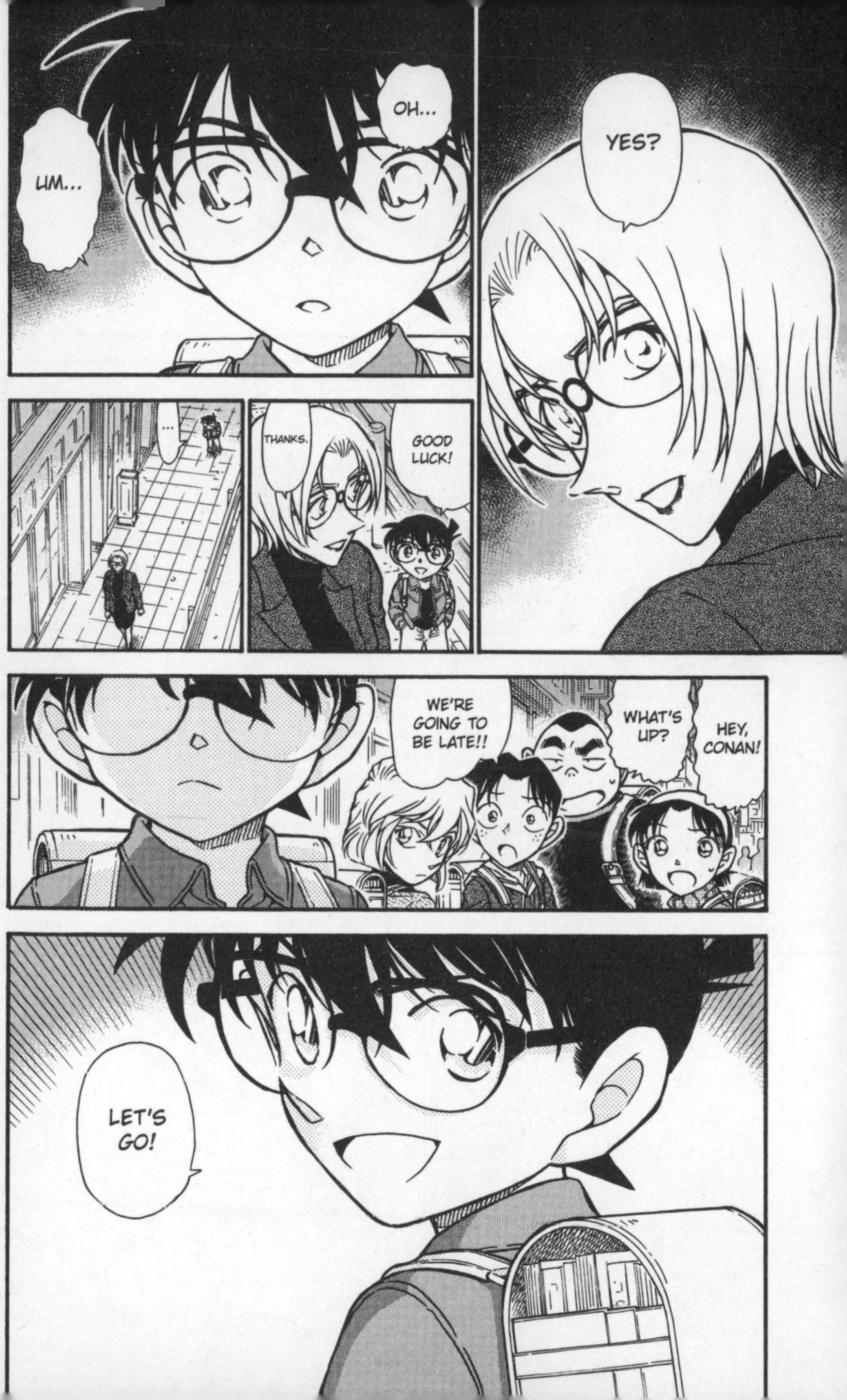
YES?
OH...
UM...
GOOD LUCK!
THANKS.
...
HEY, CONAN!
WHAT'S UP?
WE'RE GOING TO BE LATE!!
LET'S GO!

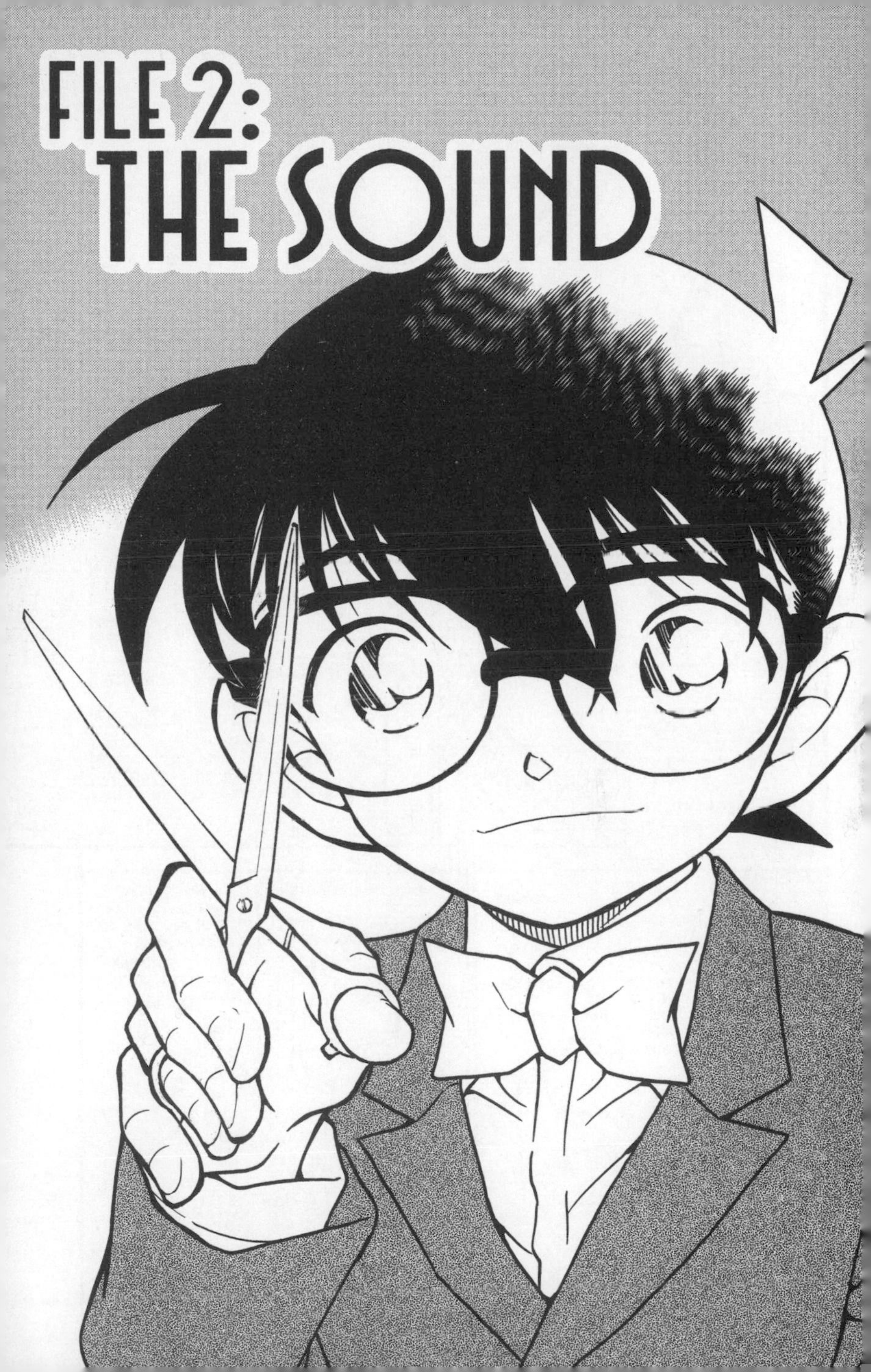
FILE 2:
THE SOUND

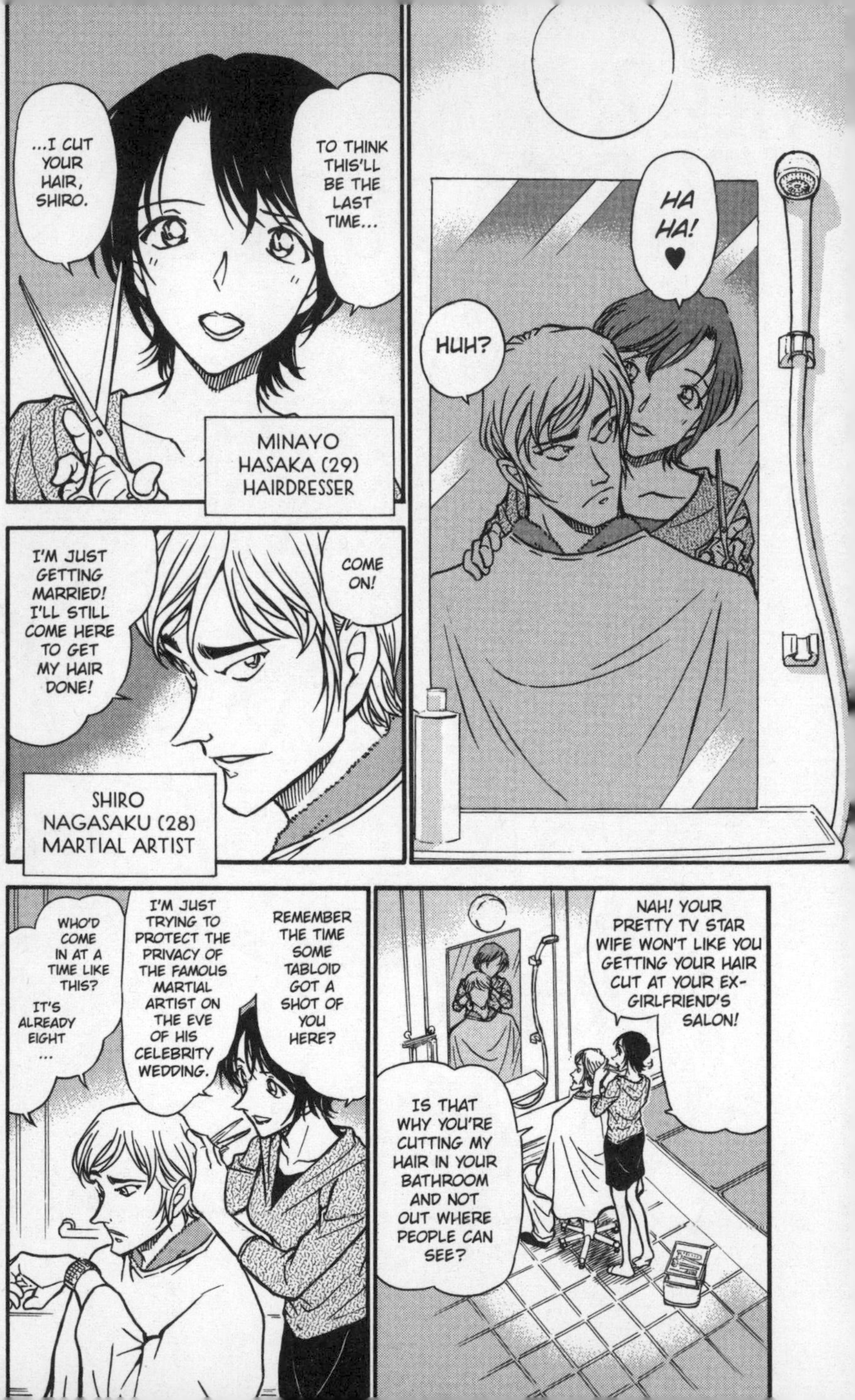
HA HA! ♥
HUH?
TO THINK THIS'LL BE THE LAST TIME...
...I CUT YOUR HAIR, SHIRO.
MINAYO HASAKA (29) HAIRDRESSER
COME ON!
I'M JUST GETTING MARRIED! I'LL STILL COME HERE TO GET MY HAIR DONE!
SHIRO NAGASAKU (28) MARTIAL ARTIST
NAH! YOUR PRETTY TV STAR WIFE WON'T LIKE YOU GETTING YOUR HAIR CUT AT YOUR EX-GIRLFRIEND'S SALON!
IS THAT WHY YOU'RE CUTTING MY HAIR IN YOUR BATHROOM AND NOT OUT WHERE PEOPLE CAN SEE?
REMEMBER THE TIME SOME TABLOID GOT A SHOT OF YOU HERE?
I'M JUST TRYING TO PROTECT THE PRIVACY OF THE FAMOUS MARTIAL ARTIST ON THE EVE OF HIS CELEBRITY WEDDING.
WHO'D COME IN AT A TIME LIKE THIS?
IT'S ALREADY EIGHT ...

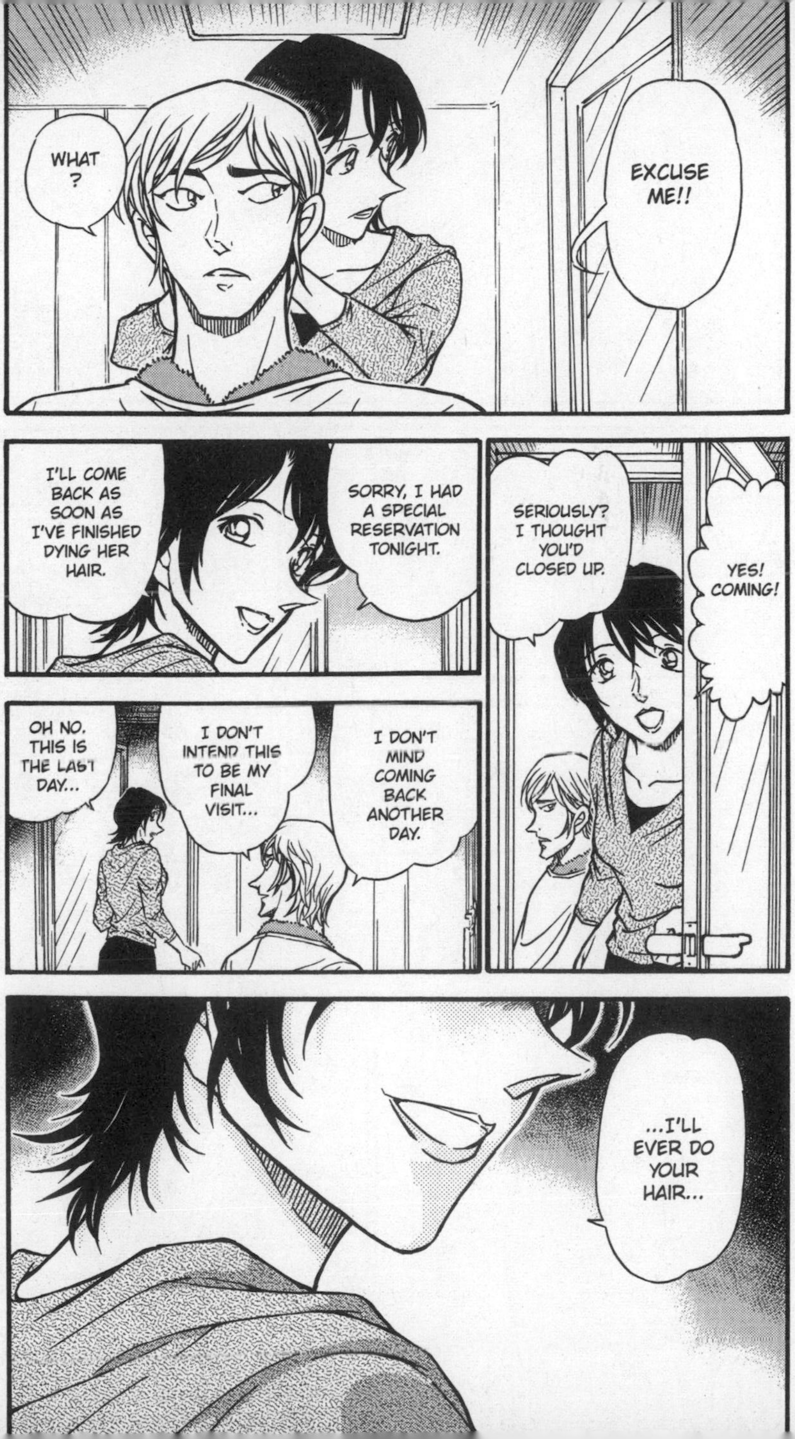
EXCUSE ME!!
WHAT ?
YES! COMING!
SERIOUSLY? I THOUGHT YOU'D CLOSED UP.
SORRY, I HAD A SPECIAL RESERVATION TONIGHT.
I'LL COME BACK AS SOON AS I'VE FINISHED DYING HER HAIR.
I DON'T MIND COMING BACK ANOTHER DAY.
I DON'T INTEND THIS TO BE MY FINAL VISIT...
OH NO. THIS IS THE LAST DAY...
...I'LL EVER DO YOUR HAIR...

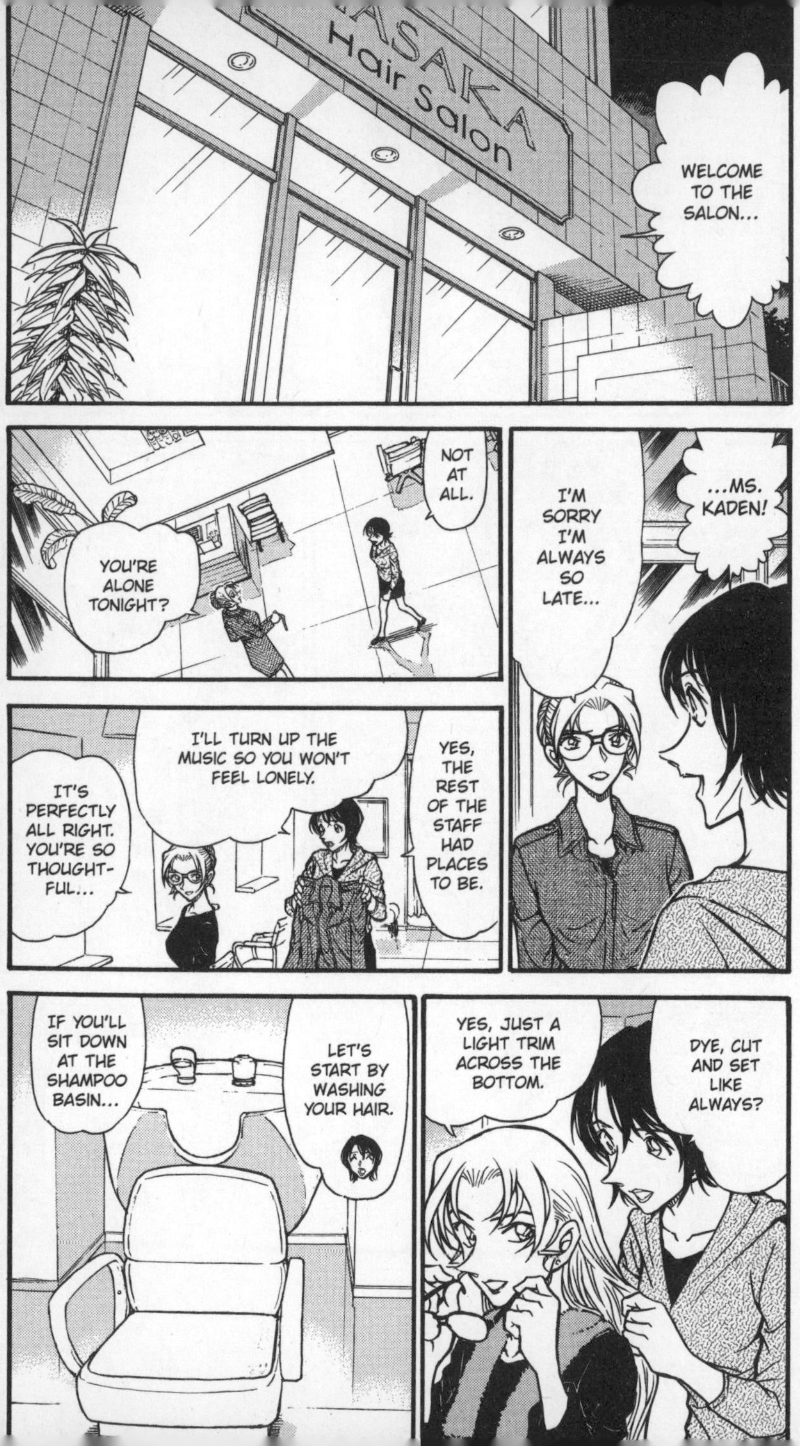
ASAKA
Hair Salon
WELCOME TO THE SALON...
...MS. KADEN!
I'M SORRY I'M ALWAYS SO LATE...
NOT AT ALL.
YOU'RE ALONE TONIGHT?
YES, THE REST OF THE STAFF HAD PLACES TO BE.
I'LL TURN UP THE MUSIC SO YOU WON'T FEEL LONELY.
IT'S PERFECTLY ALL RIGHT. YOU'RE SO THOUGHT-FUL...
DYE, CUT AND SET LIKE ALWAYS?
YES, JUST A LIGHT TRIM ACROSS THE BOTTOM.
LET'S START BY WASHING YOUR HAIR.
IF YOU'LL SIT DOWN AT THE SHAMPOO BASIN...

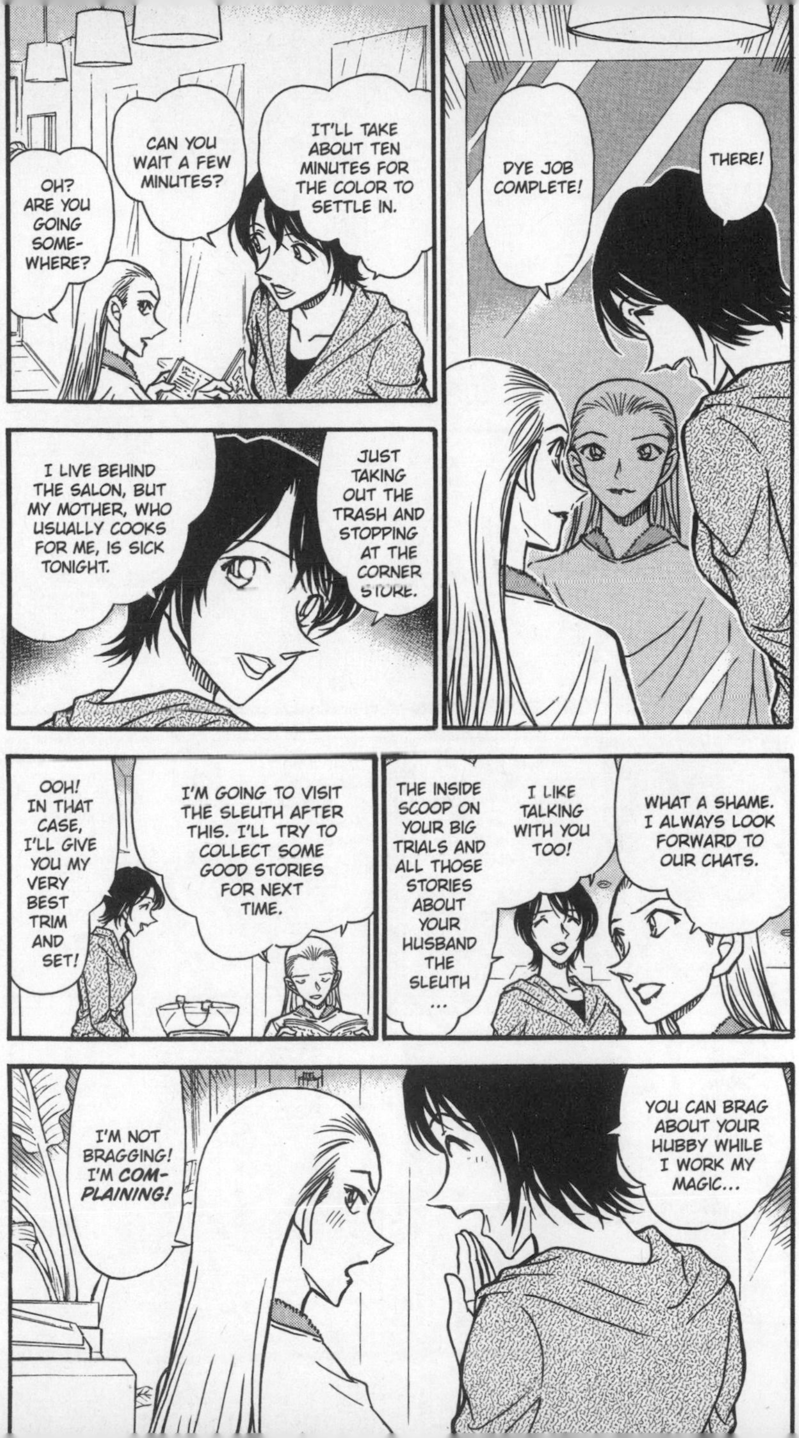
THERE!
DYE JOB COMPLETE!
IT'LL TAKE ABOUT TEN MINUTES FOR THE COLOR TO SETTLE IN.
CAN YOU WAIT A FEW MINUTES?
OH? ARE YOU GOING SOME-WHERE?
JUST TAKING OUT THE TRASH AND STOPPING AT THE CORNER STORE.
I LIVE BEHIND THE SALON, BUT MY MOTHER, WHO USUALLY COOKS FOR ME, IS SICK TONIGHT.
WHAT A SHAME. I ALWAYS LOOK FORWARD TO OUR CHATS.
I LIKE TALKING WITH YOU TOO!
THE INSIDE SCOOP ON YOUR BIG TRIALS AND ALL THOSE STORIES ABOUT YOUR HUSBAND THE SLEUTH...
I'M GOING TO VISIT THE SLEUTH AFTER THIS. I'LL TRY TO COLLECT SOME GOOD STORIES FOR NEXT TIME.
OOH! IN THAT CASE, I'LL GIVE YOU MY VERY BEST TRIM AND SET!
YOU CAN BRAG ABOUT YOUR HUBBY WHILE I WORK MY MAGIC...
I'M NOT BRAGGING! I'M *COMPLAINING!*

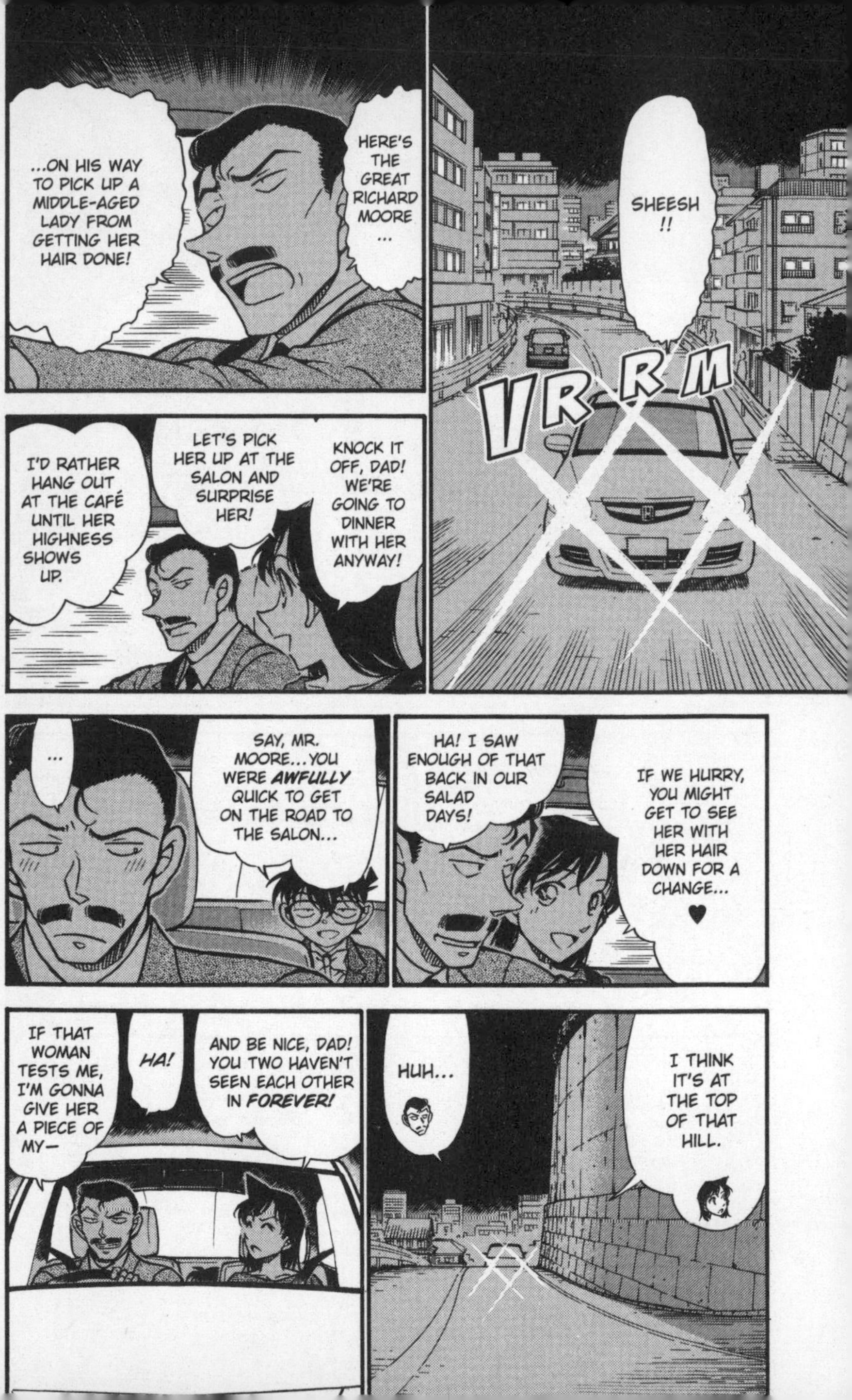

SHEESH!!
VRRM
HERE'S THE GREAT RICHARD MOORE...
...ON HIS WAY TO PICK UP A MIDDLE-AGED LADY FROM GETTING HER HAIR DONE!
KNOCK IT OFF, DAD! WE'RE GOING TO DINNER WITH HER ANYWAY!
LET'S PICK HER UP AT THE SALON AND SURPRISE HER!
I'D RATHER HANG OUT AT THE CAFÉ UNTIL HER HIGHNESS SHOWS UP.
IF WE HURRY, YOU MIGHT GET TO SEE HER WITH HER HAIR DOWN FOR A CHANGE... ♥
HA! I SAW ENOUGH OF THAT BACK IN OUR SALAD DAYS!
SAY, MR. MOORE...YOU WERE ***AWFULLY*** QUICK TO GET ON THE ROAD TO THE SALON...
...
I THINK IT'S AT THE TOP OF THAT HILL.
HUH...
AND BE NICE, DAD! YOU TWO HAVEN'T SEEN EACH OTHER IN ***FOREVER!***
HA!
IF THAT WOMAN TESTS ME, I'M GONNA GIVE HER A PIECE OF MY—

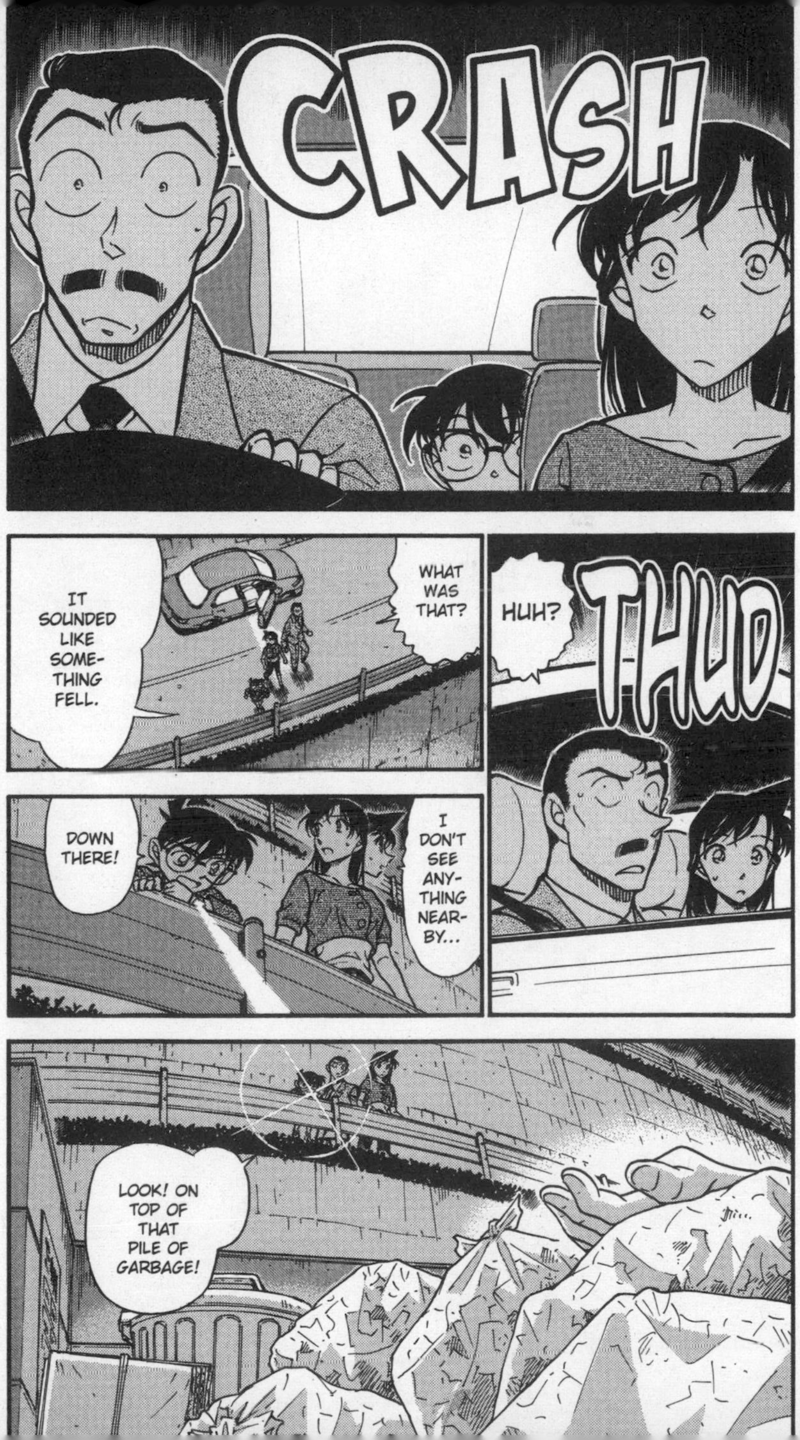
CRASH
HUH?
THUD
WHAT WAS THAT?
IT SOUNDED LIKE SOME-THING FELL.
I DON'T SEE ANY-THING NEAR-BY...
DOWN THERE!
LOOK! ON TOP OF THAT PILE OF GARBAGE!

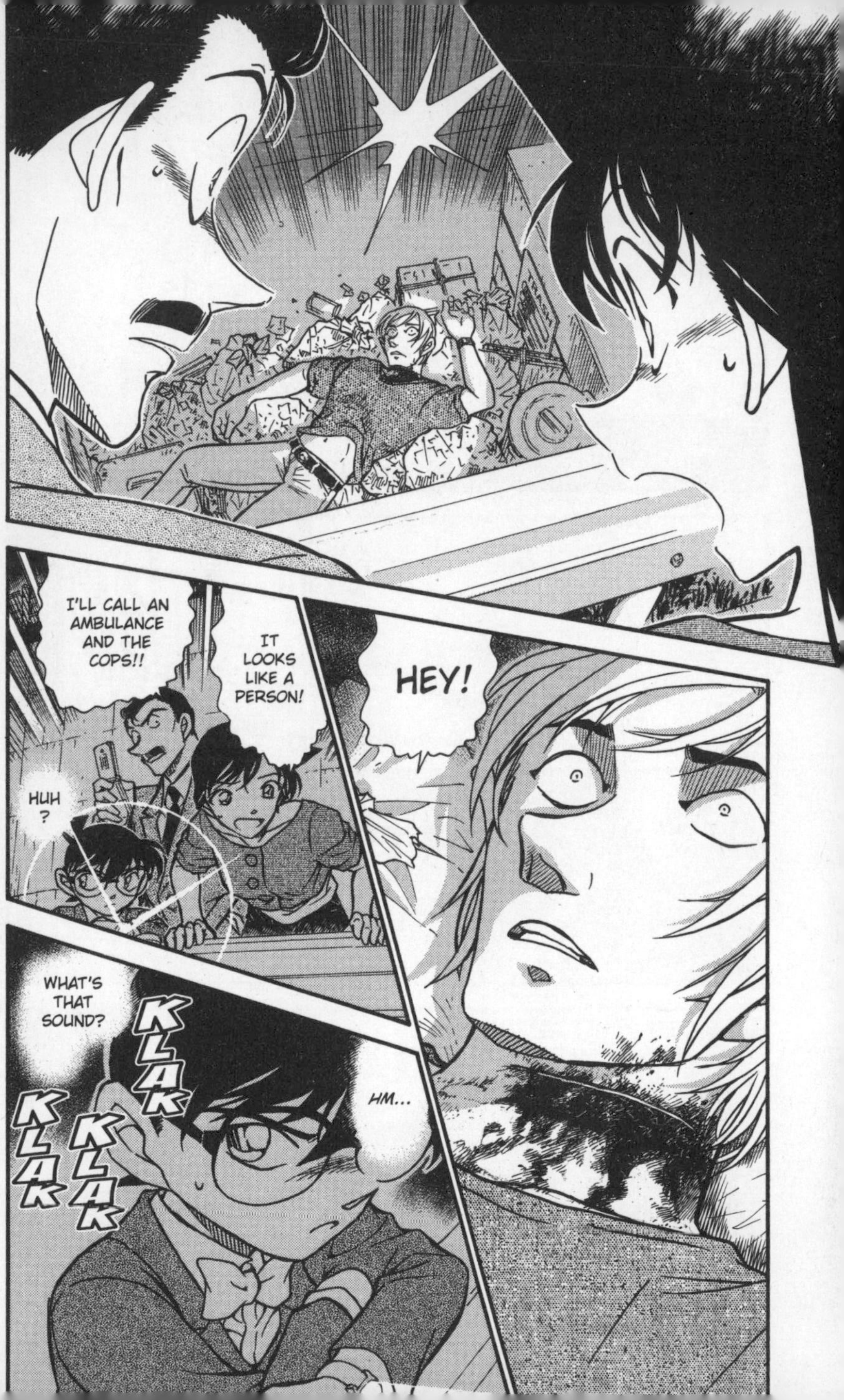
HEY!
IT LOOKS LIKE A PERSON!
I'LL CALL AN AMBULANCE AND THE COPS!!
HUH?
WHAT'S THAT SOUND?
KLAK
KLAK
KLAK
HM...

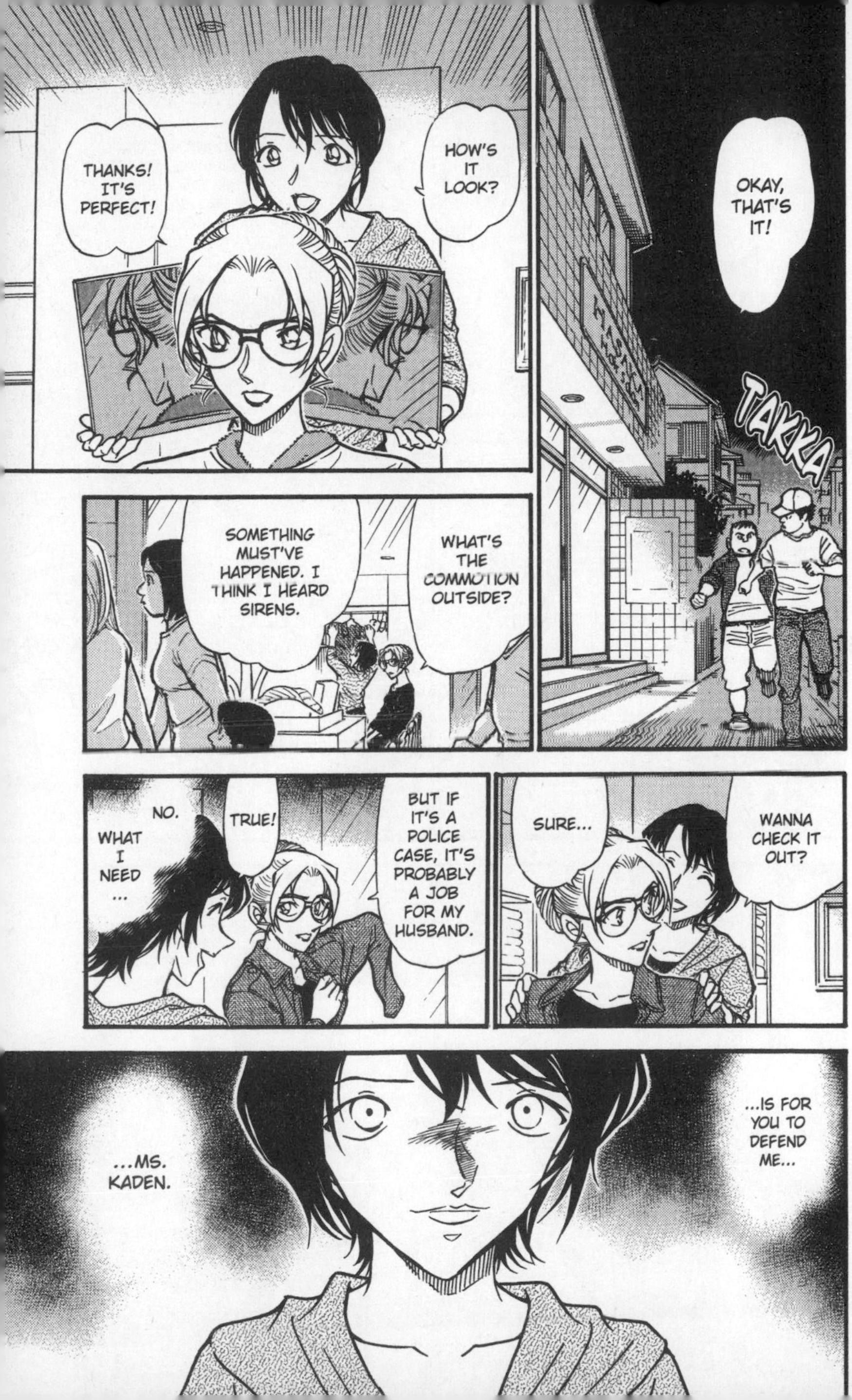
OKAY, THAT'S IT!
TAKKA
HOW'S IT LOOK?
THANKS! IT'S PERFECT!
WHAT'S THE COMMOTION OUTSIDE?
SOMETHING MUST'VE HAPPENED. I THINK I HEARD SIRENS.
WANNA CHECK IT OUT?
SURE...
BUT IF IT'S A POLICE CASE, IT'S PROBABLY A JOB FOR MY HUSBAND.
TRUE!
NO. WHAT I NEED...
...IS FOR YOU TO DEFEND ME...
...MS. KADEN.

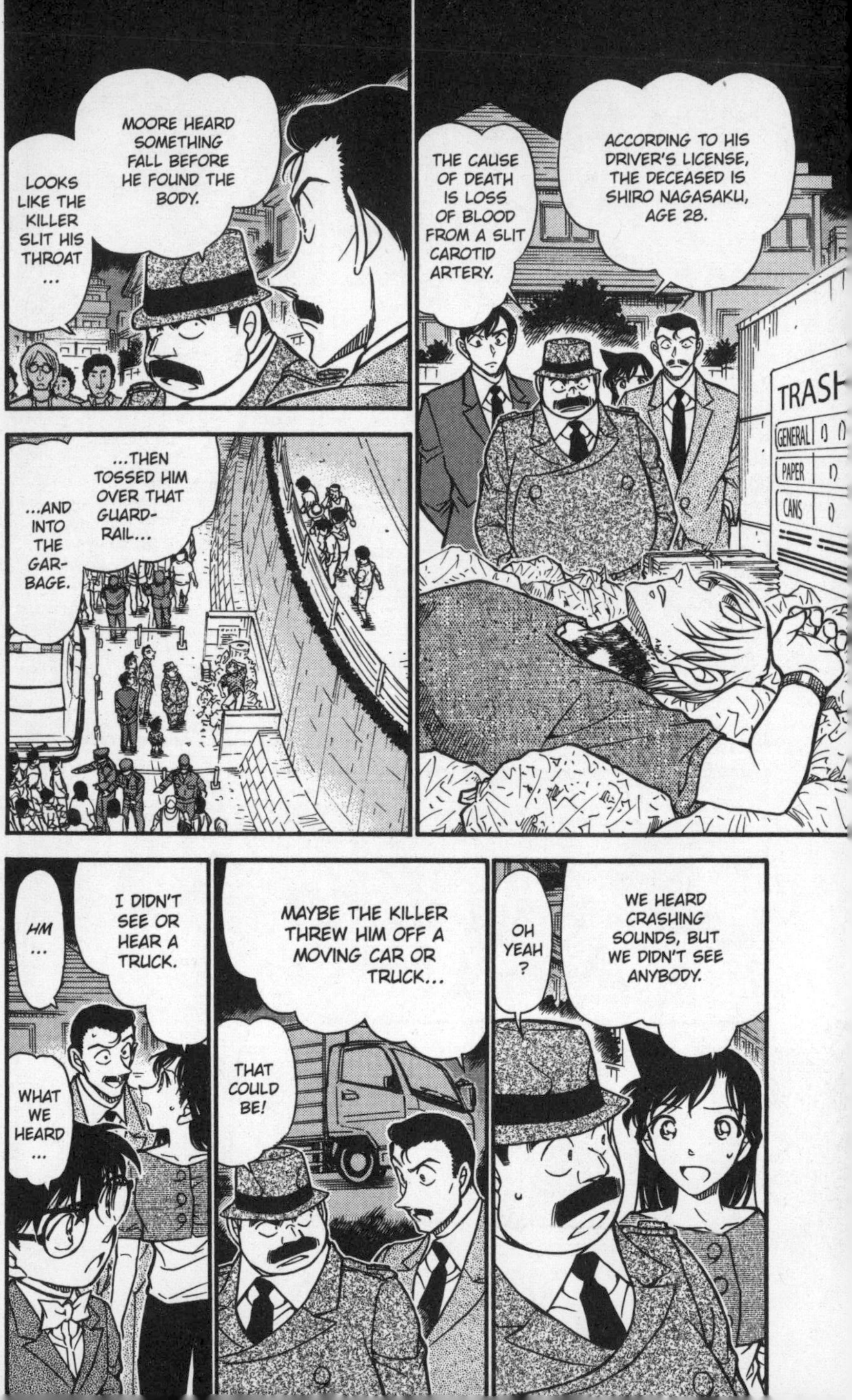
ACCORDING TO HIS DRIVER'S LICENSE, THE DECEASED IS SHIRO NAGASAKU, AGE 28.
THE CAUSE OF DEATH IS LOSS OF BLOOD FROM A SLIT CAROTID ARTERY.
TRASH
GENERAL
PAPER
CANS
MOORE HEARD SOMETHING FALL BEFORE HE FOUND THE BODY.
LOOKS LIKE THE KILLER SLIT HIS THROAT ...
...THEN TOSSED HIM OVER THAT GUARD-RAIL...
...AND INTO THE GAR-BAGE.
WE HEARD CRASHING SOUNDS, BUT WE DIDN'T SEE ANYBODY.
OH YEAH ?
MAYBE THE KILLER THREW HIM OFF A MOVING CAR OR TRUCK...
THAT COULD BE!
I DIDN'T SEE OR HEAR A TRUCK.
HM ...
WHAT WE HEARD ...

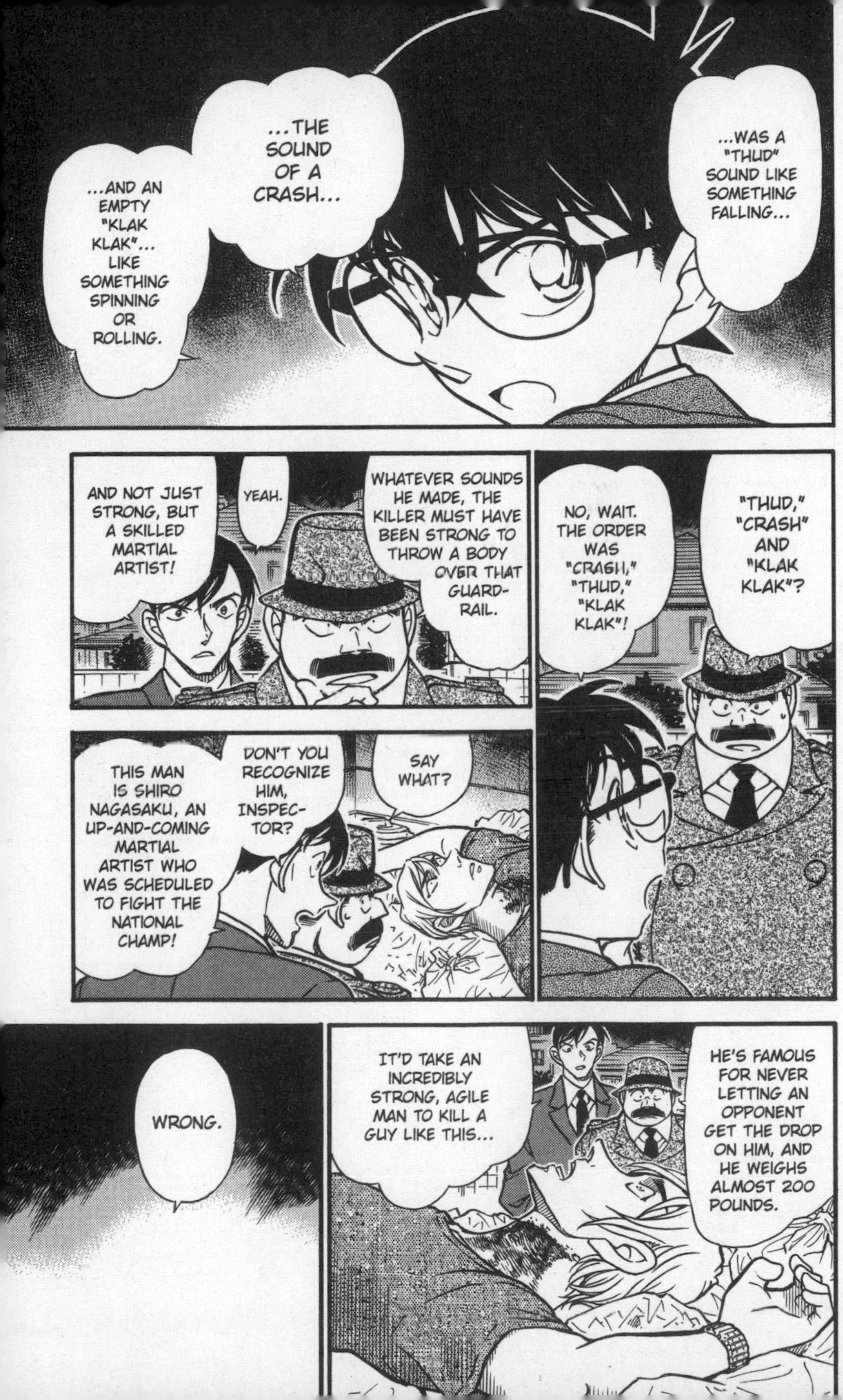
...WAS A "THUD" SOUND LIKE SOMETHING FALLING...
...THE SOUND OF A CRASH...
...AND AN EMPTY "KLAK KLAK"... LIKE SOMETHING SPINNING OR ROLLING.
"THUD," "CRASH" AND "KLAK KLAK"?
NO, WAIT. THE ORDER WAS "CRASH," "THUD," "KLAK KLAK"!
WHATEVER SOUNDS HE MADE, THE KILLER MUST HAVE BEEN STRONG TO THROW A BODY OVER THAT GUARD-RAIL.
YEAH.
AND NOT JUST STRONG, BUT A SKILLED MARTIAL ARTIST!
SAY WHAT?
DON'T YOU RECOGNIZE HIM, INSPEC-TOR?
THIS MAN IS SHIRO NAGASAKU, AN UP-AND-COMING MARTIAL ARTIST WHO WAS SCHEDULED TO FIGHT THE NATIONAL CHAMP!
HE'S FAMOUS FOR NEVER LETTING AN OPPONENT GET THE DROP ON HIM, AND HE WEIGHS ALMOST 200 POUNDS.
IT'D TAKE AN INCREDIBLY STRONG, AGILE MAN TO KILL A GUY LIKE THIS...
WRONG.

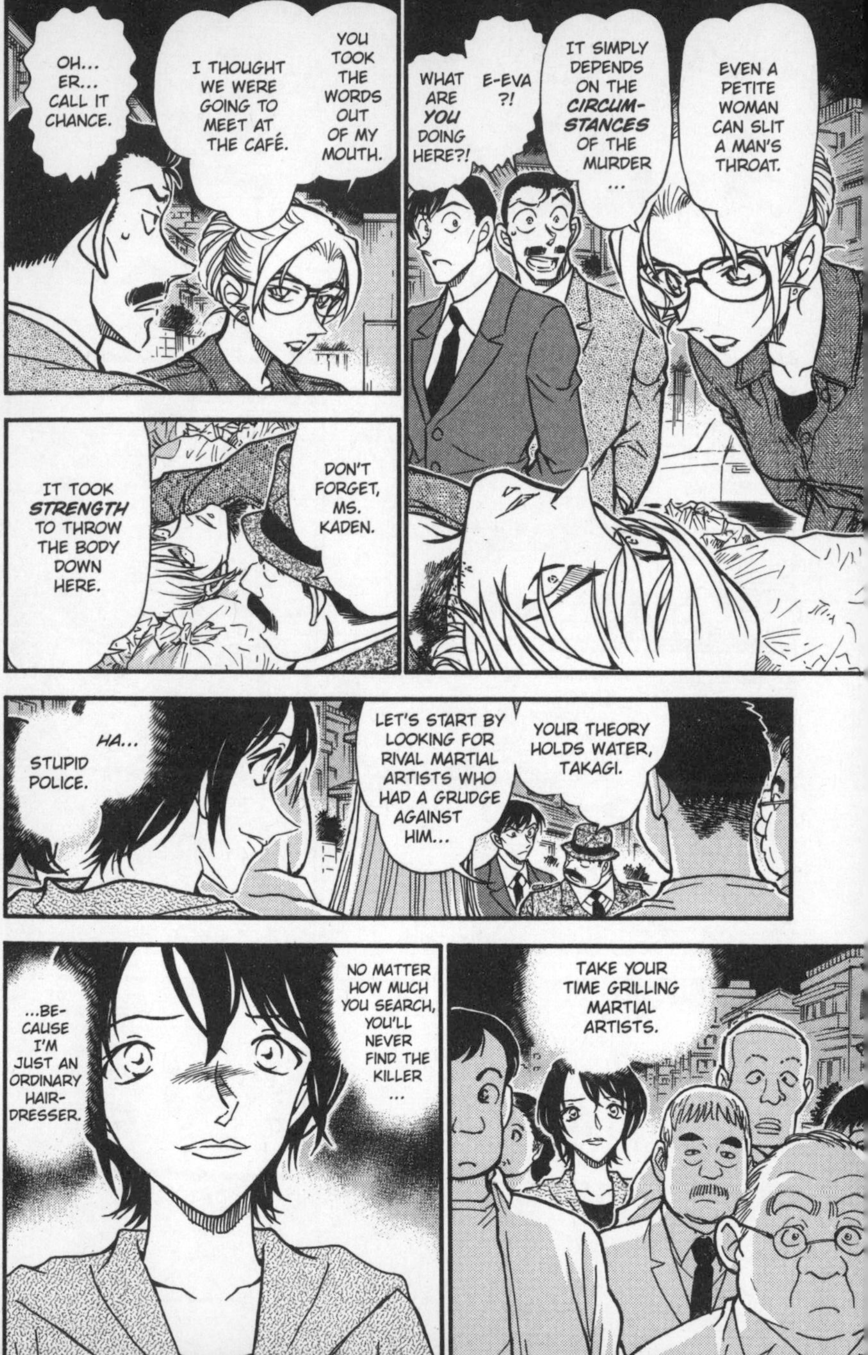
EVEN A PETITE WOMAN CAN SLIT A MAN'S THROAT.
IT SIMPLY DEPENDS ON THE CIRCUMSTANCES OF THE MURDER...
E-EVA?!
WHAT ARE YOU DOING HERE?!
YOU TOOK THE WORDS OUT OF MY MOUTH.
I THOUGHT WE WERE GOING TO MEET AT THE CAFÉ.
OH... ER... CALL IT CHANCE.
DON'T FORGET, MS. KADEN.
IT TOOK STRENGTH TO THROW THE BODY DOWN HERE.
YOUR THEORY HOLDS WATER, TAKAGI.
LET'S START BY LOOKING FOR RIVAL MARTIAL ARTISTS WHO HAD A GRUDGE AGAINST HIM...
HA...
STUPID POLICE.
TAKE YOUR TIME GRILLING MARTIAL ARTISTS.
NO MATTER HOW MUCH YOU SEARCH, YOU'LL NEVER FIND THE KILLER...
...BECAUSE I'M JUST AN ORDINARY HAIRDRESSER.

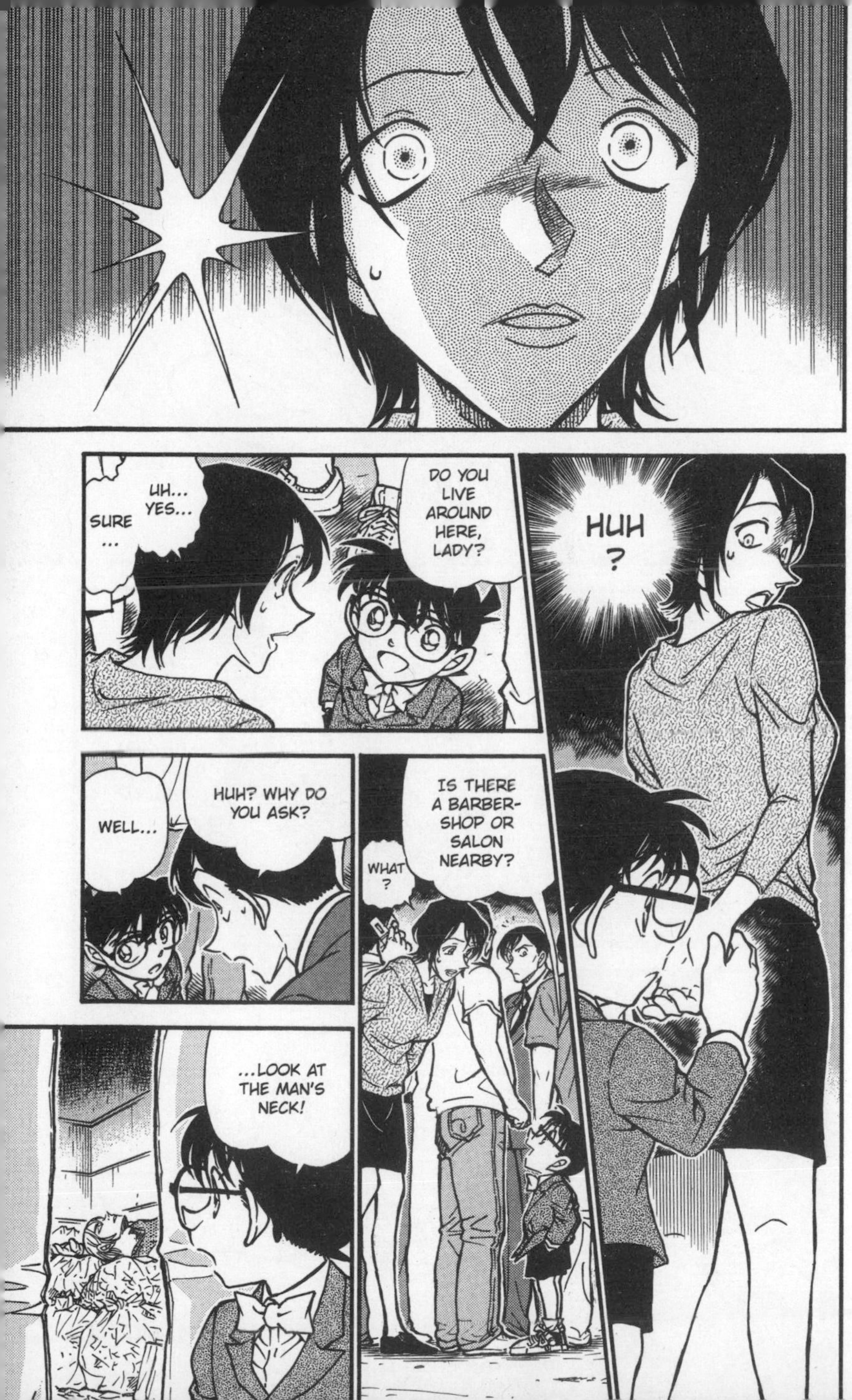
HUH ?
DO YOU LIVE AROUND HERE, LADY?
UH... YES...
SURE ...
IS THERE A BARBER-SHOP OR SALON NEARBY?
WHAT ?
HUH? WHY DO YOU ASK?
WELL...
...LOOK AT THE MAN'S NECK!

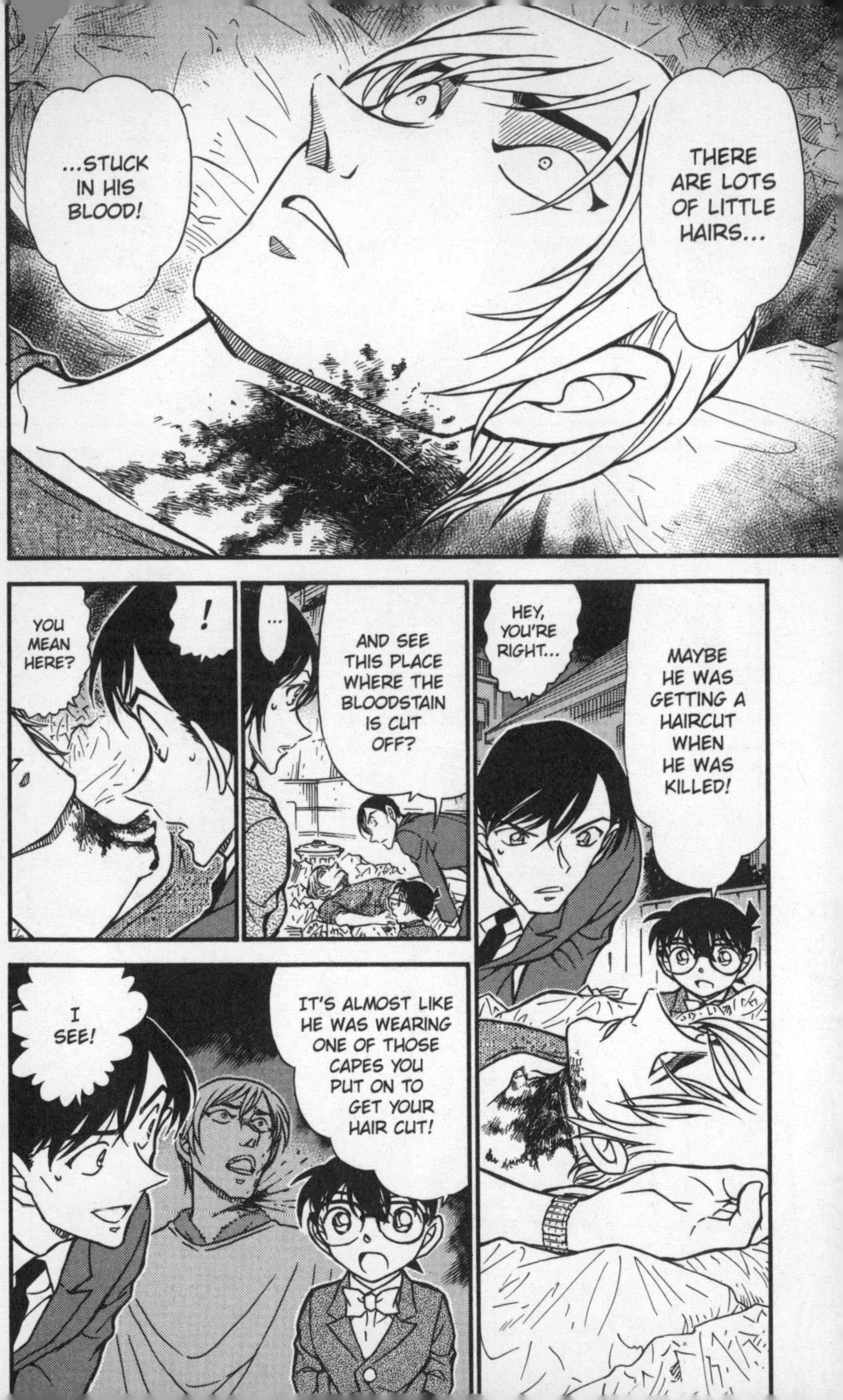
THERE ARE LOTS OF LITTLE HAIRS...
...STUCK IN HIS BLOOD!
HEY, YOU'RE RIGHT...
MAYBE HE WAS GETTING A HAIRCUT WHEN HE WAS KILLED!
AND SEE THIS PLACE WHERE THE BLOODSTAIN IS CUT OFF?
...
YOU MEAN HERE?
!
IT'S ALMOST LIKE HE WAS WEARING ONE OF THOSE CAPES YOU PUT ON TO GET YOUR HAIR CUT!
I SEE!

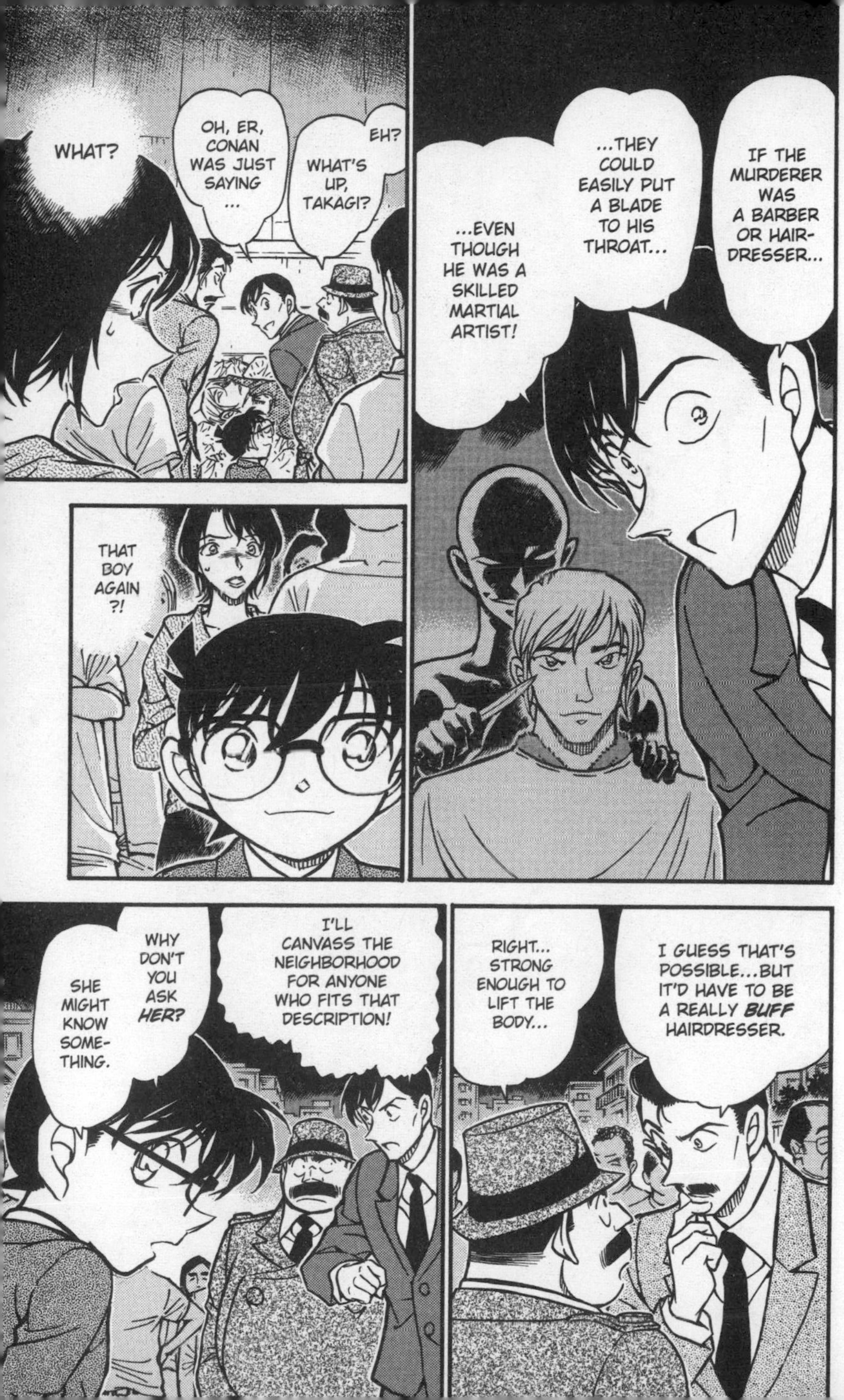
IF THE MURDERER WAS A BARBER OR HAIR-DRESSER...
...THEY COULD EASILY PUT A BLADE TO HIS THROAT...
...EVEN THOUGH HE WAS A SKILLED MARTIAL ARTIST!
EH? WHAT'S UP, TAKAGI?
OH, ER, CONAN WAS JUST SAYING ...
WHAT?
THAT BOY AGAIN ?!
I GUESS THAT'S POSSIBLE...BUT IT'D HAVE TO BE A REALLY *BUFF* HAIRDRESSER.
RIGHT... STRONG ENOUGH TO LIFT THE BODY...
I'LL CANVASS THE NEIGHBORHOOD FOR ANYONE WHO FITS THAT DESCRIPTION!
WHY DON'T YOU ASK *HER?*
SHE MIGHT KNOW SOME-THING.

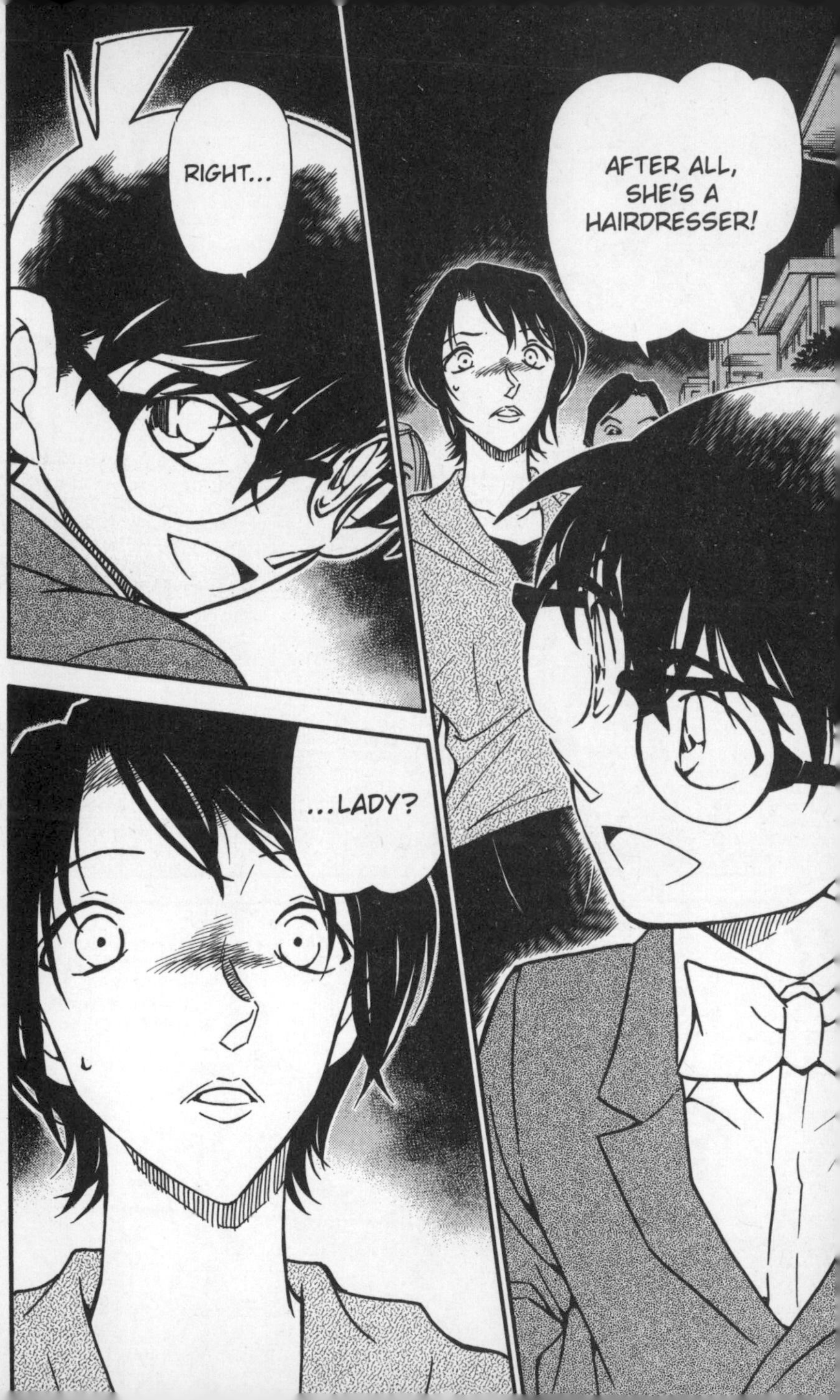
AFTER ALL, SHE'S A HAIRDRESSER!
RIGHT...
...LADY?

FILE 3: THE FLYING BODY

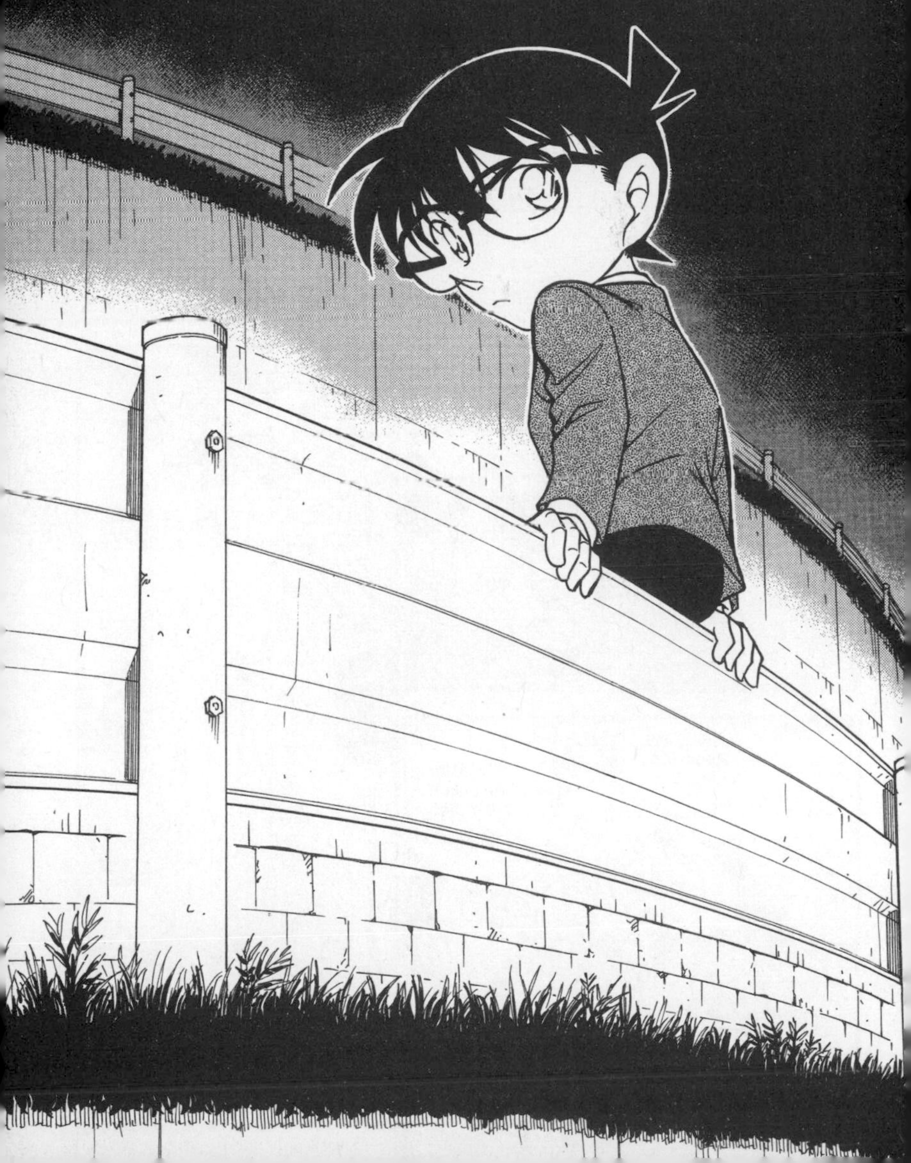

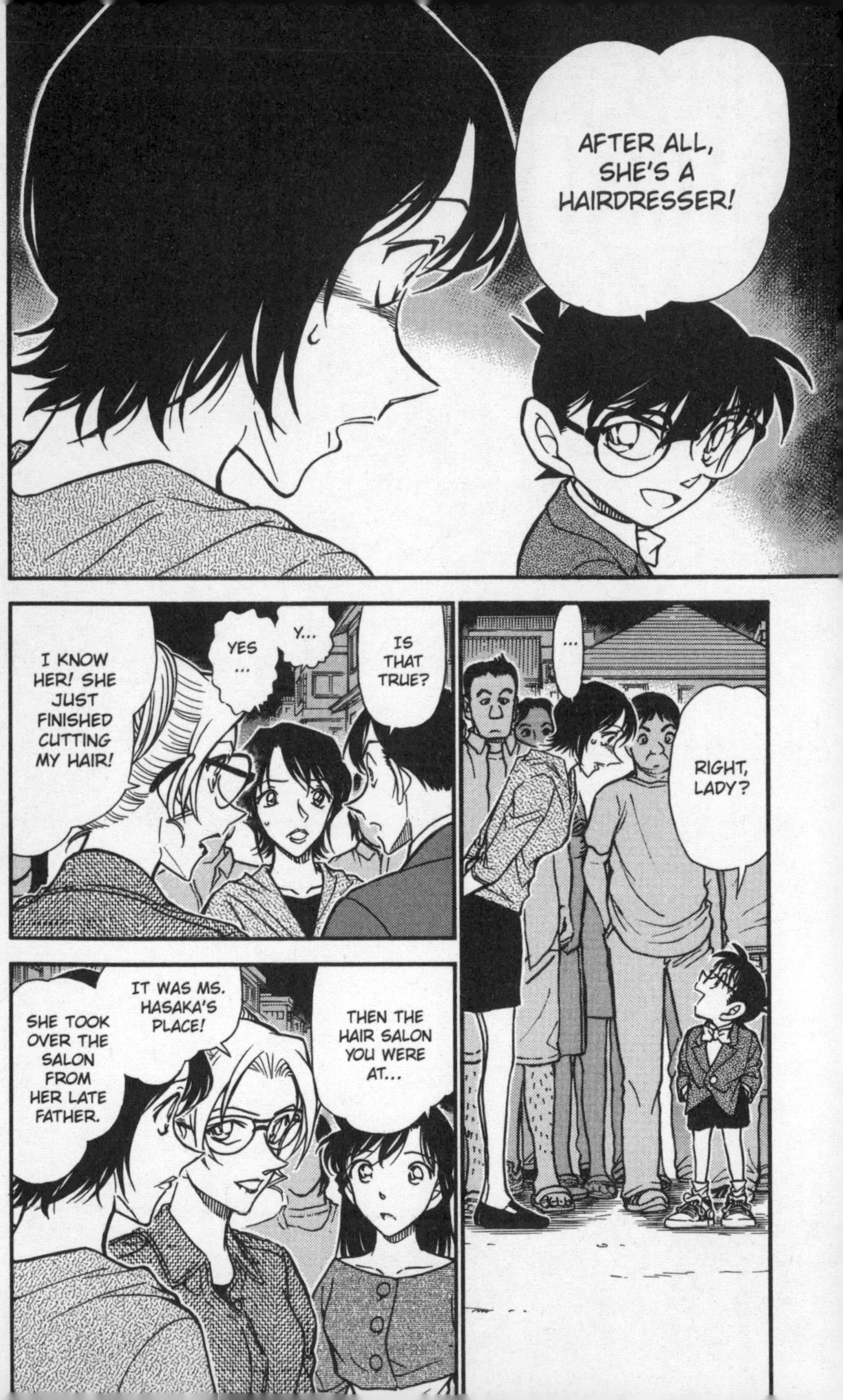
AFTER ALL, SHE'S A HAIRDRESSER!
RIGHT, LADY?
...
IS THAT TRUE?
Y...
YES ...
I KNOW HER! SHE JUST FINISHED CUTTING MY HAIR!
THEN THE HAIR SALON YOU WERE AT...
IT WAS MS. HASAKA'S PLACE!
SHE TOOK OVER THE SALON FROM HER LATE FATHER.

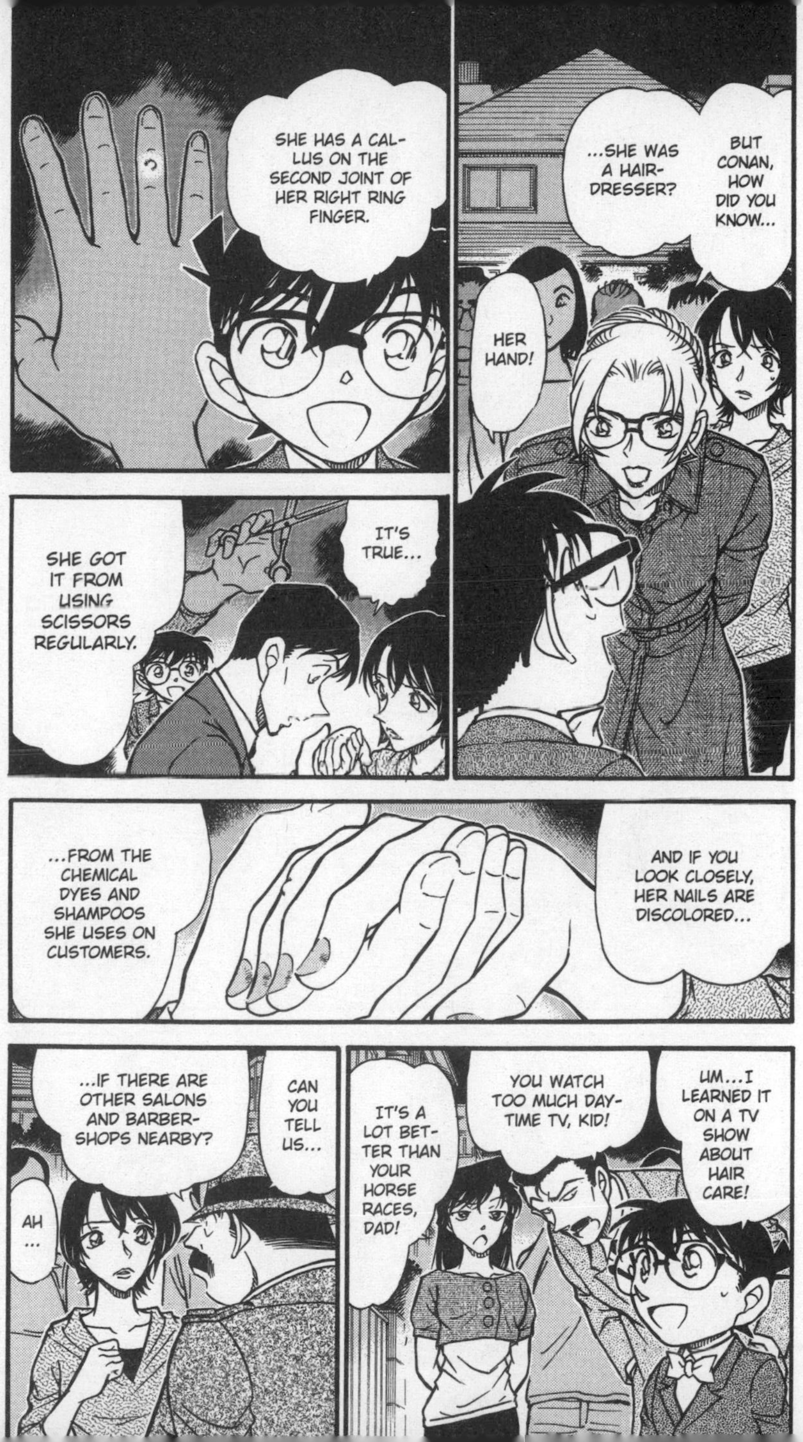
BUT CONAN, HOW DID YOU KNOW...
...SHE WAS A HAIR-DRESSER?
HER HAND!
SHE HAS A CAL-LUS ON THE SECOND JOINT OF HER RIGHT RING FINGER.
IT'S TRUE...
SHE GOT IT FROM USING SCISSORS REGULARLY.
AND IF YOU LOOK CLOSELY, HER NAILS ARE DISCOLORED...
...FROM THE CHEMICAL DYES AND SHAMPOOS SHE USES ON CUSTOMERS.
UM...I LEARNED IT ON A TV SHOW ABOUT HAIR CARE!
YOU WATCH TOO MUCH DAY-TIME TV, KID!
IT'S A LOT BET-TER THAN YOUR HORSE RACES, DAD!
CAN YOU TELL US...
...IF THERE ARE OTHER SALONS AND BARBER-SHOPS NEARBY?
AH ...

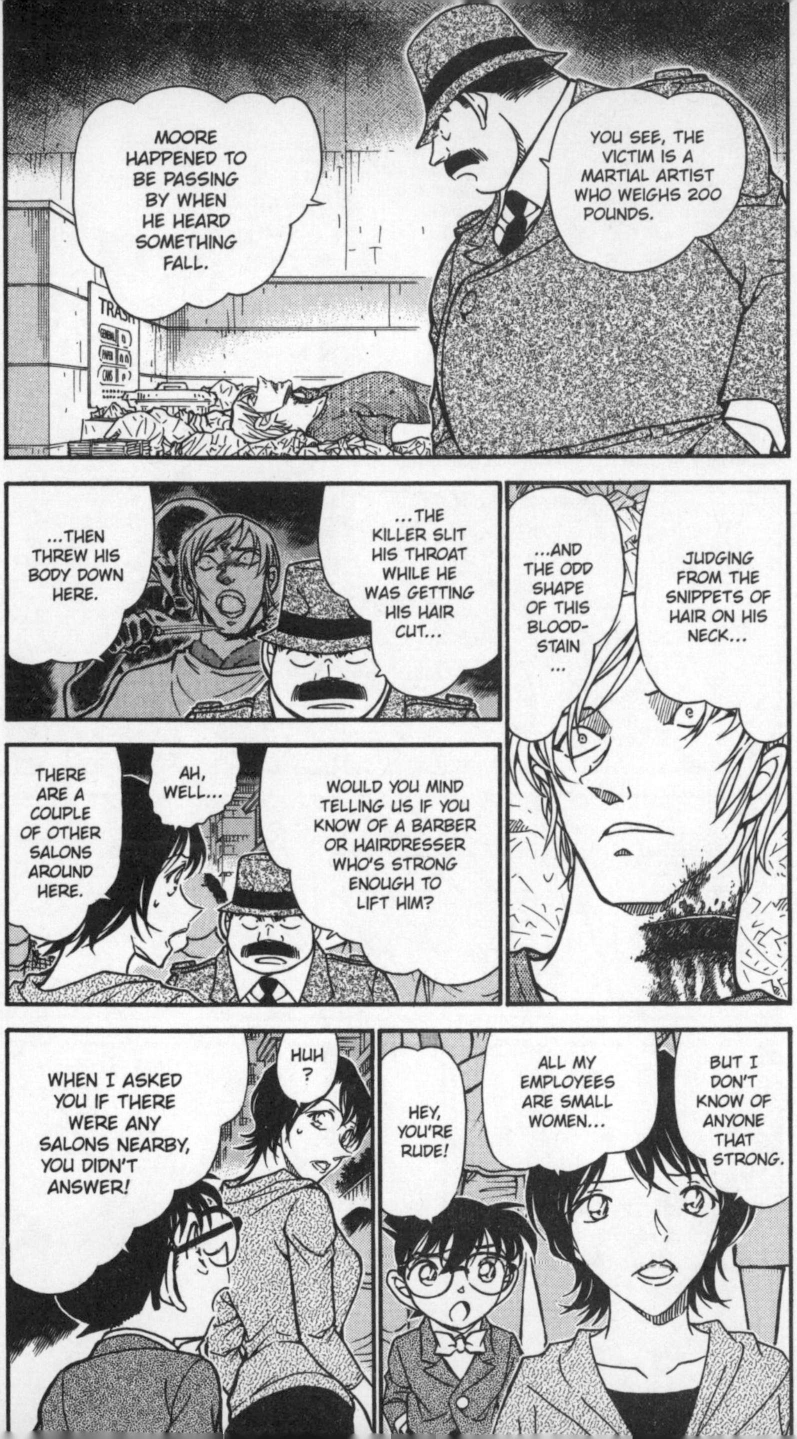
YOU SEE, THE VICTIM IS A MARTIAL ARTIST WHO WEIGHS 200 POUNDS.
MOORE HAPPENED TO BE PASSING BY WHEN HE HEARD SOMETHING FALL.
TRASH
JUDGING FROM THE SNIPPETS OF HAIR ON HIS NECK...
...AND THE ODD SHAPE OF THIS BLOOD-STAIN...
...THE KILLER SLIT HIS THROAT WHILE HE WAS GETTING HIS HAIR CUT...
...THEN THREW HIS BODY DOWN HERE.
WOULD YOU MIND TELLING US IF YOU KNOW OF A BARBER OR HAIRDRESSER WHO'S STRONG ENOUGH TO LIFT HIM?
AH, WELL...
THERE ARE A COUPLE OF OTHER SALONS AROUND HERE.
BUT I DON'T KNOW OF ANYONE THAT STRONG.
ALL MY EMPLOYEES ARE SMALL WOMEN...
HEY, YOU'RE RUDE!
HUH?
WHEN I ASKED YOU IF THERE WERE ANY SALONS NEARBY, YOU DIDN'T ANSWER!

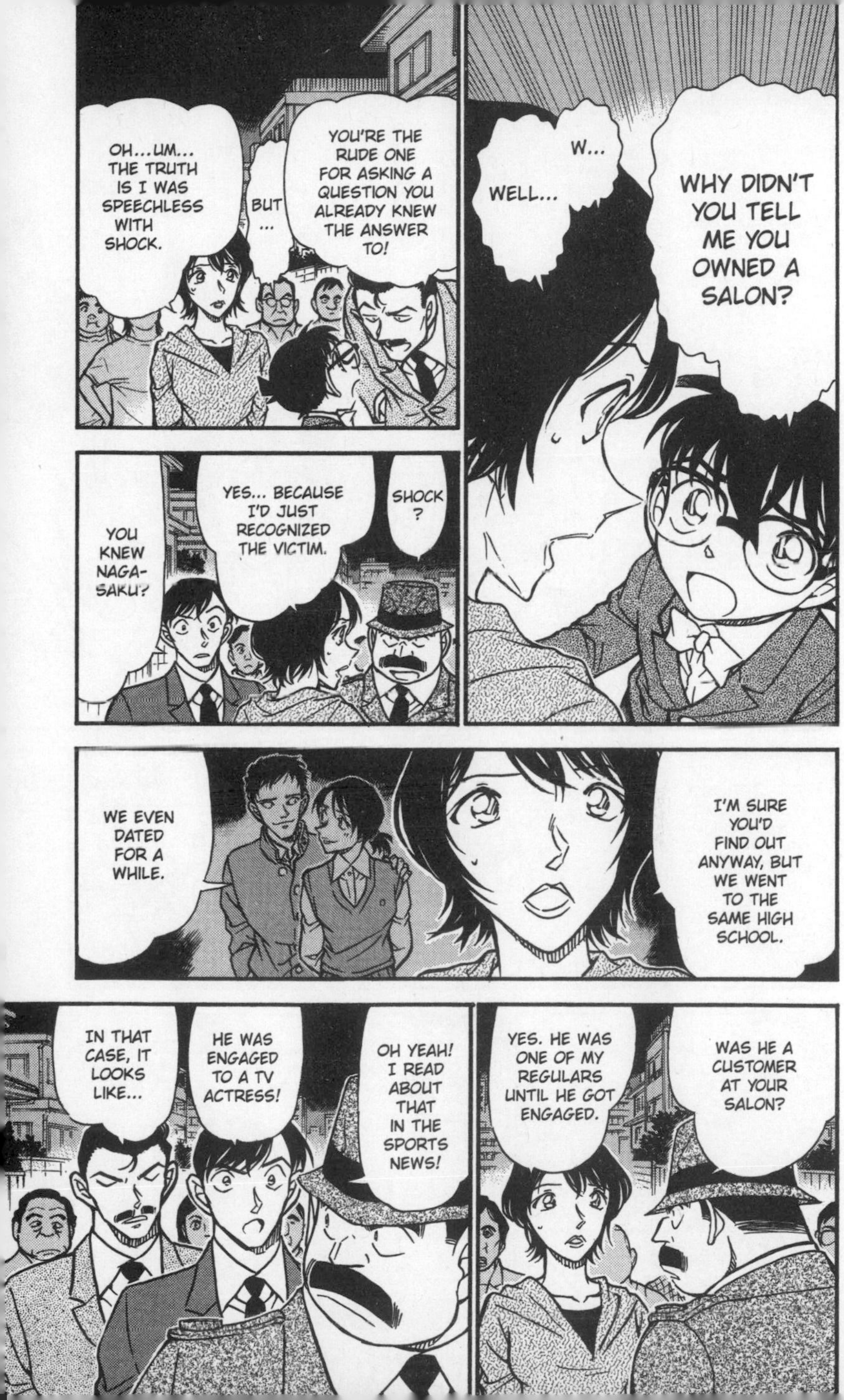
WHY DIDN'T YOU TELL ME YOU OWNED A SALON?
W... WELL...
YOU'RE THE RUDE ONE FOR ASKING A QUESTION YOU ALREADY KNEW THE ANSWER TO!
BUT ...
OH...UM... THE TRUTH IS I WAS SPEECHLESS WITH SHOCK.
SHOCK ?
YES... BECAUSE I'D JUST RECOGNIZED THE VICTIM.
YOU KNEW NAGA-SAKU?
I'M SURE YOU'D FIND OUT ANYWAY, BUT WE WENT TO THE SAME HIGH SCHOOL.
WE EVEN DATED FOR A WHILE.
WAS HE A CUSTOMER AT YOUR SALON?
YES. HE WAS ONE OF MY REGULARS UNTIL HE GOT ENGAGED.
OH YEAH! I READ ABOUT THAT IN THE SPORTS NEWS!
HE WAS ENGAGED TO A TV ACTRESS!
IN THAT CASE, IT LOOKS LIKE...

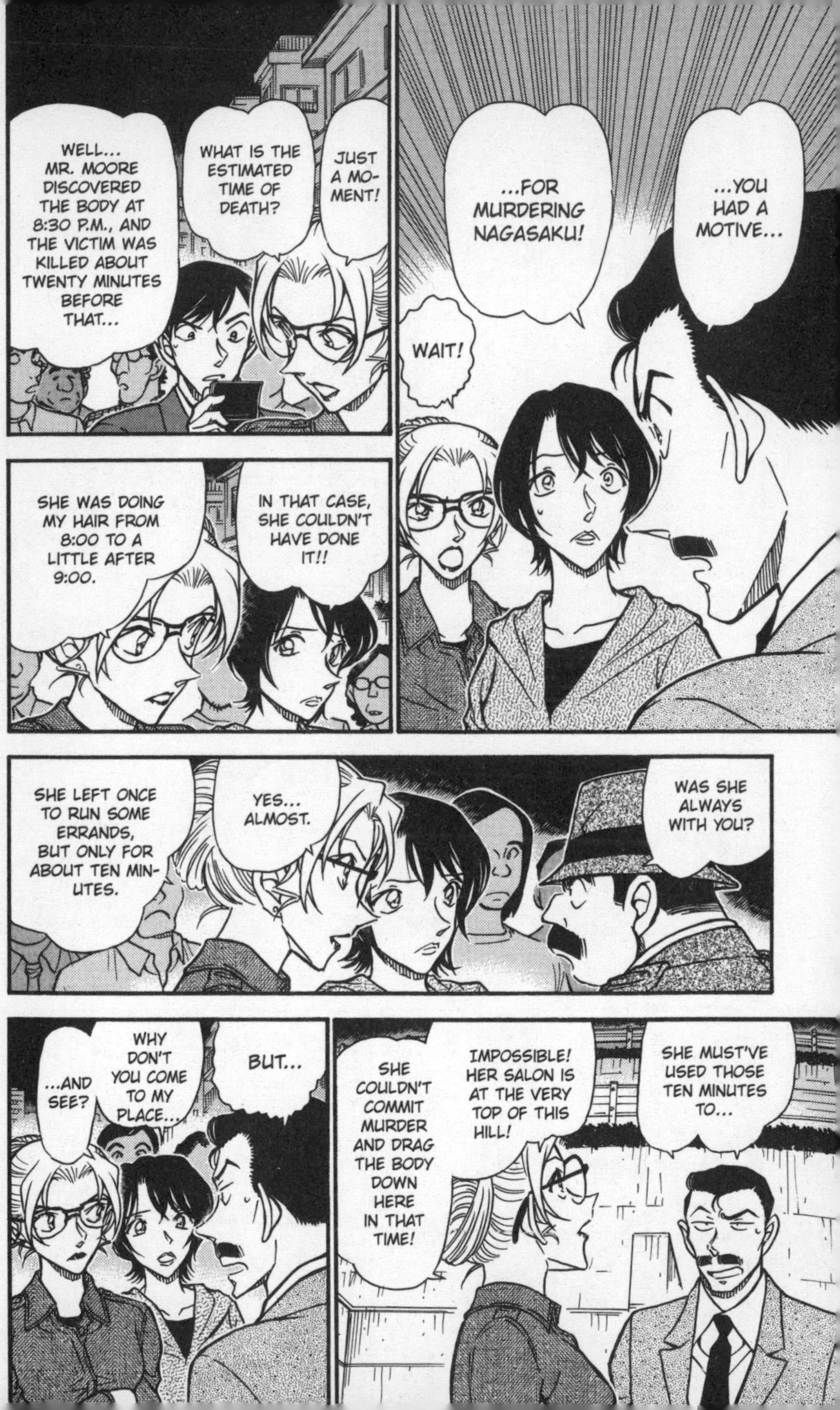
...YOU HAD A MOTIVE...
...FOR MURDERING NAGASAKU!
WAIT!
JUST A MO-MENT!
WHAT IS THE ESTIMATED TIME OF DEATH?
WELL... MR. MOORE DISCOVERED THE BODY AT 8:30 P.M., AND THE VICTIM WAS KILLED ABOUT TWENTY MINUTES BEFORE THAT...
IN THAT CASE, SHE COULDN'T HAVE DONE IT!!
SHE WAS DOING MY HAIR FROM 8:00 TO A LITTLE AFTER 9:00.
WAS SHE ALWAYS WITH YOU?
YES... ALMOST.
SHE LEFT ONCE TO RUN SOME ERRANDS, BUT ONLY FOR ABOUT TEN MIN-UTES.
SHE MUST'VE USED THOSE TEN MINUTES TO...
IMPOSSIBLE! HER SALON IS AT THE VERY TOP OF THIS HILL!
SHE COULDN'T COMMIT MURDER AND DRAG THE BODY DOWN HERE IN THAT TIME!
BUT...
WHY DON'T YOU COME TO MY PLACE...
...AND SEE?

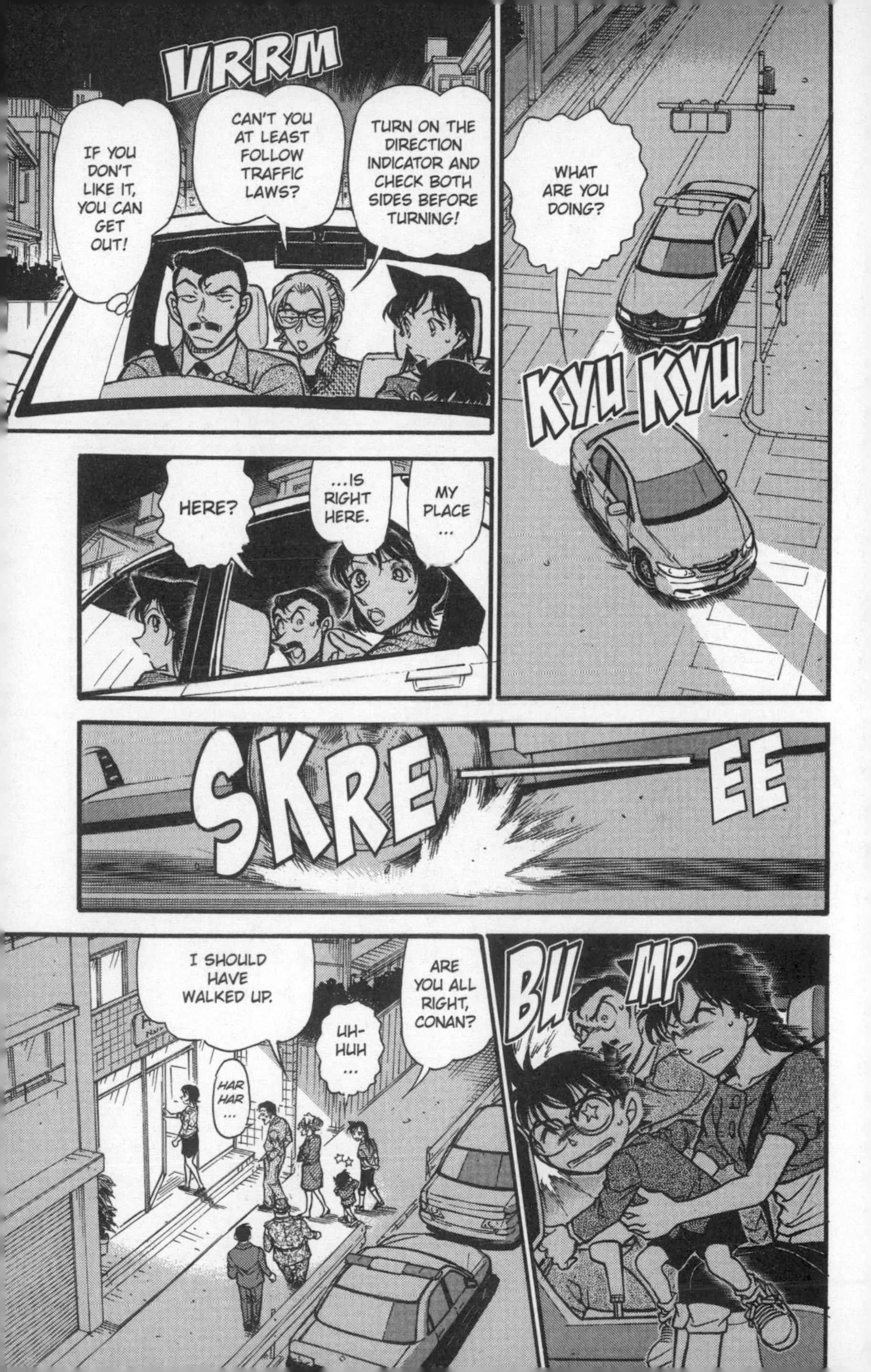
WHAT ARE YOU DOING?
KYU KYU
VRRM
TURN ON THE DIRECTION INDICATOR AND CHECK BOTH SIDES BEFORE TURNING!
CAN'T YOU AT LEAST FOLLOW TRAFFIC LAWS?
IF YOU DON'T LIKE IT, YOU CAN GET OUT!
MY PLACE ...
...IS RIGHT HERE.
HERE?
SKRE EE
BUMP
ARE YOU ALL RIGHT, CONAN?
UH-HUH ...
I SHOULD HAVE WALKED UP.
HAR HAR ...

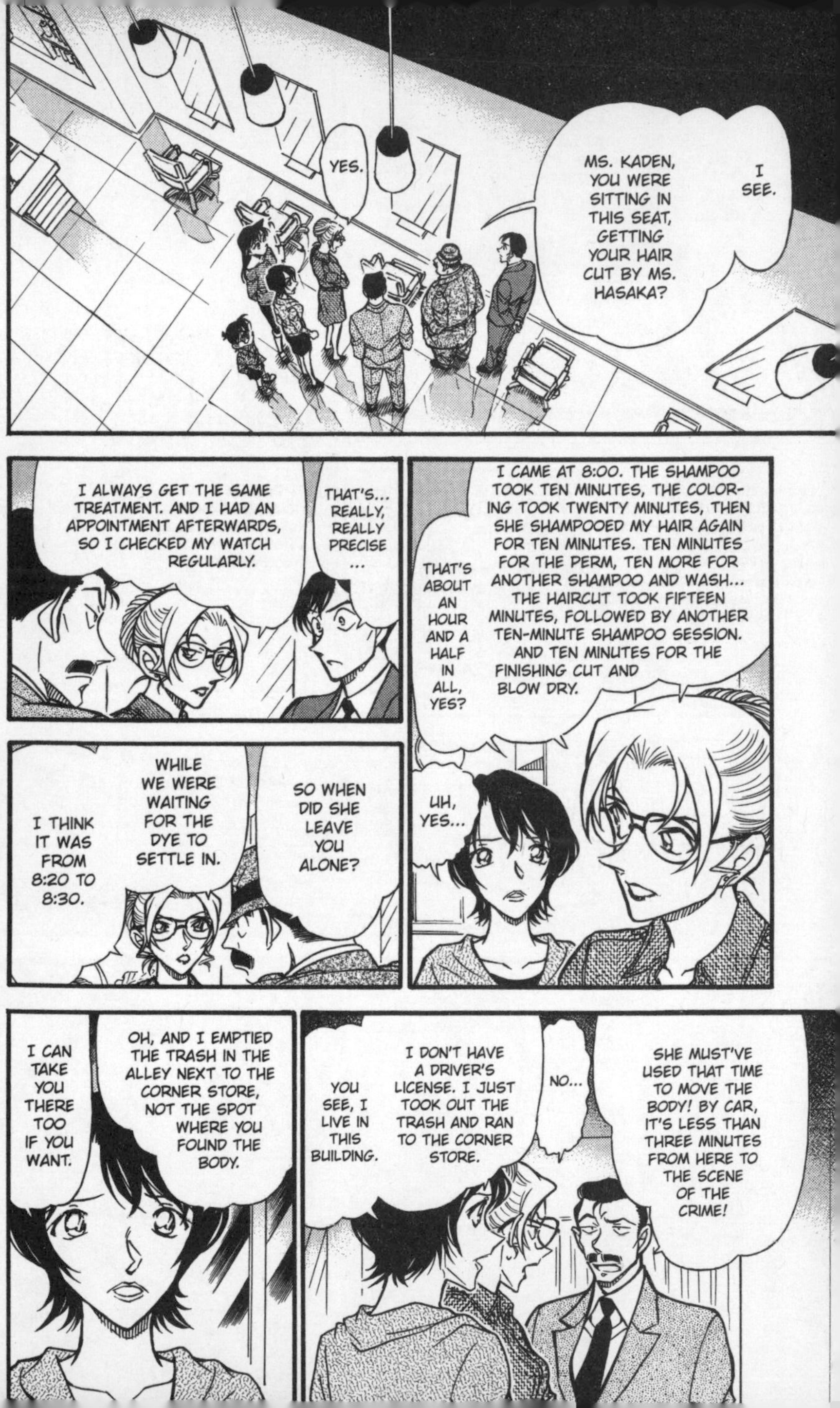
I SEE.
MS. KADEN, YOU WERE SITTING IN THIS SEAT, GETTING YOUR HAIR CUT BY MS. HASAKA?
YES.
I CAME AT 8:00. THE SHAMPOO TOOK TEN MINUTES, THE COLOR-ING TOOK TWENTY MINUTES, THEN SHE SHAMPOOED MY HAIR AGAIN FOR TEN MINUTES. TEN MINUTES FOR THE PERM, TEN MORE FOR ANOTHER SHAMPOO AND WASH... THE HAIRCUT TOOK FIFTEEN MINUTES, FOLLOWED BY ANOTHER TEN-MINUTE SHAMPOO SESSION. AND TEN MINUTES FOR THE FINISHING CUT AND BLOW DRY.
THAT'S ABOUT AN HOUR AND A HALF IN ALL, YES?
UH, YES...
THAT'S... REALLY, REALLY PRECISE...
I ALWAYS GET THE SAME TREATMENT. AND I HAD AN APPOINTMENT AFTERWARDS, SO I CHECKED MY WATCH REGULARLY.
SO WHEN DID SHE LEAVE YOU ALONE?
WHILE WE WERE WAITING FOR THE DYE TO SETTLE IN.
I THINK IT WAS FROM 8:20 TO 8:30.
SHE MUST'VE USED THAT TIME TO MOVE THE BODY! BY CAR, IT'S LESS THAN THREE MINUTES FROM HERE TO THE SCENE OF THE CRIME!
NO...
I DON'T HAVE A DRIVER'S LICENSE. I JUST TOOK OUT THE TRASH AND RAN TO THE CORNER STORE.
YOU SEE, I LIVE IN THIS BUILDING.
OH, AND I EMPTIED THE TRASH IN THE ALLEY NEXT TO THE CORNER STORE, NOT THE SPOT WHERE YOU FOUND THE BODY.
I CAN TAKE YOU THERE TOO IF YOU WANT.

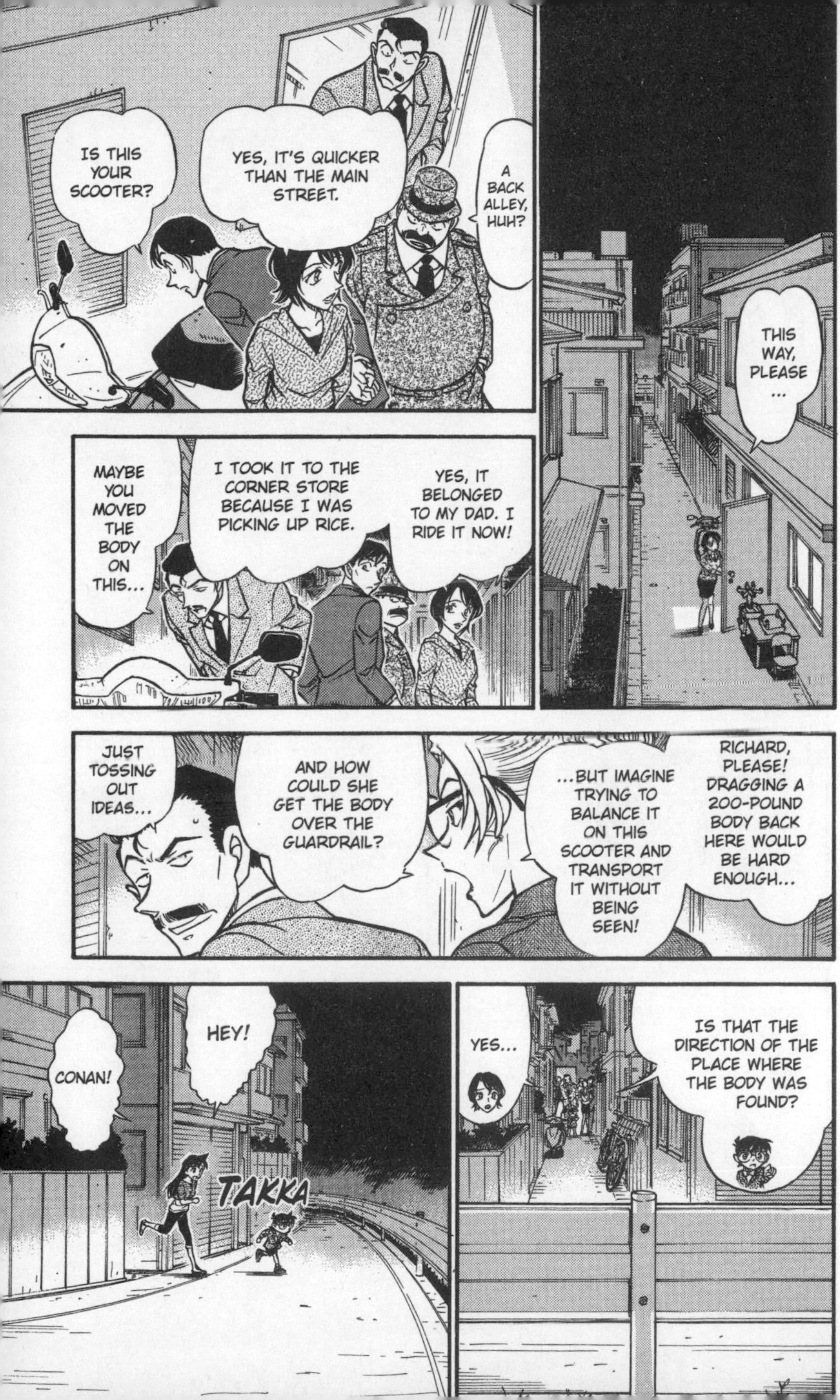
THIS WAY, PLEASE...
A BACK ALLEY, HUH?
YES, IT'S QUICKER THAN THE MAIN STREET.
IS THIS YOUR SCOOTER?
YES, IT BELONGED TO MY DAD. I RIDE IT NOW!
I TOOK IT TO THE CORNER STORE BECAUSE I WAS PICKING UP RICE.
MAYBE YOU MOVED THE BODY ON THIS...
RICHARD, PLEASE! DRAGGING A 200-POUND BODY BACK HERE WOULD BE HARD ENOUGH...
...BUT IMAGINE TRYING TO BALANCE IT ON THIS SCOOTER AND TRANSPORT IT WITHOUT BEING SEEN!
AND HOW COULD SHE GET THE BODY OVER THE GUARDRAIL?
JUST TOSSING OUT IDEAS...
IS THAT THE DIRECTION OF THE PLACE WHERE THE BODY WAS FOUND?
YES...
HEY!
CONAN!
TAKKA

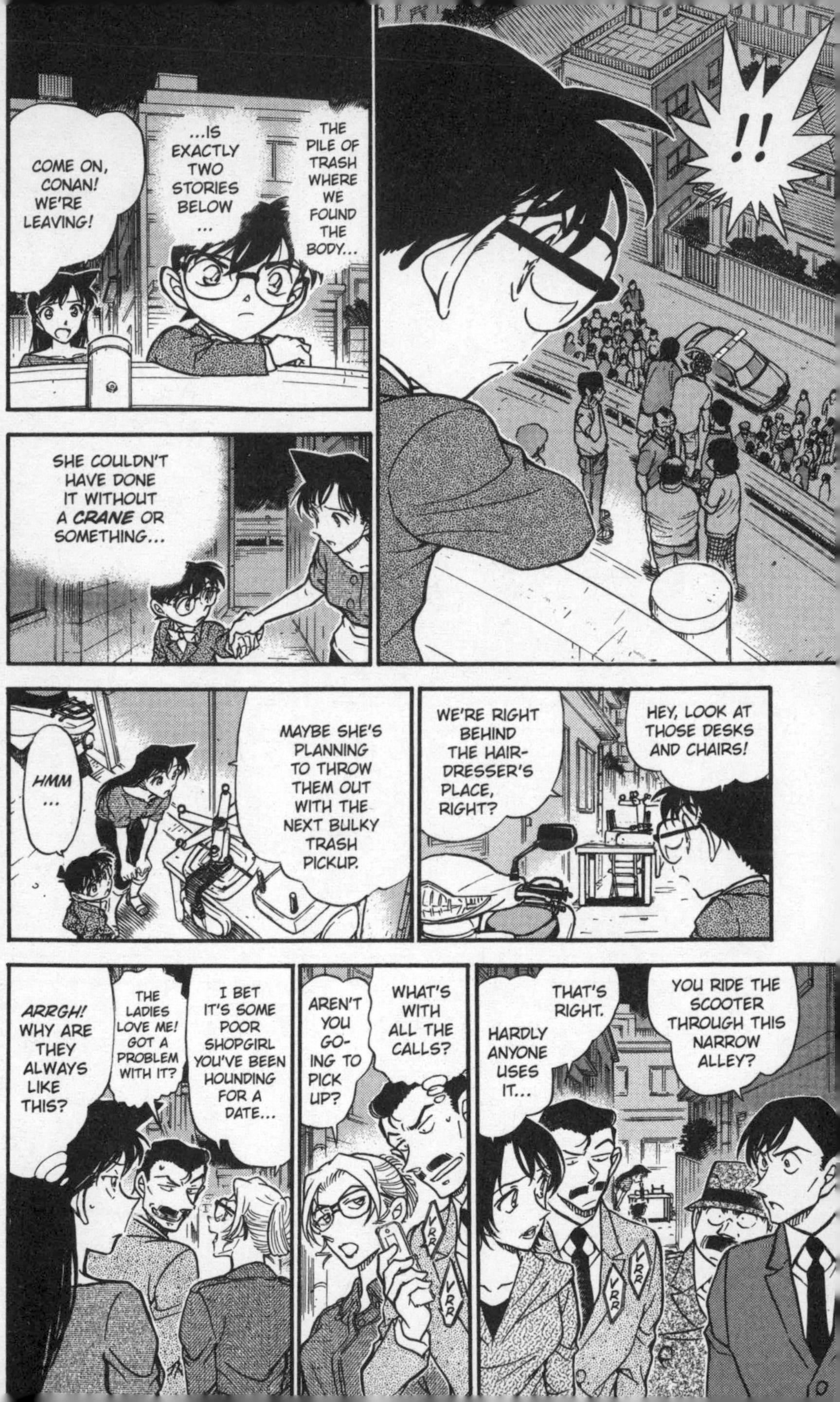
!!
THE PILE OF TRASH WHERE WE FOUND THE BODY...
...IS EXACTLY TWO STORIES BELOW...
COME ON, CONAN! WE'RE LEAVING!
SHE COULDN'T HAVE DONE IT WITHOUT A *CRANE* OR SOMETHING...
HEY, LOOK AT THOSE DESKS AND CHAIRS!
WE'RE RIGHT BEHIND THE HAIR-DRESSER'S PLACE, RIGHT?
MAYBE SHE'S PLANNING TO THROW THEM OUT WITH THE NEXT BULKY TRASH PICKUP.
HMM...
YOU RIDE THE SCOOTER THROUGH THIS NARROW ALLEY?
THAT'S RIGHT.
HARDLY ANYONE USES IT...
VRR
VRR
WHAT'S WITH ALL THE CALLS?
AREN'T YOU GOING TO PICK UP?
VRR
VRR
I BET IT'S SOME POOR SHOPGIRL YOU'VE BEEN HOUNDING FOR A DATE...
THE LADIES LOVE ME! GOT A PROBLEM WITH IT?
ARRGH! WHY ARE THEY ALWAYS LIKE THIS?

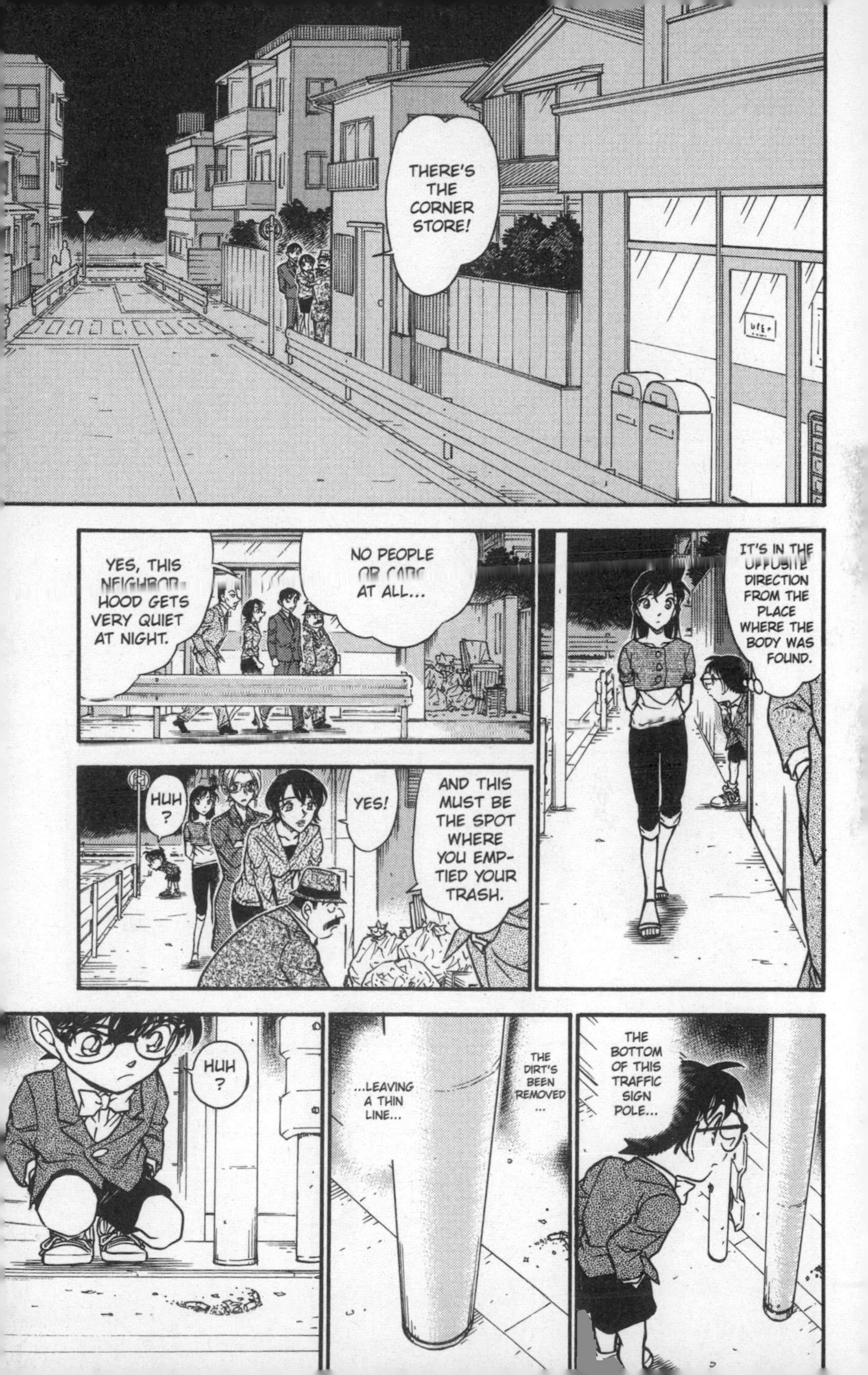
THERE'S THE CORNER STORE!
IT'S IN THE OPPOSITE DIRECTION FROM THE PLACE WHERE THE BODY WAS FOUND.
NO PEOPLE OR CARS AT ALL...
YES, THIS NEIGHBORHOOD GETS VERY QUIET AT NIGHT.
AND THIS MUST BE THE SPOT WHERE YOU EMPTIED YOUR TRASH.
YES!
HUH?
THE BOTTOM OF THIS TRAFFIC SIGN POLE...
THE DIRT'S BEEN REMOVED...
...LEAVING A THIN LINE...
HUH?

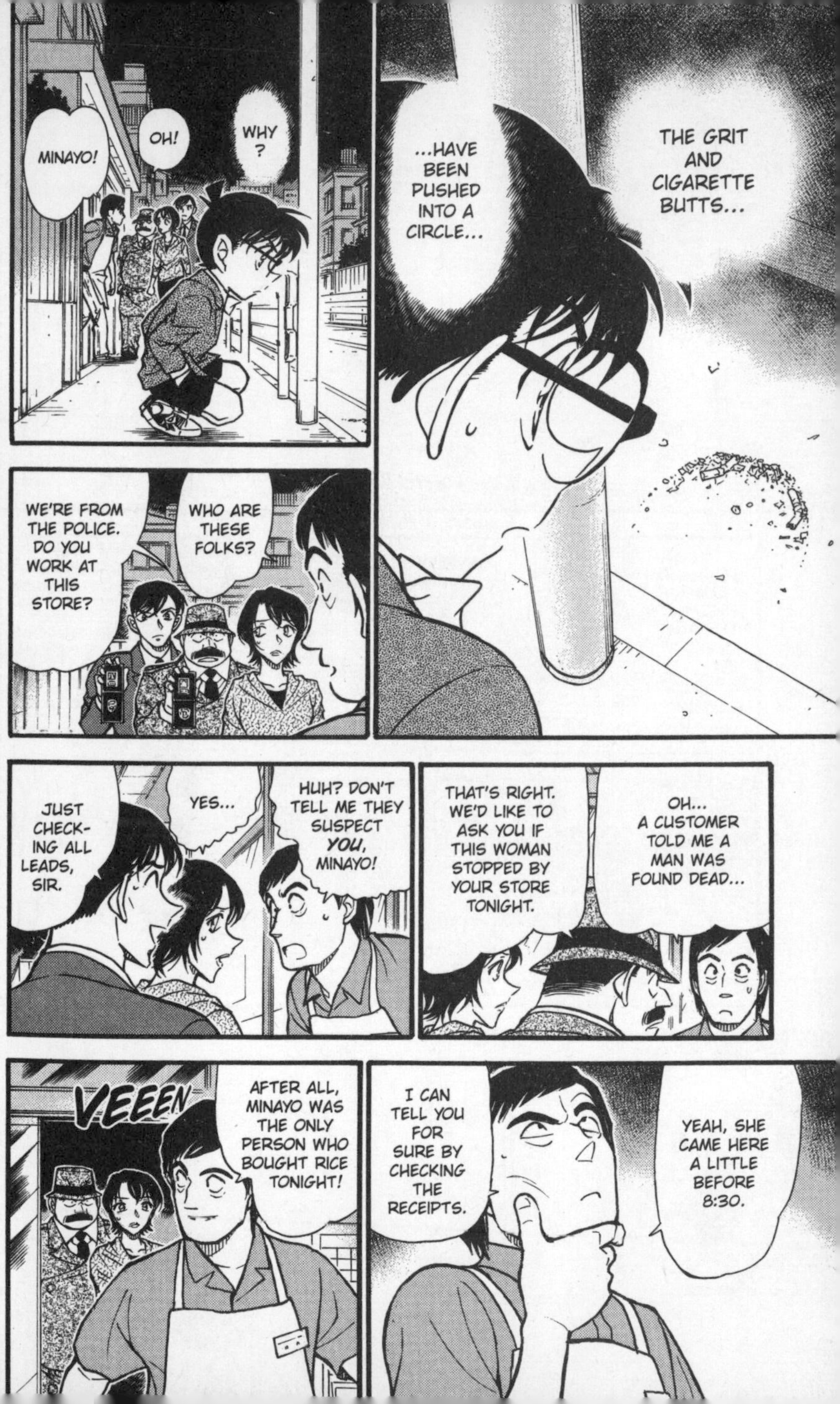
THE GRIT AND CIGARETTE BUTTS...
...HAVE BEEN PUSHED INTO A CIRCLE...
WHY?
OH!
MINAYO!
WHO ARE THESE FOLKS?
WE'RE FROM THE POLICE. DO YOU WORK AT THIS STORE?
OH... A CUSTOMER TOLD ME A MAN WAS FOUND DEAD...
THAT'S RIGHT. WE'D LIKE TO ASK YOU IF THIS WOMAN STOPPED BY YOUR STORE TONIGHT.
HUH? DON'T TELL ME THEY SUSPECT *YOU*, MINAYO!
YES...
JUST CHECKING ALL LEADS, SIR.
YEAH, SHE CAME HERE A LITTLE BEFORE 8:30.
I CAN TELL YOU FOR SURE BY CHECKING THE RECEIPTS.
AFTER ALL, MINAYO WAS THE ONLY PERSON WHO BOUGHT RICE TONIGHT!
VEEEN

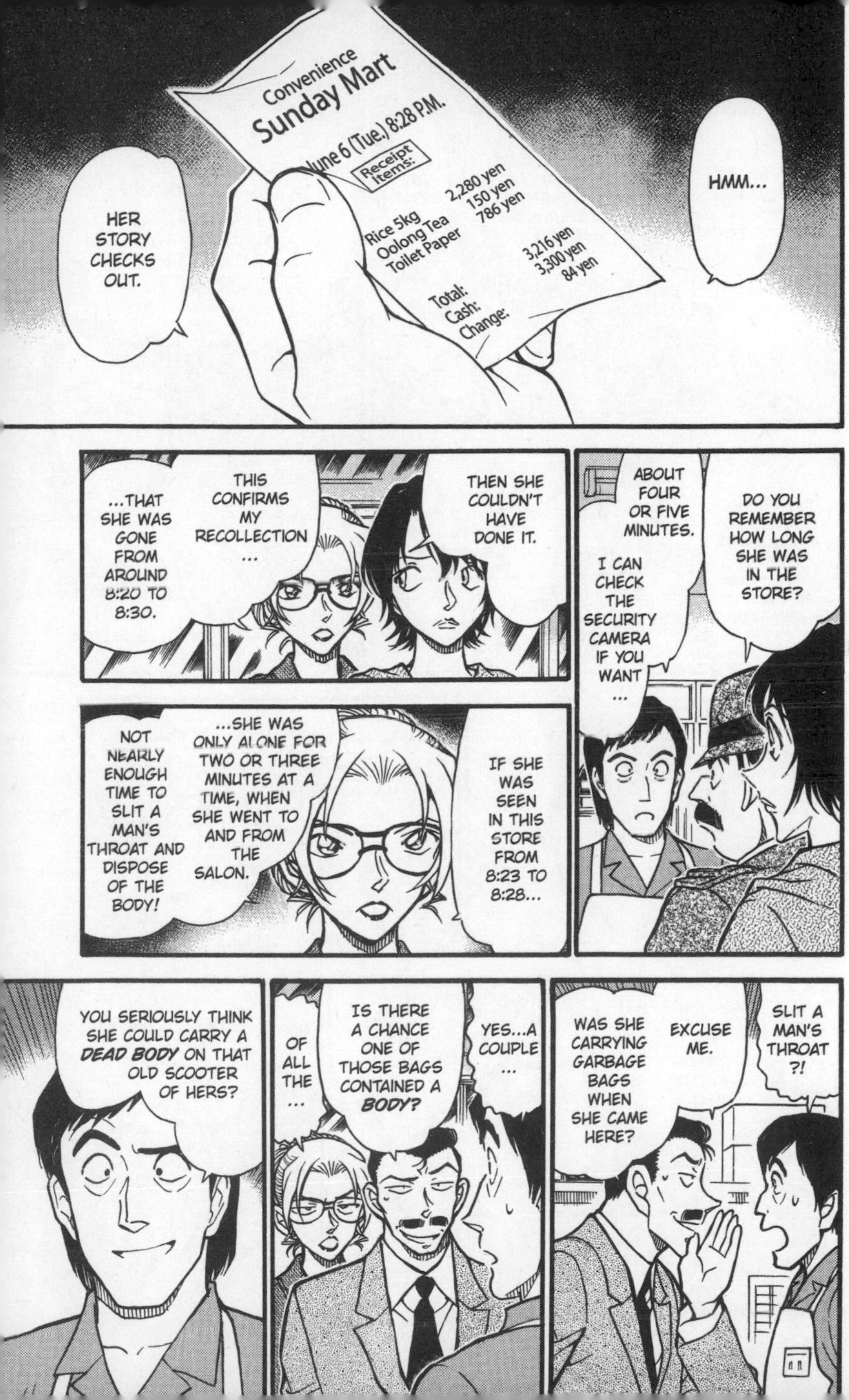
HMM...
Convenience
Sunday Mart
June 6 (Tue.) 8:28 P.M.
Receipt Items:
Rice 5kg 2,280 yen
Oolong Tea 150 yen
Toilet Paper 786 yen
Total: 3,216 yen
Cash: 3,300 yen
Change: 84 yen
HER STORY CHECKS OUT.
DO YOU REMEMBER HOW LONG SHE WAS IN THE STORE?
ABOUT FOUR OR FIVE MINUTES.
I CAN CHECK THE SECURITY CAMERA IF YOU WANT...
THEN SHE COULDN'T HAVE DONE IT.
THIS CONFIRMS MY RECOLLECTION...
...THAT SHE WAS GONE FROM AROUND 8:20 TO 8:30.
IF SHE WAS SEEN IN THIS STORE FROM 8:23 TO 8:28...
...SHE WAS ONLY ALONE FOR TWO OR THREE MINUTES AT A TIME, WHEN SHE WENT TO AND FROM THE SALON.
NOT NEARLY ENOUGH TIME TO SLIT A MAN'S THROAT AND DISPOSE OF THE BODY!
SLIT A MAN'S THROAT?!
EXCUSE ME.
WAS SHE CARRYING GARBAGE BAGS WHEN SHE CAME HERE?
YES...A COUPLE...
IS THERE A CHANCE ONE OF THOSE BAGS CONTAINED A ***BODY?***
OF ALL THE...
YOU SERIOUSLY THINK SHE COULD CARRY A ***DEAD BODY*** ON THAT OLD SCOOTER OF HERS?

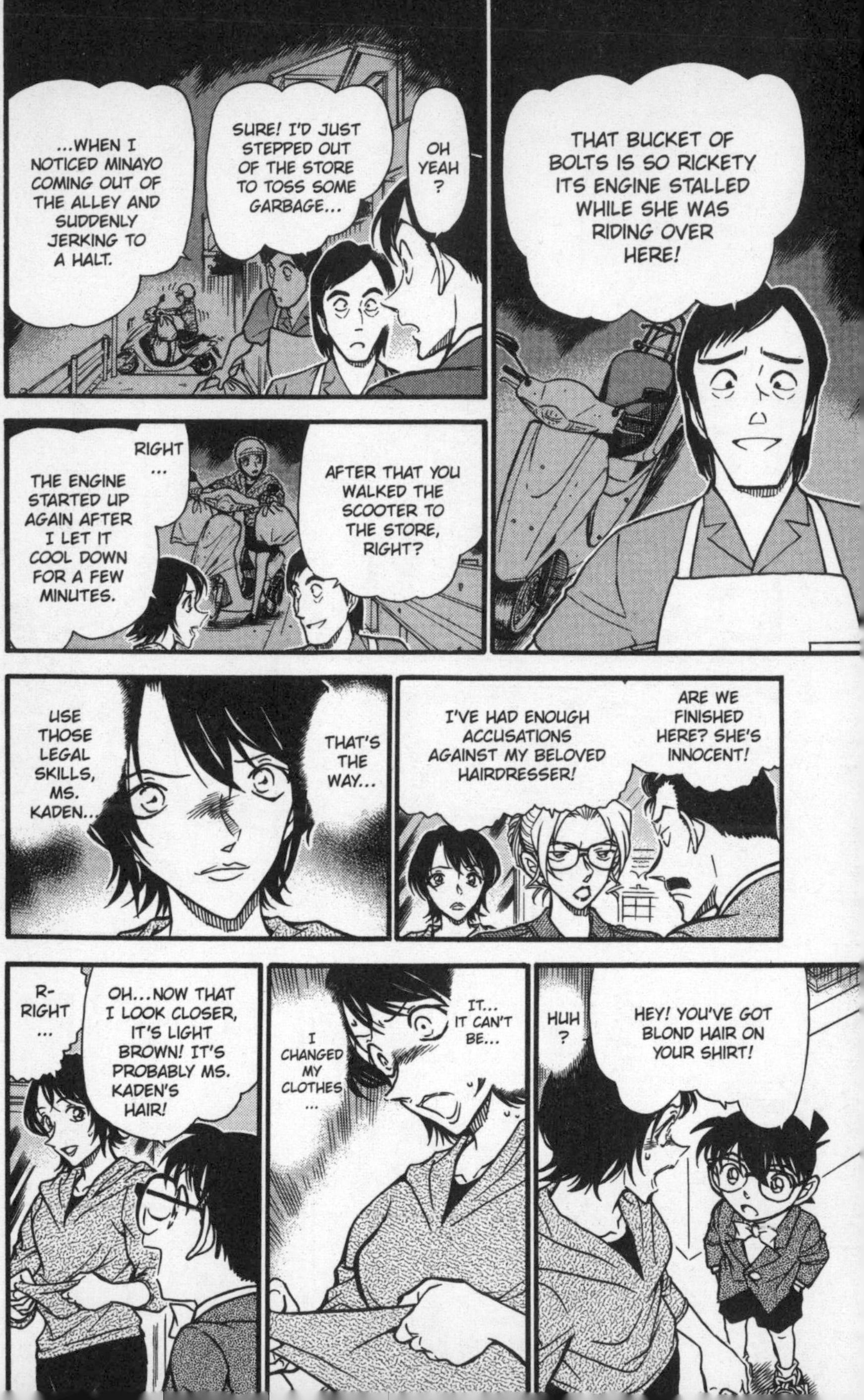
OH YEAH ?
SURE! I'D JUST STEPPED OUT OF THE STORE TO TOSS SOME GARBAGE...
...WHEN I NOTICED MINAYO COMING OUT OF THE ALLEY AND SUDDENLY JERKING TO A HALT.
THAT BUCKET OF BOLTS IS SO RICKETY ITS ENGINE STALLED WHILE SHE WAS RIDING OVER HERE!
AFTER THAT YOU WALKED THE SCOOTER TO THE STORE, RIGHT?
RIGHT ...
THE ENGINE STARTED UP AGAIN AFTER I LET IT COOL DOWN FOR A FEW MINUTES.
ARE WE FINISHED HERE? SHE'S INNOCENT!
I'VE HAD ENOUGH ACCUSATIONS AGAINST MY BELOVED HAIRDRESSER!
THAT'S THE WAY...
USE THOSE LEGAL SKILLS, MS. KADEN...
HEY! YOU'VE GOT BLOND HAIR ON YOUR SHIRT!
HUH ?
IT... IT CAN'T BE...
I CHANGED MY CLOTHES ...
OH...NOW THAT I LOOK CLOSER, IT'S LIGHT BROWN! IT'S PROBABLY MS. KADEN'S HAIR!
R-RIGHT ...

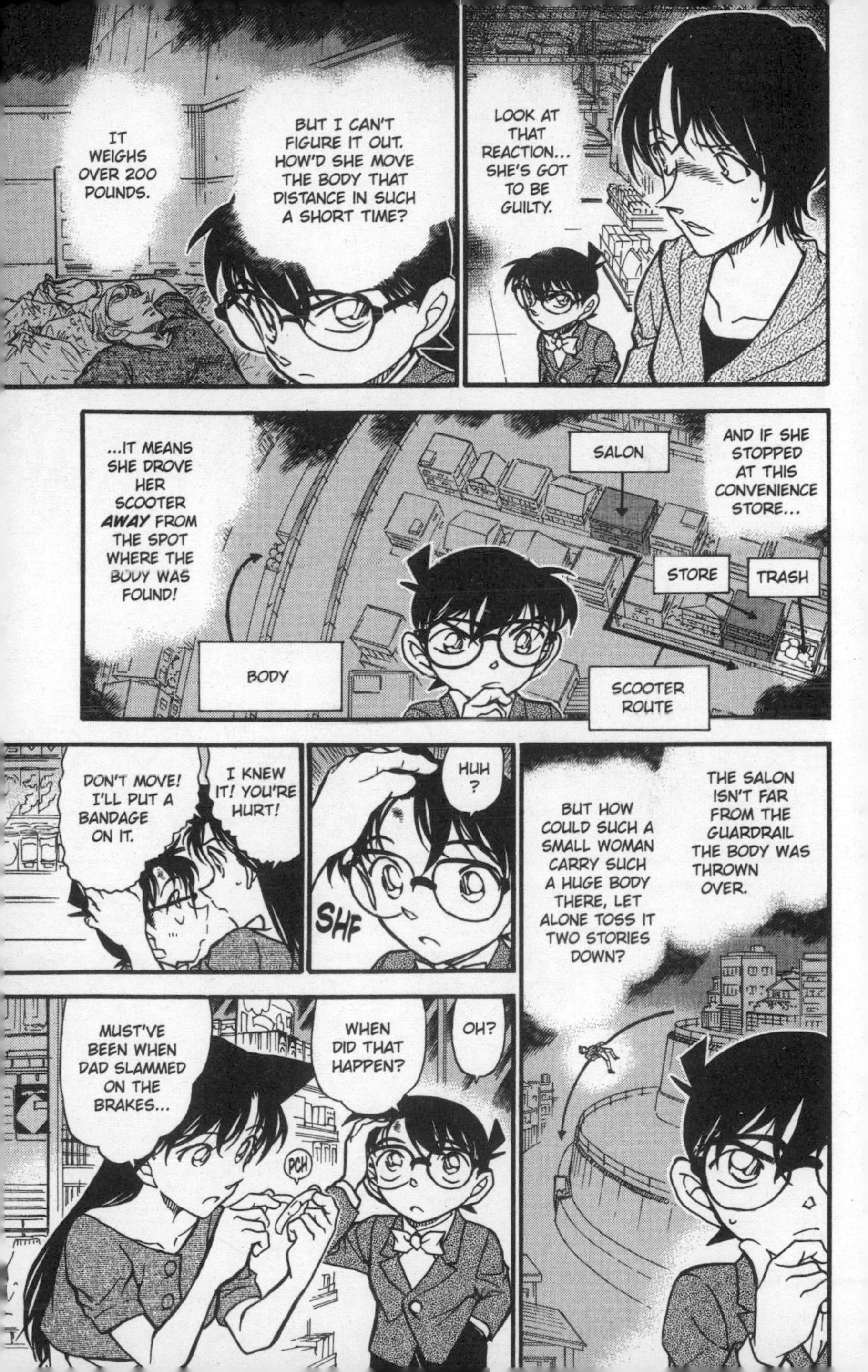
LOOK AT THAT REACTION... SHE'S GOT TO BE GUILTY.
BUT I CAN'T FIGURE IT OUT. HOW'D SHE MOVE THE BODY THAT DISTANCE IN SUCH A SHORT TIME?
IT WEIGHS OVER 200 POUNDS.
AND IF SHE STOPPED AT THIS CONVENIENCE STORE...
SALON
TRASH
STORE
SCOOTER ROUTE
...IT MEANS SHE DROVE HER SCOOTER AWAY FROM THE SPOT WHERE THE BODY WAS FOUND!
BODY
THE SALON ISN'T FAR FROM THE GUARDRAIL THE BODY WAS THROWN OVER.
BUT HOW COULD SUCH A SMALL WOMAN CARRY SUCH A HUGE BODY THERE, LET ALONE TOSS IT TWO STORIES DOWN?
HUH?
SHF
I KNEW IT! YOU'RE HURT!
DON'T MOVE! I'LL PUT A BANDAGE ON IT.
OH?
WHEN DID THAT HAPPEN?
MUST'VE BEEN WHEN DAD SLAMMED ON THE BRAKES...
PCH

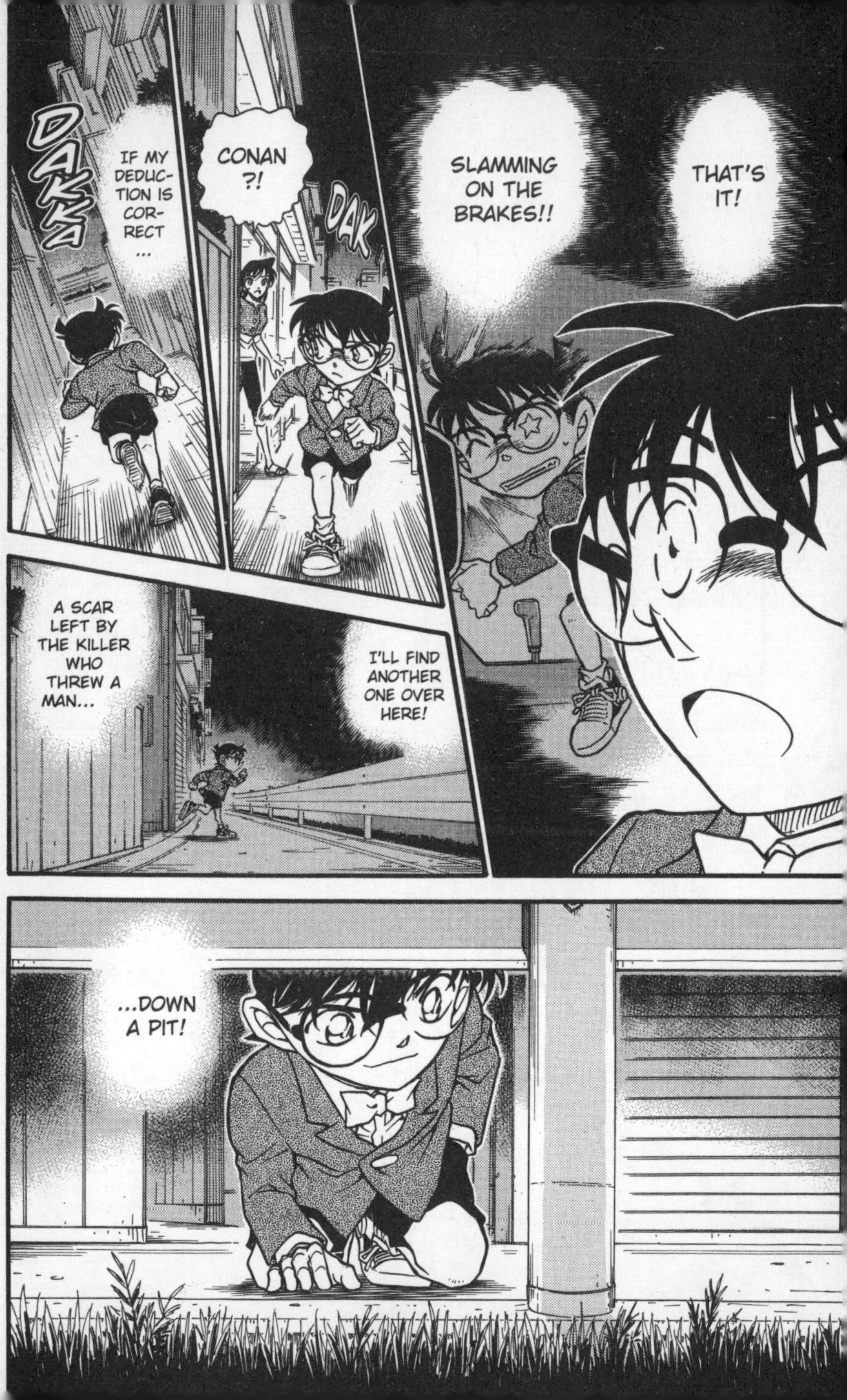
THAT'S IT!
SLAMMING ON THE BRAKES!!
CONAN ?!
DAK
DAKA
IF MY DEDUCTION IS CORRECT ...
I'LL FIND ANOTHER ONE OVER HERE!
A SCAR LEFT BY THE KILLER WHO THREW A MAN...
...DOWN A PIT!

FILE 4: MECHANICS OF AN ALIBI

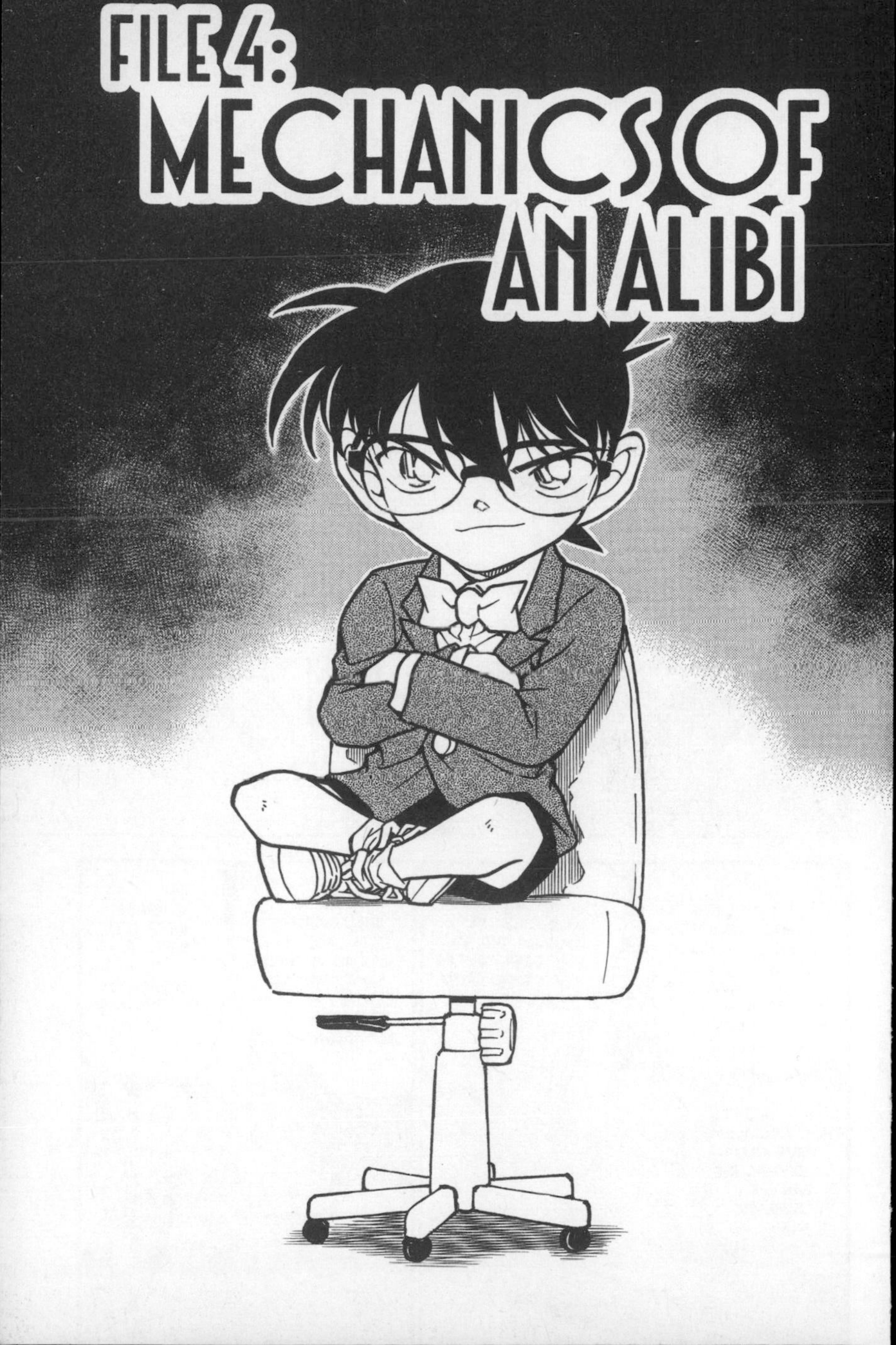

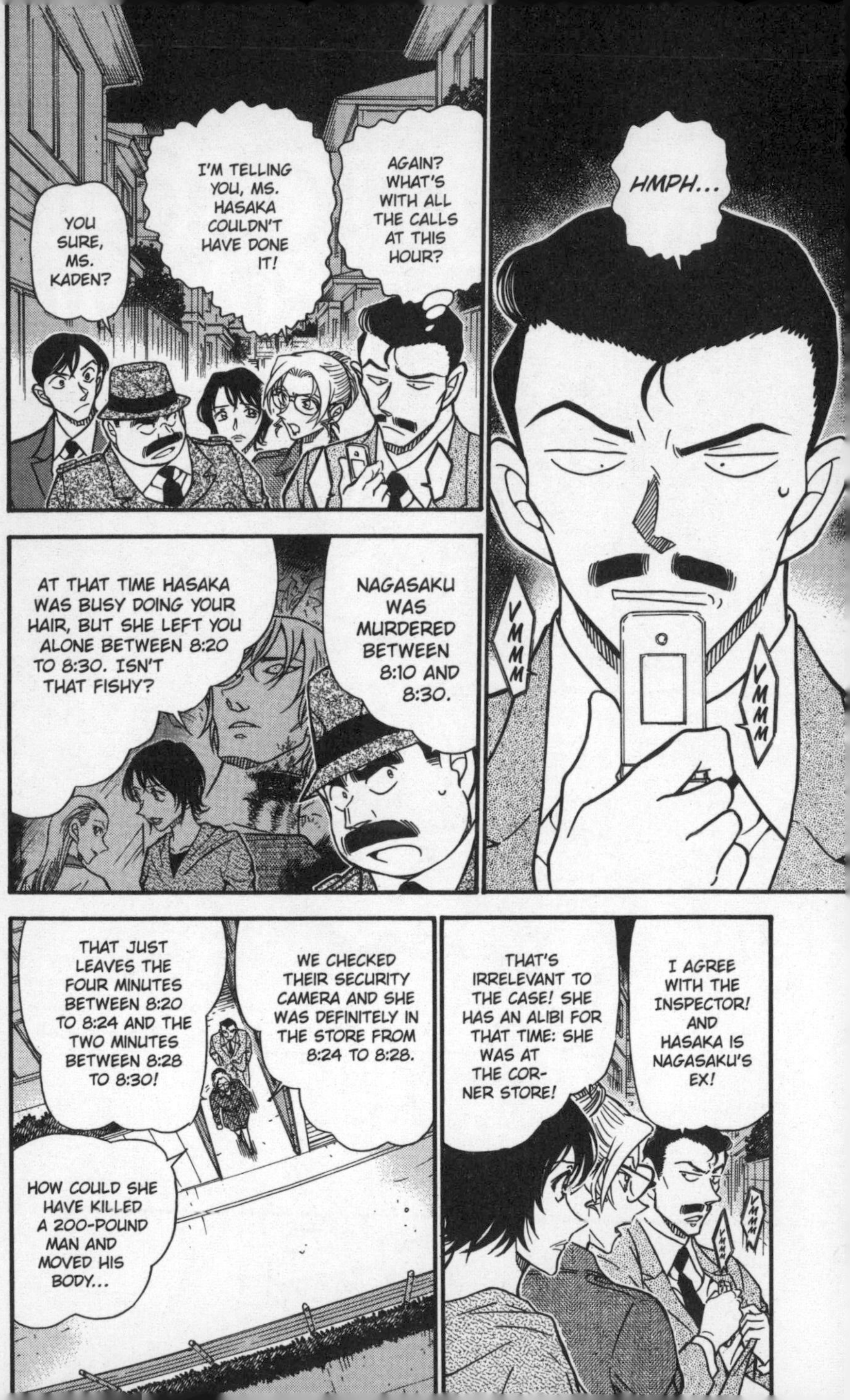
HMPH...
VMMM
VMMM
AGAIN? WHAT'S WITH ALL THE CALLS AT THIS HOUR?
I'M TELLING YOU, MS. HASAKA COULDN'T HAVE DONE IT!
YOU SURE, MS. KADEN?
NAGASAKU WAS MURDERED BETWEEN 8:10 AND 8:30.
AT THAT TIME HASAKA WAS BUSY DOING YOUR HAIR, BUT SHE LEFT YOU ALONE BETWEEN 8:20 TO 8:30. ISN'T THAT FISHY?
I AGREE WITH THE INSPECTOR! AND HASAKA IS NAGASAKU'S EX!
THAT'S IRRELEVANT TO THE CASE! SHE HAS AN ALIBI FOR THAT TIME: SHE WAS AT THE COR-NER STORE!
VMMM
WE CHECKED THEIR SECURITY CAMERA AND SHE WAS DEFINITELY IN THE STORE FROM 8:24 TO 8:28.
THAT JUST LEAVES THE FOUR MINUTES BETWEEN 8:20 TO 8:24 AND THE TWO MINUTES BETWEEN 8:28 TO 8:30!
HOW COULD SHE HAVE KILLED A 200-POUND MAN AND MOVED HIS BODY...

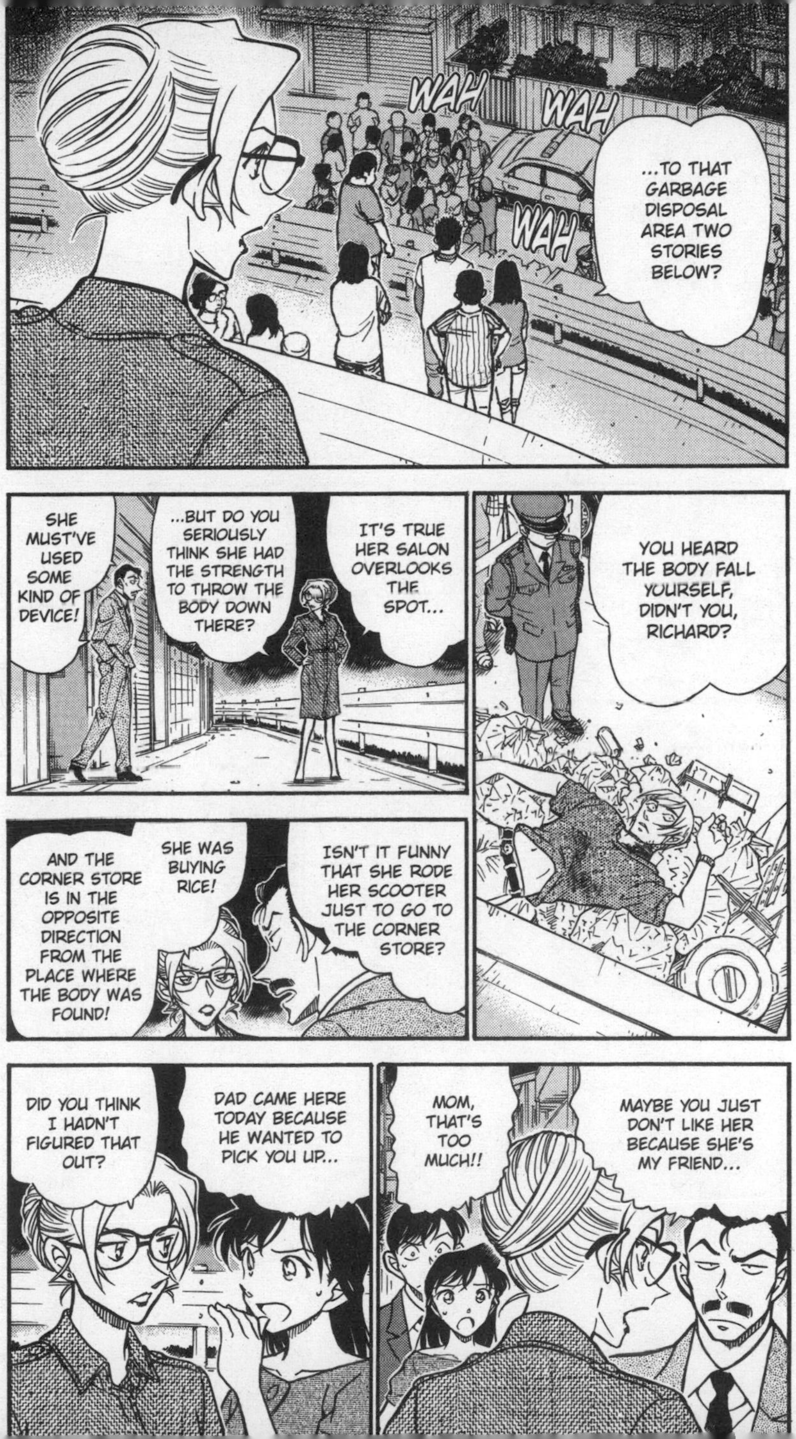
WAH
WAH
WAH
...TO THAT GARBAGE DISPOSAL AREA TWO STORIES BELOW?
YOU HEARD THE BODY FALL YOURSELF, DIDN'T YOU, RICHARD?
IT'S TRUE HER SALON OVERLOOKS THE SPOT...
...BUT DO YOU SERIOUSLY THINK SHE HAD THE STRENGTH TO THROW THE BODY DOWN THERE?
SHE MUST'VE USED SOME KIND OF DEVICE!
ISN'T IT FUNNY THAT SHE RODE HER SCOOTER JUST TO GO TO THE CORNER STORE?
SHE WAS BUYING RICE!
AND THE CORNER STORE IS IN THE OPPOSITE DIRECTION FROM THE PLACE WHERE THE BODY WAS FOUND!
MAYBE YOU JUST DON'T LIKE HER BECAUSE SHE'S MY FRIEND...
MOM, THAT'S TOO MUCH!!
DAD CAME HERE TODAY BECAUSE HE WANTED TO PICK YOU UP...
DID YOU THINK I HADN'T FIGURED THAT OUT?

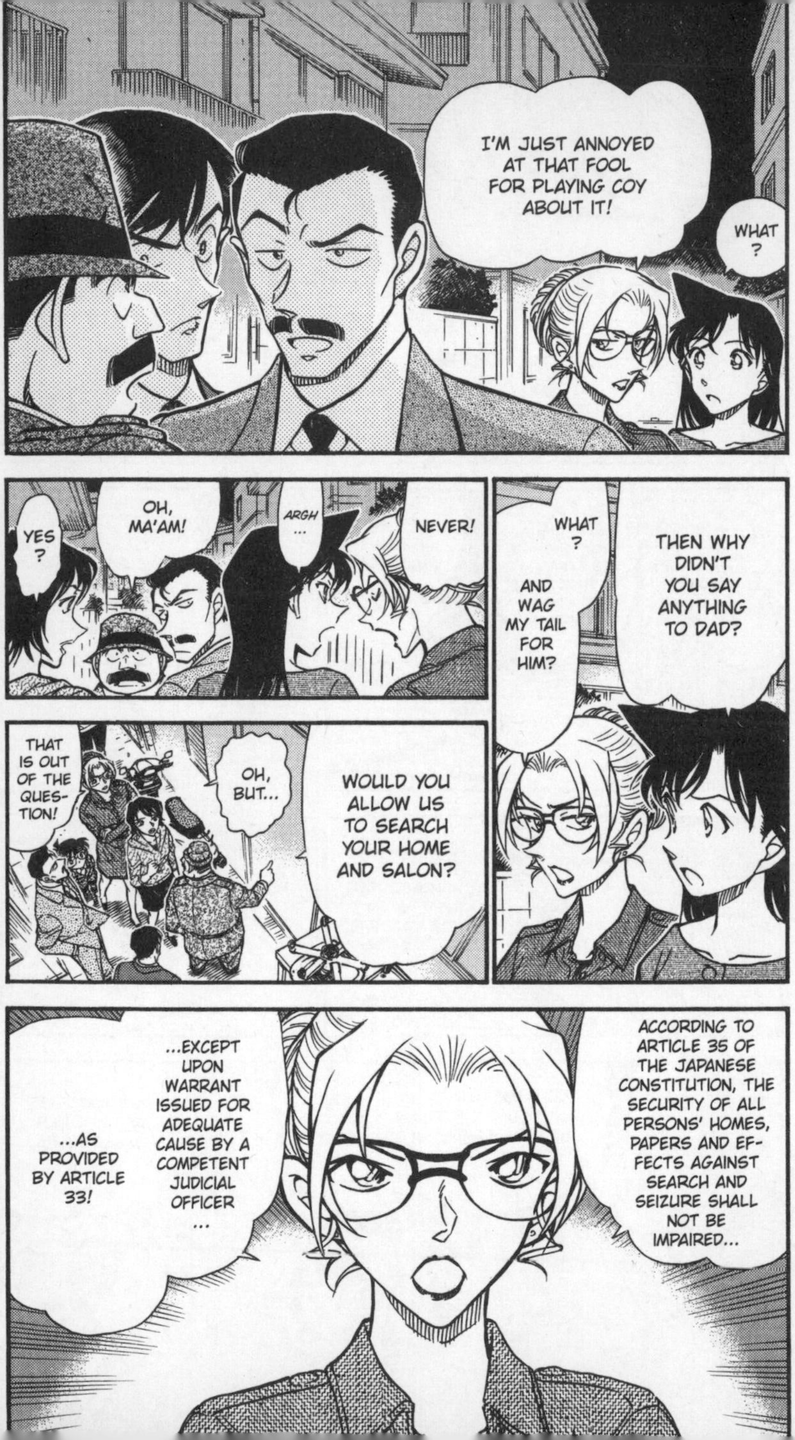
I'M JUST ANNOYED AT THAT FOOL FOR PLAYING COY ABOUT IT!
WHAT?
THEN WHY DIDN'T YOU SAY ANYTHING TO DAD?
WHAT? AND WAG MY TAIL FOR HIM?
NEVER!
ARGH...
OH, MA'AM!
YES?
WOULD YOU ALLOW US TO SEARCH YOUR HOME AND SALON?
OH, BUT...
THAT IS OUT OF THE QUES-TION!
ACCORDING TO ARTICLE 35 OF THE JAPANESE CONSTITUTION, THE SECURITY OF ALL PERSONS' HOMES, PAPERS AND EF-FECTS AGAINST SEARCH AND SEIZURE SHALL NOT BE IMPAIRED...
...EXCEPT UPON WARRANT ISSUED FOR ADEQUATE CAUSE BY A COMPETENT JUDICIAL OFFICER...
...AS PROVIDED BY ARTICLE 33!

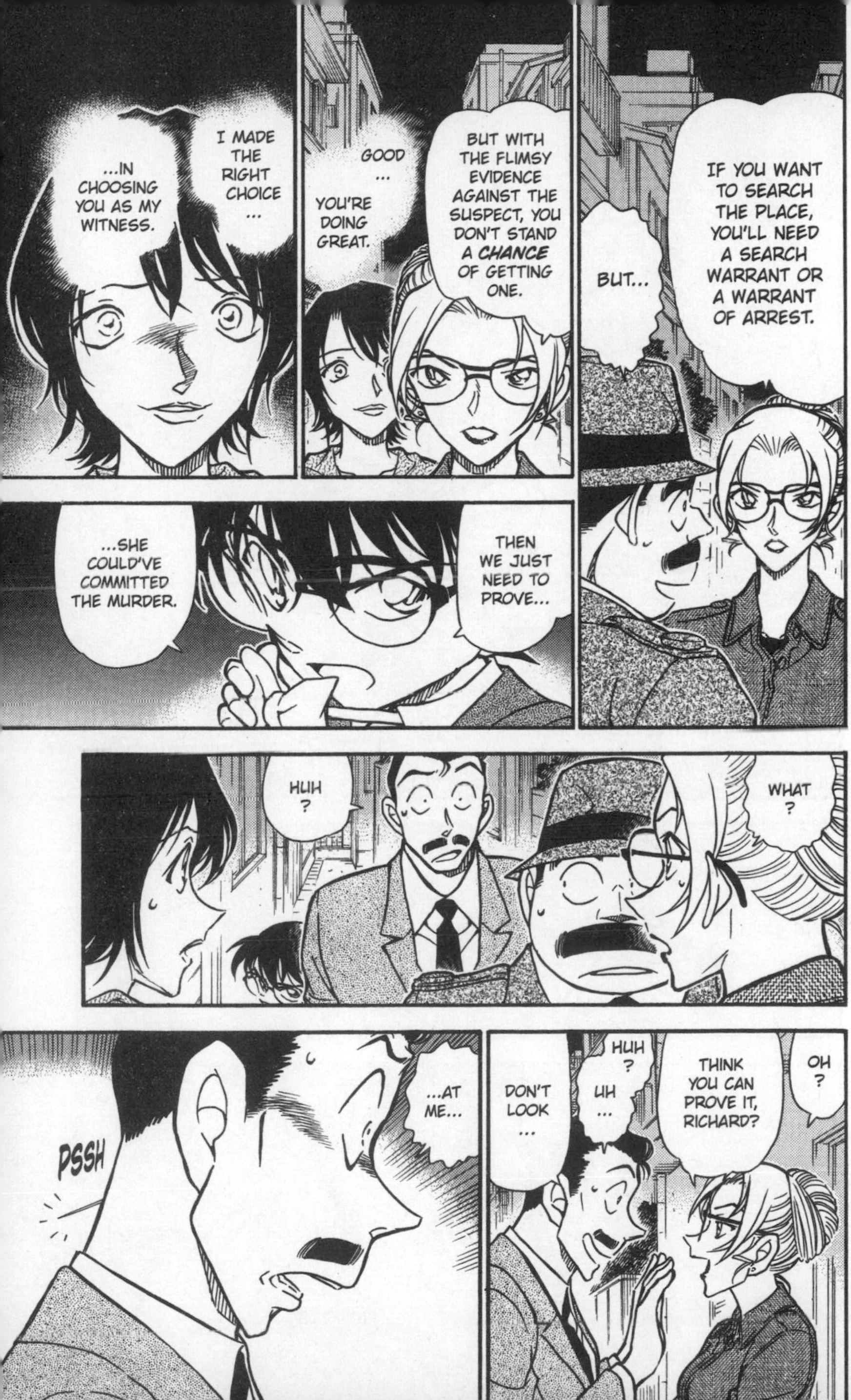
IF YOU WANT TO SEARCH THE PLACE, YOU'LL NEED A SEARCH WARRANT OR A WARRANT OF ARREST.
BUT...
BUT WITH THE FLIMSY EVIDENCE AGAINST THE SUSPECT, YOU DON'T STAND A CHANCE OF GETTING ONE.
GOOD ...
YOU'RE DOING GREAT.
I MADE THE RIGHT CHOICE ...
...IN CHOOSING YOU AS MY WITNESS.
THEN WE JUST NEED TO PROVE...
...SHE COULD'VE COMMITTED THE MURDER.
WHAT?
HUH?
OH?
THINK YOU CAN PROVE IT, RICHARD?
HUH?
UH ...
DON'T LOOK ...
...AT ME...
PSSH

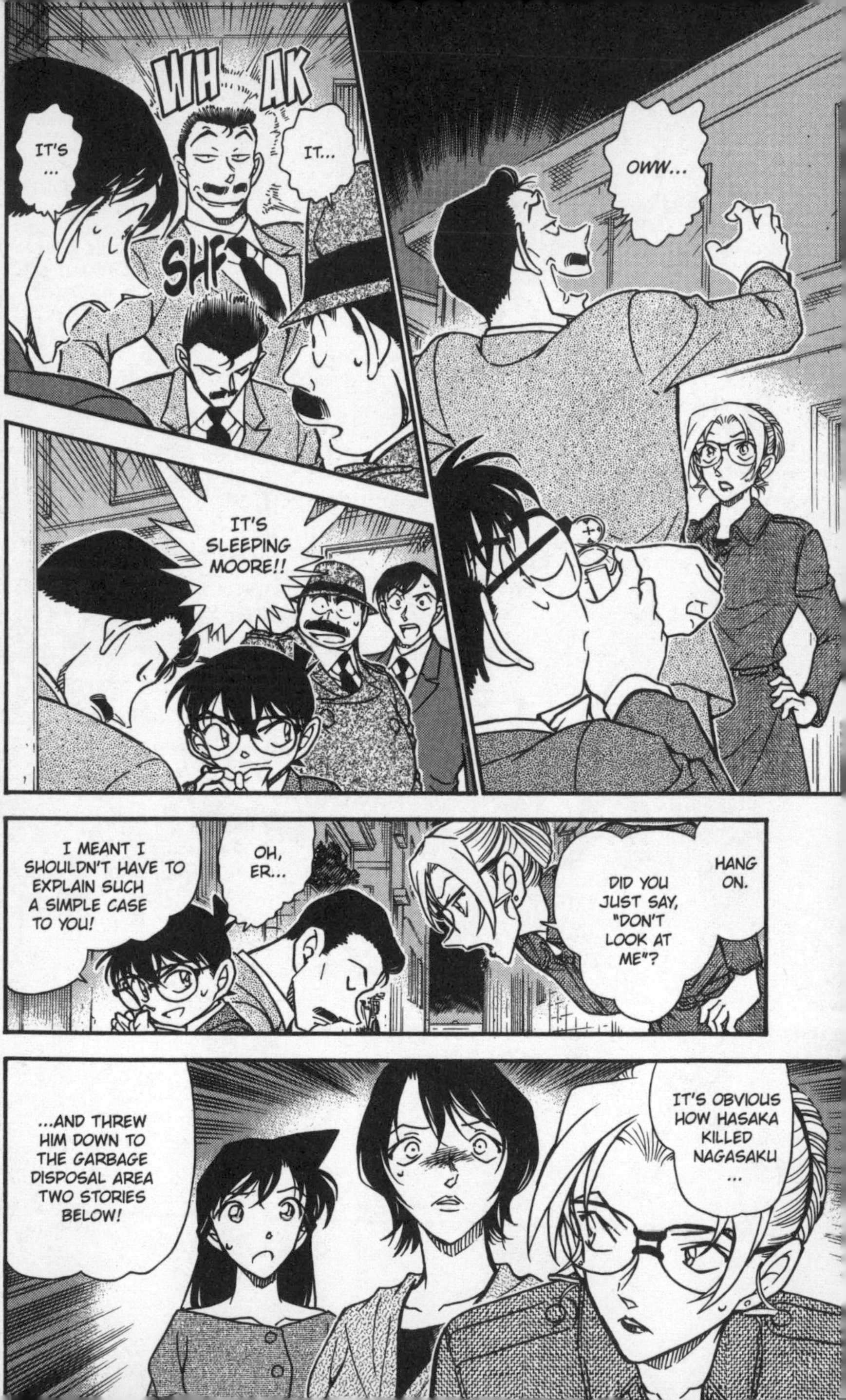
OWW...
WH AK
IT...
IT'S ...
SHF
IT'S SLEEPING MOORE!!
HANG ON.
DID YOU JUST SAY, "DON'T LOOK AT ME"?
OH, ER...
I MEANT I SHOULDN'T HAVE TO EXPLAIN SUCH A SIMPLE CASE TO YOU!
IT'S OBVIOUS HOW HASAKA KILLED NAGASAKU ...
...AND THREW HIM DOWN TO THE GARBAGE DISPOSAL AREA TWO STORIES BELOW!

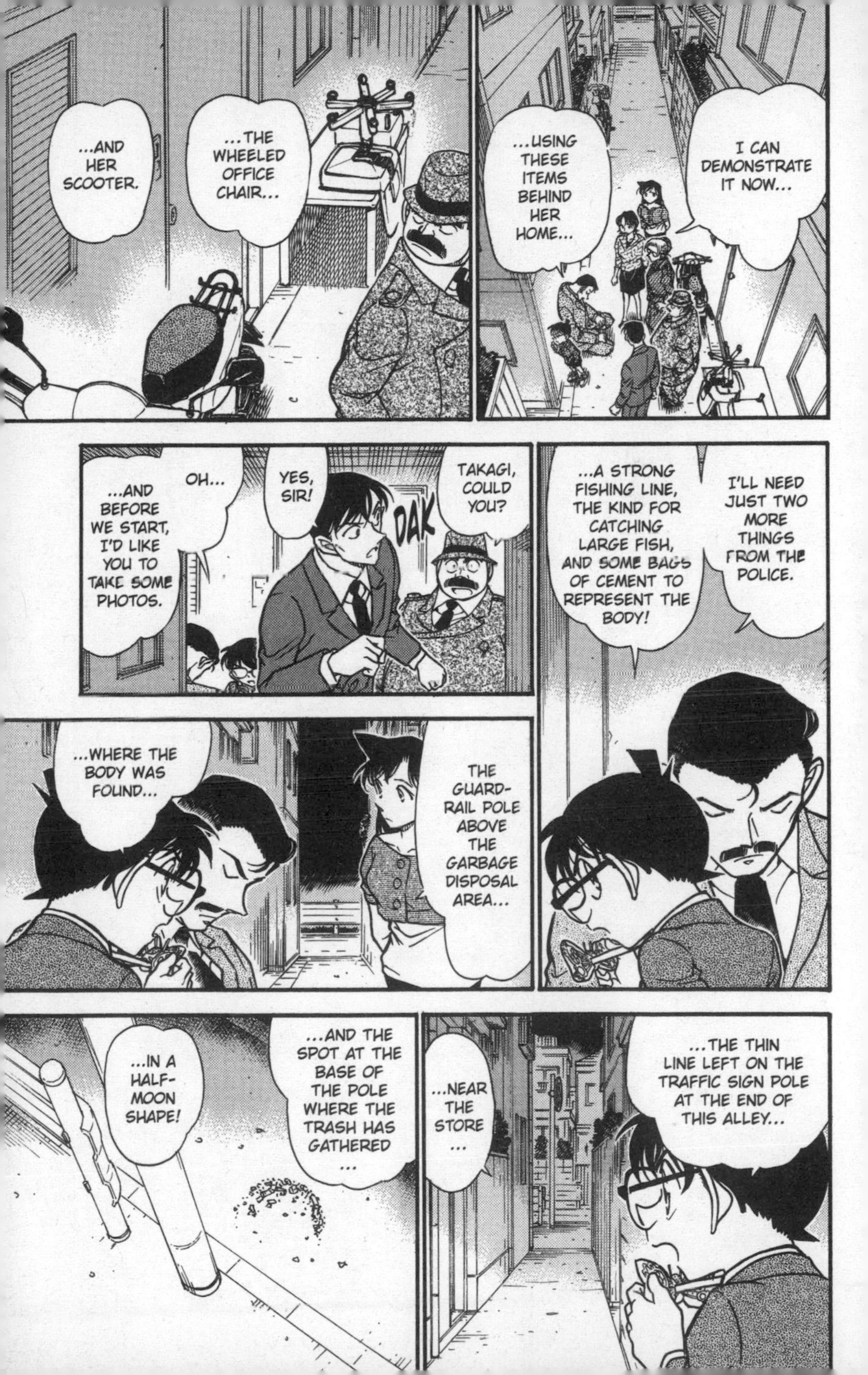
I CAN DEMONSTRATE IT NOW...
...USING THESE ITEMS BEHIND HER HOME...
...THE WHEELED OFFICE CHAIR...
...AND HER SCOOTER.
I'LL NEED JUST TWO MORE THINGS FROM THE POLICE.
...A STRONG FISHING LINE, THE KIND FOR CATCHING LARGE FISH, AND SOME BAGS OF CEMENT TO REPRESENT THE BODY!
TAKAGI, COULD YOU?
DAK
YES, SIR!
OH...
...AND BEFORE WE START, I'D LIKE YOU TO TAKE SOME PHOTOS.
THE GUARD-RAIL POLE ABOVE THE GARBAGE DISPOSAL AREA...
...WHERE THE BODY WAS FOUND...
...THE THIN LINE LEFT ON THE TRAFFIC SIGN POLE AT THE END OF THIS ALLEY...
...NEAR THE STORE ...
...AND THE SPOT AT THE BASE OF THE POLE WHERE THE TRASH HAS GATHERED ...
...IN A HALF-MOON SHAPE!

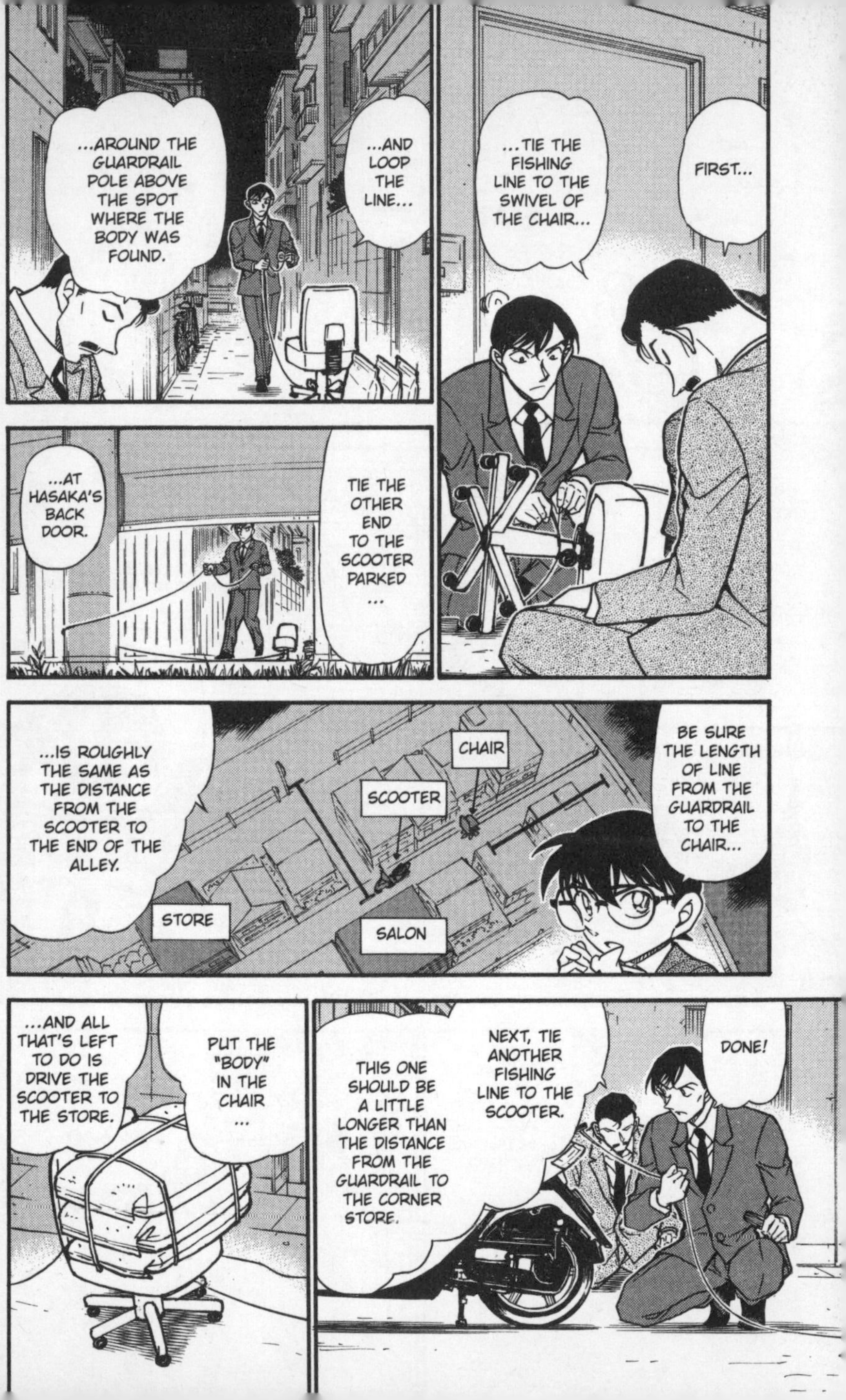
FIRST...
...TIE THE FISHING LINE TO THE SWIVEL OF THE CHAIR...
...AND LOOP THE LINE...
...AROUND THE GUARDRAIL POLE ABOVE THE SPOT WHERE THE BODY WAS FOUND.
TIE THE OTHER END TO THE SCOOTER PARKED ...
...AT HASAKA'S BACK DOOR.
BE SURE THE LENGTH OF LINE FROM THE GUARDRAIL TO THE CHAIR...
CHAIR
SCOOTER
STORE
SALON
...IS ROUGHLY THE SAME AS THE DISTANCE FROM THE SCOOTER TO THE END OF THE ALLEY.
DONE!
NEXT, TIE ANOTHER FISHING LINE TO THE SCOOTER.
THIS ONE SHOULD BE A LITTLE LONGER THAN THE DISTANCE FROM THE GUARDRAIL TO THE CORNER STORE.
PUT THE "BODY" IN THE CHAIR ...
...AND ALL THAT'S LEFT TO DO IS DRIVE THE SCOOTER TO THE STORE.

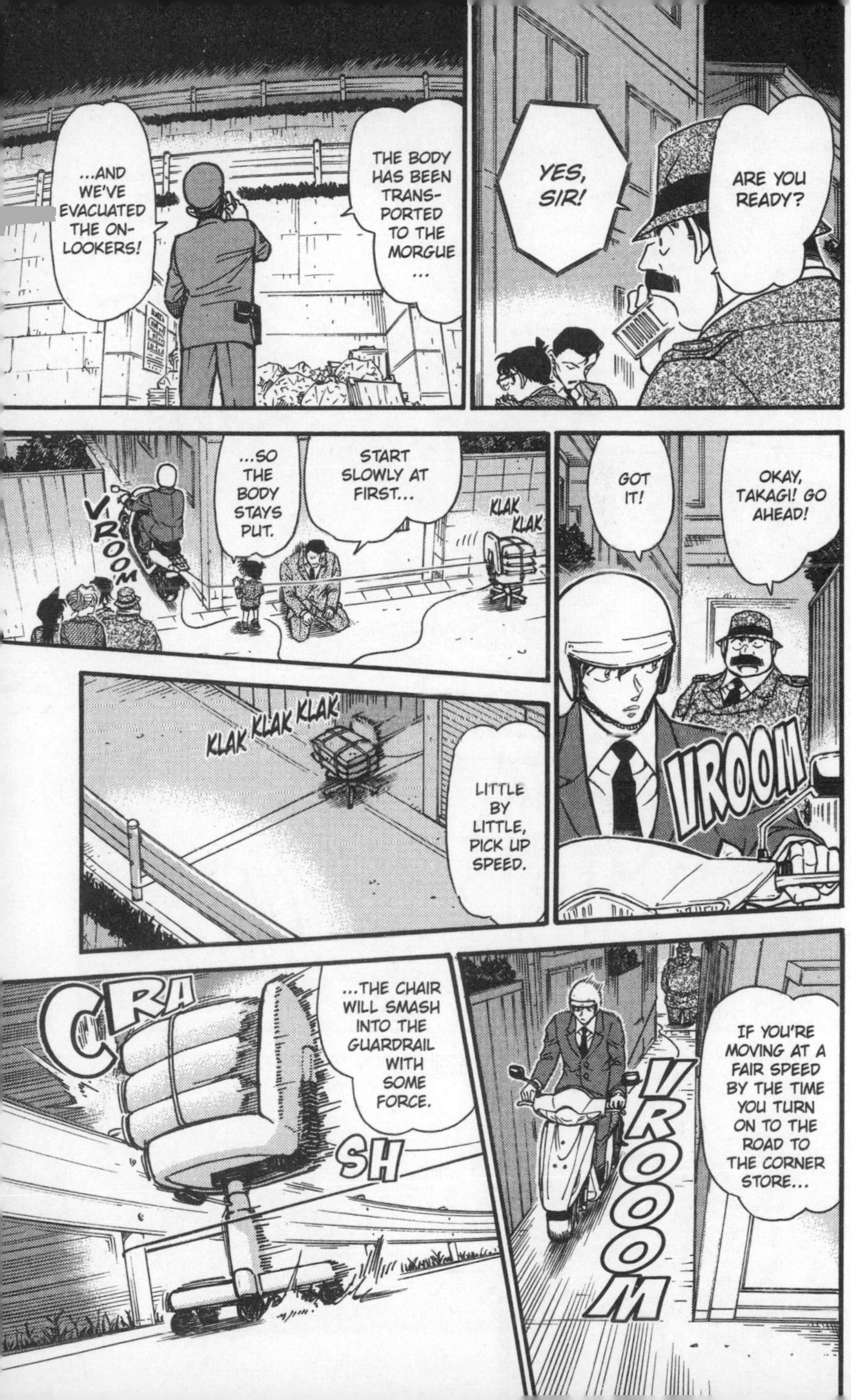
ARE YOU READY?
YES, SIR!
THE BODY HAS BEEN TRANS-PORTED TO THE MORGUE...
...AND WE'VE EVACUATED THE ON-LOOKERS!
OKAY, TAKAGI! GO AHEAD!
GOT IT!
VROOM
START SLOWLY AT FIRST...
...SO THE BODY STAYS PUT.
KLAK KLAK
VROOM
LITTLE BY LITTLE, PICK UP SPEED.
KLAK KLAK KLAK
IF YOU'RE MOVING AT A FAIR SPEED BY THE TIME YOU TURN ON TO THE ROAD TO THE CORNER STORE...
VROOOOM
...THE CHAIR WILL SMASH INTO THE GUARDRAIL WITH SOME FORCE.
CRA
SH

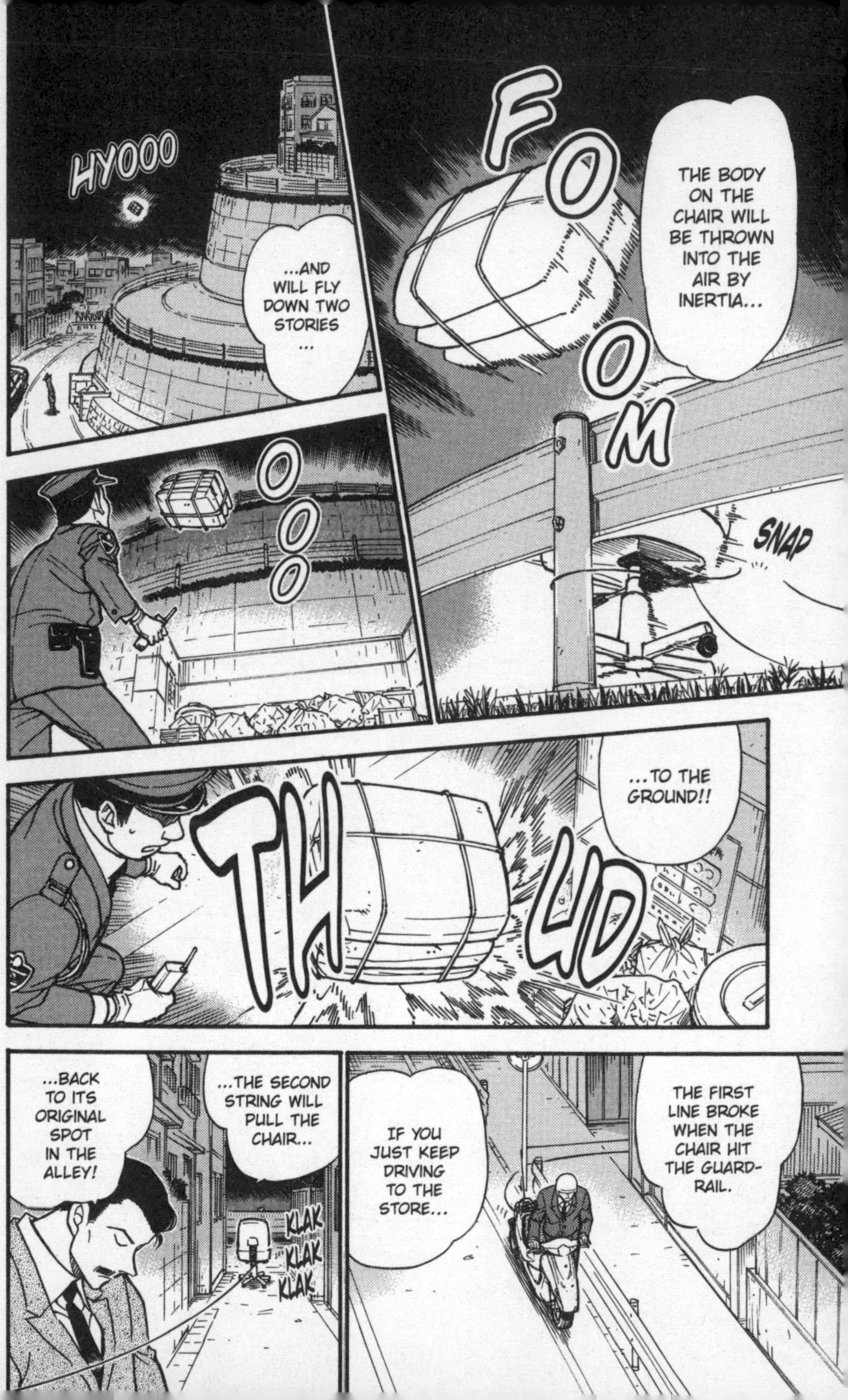
FOOM
THE BODY ON THE CHAIR WILL BE THROWN INTO THE AIR BY INERTIA...
SNAP
HYOOO
...AND WILL FLY DOWN TWO STORIES ...
OOOO
THUD
...TO THE GROUND!!
THE FIRST LINE BROKE WHEN THE CHAIR HIT THE GUARD-RAIL.
IF YOU JUST KEEP DRIVING TO THE STORE...
...THE SECOND STRING WILL PULL THE CHAIR...
KLAK KLAK KLAK
...BACK TO ITS ORIGINAL SPOT IN THE ALLEY!

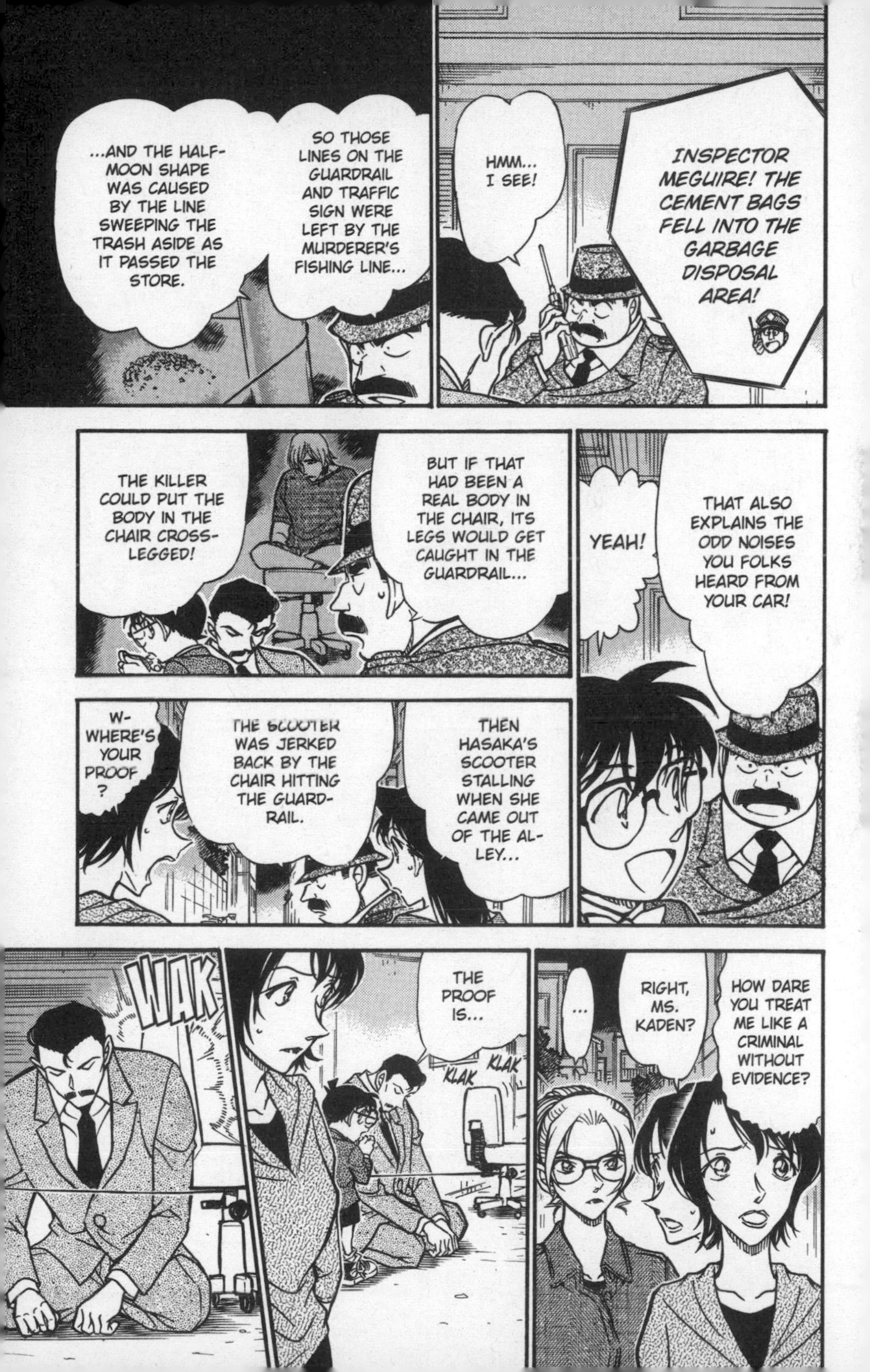
INSPECTOR MEGUIRE! THE CEMENT BAGS FELL INTO THE GARBAGE DISPOSAL AREA!
HMM... I SEE!
SO THOSE LINES ON THE GUARDRAIL AND TRAFFIC SIGN WERE LEFT BY THE MURDERER'S FISHING LINE...
...AND THE HALF-MOON SHAPE WAS CAUSED BY THE LINE SWEEPING THE TRASH ASIDE AS IT PASSED THE STORE.
THAT ALSO EXPLAINS THE ODD NOISES YOU FOLKS HEARD FROM YOUR CAR!
YEAH!
BUT IF THAT HAD BEEN A REAL BODY IN THE CHAIR, ITS LEGS WOULD GET CAUGHT IN THE GUARDRAIL...
THE KILLER COULD PUT THE BODY IN THE CHAIR CROSS-LEGGED!
THEN HASAKA'S SCOOTER STALLING WHEN SHE CAME OUT OF THE AL-LEY...
THE SCOOTER WAS JERKED BACK BY THE CHAIR HITTING THE GUARD-RAIL.
W-WHERE'S YOUR PROOF?
HOW DARE YOU TREAT ME LIKE A CRIMINAL WITHOUT EVIDENCE?
RIGHT, MS. KADEN?
...
THE PROOF IS...
KLAK
KLAK
WAK

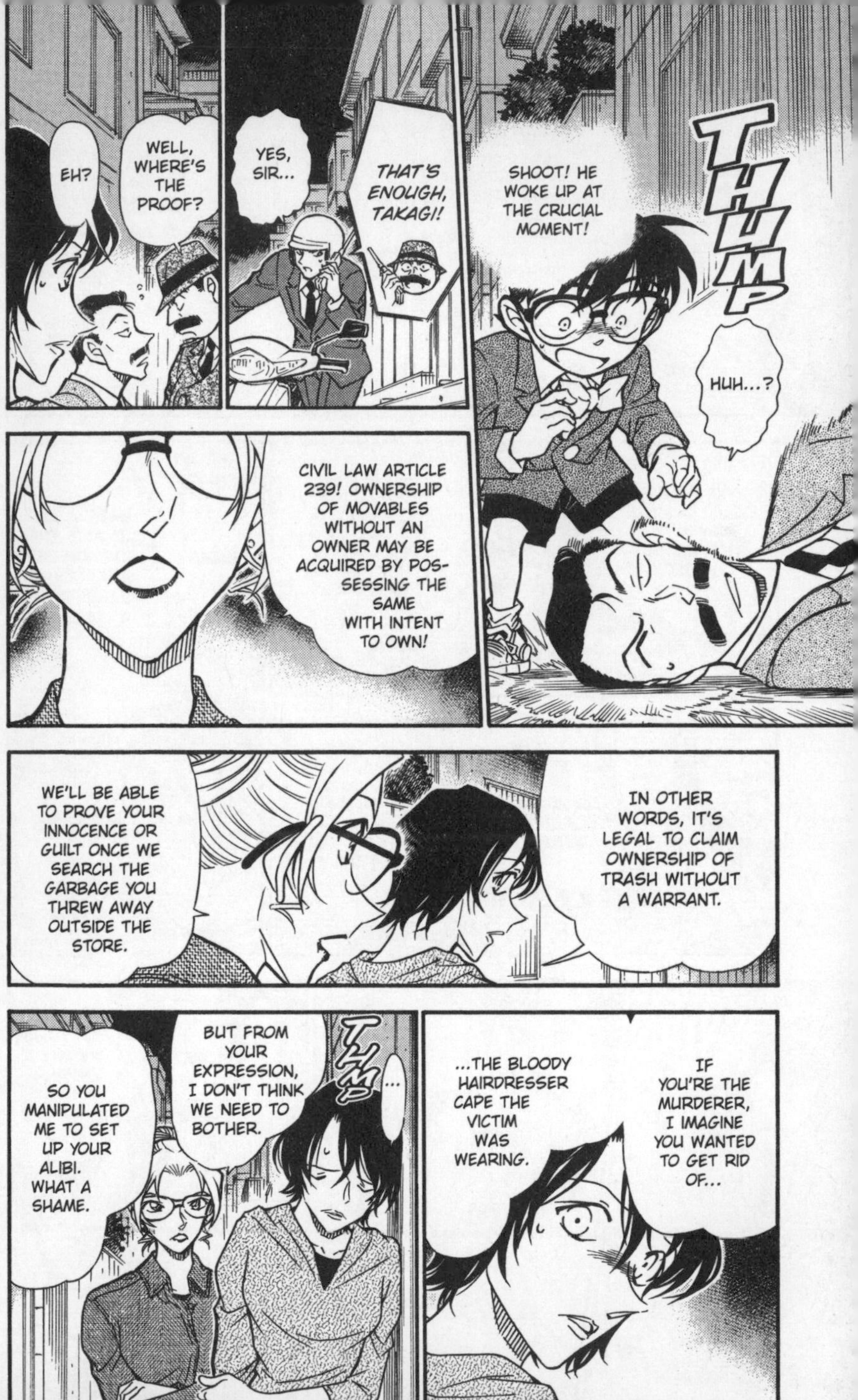
THUMP
SHOOT! HE WOKE UP AT THE CRUCIAL MOMENT!
HUH...?
THAT'S ENOUGH, TAKAGI!
YES, SIR...
WELL, WHERE'S THE PROOF?
EH?
CIVIL LAW ARTICLE 239! OWNERSHIP OF MOVABLES WITHOUT AN OWNER MAY BE ACQUIRED BY POS-SESSING THE SAME WITH INTENT TO OWN!
IN OTHER WORDS, IT'S LEGAL TO CLAIM OWNERSHIP OF TRASH WITHOUT A WARRANT.
WE'LL BE ABLE TO PROVE YOUR INNOCENCE OR GUILT ONCE WE SEARCH THE GARBAGE YOU THREW AWAY OUTSIDE THE STORE.
IF YOU'RE THE MURDERER, I IMAGINE YOU WANTED TO GET RID OF...
...THE BLOODY HAIRDRESSER CAPE THE VICTIM WAS WEARING.
THUMP
...
BUT FROM YOUR EXPRESSION, I DON'T THINK WE NEED TO BOTHER.
SO YOU MANIPULATED ME TO SET UP YOUR ALIBI. WHAT A SHAME.

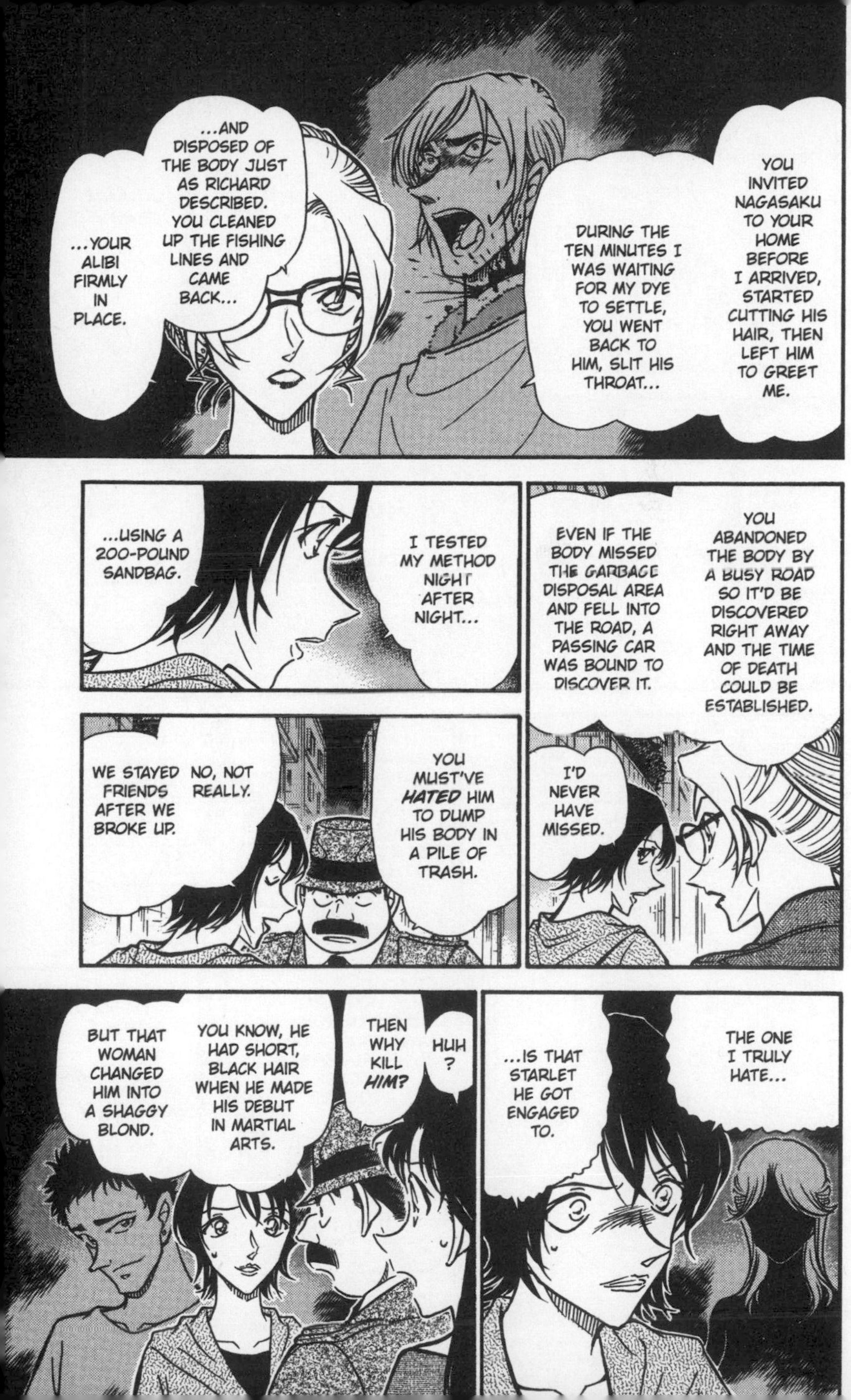
YOU INVITED NAGASAKU TO YOUR HOME BEFORE I ARRIVED, STARTED CUTTING HIS HAIR, THEN LEFT HIM TO GREET ME.
DURING THE TEN MINUTES I WAS WAITING FOR MY DYE TO SETTLE, YOU WENT BACK TO HIM, SLIT HIS THROAT...
...AND DISPOSED OF THE BODY JUST AS RICHARD DESCRIBED. YOU CLEANED UP THE FISHING LINES AND CAME BACK...
...YOUR ALIBI FIRMLY IN PLACE.
YOU ABANDONED THE BODY BY A BUSY ROAD SO IT'D BE DISCOVERED RIGHT AWAY AND THE TIME OF DEATH COULD BE ESTABLISHED.
EVEN IF THE BODY MISSED THE GARBAGE DISPOSAL AREA AND FELL INTO THE ROAD, A PASSING CAR WAS BOUND TO DISCOVER IT.
I TESTED MY METHOD NIGHT AFTER NIGHT...
...USING A 200-POUND SANDBAG.
I'D NEVER HAVE MISSED.
YOU MUST'VE *HATED* HIM TO DUMP HIS BODY IN A PILE OF TRASH.
NO, NOT REALLY.
WE STAYED FRIENDS AFTER WE BROKE UP.
THE ONE I TRULY HATE...
...IS THAT STARLET HE GOT ENGAGED TO.
HUH?
THEN WHY KILL *HIM?*
YOU KNOW, HE HAD SHORT, BLACK HAIR WHEN HE MADE HIS DEBUT IN MARTIAL ARTS.
BUT THAT WOMAN CHANGED HIM INTO A SHAGGY BLOND.

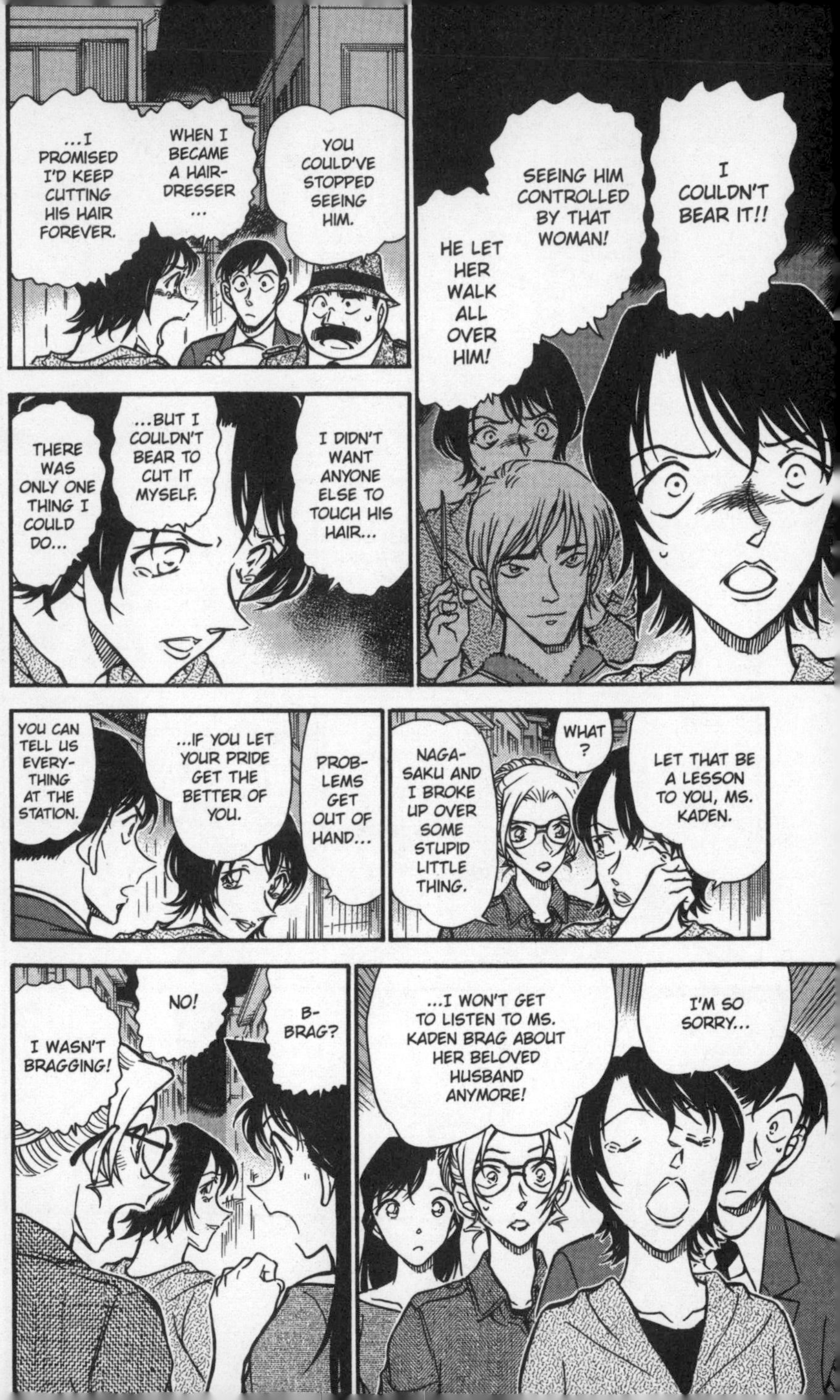
I COULDN'T BEAR IT!!
SEEING HIM CONTROLLED BY THAT WOMAN!
HE LET HER WALK ALL OVER HIM!
YOU COULD'VE STOPPED SEEING HIM.
WHEN I BECAME A HAIRDRESSER...
...I PROMISED I'D KEEP CUTTING HIS HAIR FOREVER.
I DIDN'T WANT ANYONE ELSE TO TOUCH HIS HAIR...
...BUT I COULDN'T BEAR TO CUT IT MYSELF.
THERE WAS ONLY ONE THING I COULD DO...
LET THAT BE A LESSON TO YOU, MS. KADEN.
WHAT?
NAGASAKU AND I BROKE UP OVER SOME STUPID LITTLE THING.
PROBLEMS GET OUT OF HAND...
...IF YOU LET YOUR PRIDE GET THE BETTER OF YOU.
YOU CAN TELL US EVERYTHING AT THE STATION.
I'M SO SORRY...
...I WON'T GET TO LISTEN TO MS. KADEN BRAG ABOUT HER BELOVED HUSBAND ANYMORE!
B-BRAG?
NO!
I WASN'T BRAGGING!

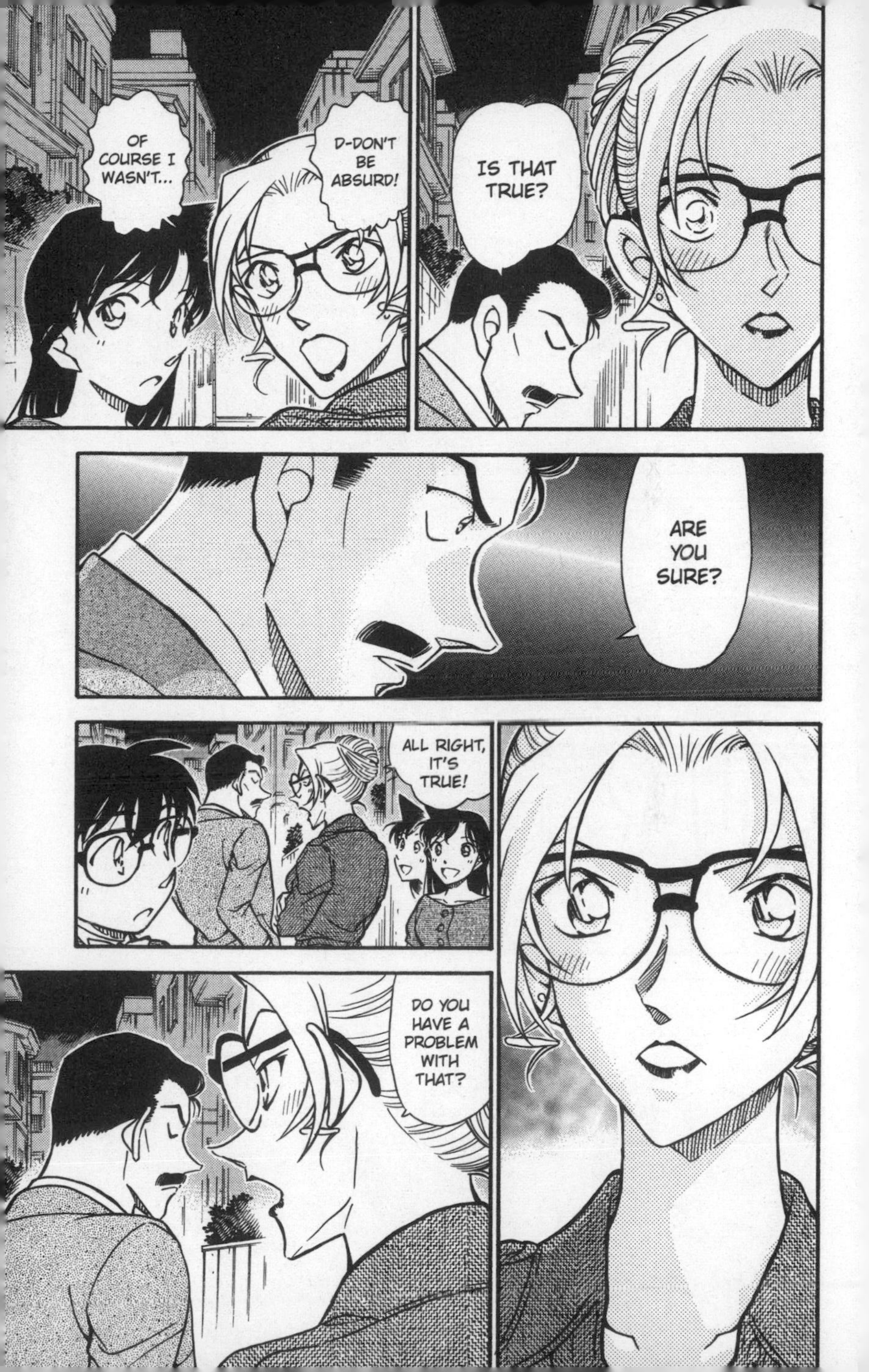
IS THAT TRUE?
D-DON'T BE ABSURD!
OF COURSE I WASN'T...
ARE YOU SURE?
ALL RIGHT, IT'S TRUE!
DO YOU HAVE A PROBLEM WITH THAT?

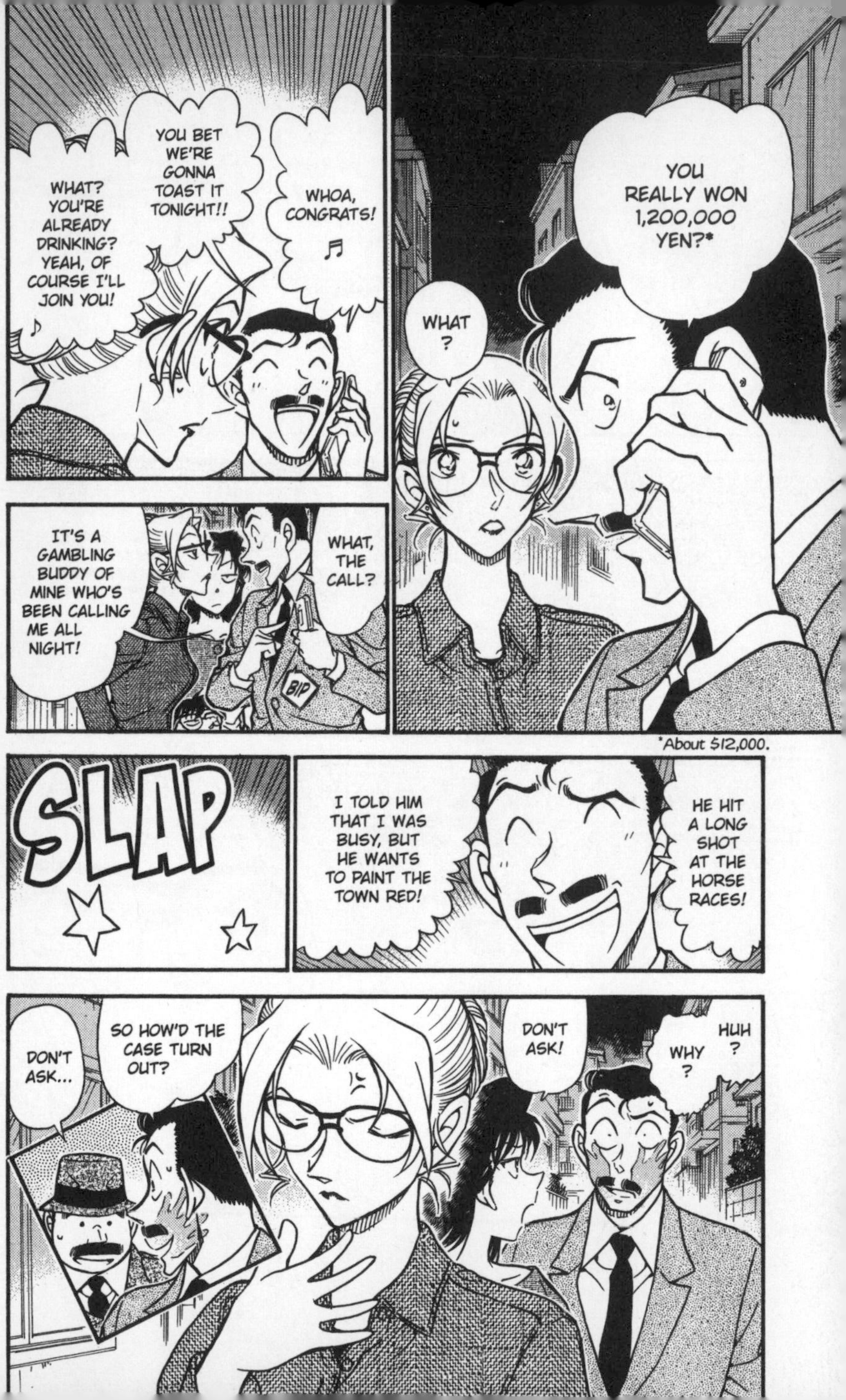
YOU REALLY WON 1,200,000 YEN?*
WHAT ?
WHOA, CONGRATS! ♪
YOU BET WE'RE GONNA TOAST IT TONIGHT!!
WHAT? YOU'RE ALREADY DRINKING? YEAH, OF COURSE I'LL JOIN YOU! ♪
WHAT, THE CALL?
IT'S A GAMBLING BUDDY OF MINE WHO'S BEEN CALLING ME ALL NIGHT!
BIP
HE HIT A LONG SHOT AT THE HORSE RACES!
I TOLD HIM THAT I WAS BUSY, BUT HE WANTS TO PAINT THE TOWN RED!
SLAP
HUH ?
WHY ?
DON'T ASK!
SO HOW'D THE CASE TURN OUT?
DON'T ASK...

*About $12,000.

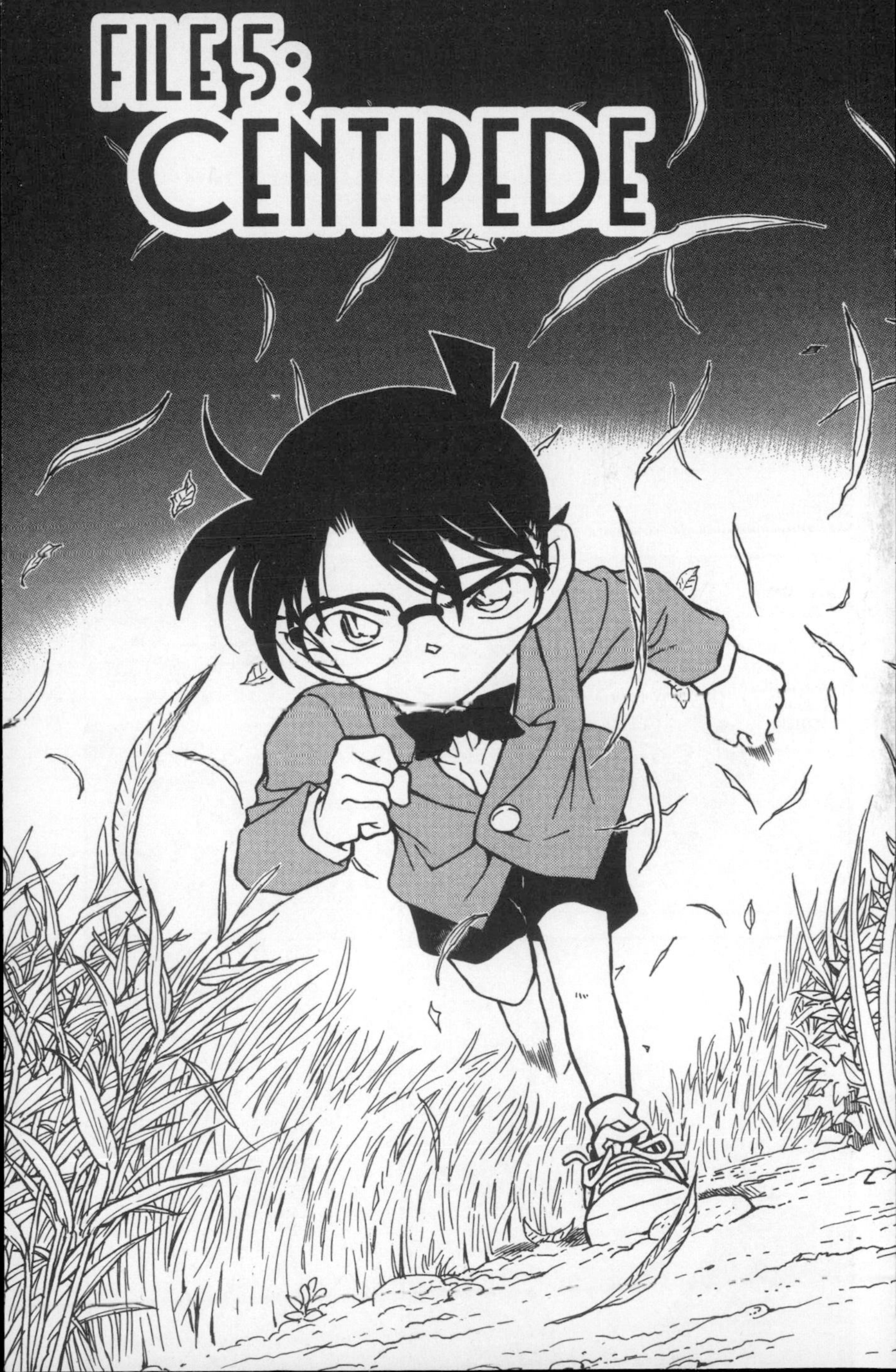
FILE 5:
CENTIPEDE

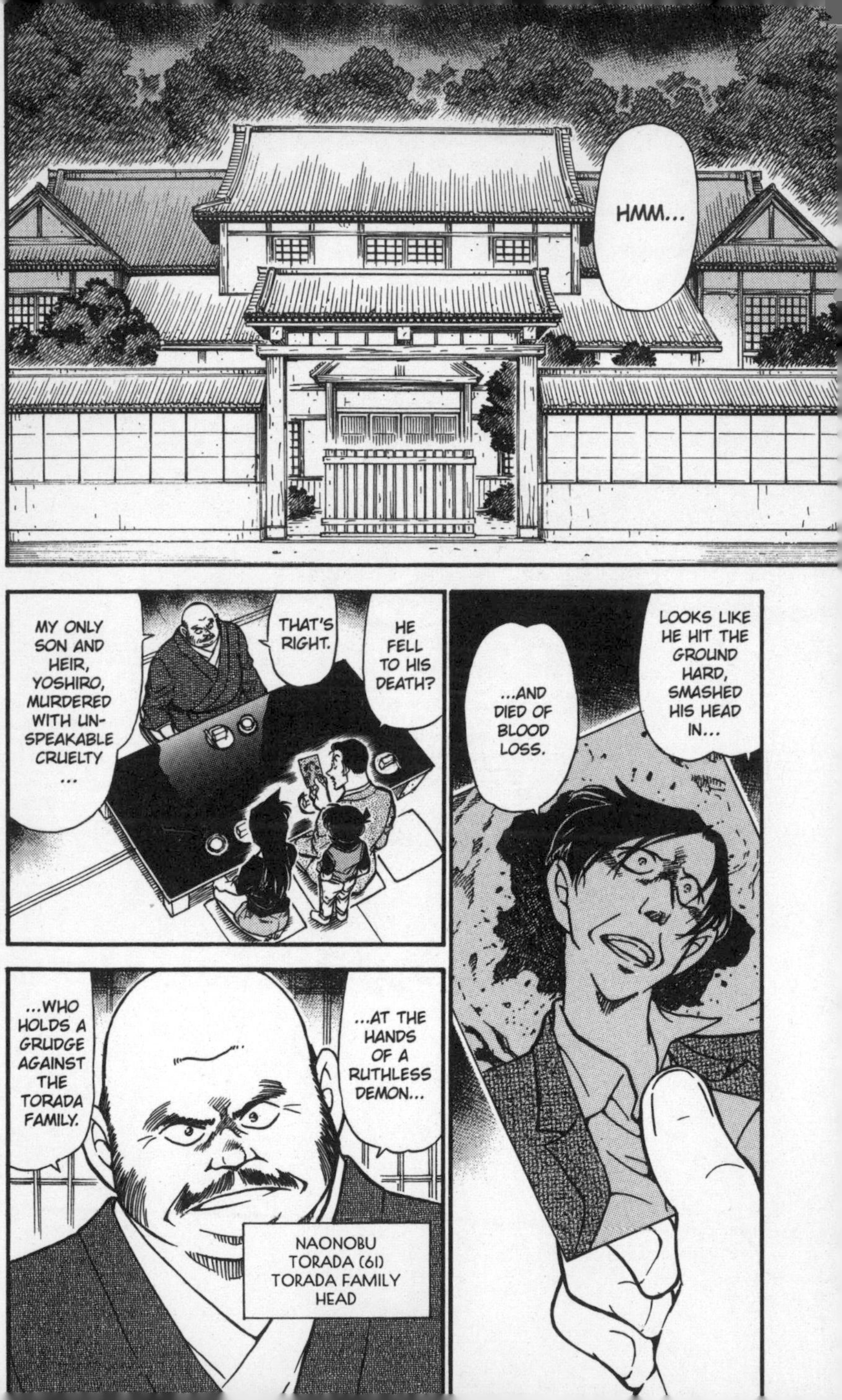
HMM...
LOOKS LIKE HE HIT THE GROUND HARD, SMASHED HIS HEAD IN...
...AND DIED OF BLOOD LOSS.
HE FELL TO HIS DEATH?
THAT'S RIGHT.
MY ONLY SON AND HEIR, YOSHIRO, MURDERED WITH UN-SPEAKABLE CRUELTY ...
...AT THE HANDS OF A RUTHLESS DEMON...
...WHO HOLDS A GRUDGE AGAINST THE TORADA FAMILY.
NAONOBU TORADA (61) TORADA FAMILY HEAD

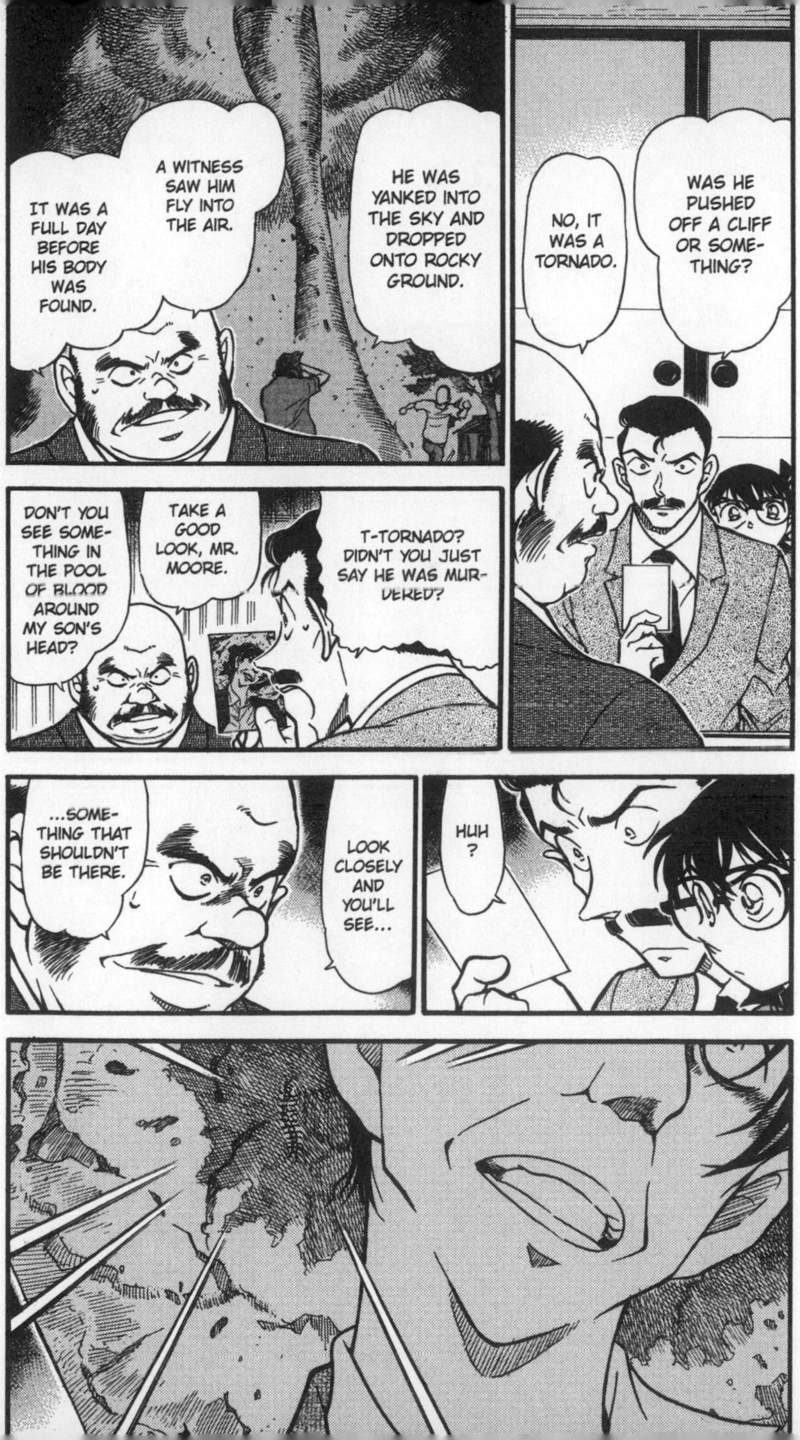
WAS HE PUSHED OFF A CLIFF OR SOME-THING?
NO, IT WAS A TORNADO.
HE WAS YANKED INTO THE SKY AND DROPPED ONTO ROCKY GROUND.
A WITNESS SAW HIM FLY INTO THE AIR.
IT WAS A FULL DAY BEFORE HIS BODY WAS FOUND.
T-TORNADO? DIDN'T YOU JUST SAY HE WAS MUR-DERED?
TAKE A GOOD LOOK, MR. MOORE.
DON'T YOU SEE SOME-THING IN THE POOL OF BLOOD AROUND MY SON'S HEAD?
HUH?
LOOK CLOSELY AND YOU'LL SEE...
...SOME-THING THAT SHOULDN'T BE THERE.

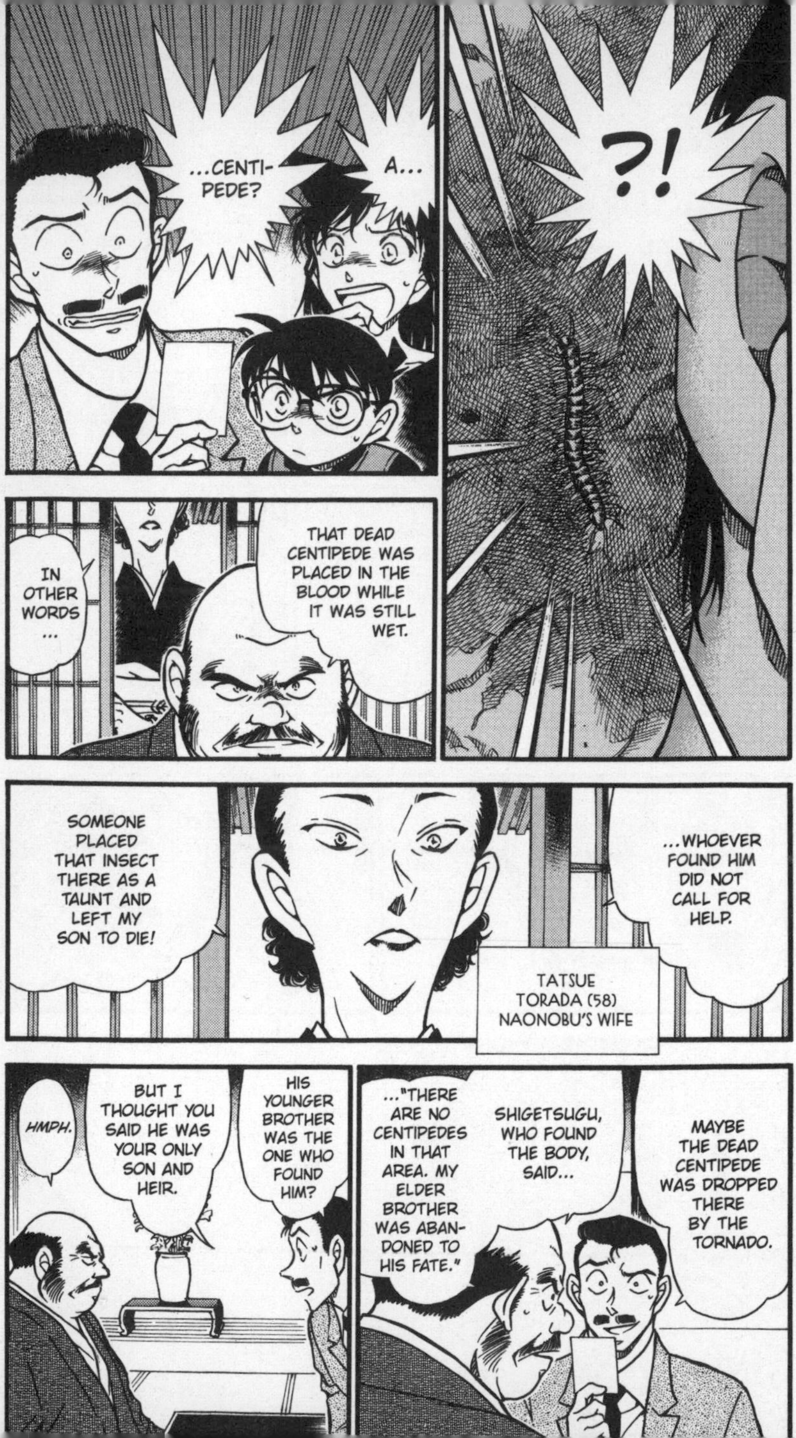
?!
A...
...CENTI-PEDE?
THAT DEAD CENTIPEDE WAS PLACED IN THE BLOOD WHILE IT WAS STILL WET.
IN OTHER WORDS ...
...WHOEVER FOUND HIM DID NOT CALL FOR HELP.
TATSUE TORADA (58) NAONOBU'S WIFE
SOMEONE PLACED THAT INSECT THERE AS A TAUNT AND LEFT MY SON TO DIE!
MAYBE THE DEAD CENTIPEDE WAS DROPPED THERE BY THE TORNADO.
SHIGETSUGU, WHO FOUND THE BODY, SAID...
..."THERE ARE NO CENTIPEDES IN THAT AREA. MY ELDER BROTHER WAS ABAN-DONED TO HIS FATE."
HIS YOUNGER BROTHER WAS THE ONE WHO FOUND HIM?
BUT I THOUGHT YOU SAID HE WAS YOUR ONLY SON AND HEIR.
HMPH.

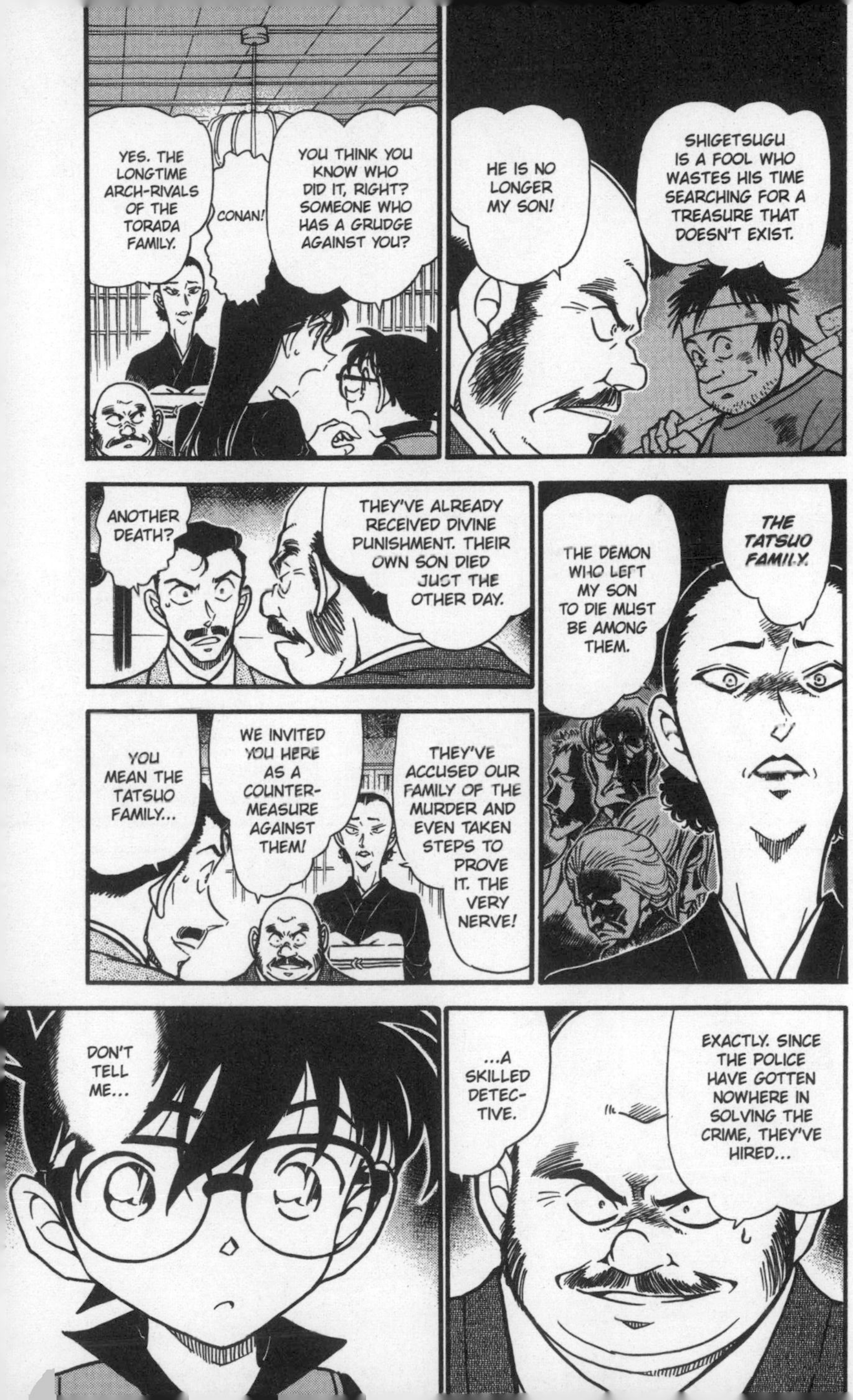
SHIGETSUGU IS A FOOL WHO WASTES HIS TIME SEARCHING FOR A TREASURE THAT DOESN'T EXIST.
HE IS NO LONGER MY SON!
YOU THINK YOU KNOW WHO DID IT, RIGHT? SOMEONE WHO HAS A GRUDGE AGAINST YOU?
CONAN!
YES. THE LONGTIME ARCH-RIVALS OF THE TORADA FAMILY.
THE TATSUO FAMILY.
THE DEMON WHO LEFT MY SON TO DIE MUST BE AMONG THEM.
THEY'VE ALREADY RECEIVED DIVINE PUNISHMENT. THEIR OWN SON DIED JUST THE OTHER DAY.
ANOTHER DEATH?
THEY'VE ACCUSED OUR FAMILY OF THE MURDER AND EVEN TAKEN STEPS TO PROVE IT. THE VERY NERVE!
WE INVITED YOU HERE AS A COUNTER-MEASURE AGAINST THEM!
YOU MEAN THE TATSUO FAMILY...
EXACTLY. SINCE THE POLICE HAVE GOTTEN NOWHERE IN SOLVING THE CRIME, THEY'VE HIRED...
...A SKILLED DETECTIVE.
DON'T TELL ME...

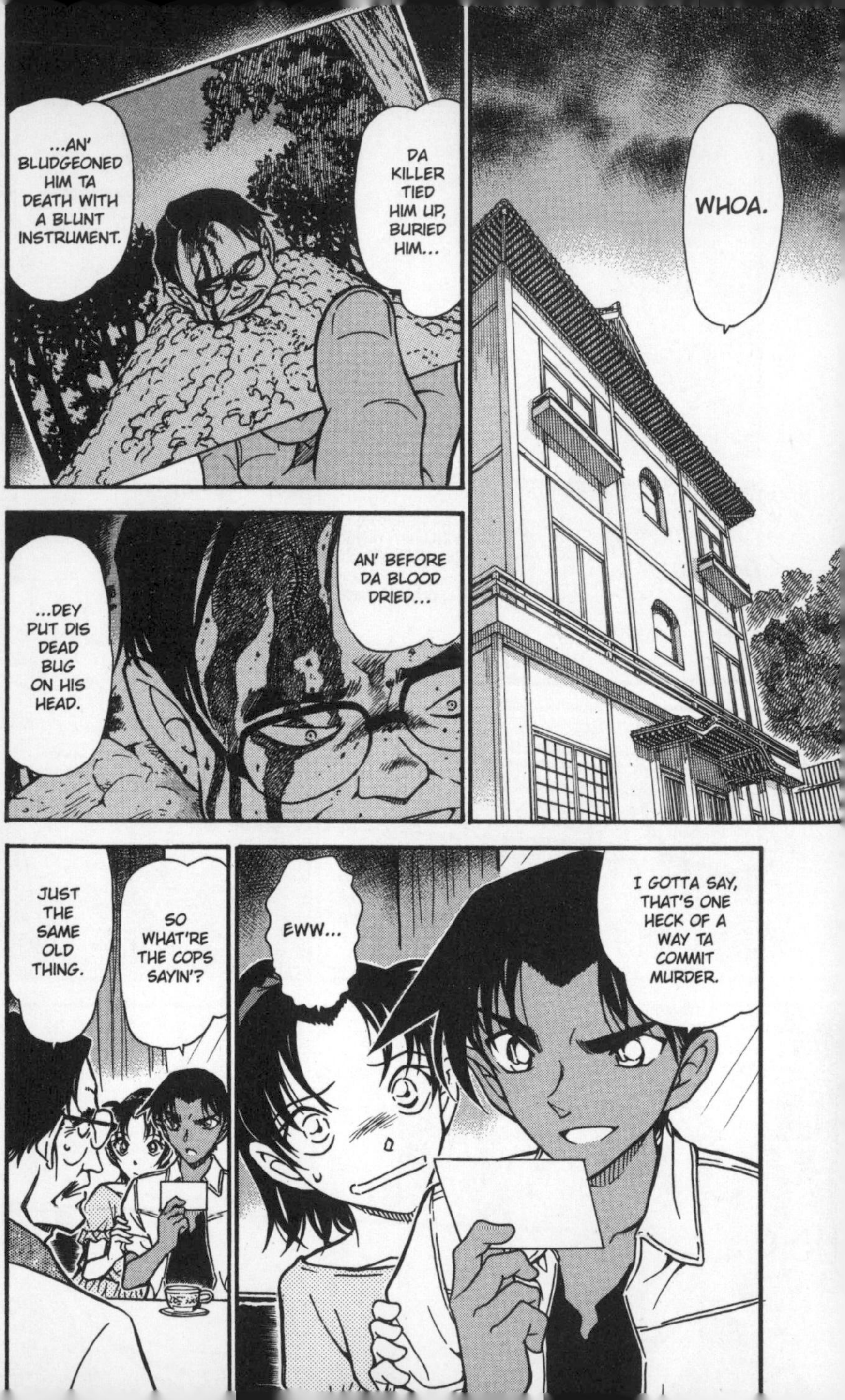
WHOA.
DA KILLER TIED HIM UP, BURIED HIM...
...AN' BLUDGEONED HIM TA DEATH WITH A BLUNT INSTRUMENT.
AN' BEFORE DA BLOOD DRIED...
...DEY PUT DIS DEAD BUG ON HIS HEAD.
I GOTTA SAY, THAT'S ONE HECK OF A WAY TA COMMIT MURDER.
EWW...
SO WHAT'RE THE COPS SAYIN'?
JUST THE SAME OLD THING.

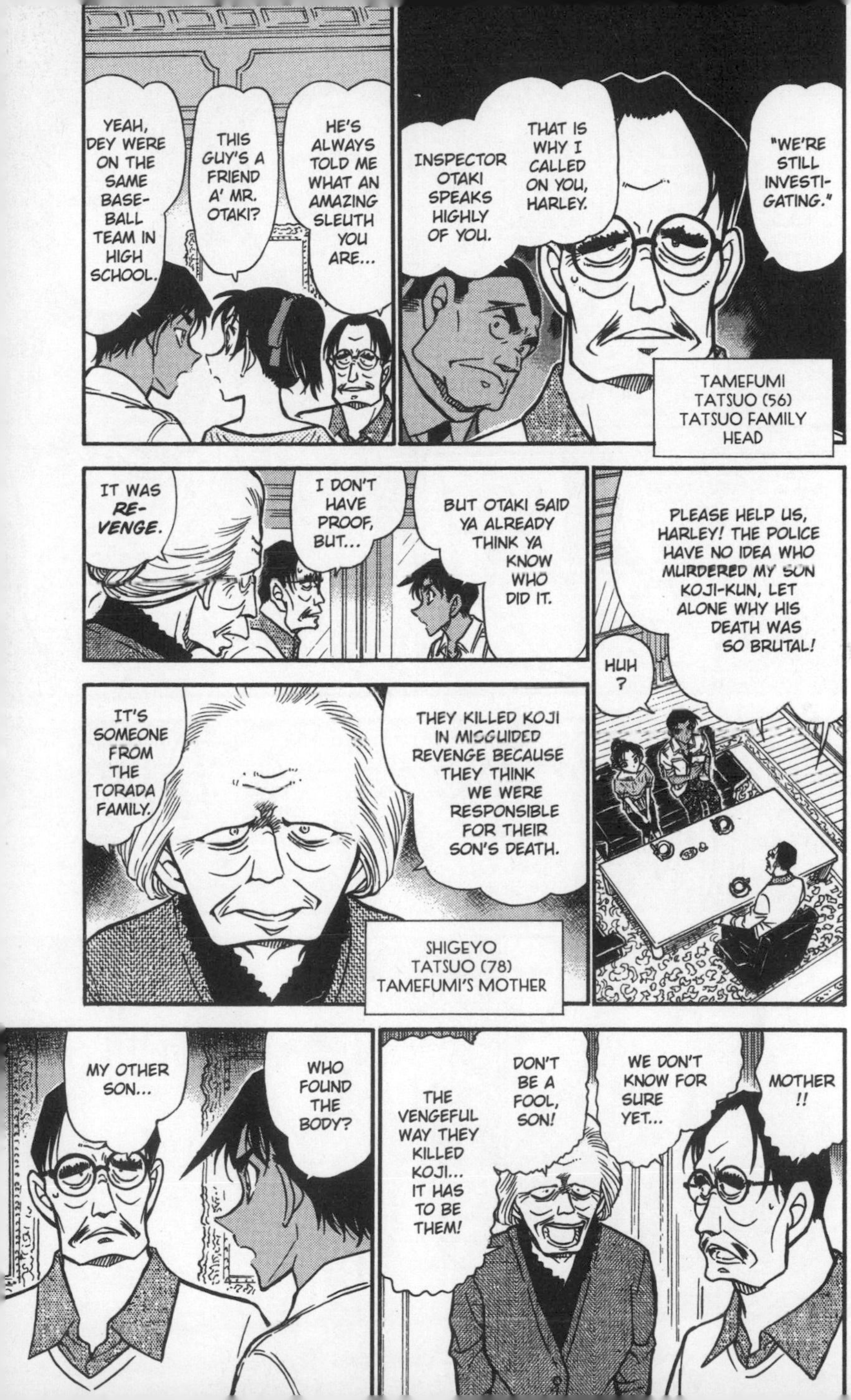
"WE'RE STILL INVESTI-GATING."
THAT IS WHY I CALLED ON YOU, HARLEY.
INSPECTOR OTAKI SPEAKS HIGHLY OF YOU.
TAMEFUMI TATSUO (56) TATSUO FAMILY HEAD
HE'S ALWAYS TOLD ME WHAT AN AMAZING SLEUTH YOU ARE...
THIS GUY'S A FRIEND A' MR. OTAKI?
YEAH, DEY WERE ON THE SAME BASE-BALL TEAM IN HIGH SCHOOL.
PLEASE HELP US, HARLEY! THE POLICE HAVE NO IDEA WHO MURDERED MY SON KOJI-KUN, LET ALONE WHY HIS DEATH WAS SO BRUTAL!
HUH?
BUT OTAKI SAID YA ALREADY THINK YA KNOW WHO DID IT.
I DON'T HAVE PROOF, BUT...
IT WAS *RE-VENGE*.
THEY KILLED KOJI IN MISGUIDED REVENGE BECAUSE THEY THINK WE WERE RESPONSIBLE FOR THEIR SON'S DEATH.
IT'S SOMEONE FROM THE TORADA FAMILY.
SHIGEYO TATSUO (78) TAMEFUMI'S MOTHER
MOTHER!!
WE DON'T KNOW FOR SURE YET...
DON'T BE A FOOL, SON!
THE VENGEFUL WAY THEY KILLED KOJI... IT HAS TO BE THEM!
WHO FOUND THE BODY?
MY OTHER SON...

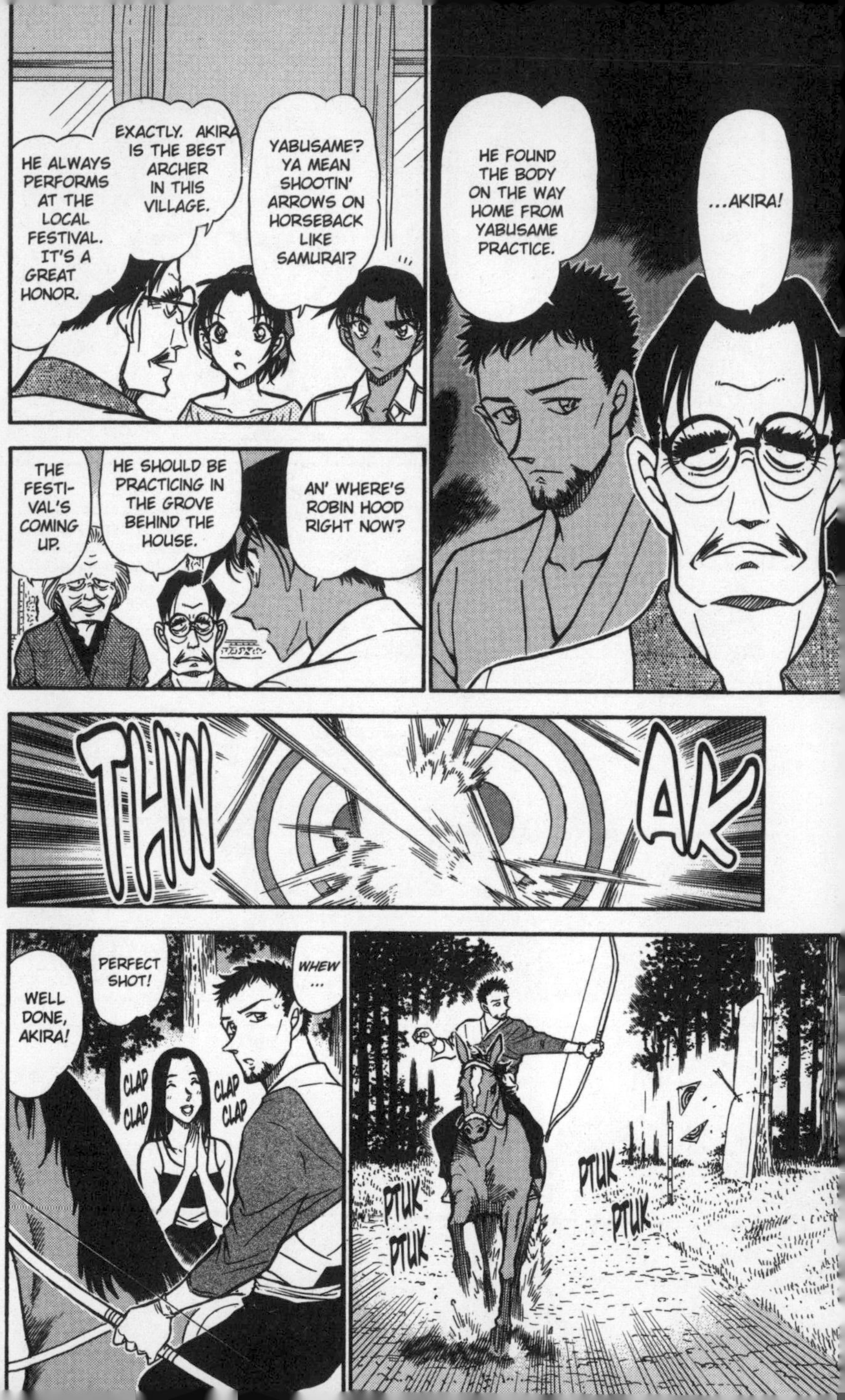
...AKIRA!
HE FOUND THE BODY ON THE WAY HOME FROM YABUSAME PRACTICE.
YABUSAME? YA MEAN SHOOTIN' ARROWS ON HORSEBACK LIKE SAMURAI?
EXACTLY. AKIRA IS THE BEST ARCHER IN THIS VILLAGE.
HE ALWAYS PERFORMS AT THE LOCAL FESTIVAL. IT'S A GREAT HONOR.
AN' WHERE'S ROBIN HOOD RIGHT NOW?
HE SHOULD BE PRACTICING IN THE GROVE BEHIND THE HOUSE.
THE FESTI-VAL'S COMING UP.
THWAK
PTUK
PTUK
PTUK
PTUK
WHEW ...
PERFECT SHOT!
WELL DONE, AKIRA!
CLAP CLAP
CLAP CLAP

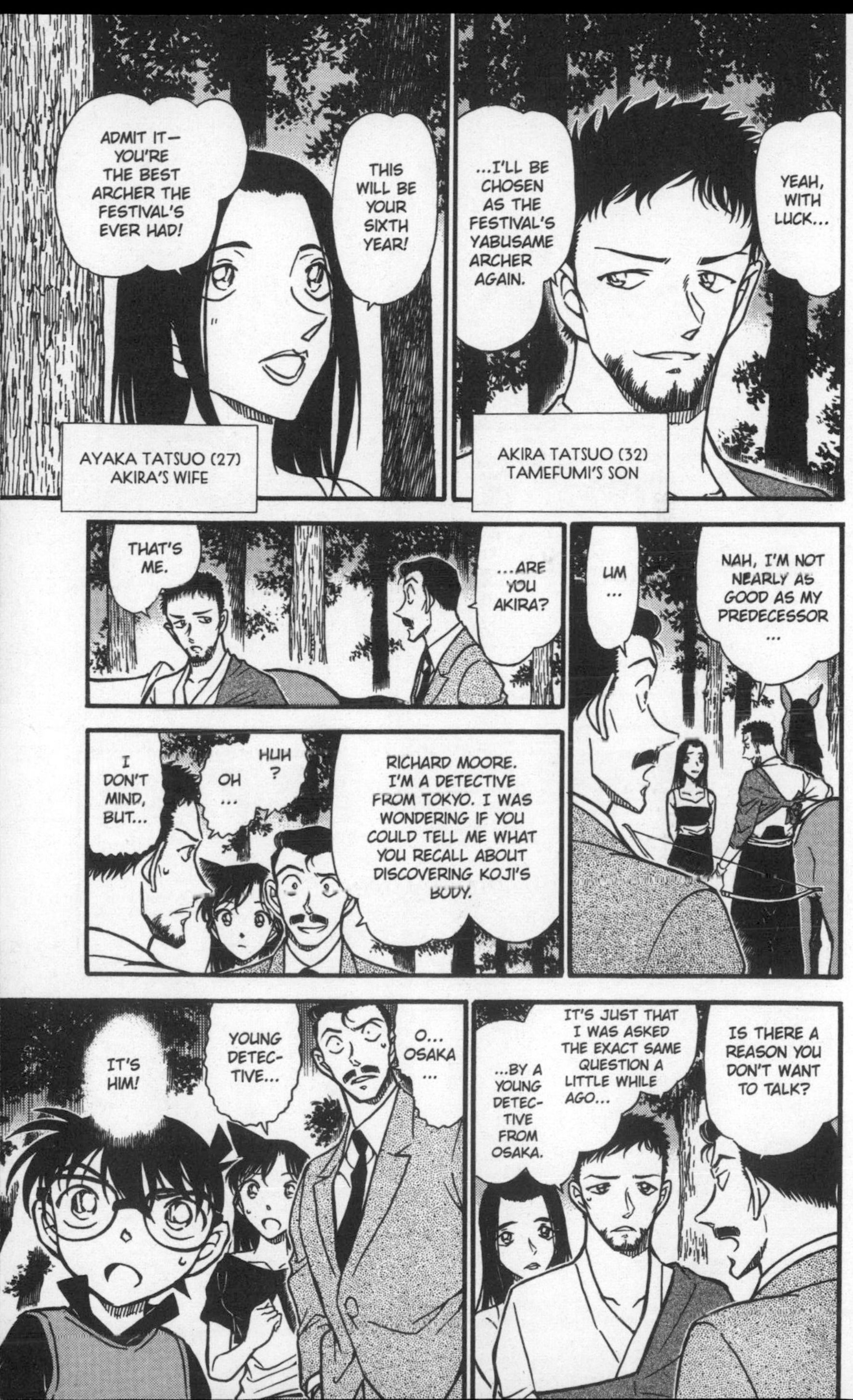
YEAH, WITH LUCK...
...I'LL BE CHOSEN AS THE FESTIVAL'S YABUSAME ARCHER AGAIN.
AKIRA TATSUO (32) TAMEFUMI'S SON
THIS WILL BE YOUR SIXTH YEAR!
ADMIT IT— YOU'RE THE BEST ARCHER THE FESTIVAL'S EVER HAD!
AYAKA TATSUO (27) AKIRA'S WIFE
NAH, I'M NOT NEARLY AS GOOD AS MY PREDECESSOR...
UM...
...ARE YOU AKIRA?
THAT'S ME.
RICHARD MOORE. I'M A DETECTIVE FROM TOKYO. I WAS WONDERING IF YOU COULD TELL ME WHAT YOU RECALL ABOUT DISCOVERING KOJI'S BODY.
HUH?
OH...
I DON'T MIND, BUT...
IS THERE A REASON YOU DON'T WANT TO TALK?
IT'S JUST THAT I WAS ASKED THE EXACT SAME QUESTION A LITTLE WHILE AGO...
...BY A YOUNG DETECTIVE FROM OSAKA.
O... OSAKA...
YOUNG DETECTIVE...
IT'S HIM!

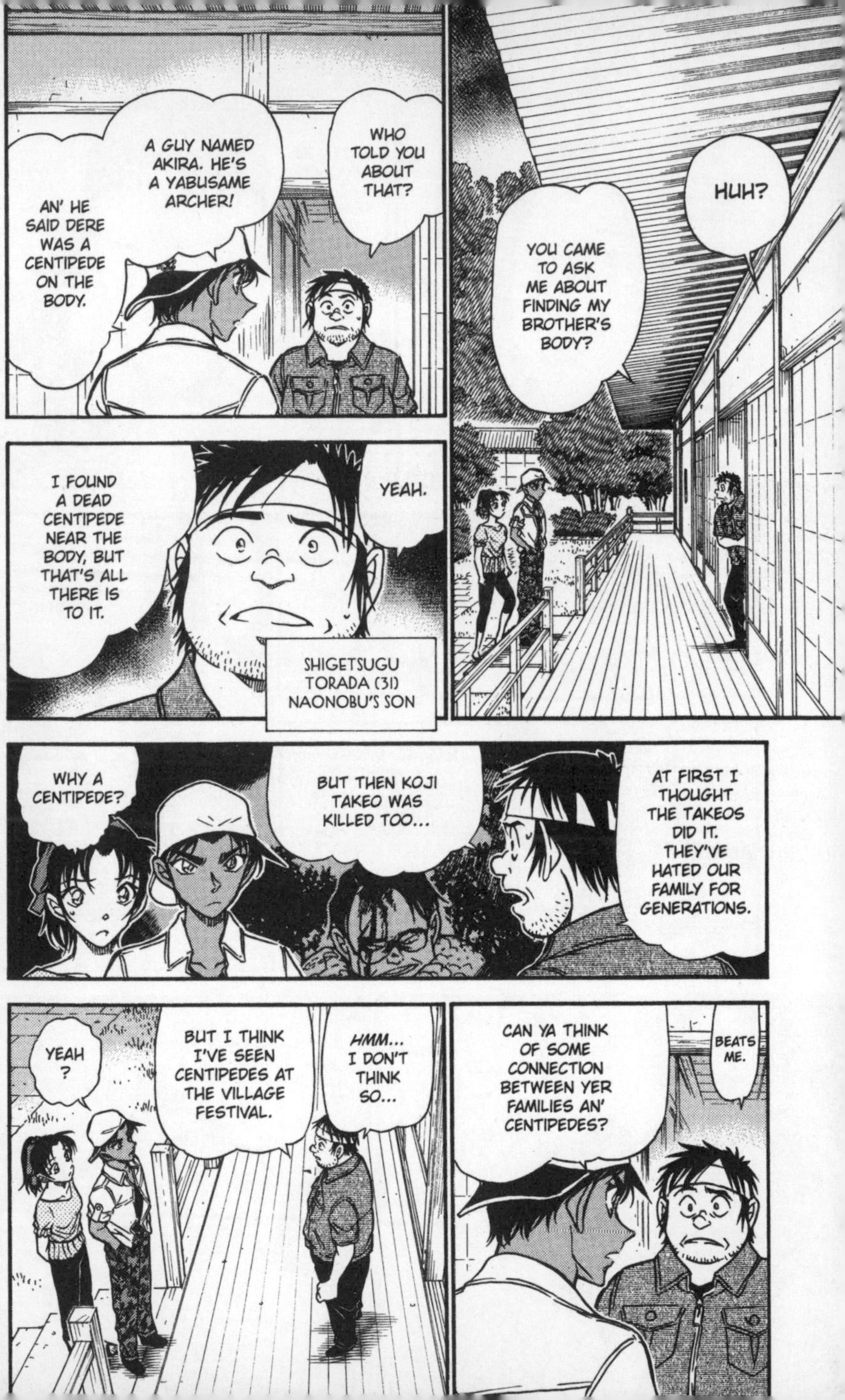
HUH?
YOU CAME TO ASK ME ABOUT FINDING MY BROTHER'S BODY?
WHO TOLD YOU ABOUT THAT?
A GUY NAMED AKIRA. HE'S A YABUSAME ARCHER!
AN' HE SAID DERE WAS A CENTIPEDE ON THE BODY.
YEAH.
I FOUND A DEAD CENTIPEDE NEAR THE BODY, BUT THAT'S ALL THERE IS TO IT.
SHIGETSUGU TORADA (31) NAONOBU'S SON
AT FIRST I THOUGHT THE TAKEOS DID IT. THEY'VE HATED OUR FAMILY FOR GENERATIONS.
BUT THEN KOJI TAKEO WAS KILLED TOO...
WHY A CENTIPEDE?
BEATS ME.
CAN YA THINK OF SOME CONNECTION BETWEEN YER FAMILIES AN' CENTIPEDES?
HMM... I DON'T THINK SO...
BUT I THINK I'VE SEEN CENTIPEDES AT THE VILLAGE FESTIVAL.
YEAH?

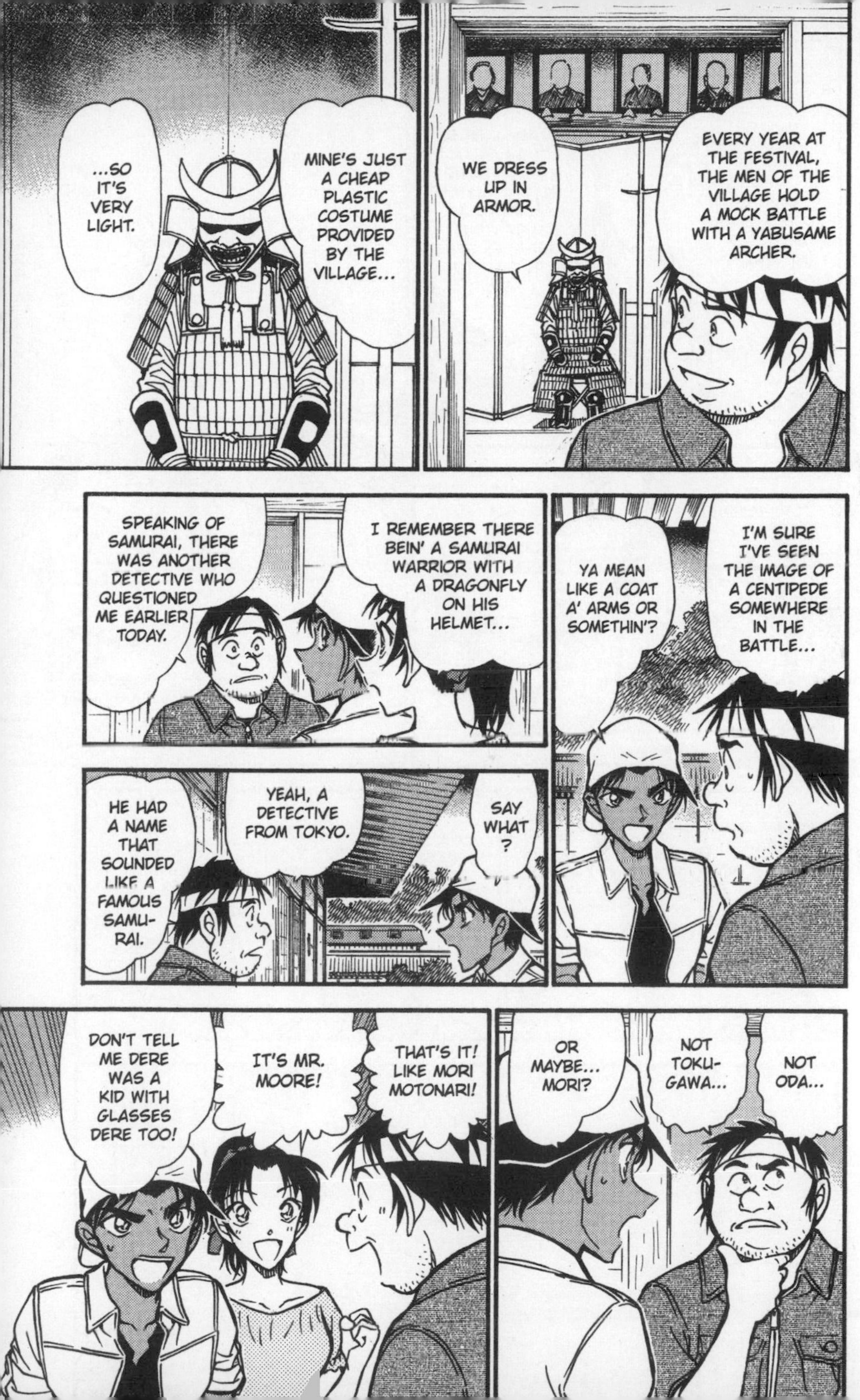
EVERY YEAR AT THE FESTIVAL, THE MEN OF THE VILLAGE HOLD A MOCK BATTLE WITH A YABUSAME ARCHER.
WE DRESS UP IN ARMOR.
MINE'S JUST A CHEAP PLASTIC COSTUME PROVIDED BY THE VILLAGE...
...SO IT'S VERY LIGHT.
I'M SURE I'VE SEEN THE IMAGE OF A CENTIPEDE SOMEWHERE IN THE BATTLE...
YA MEAN LIKE A COAT A' ARMS OR SOMETHIN'?
I REMEMBER THERE BEIN' A SAMURAI WARRIOR WITH A DRAGONFLY ON HIS HELMET...
SPEAKING OF SAMURAI, THERE WAS ANOTHER DETECTIVE WHO QUESTIONED ME EARLIER TODAY.
SAY WHAT?
YEAH, A DETECTIVE FROM TOKYO.
HE HAD A NAME THAT SOUNDED LIKE A FAMOUS SAMURAI.
NOT ODA...
NOT TOKUGAWA...
OR MAYBE... MORI?
THAT'S IT! LIKE MORI MOTONARI!
IT'S MR. MOORE!
DON'T TELL ME DERE WAS A KID WITH GLASSES DERE TOO!

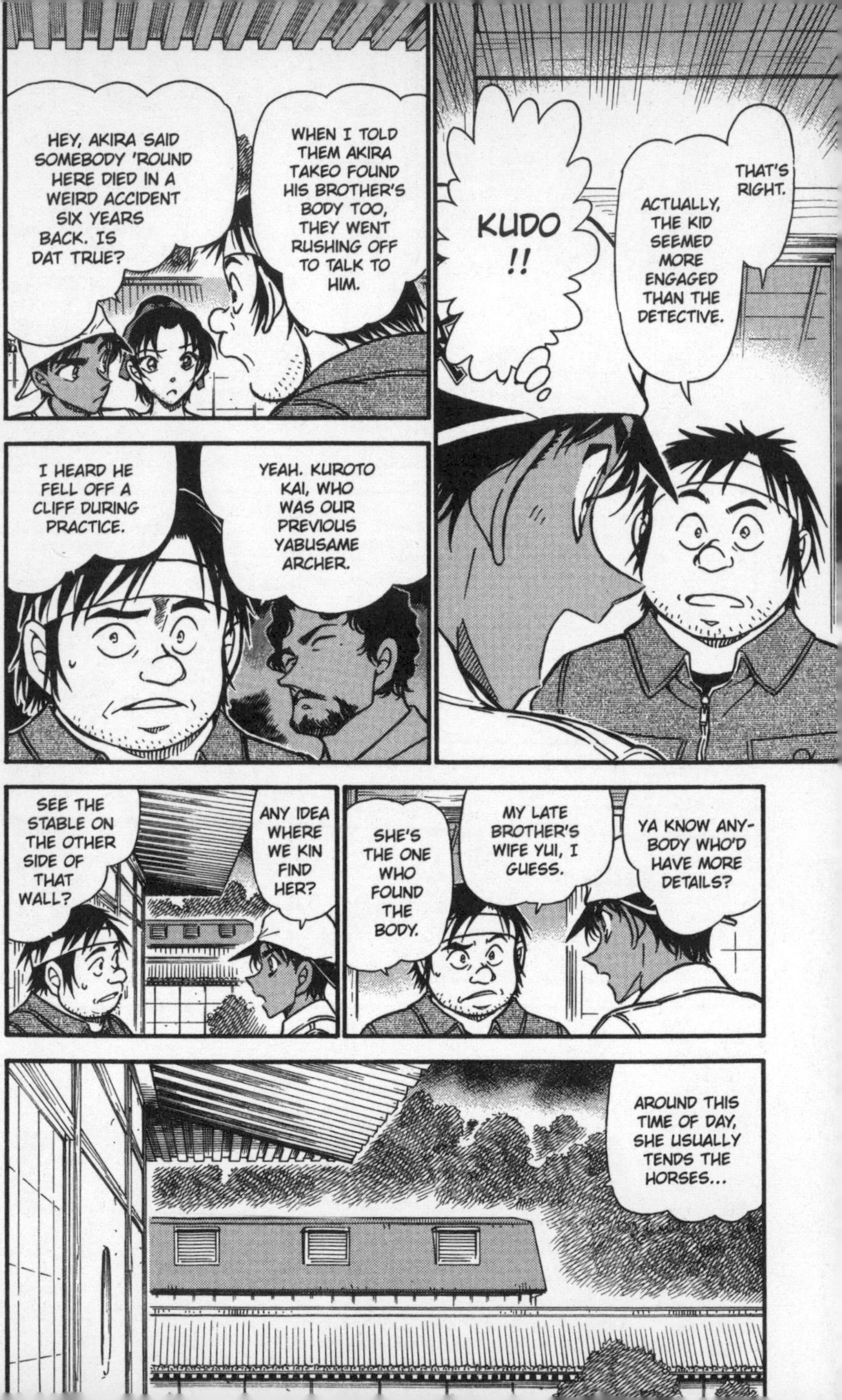
THAT'S RIGHT.
ACTUALLY, THE KID SEEMED MORE ENGAGED THAN THE DETECTIVE.
KUDO !!
WHEN I TOLD THEM AKIRA TAKEO FOUND HIS BROTHER'S BODY TOO, THEY WENT RUSHING OFF TO TALK TO HIM.
HEY, AKIRA SAID SOMEBODY 'ROUND HERE DIED IN A WEIRD ACCIDENT SIX YEARS BACK. IS DAT TRUE?
YEAH. KUROTO KAI, WHO WAS OUR PREVIOUS YABUSAME ARCHER.
I HEARD HE FELL OFF A CLIFF DURING PRACTICE.
YA KNOW ANY-BODY WHO'D HAVE MORE DETAILS?
MY LATE BROTHER'S WIFE YUI, I GUESS.
SHE'S THE ONE WHO FOUND THE BODY.
ANY IDEA WHERE WE KIN FIND HER?
SEE THE STABLE ON THE OTHER SIDE OF THAT WALL?
AROUND THIS TIME OF DAY, SHE USUALLY TENDS THE HORSES...

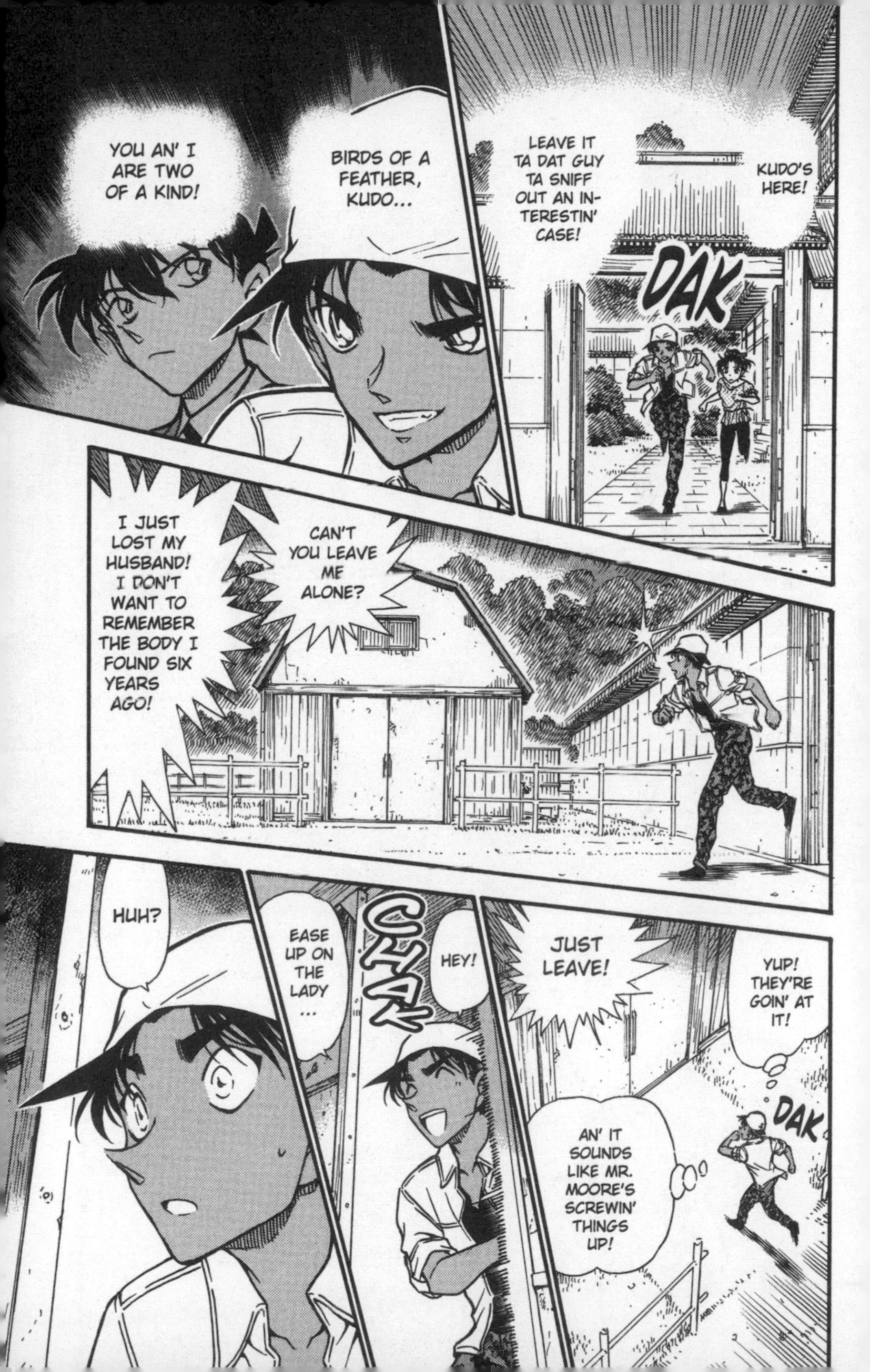
KUDO'S HERE!
LEAVE IT TA DAT GUY TA SNIFF OUT AN IN-TERESTIN' CASE!
DAK
BIRDS OF A FEATHER, KUDO...
YOU AN' I ARE TWO OF A KIND!
CAN'T YOU LEAVE ME ALONE?
I JUST LOST MY HUSBAND! I DON'T WANT TO REMEMBER THE BODY I FOUND SIX YEARS AGO!
YUP! THEY'RE GOIN' AT IT!
JUST LEAVE!
DAK
AN' IT SOUNDS LIKE MR. MOORE'S SCREWIN' THINGS UP!
HEY!
CHAK
EASE UP ON THE LADY ...
HUH?

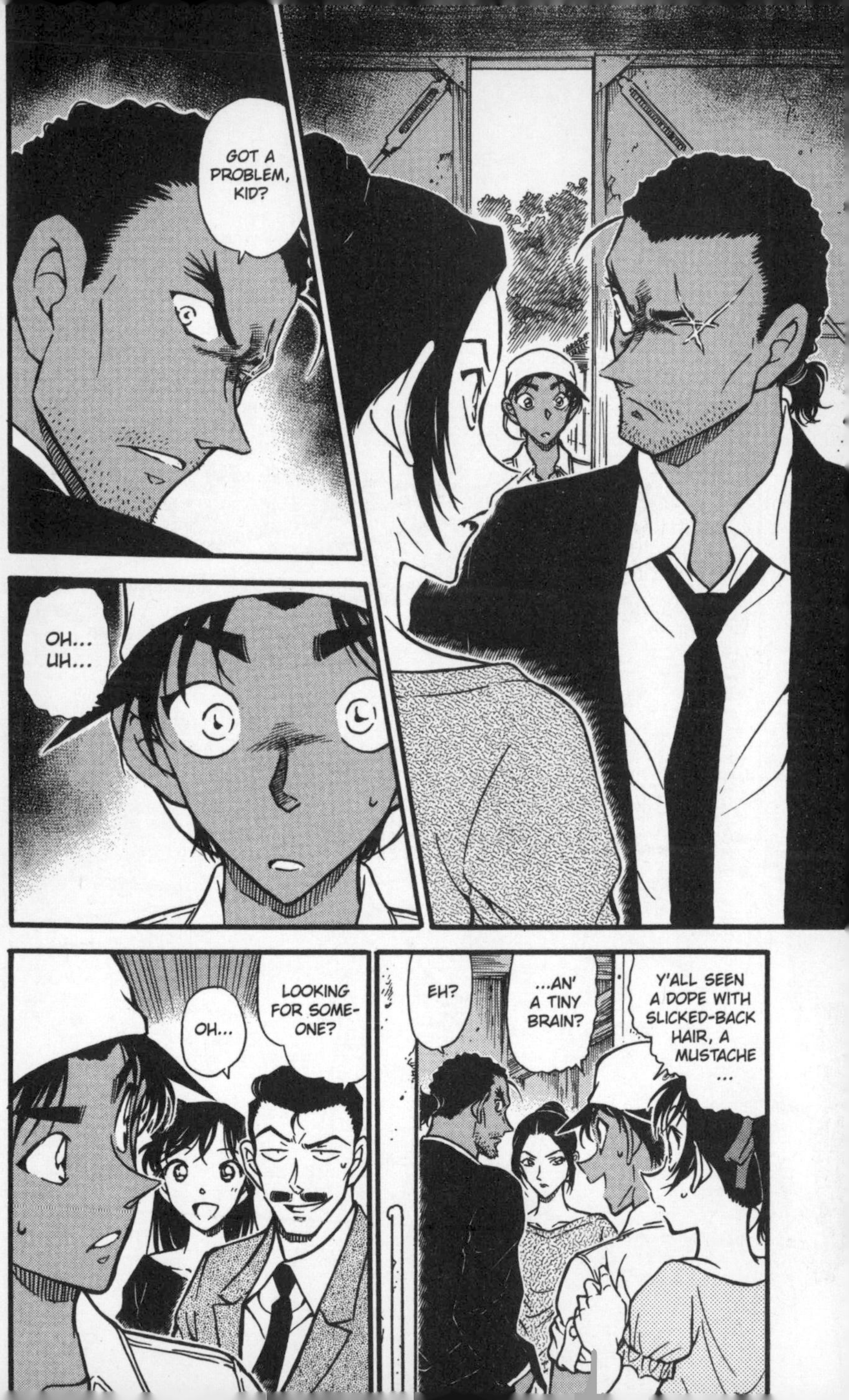
GOT A PROBLEM, KID?
OH... UH...
Y'ALL SEEN A DOPE WITH SLICKED-BACK HAIR, A MUSTACHE ...
...AN' A TINY BRAIN?
EH?
LOOKING FOR SOME-ONE?
OH...

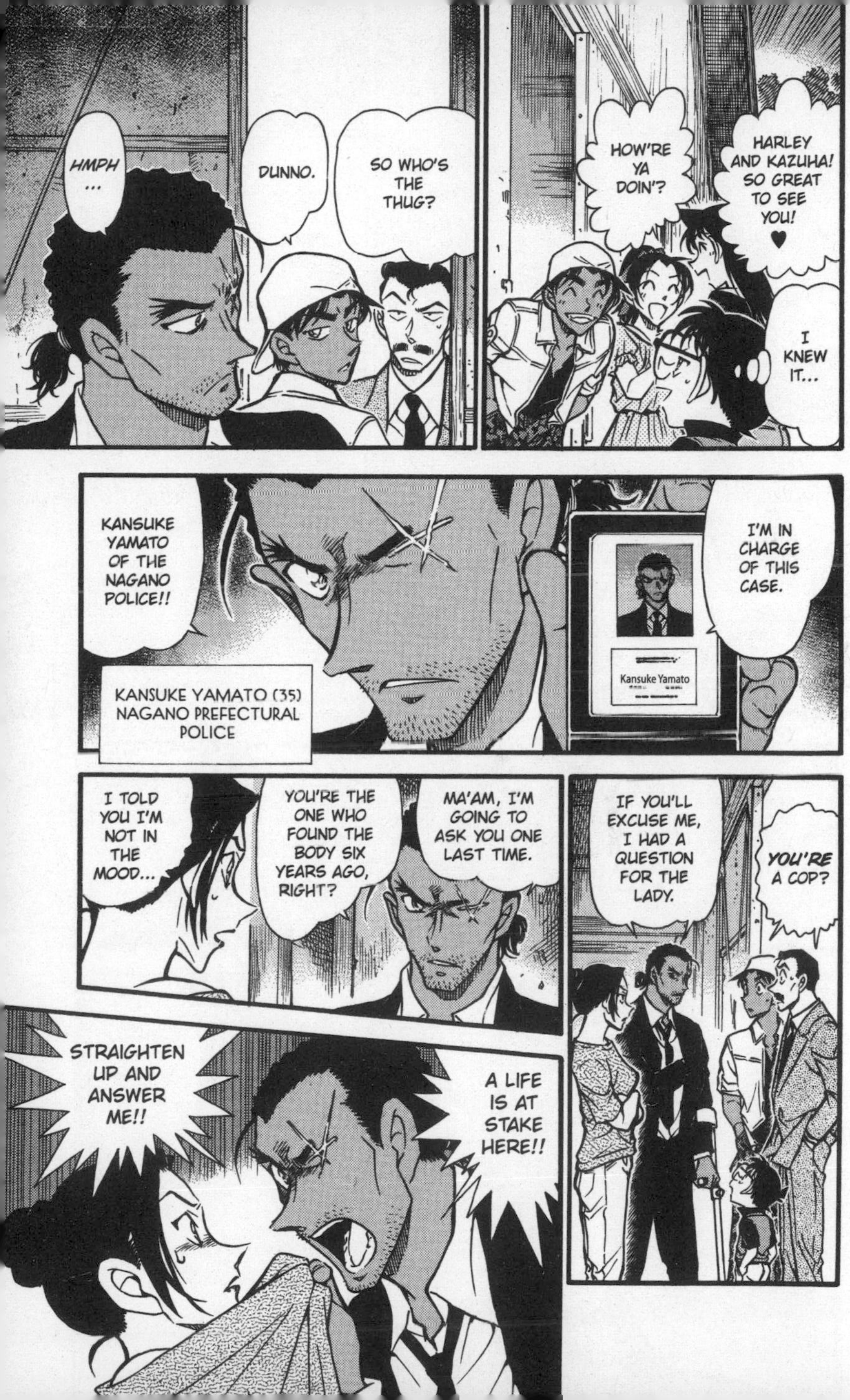
HARLEY AND KAZUHA! SO GREAT TO SEE YOU! ♥
HOW'RE YA DOIN'?
I KNEW IT...
SO WHO'S THE THUG?
DUNNO.
HMPH ...
I'M IN CHARGE OF THIS CASE.
Kansuke Yamato
KANSUKE YAMATO OF THE NAGANO POLICE!!
KANSUKE YAMATO (35) NAGANO PREFECTURAL POLICE
YOU'RE A COP?
IF YOU'LL EXCUSE ME, I HAD A QUESTION FOR THE LADY.
MA'AM, I'M GOING TO ASK YOU ONE LAST TIME.
YOU'RE THE ONE WHO FOUND THE BODY SIX YEARS AGO, RIGHT?
I TOLD YOU I'M NOT IN THE MOOD...
A LIFE IS AT STAKE HERE!!
STRAIGHTEN UP AND ANSWER ME!!

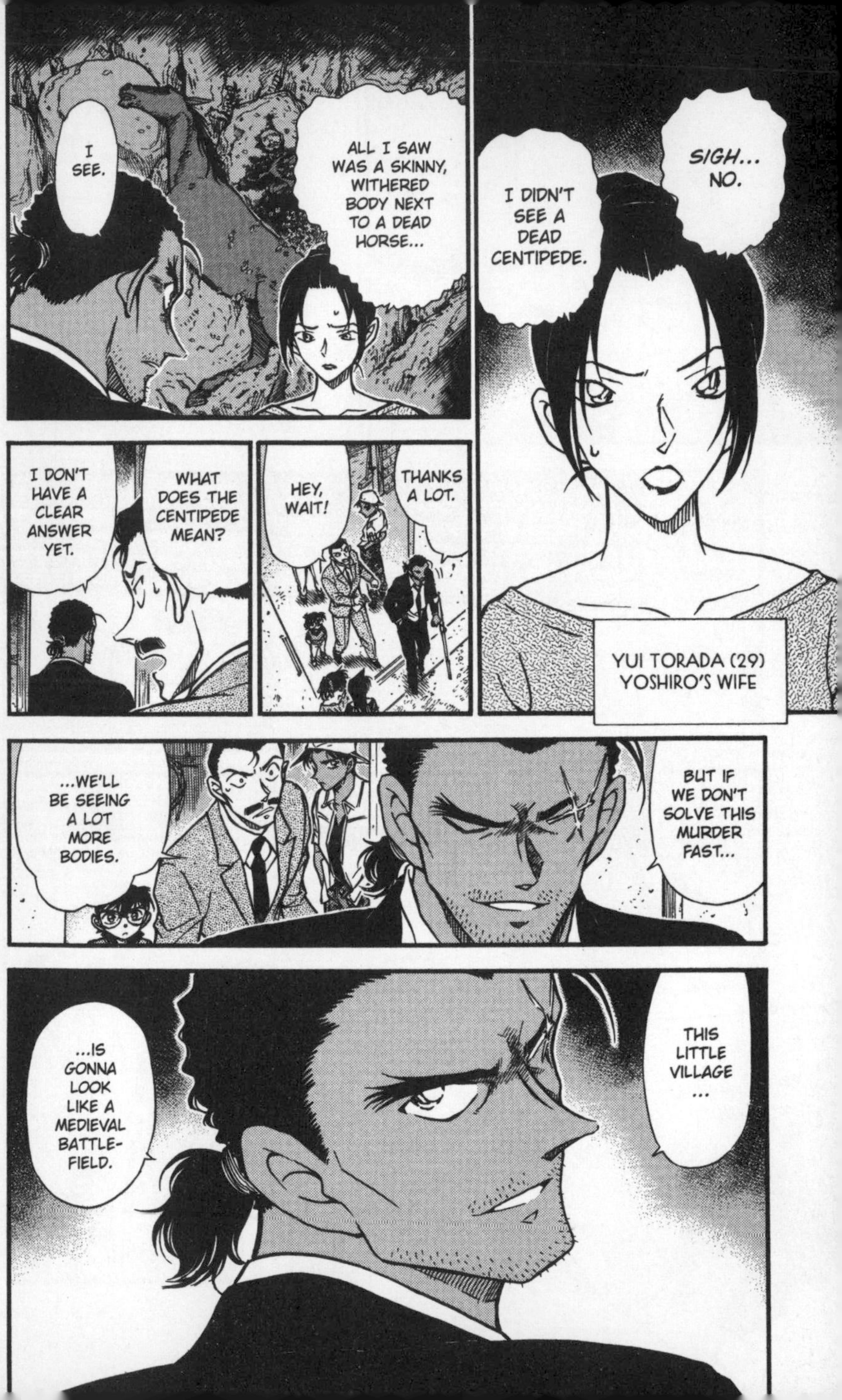
SIGH... NO.
I DIDN'T SEE A DEAD CENTIPEDE.
YUI TORADA (29) YOSHIRO'S WIFE
ALL I SAW WAS A SKINNY, WITHERED BODY NEXT TO A DEAD HORSE...
I SEE.
THANKS A LOT.
HEY, WAIT!
WHAT DOES THE CENTIPEDE MEAN?
I DON'T HAVE A CLEAR ANSWER YET.
BUT IF WE DON'T SOLVE THIS MURDER FAST...
...WE'LL BE SEEING A LOT MORE BODIES.
THIS LITTLE VILLAGE...
...IS GONNA LOOK LIKE A MEDIEVAL BATTLE-FIELD.

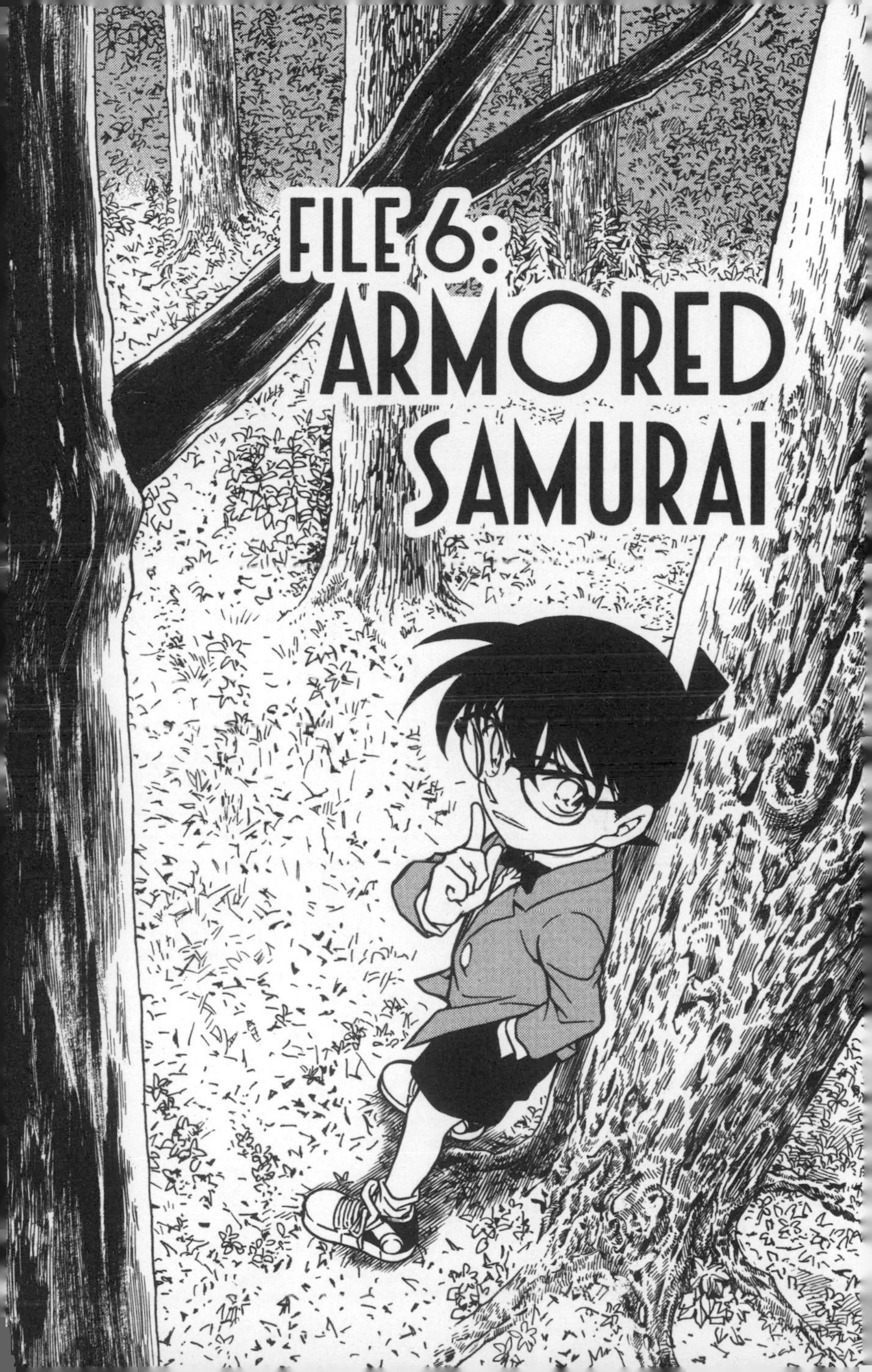
FILE 6:
ARMORED
SAMURAI

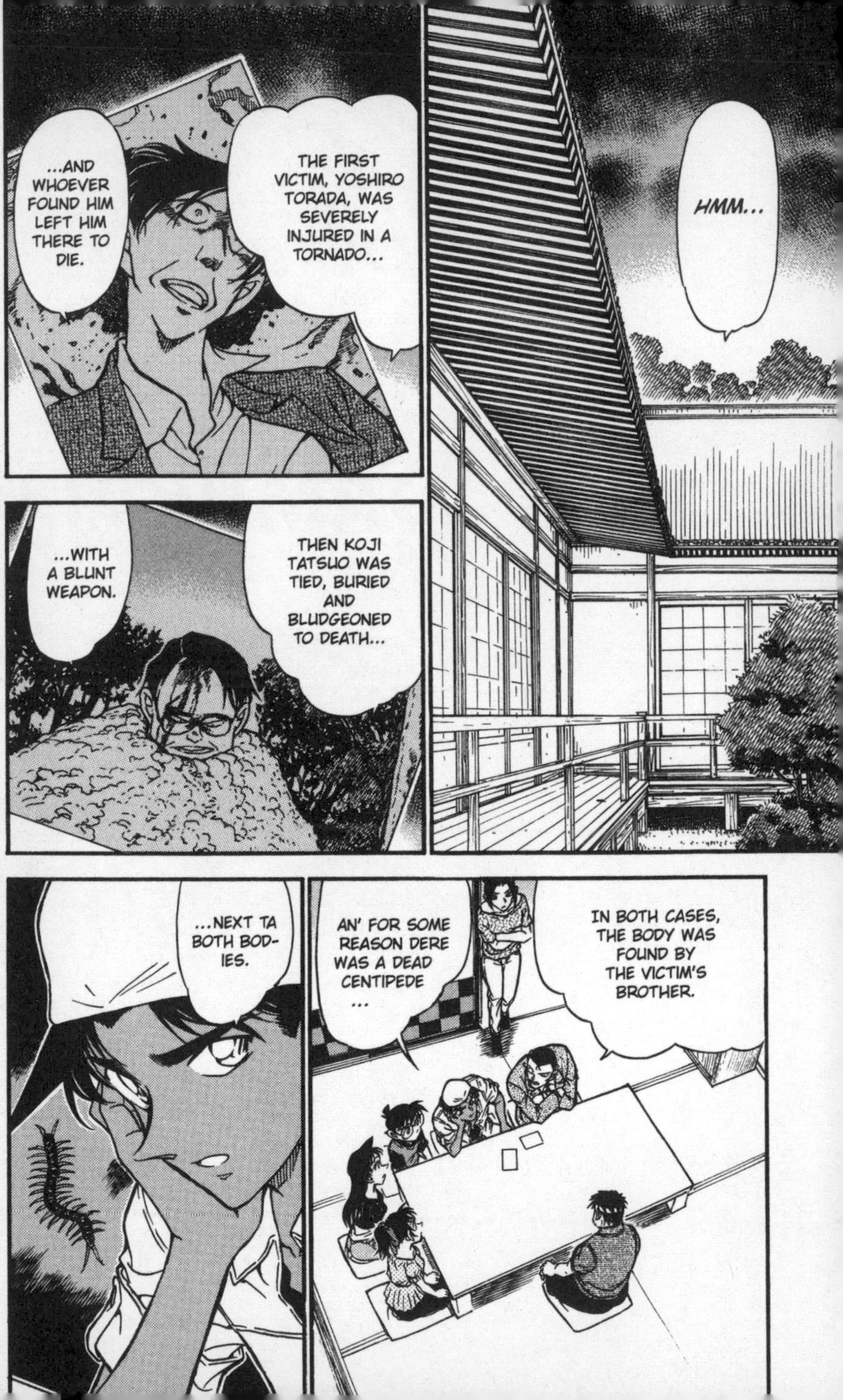
HMM...
THE FIRST VICTIM, YOSHIRO TORADA, WAS SEVERELY INJURED IN A TORNADO...
...AND WHOEVER FOUND HIM LEFT HIM THERE TO DIE.
THEN KOJI TATSUO WAS TIED, BURIED AND BLUDGEONED TO DEATH...
...WITH A BLUNT WEAPON.
IN BOTH CASES, THE BODY WAS FOUND BY THE VICTIM'S BROTHER.
AN' FOR SOME REASON DERE WAS A DEAD CENTIPEDE ...
...NEXT TA BOTH BOD-IES.

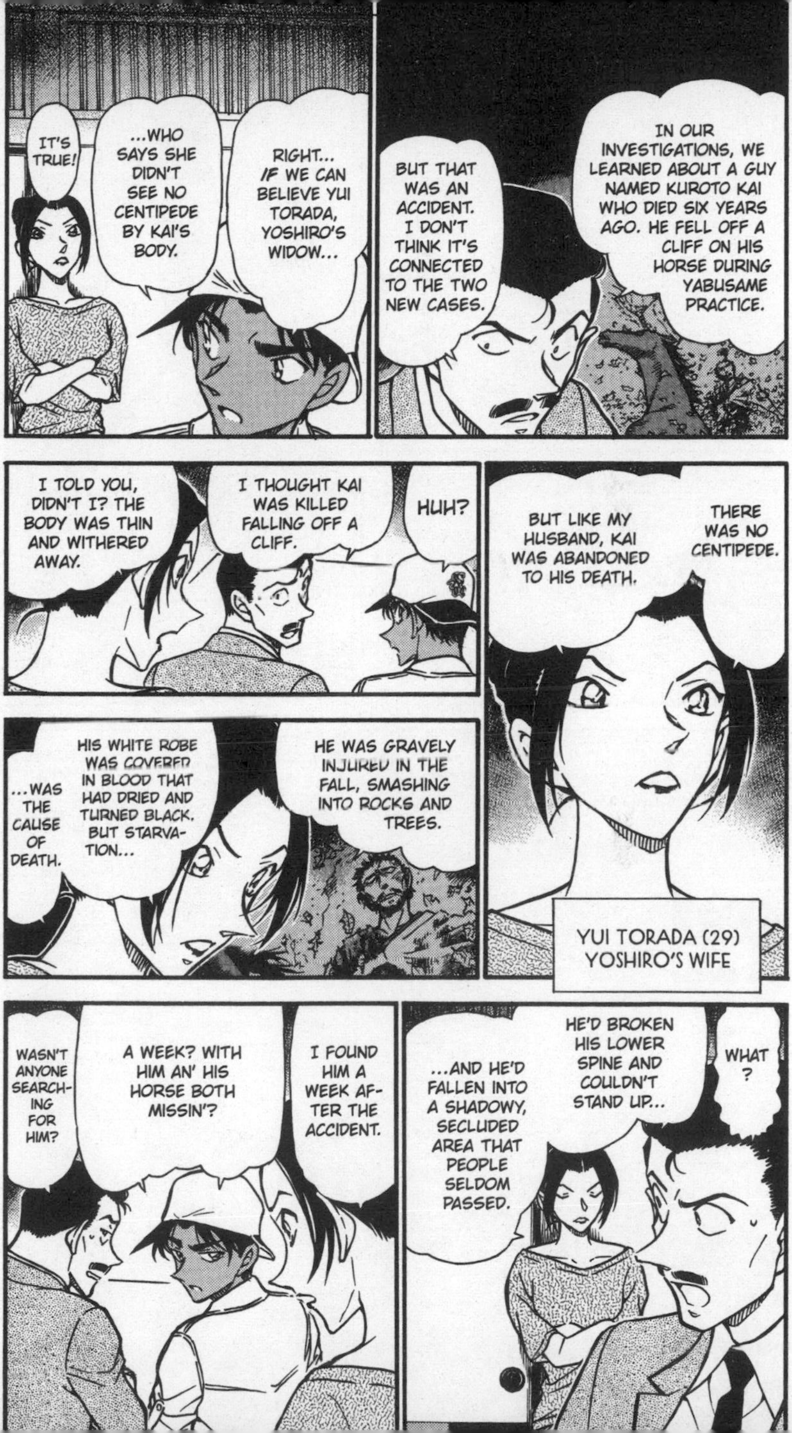
IN OUR INVESTIGATIONS, WE LEARNED ABOUT A GUY NAMED KUROTO KAI WHO DIED SIX YEARS AGO. HE FELL OFF A CLIFF ON HIS HORSE DURING YABUSAME PRACTICE.
BUT THAT WAS AN ACCIDENT. I DON'T THINK IT'S CONNECTED TO THE TWO NEW CASES.
RIGHT... *IF* WE CAN BELIEVE YUI TORADA, YOSHIRO'S WIDOW...
...WHO SAYS SHE DIDN'T SEE NO CENTIPEDE BY KAI'S BODY.
IT'S TRUE!
THERE WAS NO CENTIPEDE.
BUT LIKE MY HUSBAND, KAI WAS ABANDONED TO HIS DEATH.
YUI TORADA (29) YOSHIRO'S WIFE
HUH?
I THOUGHT KAI WAS KILLED FALLING OFF A CLIFF.
I TOLD YOU, DIDN'T I? THE BODY WAS THIN AND WITHERED AWAY.
HE WAS GRAVELY INJURED IN THE FALL, SMASHING INTO ROCKS AND TREES.
HIS WHITE ROBE WAS COVERED IN BLOOD THAT HAD DRIED AND TURNED BLACK. BUT STARVATION...
...WAS THE CAUSE OF DEATH.
WHAT?
HE'D BROKEN HIS LOWER SPINE AND COULDN'T STAND UP...
...AND HE'D FALLEN INTO A SHADOWY, SECLUDED AREA THAT PEOPLE SELDOM PASSED.
I FOUND HIM A WEEK AFTER THE ACCIDENT.
A WEEK? WITH HIM AN' HIS HORSE BOTH MISSIN'?
WASN'T ANYONE SEARCHING FOR HIM?

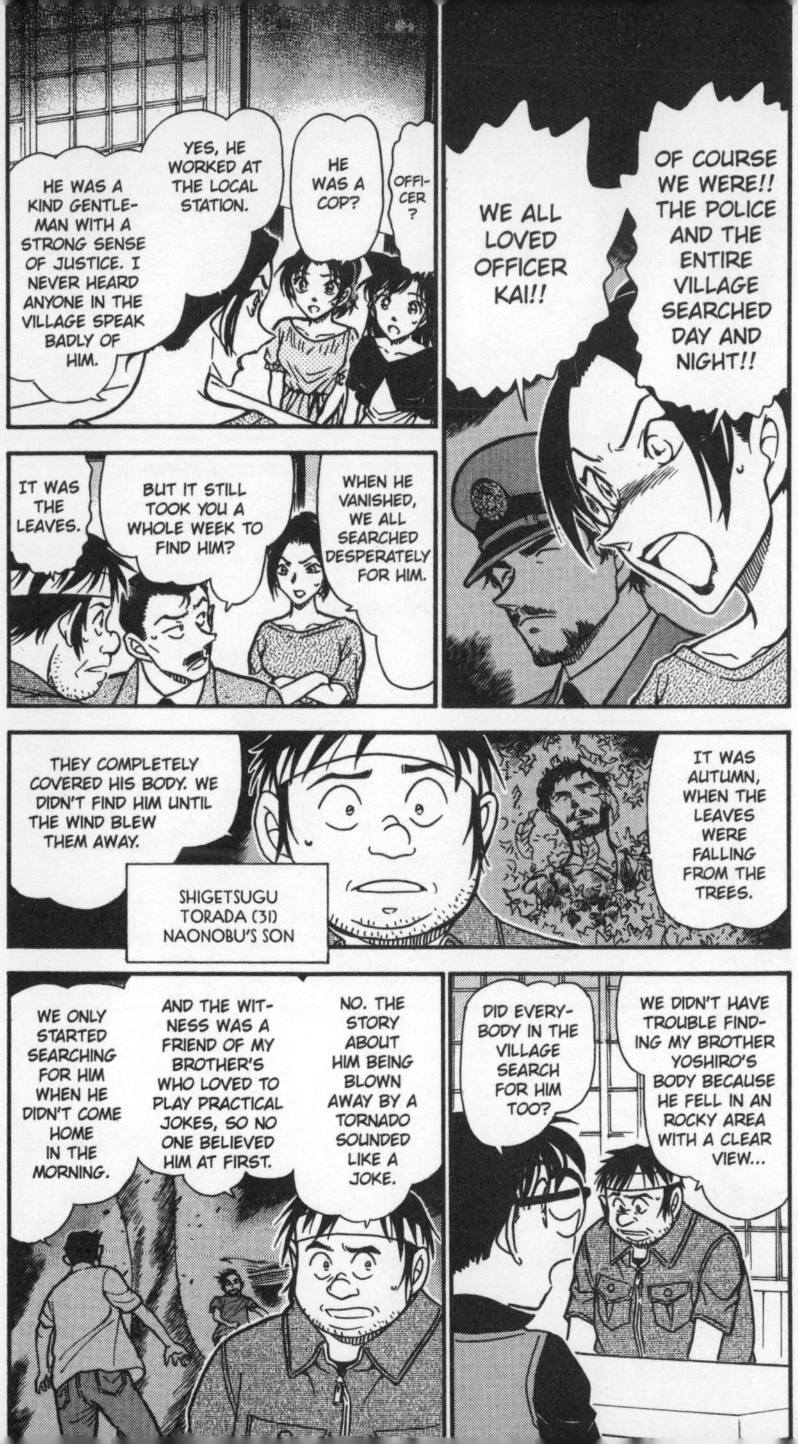
OF COURSE WE WERE!! THE POLICE AND THE ENTIRE VILLAGE SEARCHED DAY AND NIGHT!!
WE ALL LOVED OFFICER KAI!!
OFFICER?
HE WAS A COP?
YES, HE WORKED AT THE LOCAL STATION.
HE WAS A KIND GENTLEMAN WITH A STRONG SENSE OF JUSTICE. I NEVER HEARD ANYONE IN THE VILLAGE SPEAK BADLY OF HIM.
WHEN HE VANISHED, WE ALL SEARCHED DESPERATELY FOR HIM.
BUT IT STILL TOOK YOU A WHOLE WEEK TO FIND HIM?
IT WAS THE LEAVES.
IT WAS AUTUMN, WHEN THE LEAVES WERE FALLING FROM THE TREES.
THEY COMPLETELY COVERED HIS BODY. WE DIDN'T FIND HIM UNTIL THE WIND BLEW THEM AWAY.
SHIGETSUGU TORADA (31) NAONOBU'S SON
WE DIDN'T HAVE TROUBLE FINDING MY BROTHER YOSHIRO'S BODY BECAUSE HE FELL IN AN ROCKY AREA WITH A CLEAR VIEW...
DID EVERYBODY IN THE VILLAGE SEARCH FOR HIM TOO?
NO. THE STORY ABOUT HIM BEING BLOWN AWAY BY A TORNADO SOUNDED LIKE A JOKE.
AND THE WITNESS WAS A FRIEND OF MY BROTHER'S WHO LOVED TO PLAY PRACTICAL JOKES, SO NO ONE BELIEVED HIM AT FIRST.
WE ONLY STARTED SEARCHING FOR HIM WHEN HE DIDN'T COME HOME IN THE MORNING.

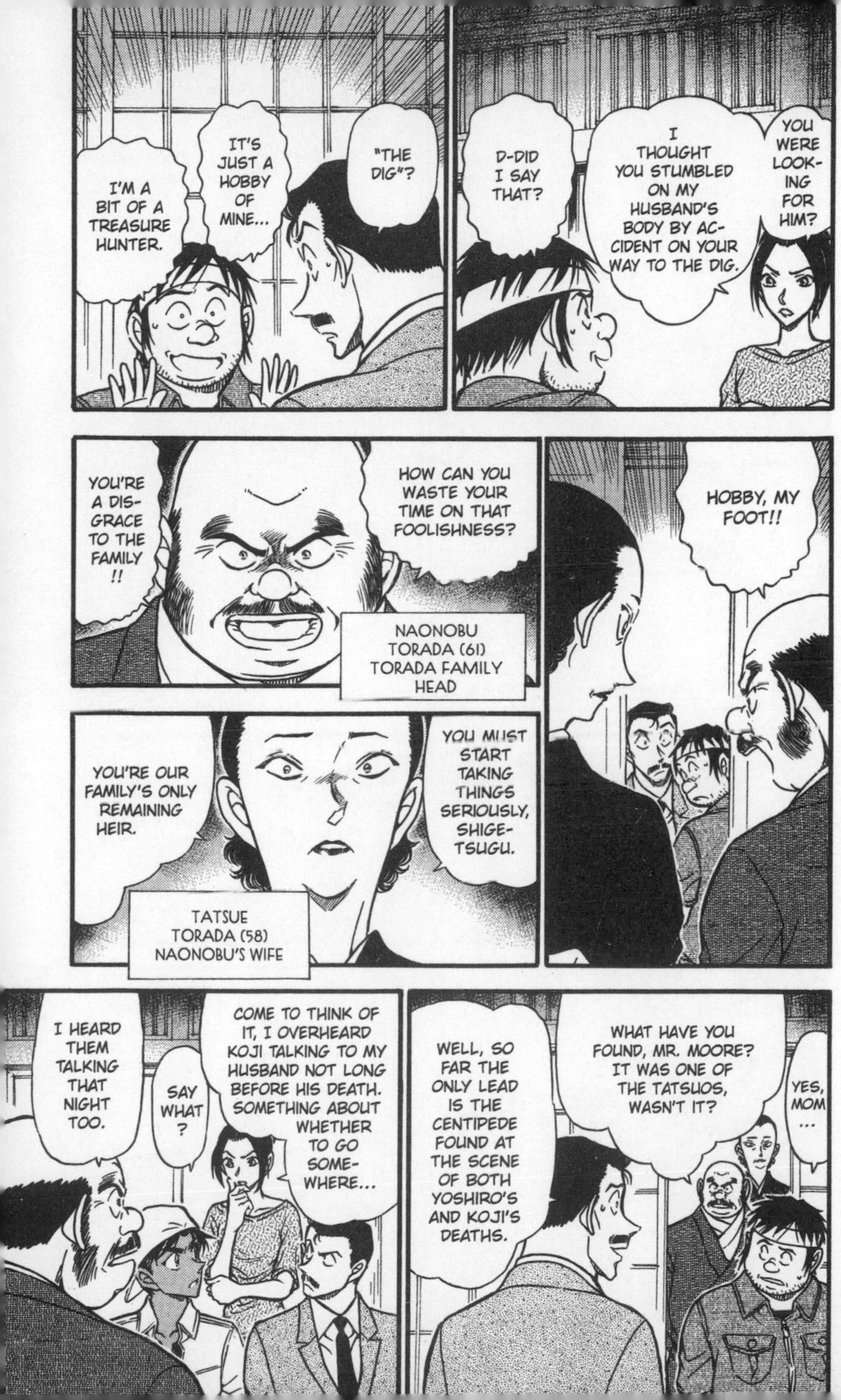
YOU WERE LOOKING FOR HIM?
I THOUGHT YOU STUMBLED ON MY HUSBAND'S BODY BY ACCIDENT ON YOUR WAY TO THE DIG.
D-DID I SAY THAT?
"THE DIG"?
IT'S JUST A HOBBY OF MINE...
I'M A BIT OF A TREASURE HUNTER.
HOBBY, MY FOOT!!
HOW CAN YOU WASTE YOUR TIME ON THAT FOOLISHNESS?
YOU'RE A DISGRACE TO THE FAMILY!!
NAONOBU TORADA (61) TORADA FAMILY HEAD
YOU MUST START TAKING THINGS SERIOUSLY, SHIGETSUGU.
YOU'RE OUR FAMILY'S ONLY REMAINING HEIR.
TATSUE TORADA (58) NAONOBU'S WIFE
YES, MOM...
WHAT HAVE YOU FOUND, MR. MOORE? IT WAS ONE OF THE TATSUOS, WASN'T IT?
WELL, SO FAR THE ONLY LEAD IS THE CENTIPEDE FOUND AT THE SCENE OF BOTH YOSHIRO'S AND KOJI'S DEATHS.
COME TO THINK OF IT, I OVERHEARD KOJI TALKING TO MY HUSBAND NOT LONG BEFORE HIS DEATH. SOMETHING ABOUT WHETHER TO GO SOMEWHERE...
SAY WHAT?
I HEARD THEM TALKING THAT NIGHT TOO.

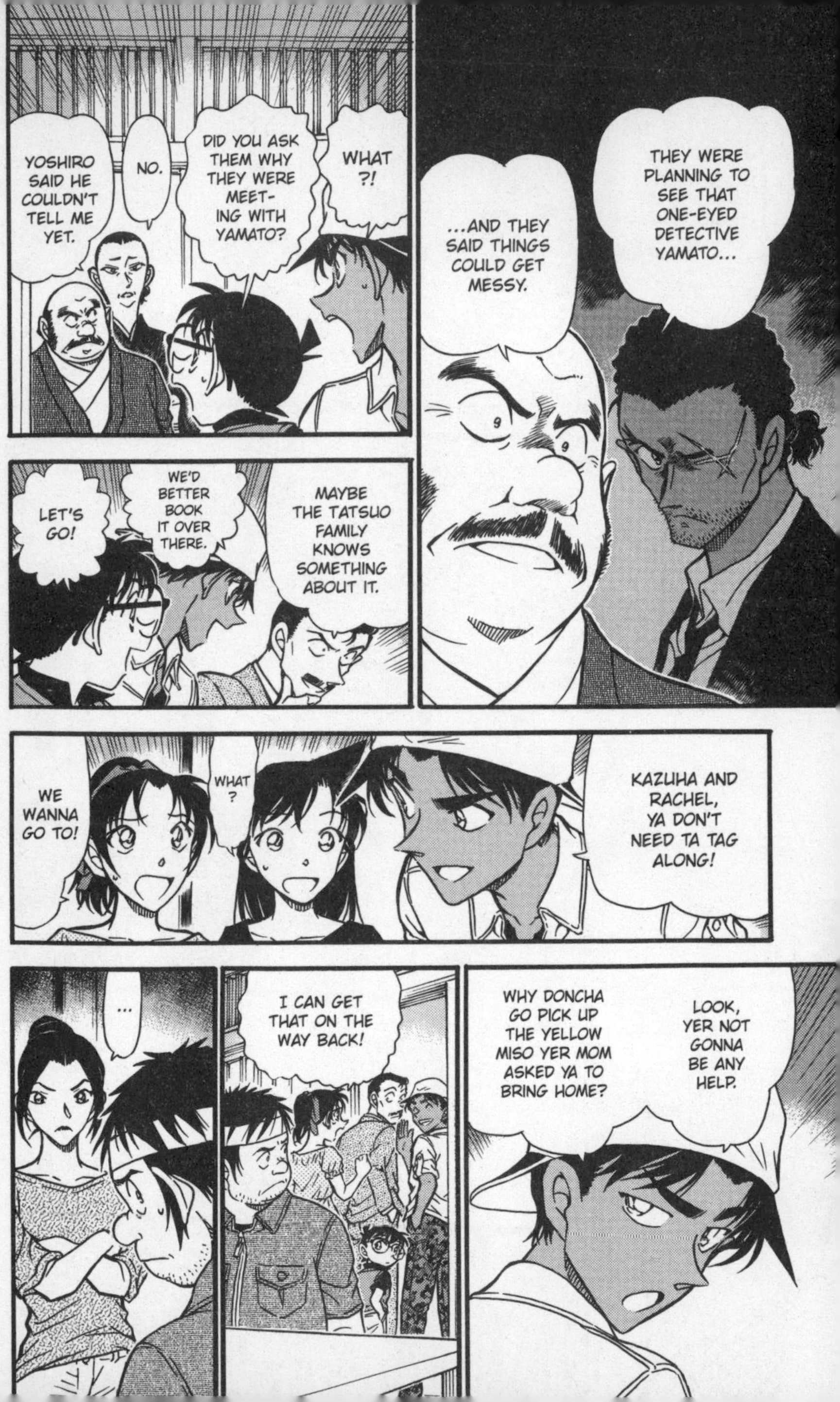
THEY WERE PLANNING TO SEE THAT ONE-EYED DETECTIVE YAMATO...
...AND THEY SAID THINGS COULD GET MESSY.
WHAT ?!
DID YOU ASK THEM WHY THEY WERE MEET-ING WITH YAMATO?
NO.
YOSHIRO SAID HE COULDN'T TELL ME YET.
MAYBE THE TATSUO FAMILY KNOWS SOMETHING ABOUT IT.
WE'D BETTER BOOK IT OVER THERE.
LET'S GO!
KAZUHA AND RACHEL, YA DON'T NEED TA TAG ALONG!
WHAT ?
WE WANNA GO TO!
LOOK, YER NOT GONNA BE ANY HELP.
WHY DONCHA GO PICK UP THE YELLOW MISO YER MOM ASKED YA TO BRING HOME?
I CAN GET THAT ON THE WAY BACK!
...

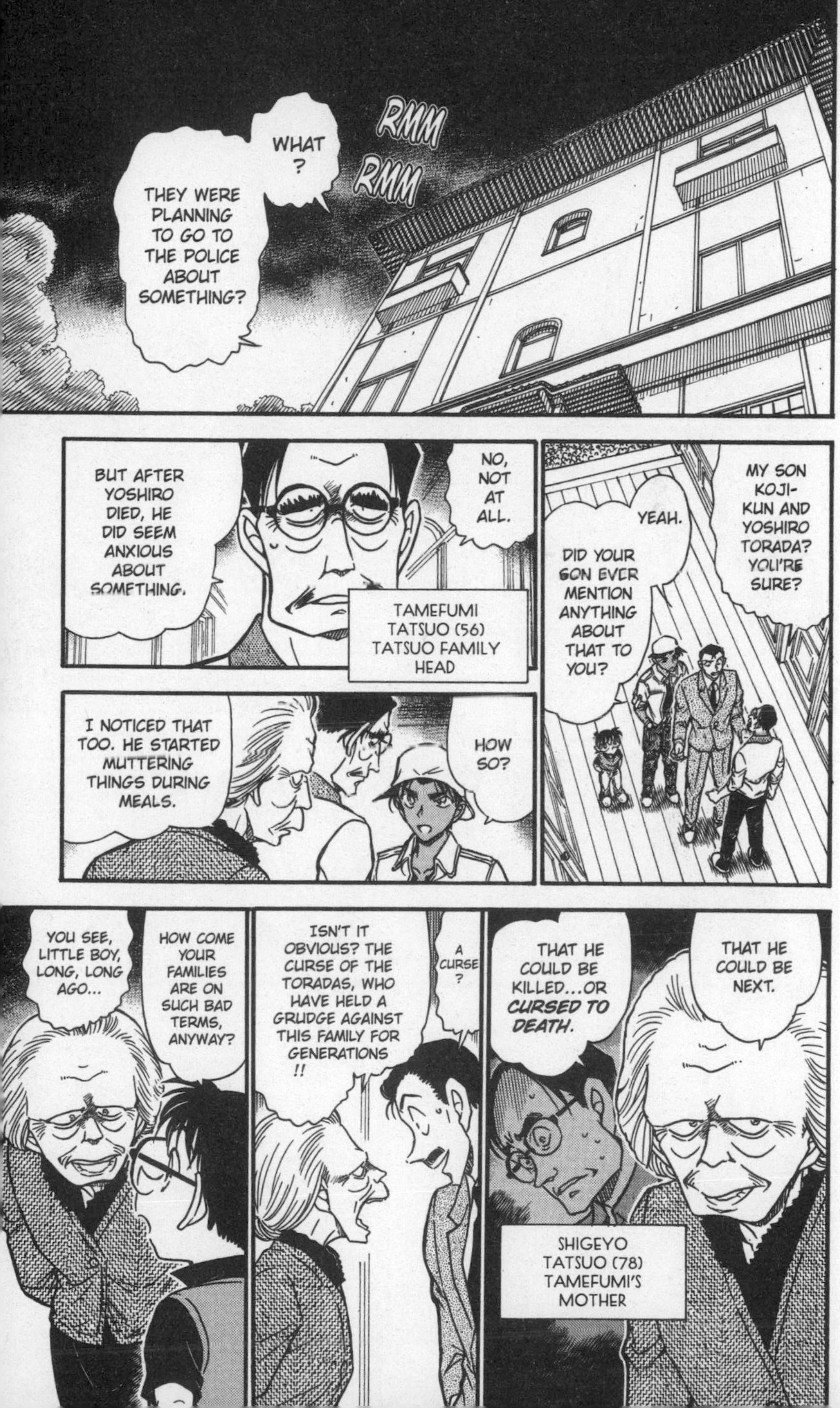
RMM RMM
WHAT ?
THEY WERE PLANNING TO GO TO THE POLICE ABOUT SOMETHING?
MY SON KOJI-KUN AND YOSHIRO TORADA? YOU'RE SURE?
YEAH.
DID YOUR SON EVER MENTION ANYTHING ABOUT THAT TO YOU?
NO, NOT AT ALL.
BUT AFTER YOSHIRO DIED, HE DID SEEM ANXIOUS ABOUT SOMETHING.
TAMEFUMI TATSUO (56) TATSUO FAMILY HEAD
HOW SO?
I NOTICED THAT TOO. HE STARTED MUTTERING THINGS DURING MEALS.
THAT HE COULD BE NEXT.
THAT HE COULD BE KILLED...OR *CURSED TO DEATH*.
SHIGEYO TATSUO (78) TAMEFUMI'S MOTHER
A CURSE ?
ISN'T IT OBVIOUS? THE CURSE OF THE TORADAS, WHO HAVE HELD A GRUDGE AGAINST THIS FAMILY FOR GENERATIONS !!
HOW COME YOUR FAMILIES ARE ON SUCH BAD TERMS, ANYWAY?
YOU SEE, LITTLE BOY, LONG, LONG AGO...

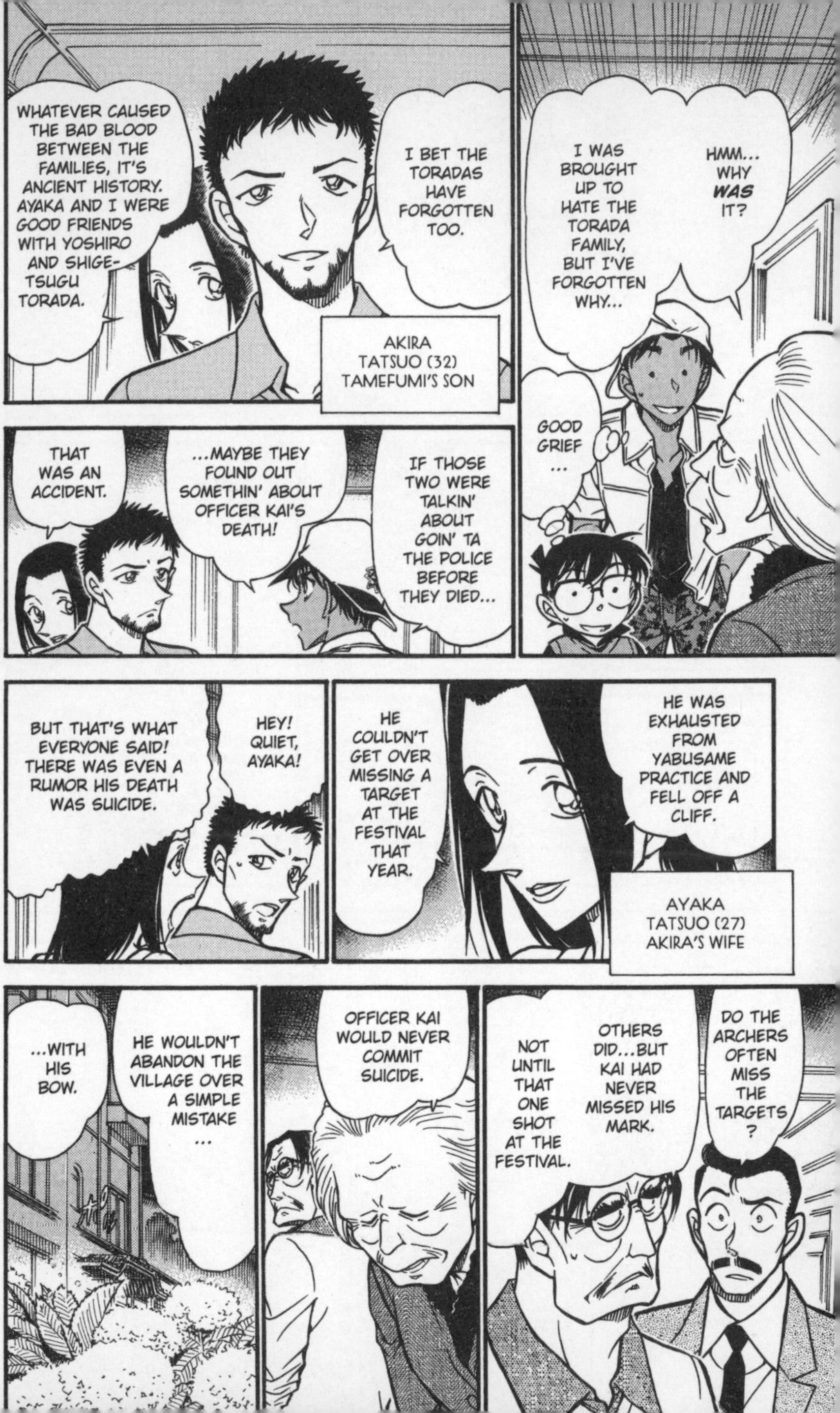
HMM... WHY *WAS* IT?
I WAS BROUGHT UP TO HATE THE TORADA FAMILY, BUT I'VE FORGOTTEN WHY...
GOOD GRIEF...
WHATEVER CAUSED THE BAD BLOOD BETWEEN THE FAMILIES, IT'S ANCIENT HISTORY. AYAKA AND I WERE GOOD FRIENDS WITH YOSHIRO AND SHIGE-TSUGU TORADA.
I BET THE TORADAS HAVE FORGOTTEN TOO.
AKIRA TATSUO (32) TAMEFUMI'S SON
IF THOSE TWO WERE TALKIN' ABOUT GOIN' TA THE POLICE BEFORE THEY DIED...
...MAYBE THEY FOUND OUT SOMETHIN' ABOUT OFFICER KAI'S DEATH!
THAT WAS AN ACCIDENT.
HE WAS EXHAUSTED FROM YABUSAME PRACTICE AND FELL OFF A CLIFF.
HE COULDN'T GET OVER MISSING A TARGET AT THE FESTIVAL THAT YEAR.
AYAKA TATSUO (27) AKIRA'S WIFE
HEY! QUIET, AYAKA!
BUT THAT'S WHAT EVERYONE SAID! THERE WAS EVEN A RUMOR HIS DEATH WAS SUICIDE.
DO THE ARCHERS OFTEN MISS THE TARGETS?
OTHERS DID...BUT KAI HAD NEVER MISSED HIS MARK.
NOT UNTIL THAT ONE SHOT AT THE FESTIVAL.
OFFICER KAI WOULD NEVER COMMIT SUICIDE.
HE WOULDN'T ABANDON THE VILLAGE OVER A SIMPLE MISTAKE...
...WITH HIS BOW.

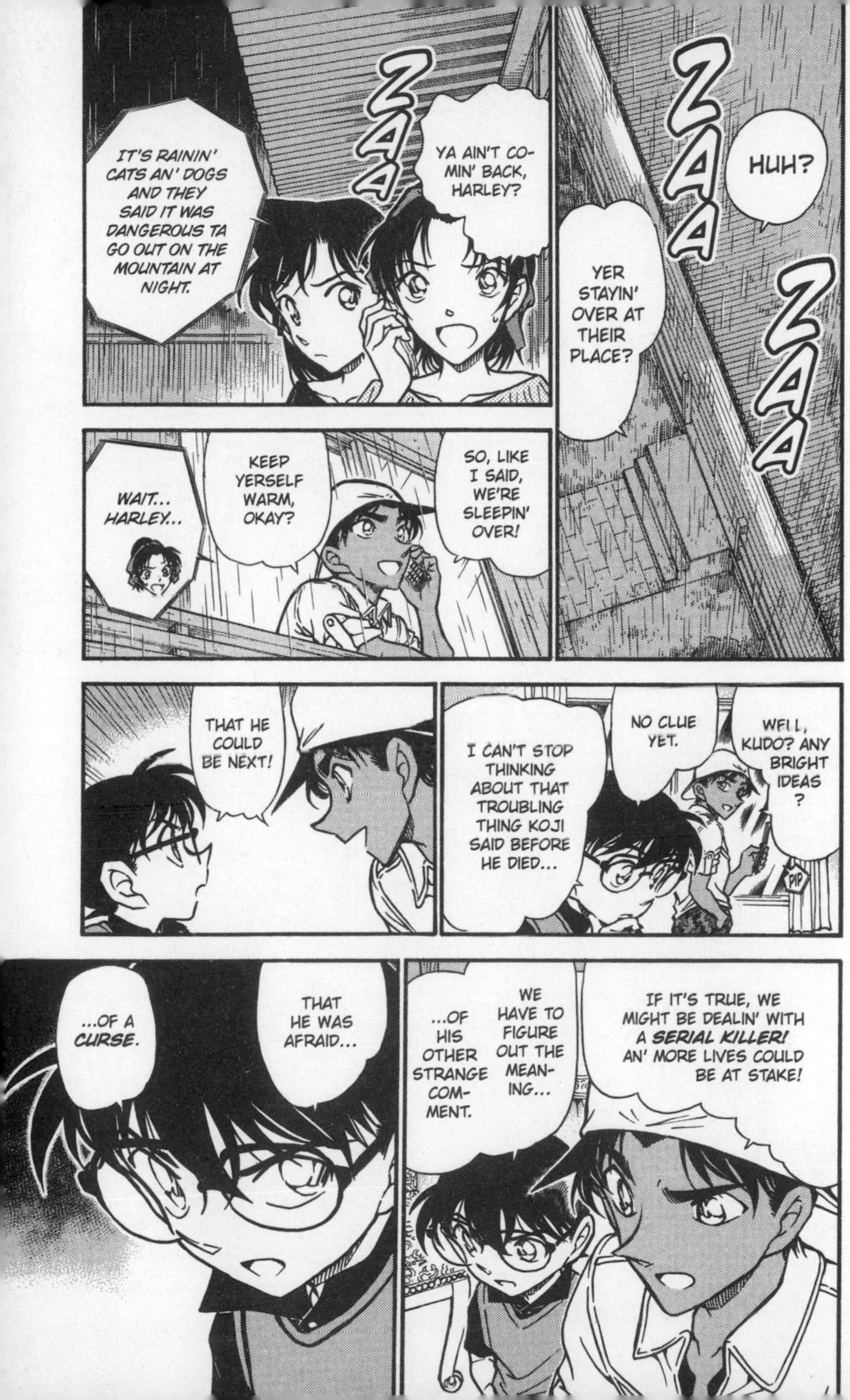
ZAAA
HUH?
YER STAYIN' OVER AT THEIR PLACE?
ZAAA
ZAAA
YA AIN'T COMIN' BACK, HARLEY?
IT'S RAININ' CATS AN' DOGS AND THEY SAID IT WAS DANGEROUS TA GO OUT ON THE MOUNTAIN AT NIGHT.
SO, LIKE I SAID, WE'RE SLEEPIN' OVER!
KEEP YERSELF WARM, OKAY?
WAIT... HARLEY...
WELL, KUDO? ANY BRIGHT IDEAS?
NO CLUE YET.
PIP
I CAN'T STOP THINKING ABOUT THAT TROUBLING THING KOJI SAID BEFORE HE DIED...
THAT HE COULD BE NEXT!
IF IT'S TRUE, WE MIGHT BE DEALIN' WITH A SERIAL KILLER! AN' MORE LIVES COULD BE AT STAKE!
WE HAVE TO FIGURE OUT THE MEANING...
...OF HIS OTHER STRANGE COMMENT.
THAT HE WAS AFRAID...
...OF A CURSE.

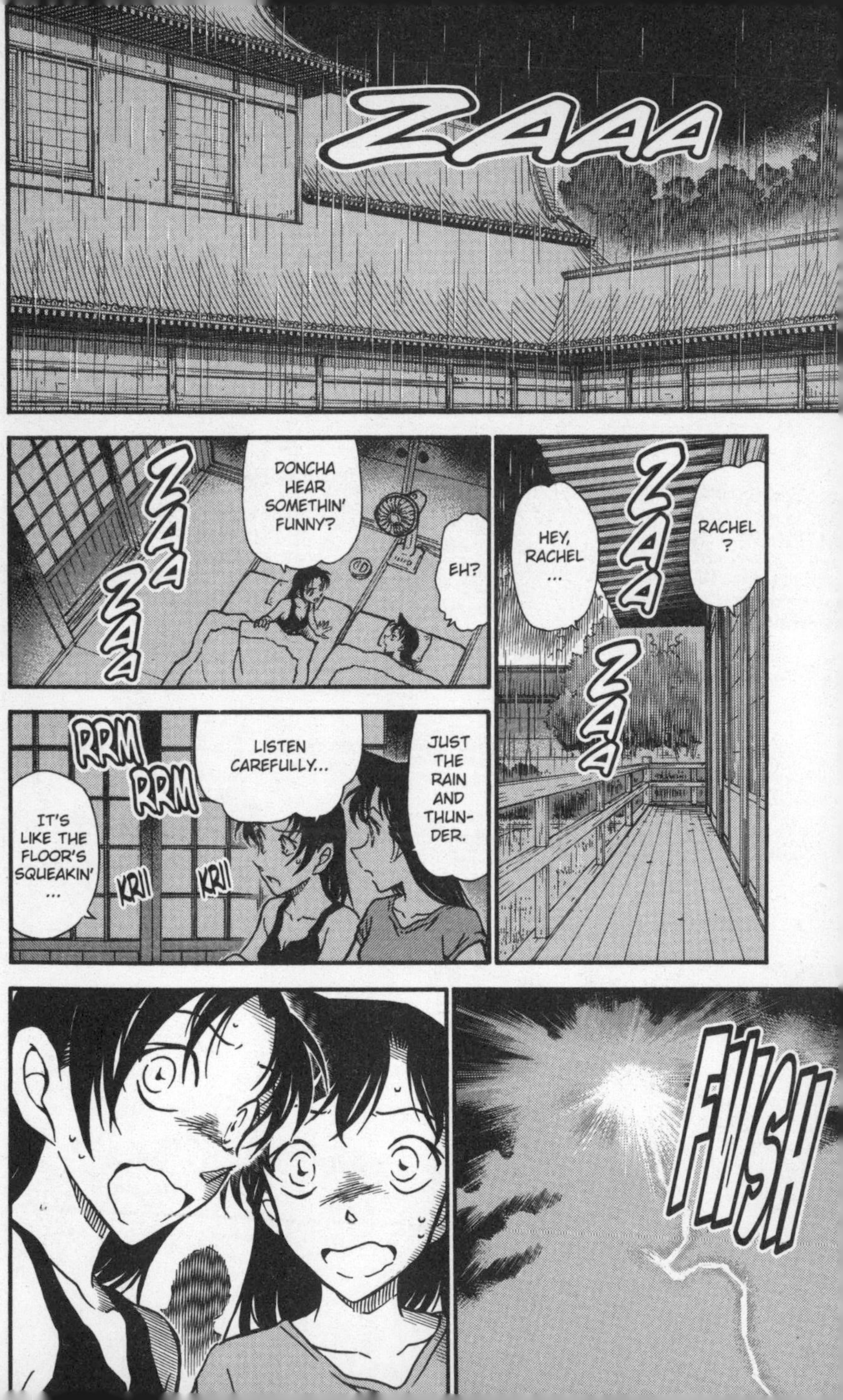
ZAAA
RACHEL ?
ZAAA
HEY, RACHEL ...
ZAAA
DONCHA HEAR SOMETHIN' FUNNY?
EH?
ZAAA
ZAAA
JUST THE RAIN AND THUN-DER.
LISTEN CAREFULLY...
RRM RRM
IT'S LIKE THE FLOOR'S SQUEAKIN' ...
KRII KRII
FLISH

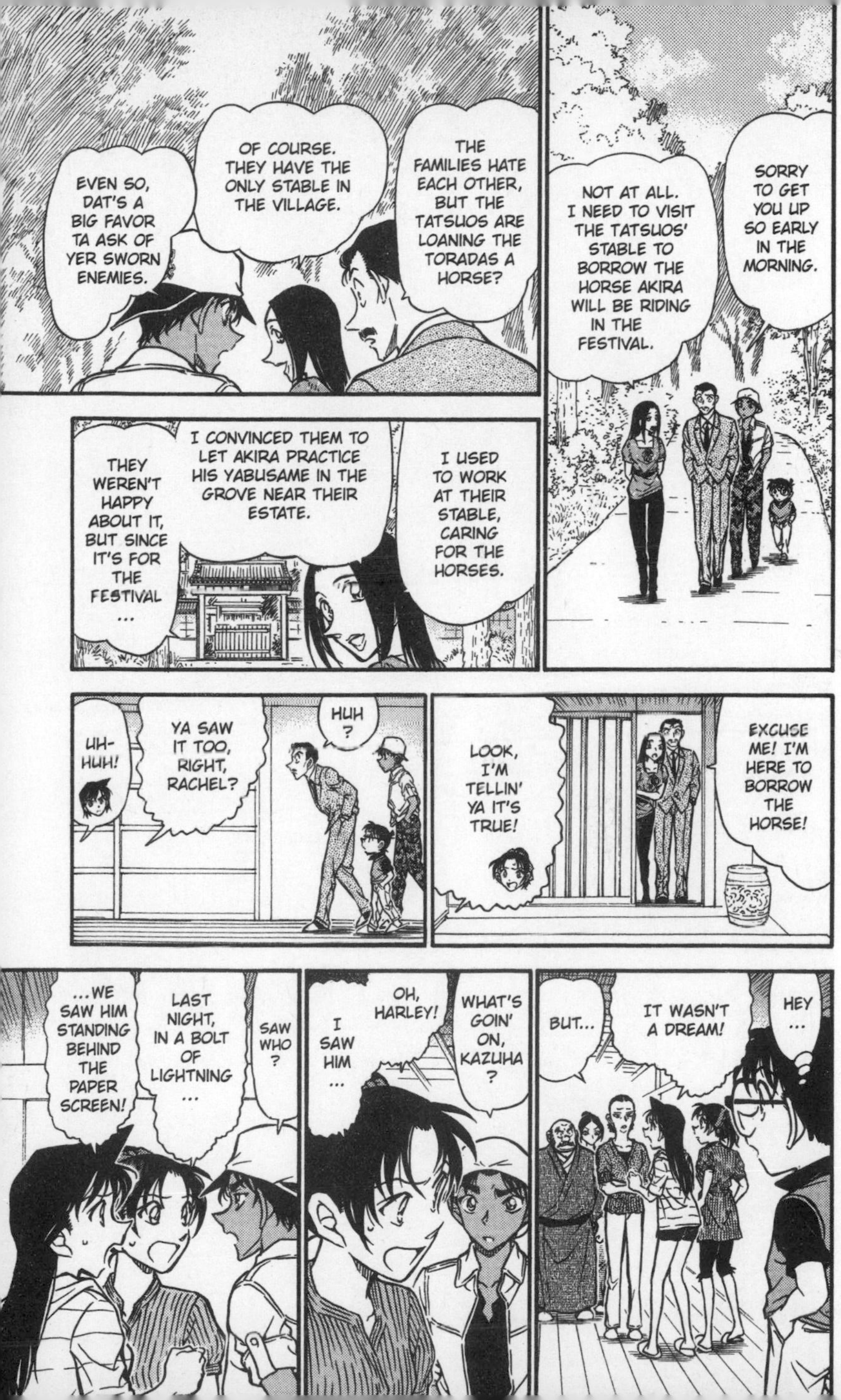
SORRY TO GET YOU UP SO EARLY IN THE MORNING.
NOT AT ALL. I NEED TO VISIT THE TATSUOS' STABLE TO BORROW THE HORSE AKIRA WILL BE RIDING IN THE FESTIVAL.
THE FAMILIES HATE EACH OTHER, BUT THE TATSUOS ARE LOANING THE TORADAS A HORSE?
OF COURSE. THEY HAVE THE ONLY STABLE IN THE VILLAGE.
EVEN SO, DAT'S A BIG FAVOR TA ASK OF YER SWORN ENEMIES.
I USED TO WORK AT THEIR STABLE, CARING FOR THE HORSES.
I CONVINCED THEM TO LET AKIRA PRACTICE HIS YABUSAME IN THE GROVE NEAR THEIR ESTATE.
THEY WEREN'T HAPPY ABOUT IT, BUT SINCE IT'S FOR THE FESTIVAL...
EXCUSE ME! I'M HERE TO BORROW THE HORSE!
LOOK, I'M TELLIN' YA IT'S TRUE!
HUH?
YA SAW IT TOO, RIGHT, RACHEL?
UH-HUH!
HEY...
IT WASN'T A DREAM!
BUT...
WHAT'S GOIN' ON, KAZUHA?
OH, HARLEY!
I SAW HIM...
SAW WHO?
LAST NIGHT, IN A BOLT OF LIGHTNING...
...WE SAW HIM STANDING BEHIND THE PAPER SCREEN!

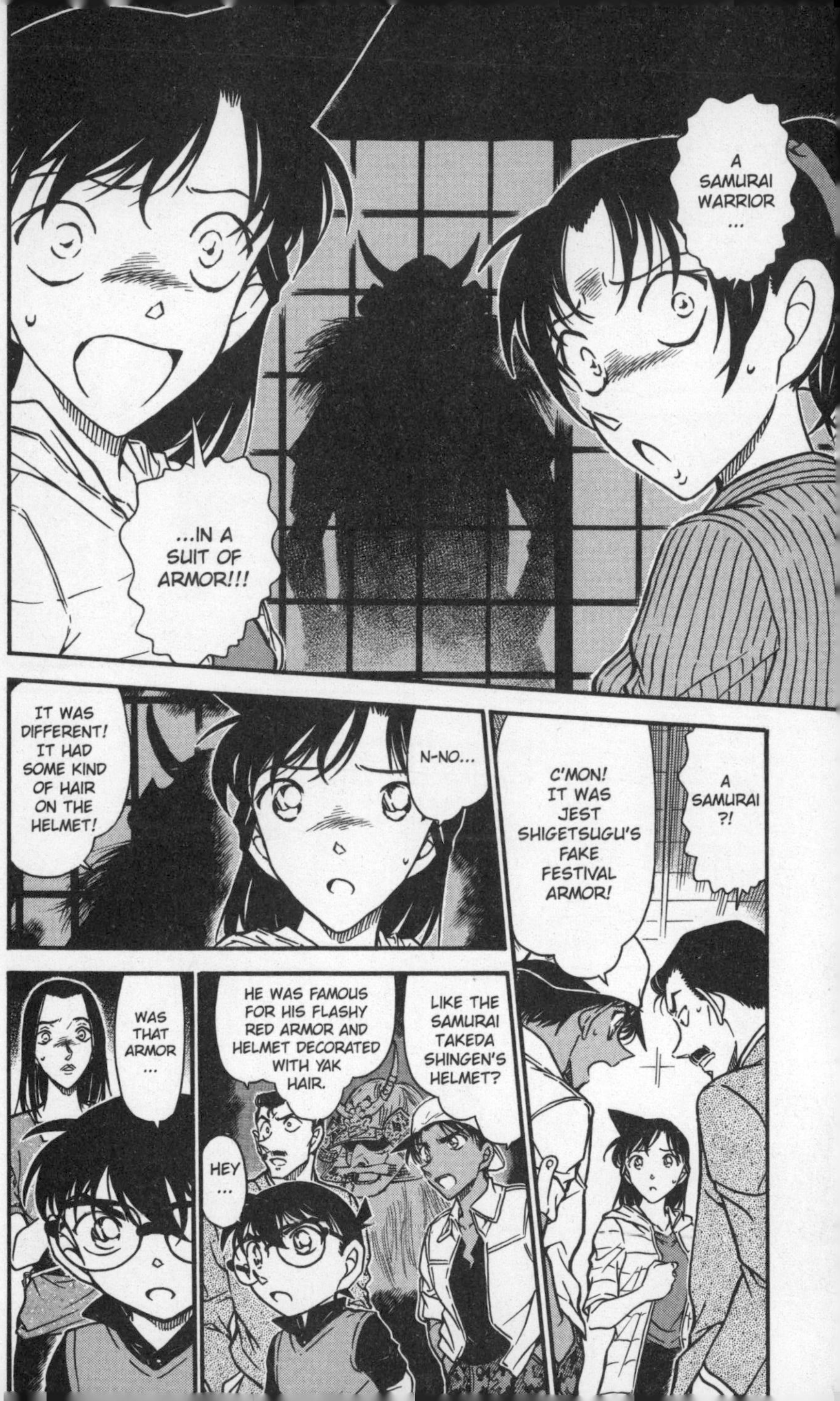
A SAMURAI WARRIOR ...
...IN A SUIT OF ARMOR!!!
A SAMURAI ?!
C'MON! IT WAS JEST SHIGETSUGU'S FAKE FESTIVAL ARMOR!
N-NO...
IT WAS DIFFERENT! IT HAD SOME KIND OF HAIR ON THE HELMET!
LIKE THE SAMURAI TAKEDA SHINGEN'S HELMET?
HE WAS FAMOUS FOR HIS FLASHY RED ARMOR AND HELMET DECORATED WITH YAK HAIR.
HEY ...
WAS THAT ARMOR ...

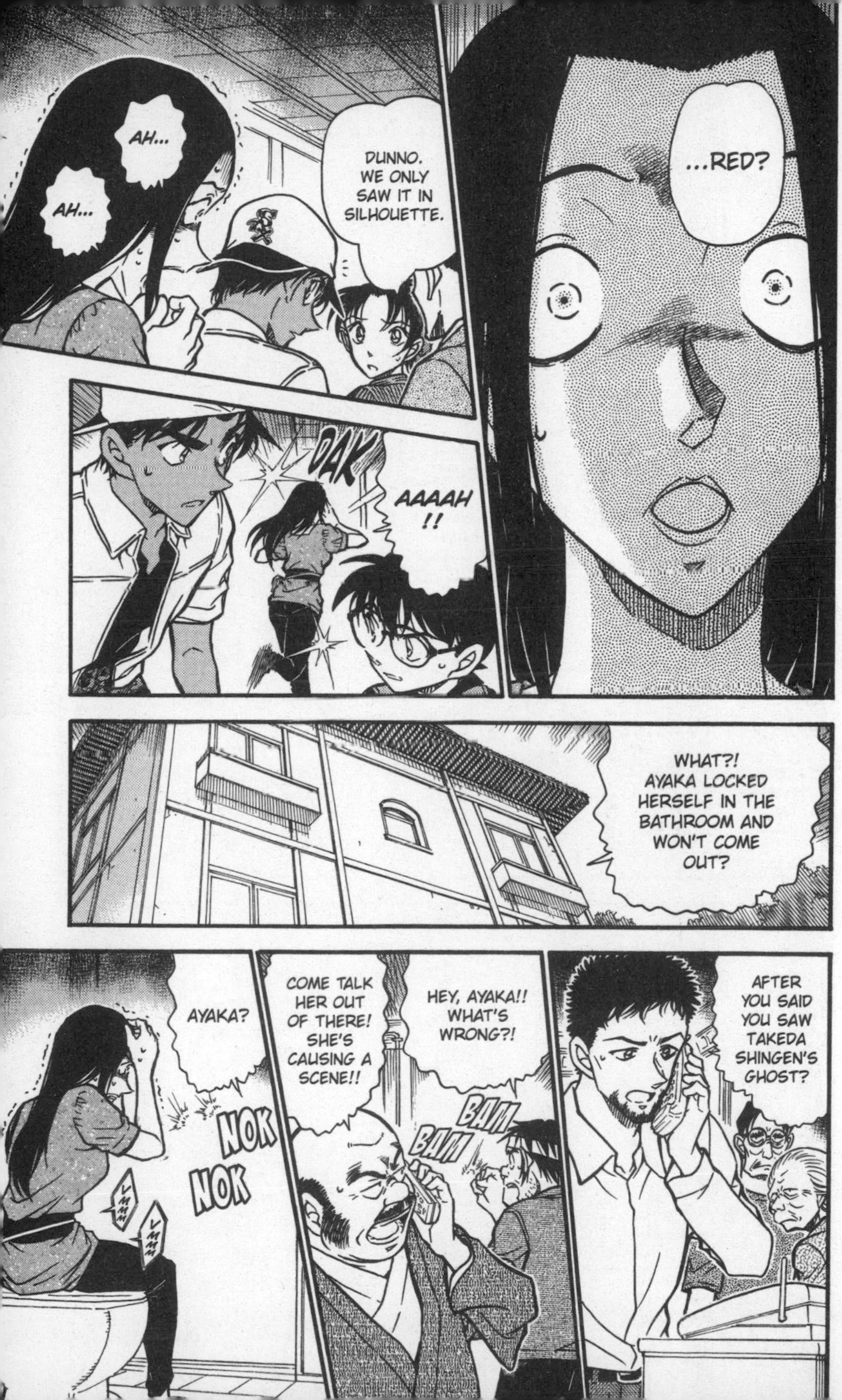
...RED?
DUNNO. WE ONLY SAW IT IN SILHOUETTE.
AH...
AH...
DAK
AAAAH!!
WHAT?! AYAKA LOCKED HERSELF IN THE BATHROOM AND WON'T COME OUT?
AFTER YOU SAID YOU SAW TAKEDA SHINGEN'S GHOST?
HEY, AYAKA!! WHAT'S WRONG?!
COME TALK HER OUT OF THERE! SHE'S CAUSING A SCENE!!
BAM
BAM
AYAKA?
NOK
NOK
VMMM
VMMM

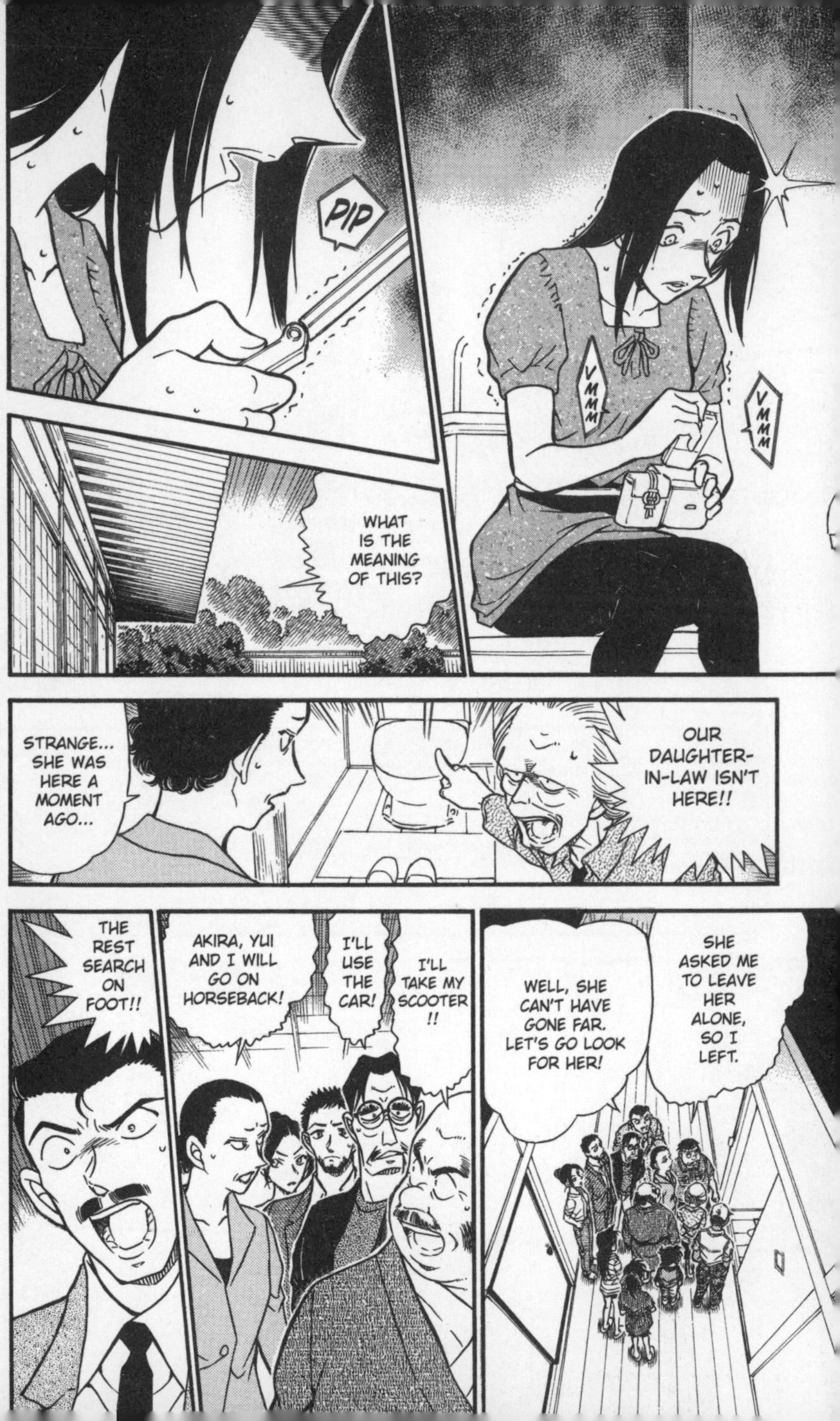
VMMM
VMMM
PIP
WHAT IS THE MEANING OF THIS?
OUR DAUGHTER-IN-LAW ISN'T HERE!!
STRANGE... SHE WAS HERE A MOMENT AGO...
SHE ASKED ME TO LEAVE HER ALONE, SO I LEFT.
WELL, SHE CAN'T HAVE GONE FAR. LET'S GO LOOK FOR HER!
I'LL TAKE MY SCOOTER !!
I'LL USE THE CAR!
AKIRA, YUI AND I WILL GO ON HORSEBACK!
THE REST SEARCH ON FOOT!!

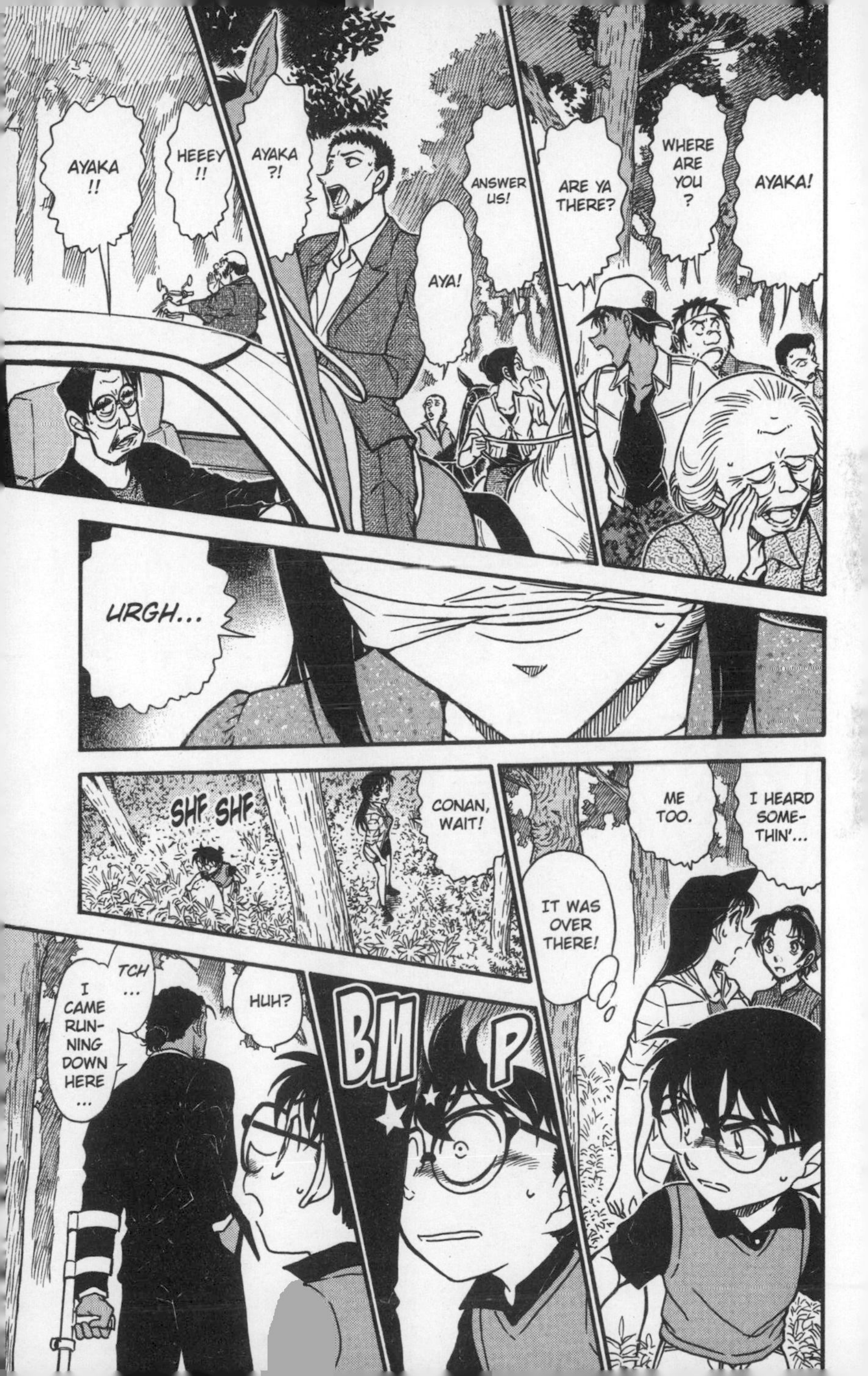
AYAKA!
WHERE ARE YOU ?
ARE YA THERE?
ANSWER US!
AYA!
AYAKA ?!
HEEEY !!
AYAKA !!
URGH...
I HEARD SOME-THIN'...
ME TOO.
IT WAS OVER THERE!
CONAN, WAIT!
SHF SHF
BMP
HUH?
TCH ...
I CAME RUN-NING DOWN HERE ...

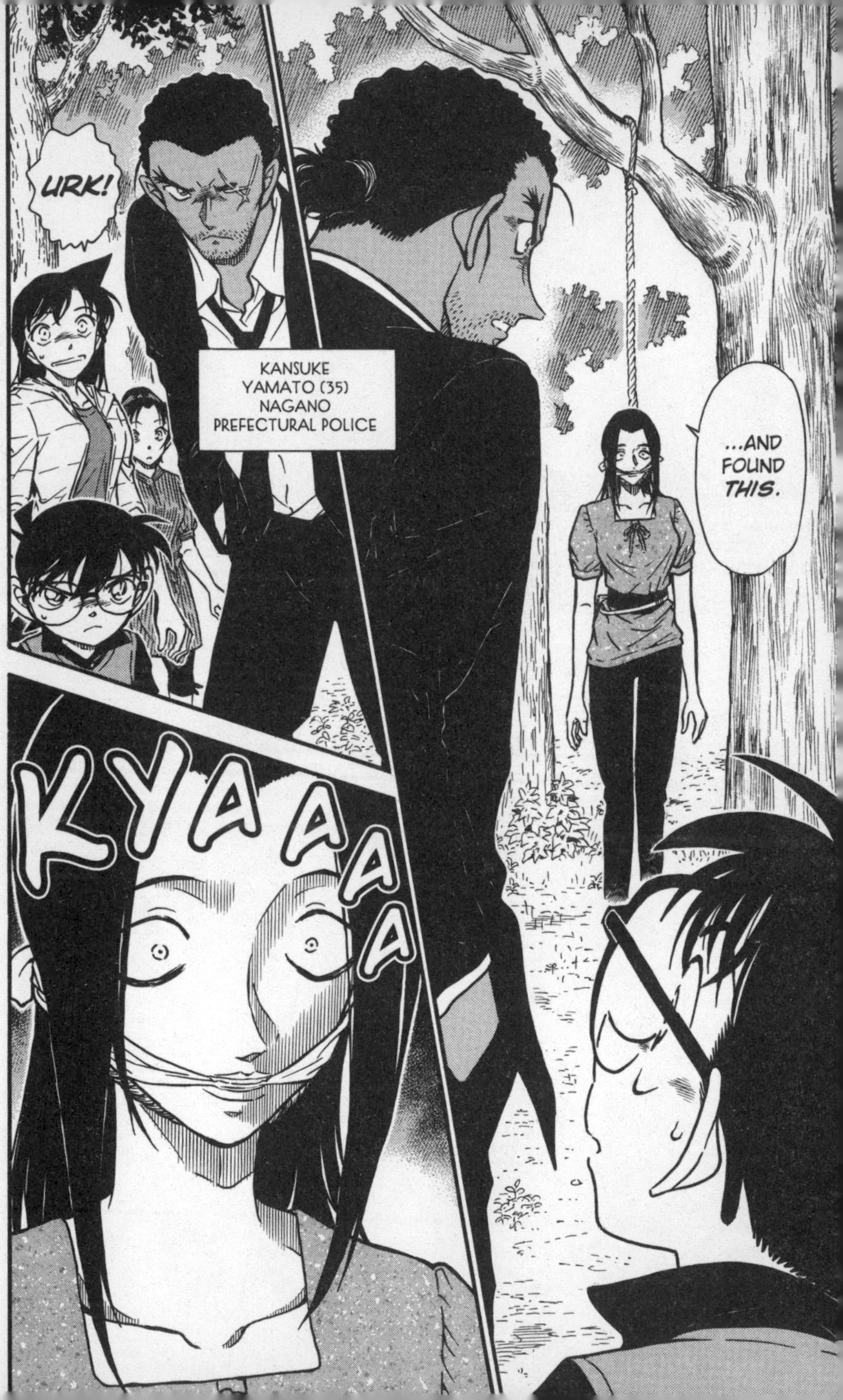
...AND FOUND THIS.
KANSUKE YAMATO (35) NAGANO PREFECTURAL POLICE
URK!
KYAAAAA

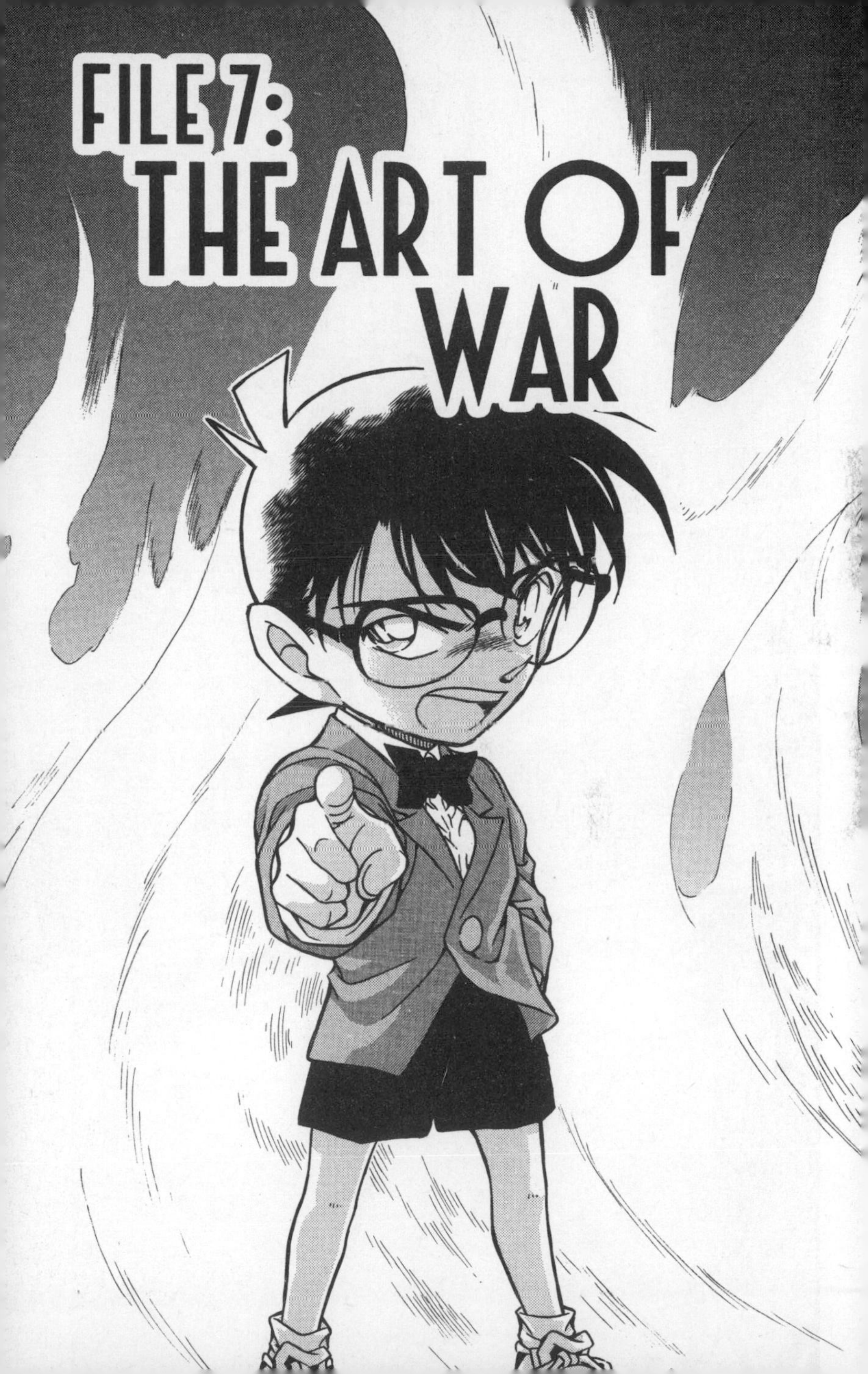
FILE 7:
THE ART OF WAR

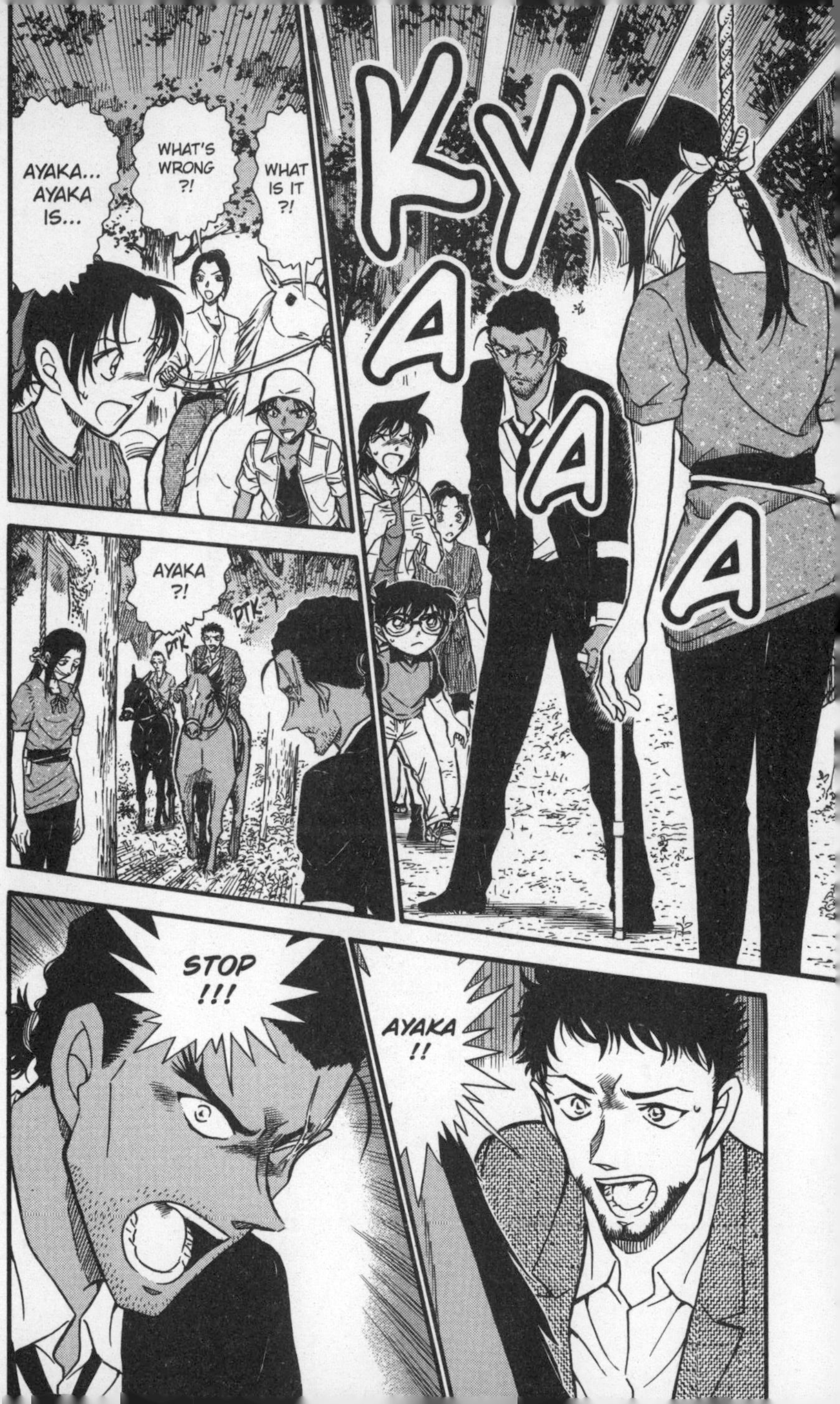
KYAAAA
WHAT IS IT ?!
WHAT'S WRONG ?!
AYAKA... AYAKA IS...
AYAKA ?!
PTK
PTK
AYAKA !!
STOP !!!

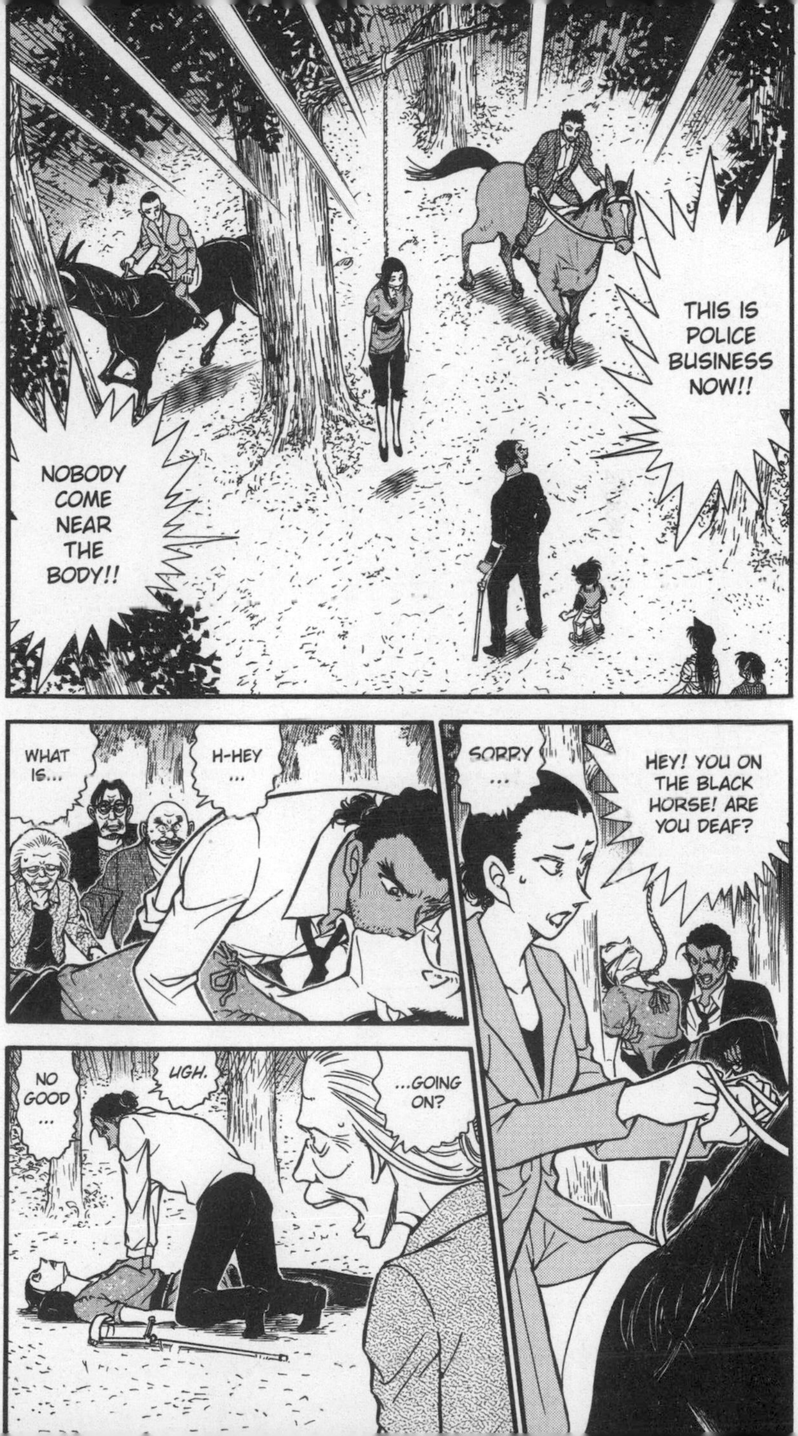
THIS IS POLICE BUSINESS NOW!!
NOBODY COME NEAR THE BODY!!
HEY! YOU ON THE BLACK HORSE! ARE YOU DEAF?
SORRY ...
H-HEY ...
WHAT IS...
...GOING ON?
UGH.
NO GOOD ...

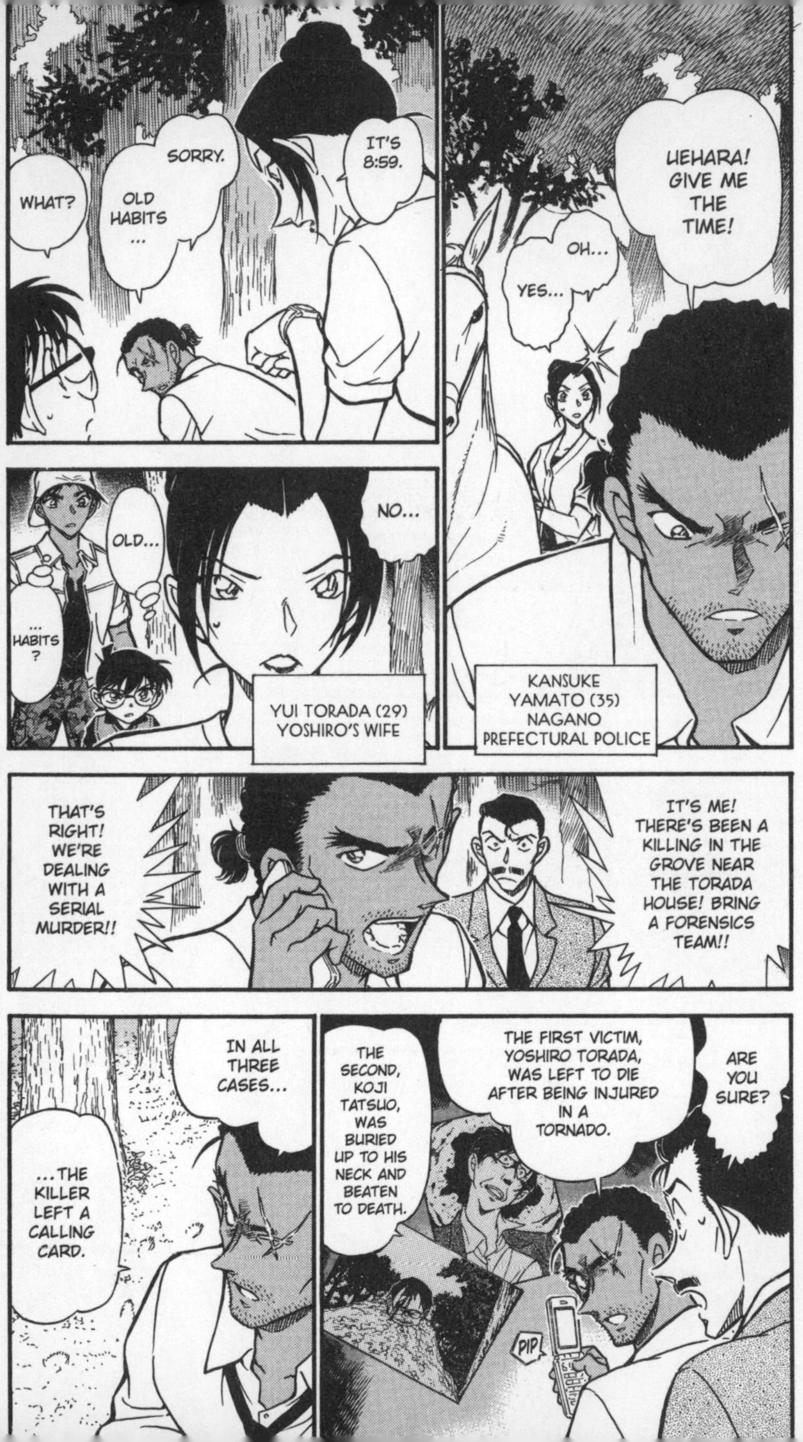
UEHARA! GIVE ME THE TIME!
OH...
YES...
KANSUKE YAMATO (35) NAGANO PREFECTURAL POLICE
IT'S 8:59.
SORRY.
OLD HABITS ...
WHAT?
NO...
OLD...
... HABITS ?
YUI TORADA (29) YOSHIRO'S WIFE
IT'S ME! THERE'S BEEN A KILLING IN THE GROVE NEAR THE TORADA HOUSE! BRING A FORENSICS TEAM!!
THAT'S RIGHT! WE'RE DEALING WITH A SERIAL MURDER!!
ARE YOU SURE?
THE FIRST VICTIM, YOSHIRO TORADA, WAS LEFT TO DIE AFTER BEING INJURED IN A TORNADO.
THE SECOND, KOJI TATSUO, WAS BURIED UP TO HIS NECK AND BEATEN TO DEATH.
PIP
IN ALL THREE CASES...
...THE KILLER LEFT A CALLING CARD.

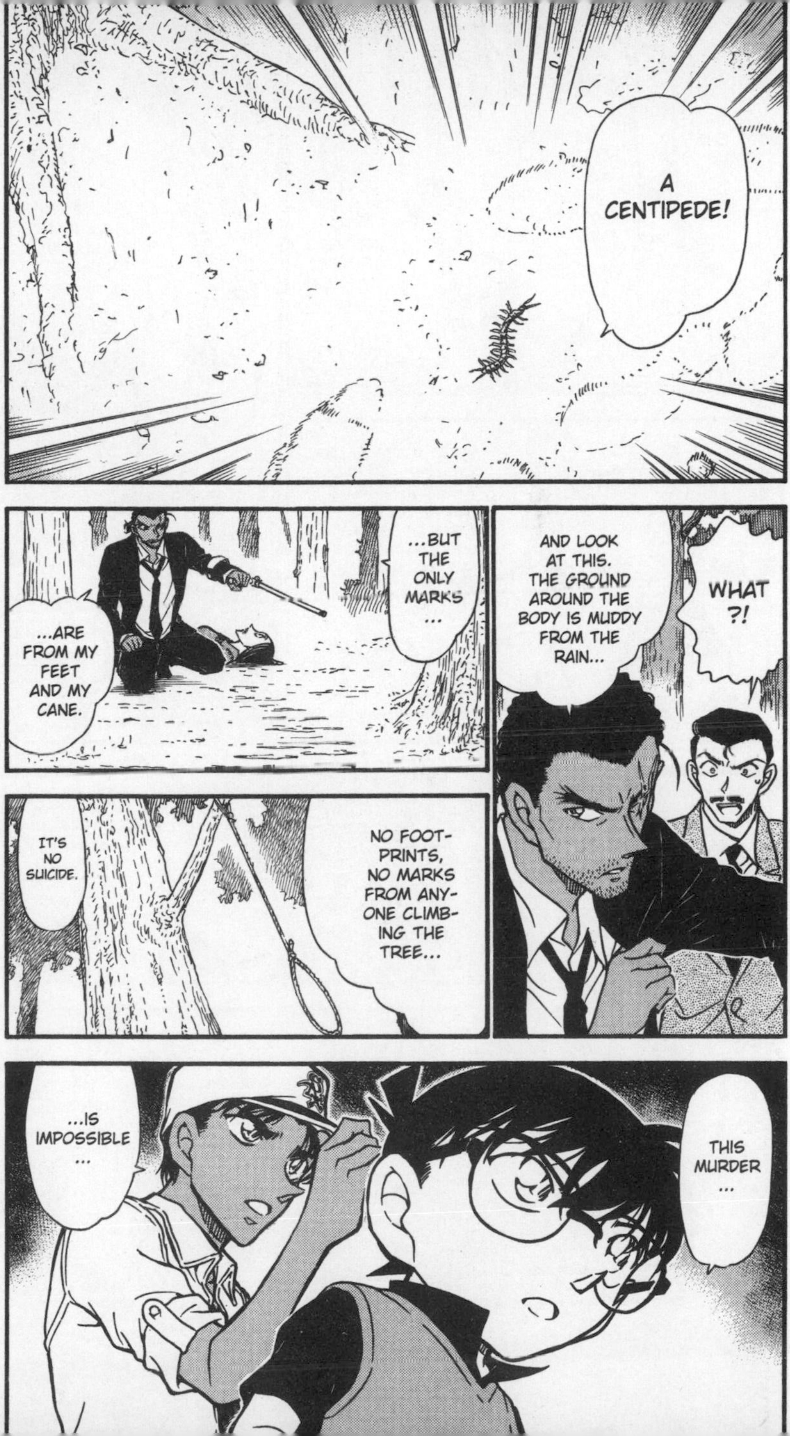
A CENTIPEDE!
WHAT?!
AND LOOK AT THIS. THE GROUND AROUND THE BODY IS MUDDY FROM THE RAIN...
...BUT THE ONLY MARKS...
...ARE FROM MY FEET AND MY CANE.
NO FOOT-PRINTS, NO MARKS FROM ANY-ONE CLIMBING THE TREE...
IT'S NO SUICIDE.
THIS MURDER...
...IS IMPOSSIBLE...

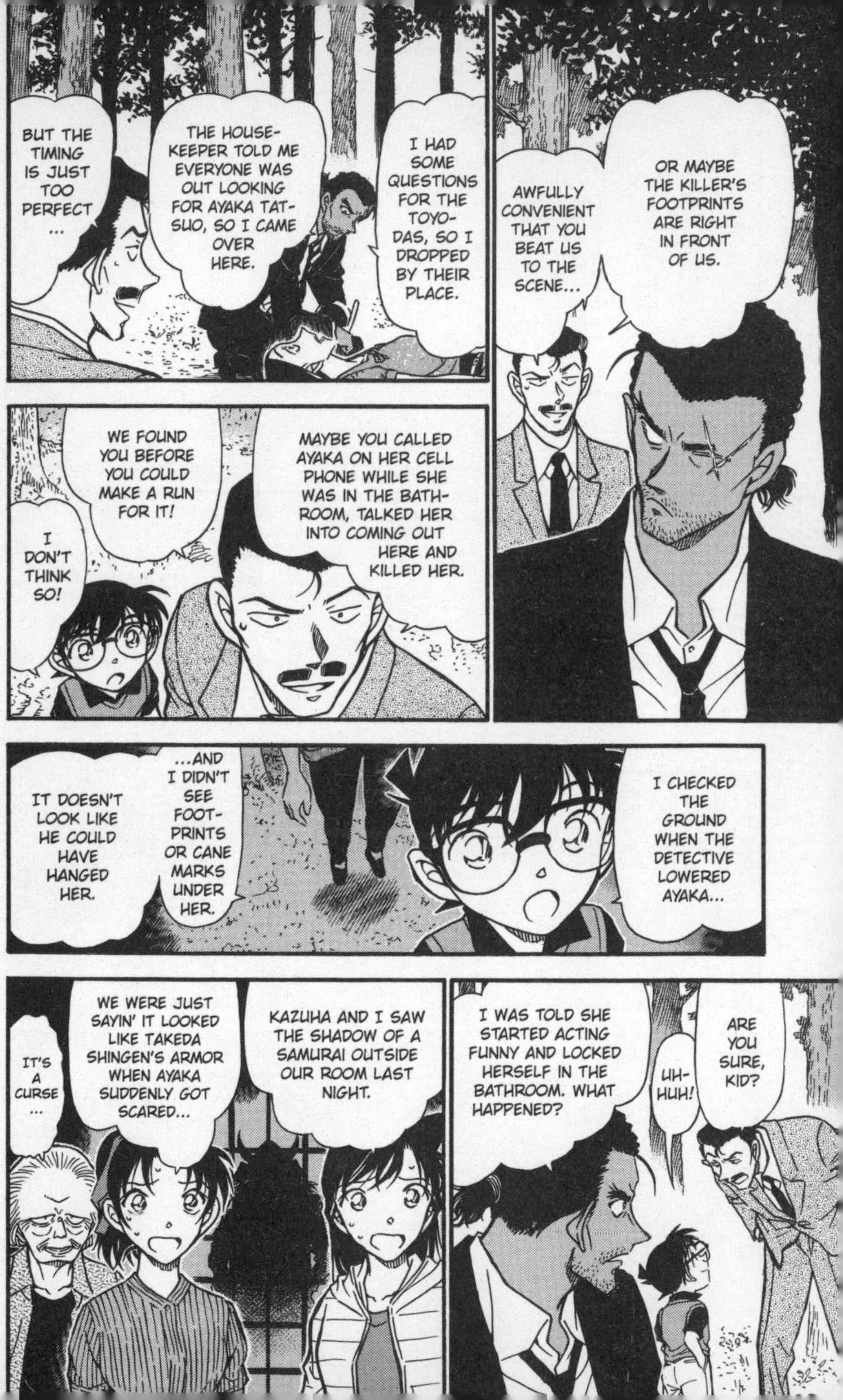
OR MAYBE THE KILLER'S FOOTPRINTS ARE RIGHT IN FRONT OF US.
AWFULLY CONVENIENT THAT YOU BEAT US TO THE SCENE...
I HAD SOME QUESTIONS FOR THE TOYODAS, SO I DROPPED BY THEIR PLACE.
THE HOUSEKEEPER TOLD ME EVERYONE WAS OUT LOOKING FOR AYAKA TATSUO, SO I CAME OVER HERE.
BUT THE TIMING IS JUST TOO PERFECT...
MAYBE YOU CALLED AYAKA ON HER CELL PHONE WHILE SHE WAS IN THE BATHROOM, TALKED HER INTO COMING OUT HERE AND KILLED HER.
WE FOUND YOU BEFORE YOU COULD MAKE A RUN FOR IT!
I DON'T THINK SO!
I CHECKED THE GROUND WHEN THE DETECTIVE LOWERED AYAKA...
...AND I DIDN'T SEE FOOTPRINTS OR CANE MARKS UNDER HER.
IT DOESN'T LOOK LIKE HE COULD HAVE HANGED HER.
ARE YOU SURE, KID?
UH-HUH!
I WAS TOLD SHE STARTED ACTING FUNNY AND LOCKED HERSELF IN THE BATHROOM. WHAT HAPPENED?
KAZUHA AND I SAW THE SHADOW OF A SAMURAI OUTSIDE OUR ROOM LAST NIGHT.
WE WERE JUST SAYIN' IT LOOKED LIKE TAKEDA SHINGEN'S ARMOR WHEN AYAKA SUDDENLY GOT SCARED...
IT'S A CURSE...

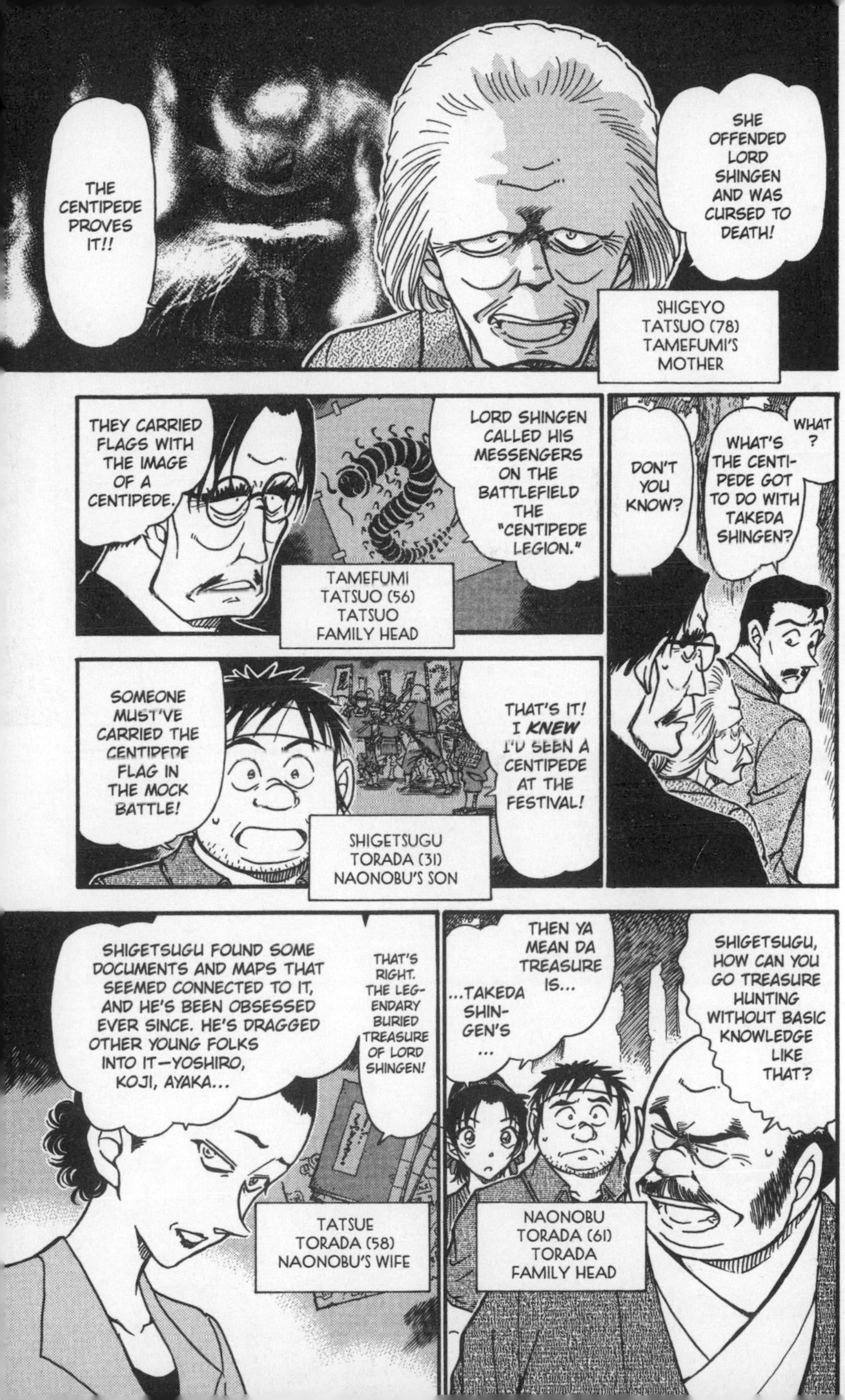
SHE OFFENDED LORD SHINGEN AND WAS CURSED TO DEATH!
SHIGEYO TATSUO (78) TAMEFUMI'S MOTHER
THE CENTIPEDE PROVES IT!!
WHAT?
WHAT'S THE CENTI-PEDE GOT TO DO WITH TAKEDA SHINGEN?
DON'T YOU KNOW?
LORD SHINGEN CALLED HIS MESSENGERS ON THE BATTLEFIELD THE "CENTIPEDE LEGION."
TAMEFUMI TATSUO (56) TATSUO FAMILY HEAD
THEY CARRIED FLAGS WITH THE IMAGE OF A CENTIPEDE.
THAT'S IT! I *KNEW* I'D SEEN A CENTIPEDE AT THE FESTIVAL!
SHIGETSUGU TORADA (31) NAONOBU'S SON
SOMEONE MUST'VE CARRIED THE CENTIPEDE FLAG IN THE MOCK BATTLE!
SHIGETSUGU, HOW CAN YOU GO TREASURE HUNTING WITHOUT BASIC KNOWLEDGE LIKE THAT?
THEN YA MEAN DA TREASURE IS...
...TAKEDA SHIN-GEN'S ...
NAONOBU TORADA (61) TORADA FAMILY HEAD
THAT'S RIGHT. THE LEG-ENDARY BURIED TREASURE OF LORD SHINGEN!
SHIGETSUGU FOUND SOME DOCUMENTS AND MAPS THAT SEEMED CONNECTED TO IT, AND HE'S BEEN OBSESSED EVER SINCE. HE'S DRAGGED OTHER YOUNG FOLKS INTO IT—YOSHIRO, KOJI, AYAKA...
TATSUE TORADA (58) NAONOBU'S WIFE

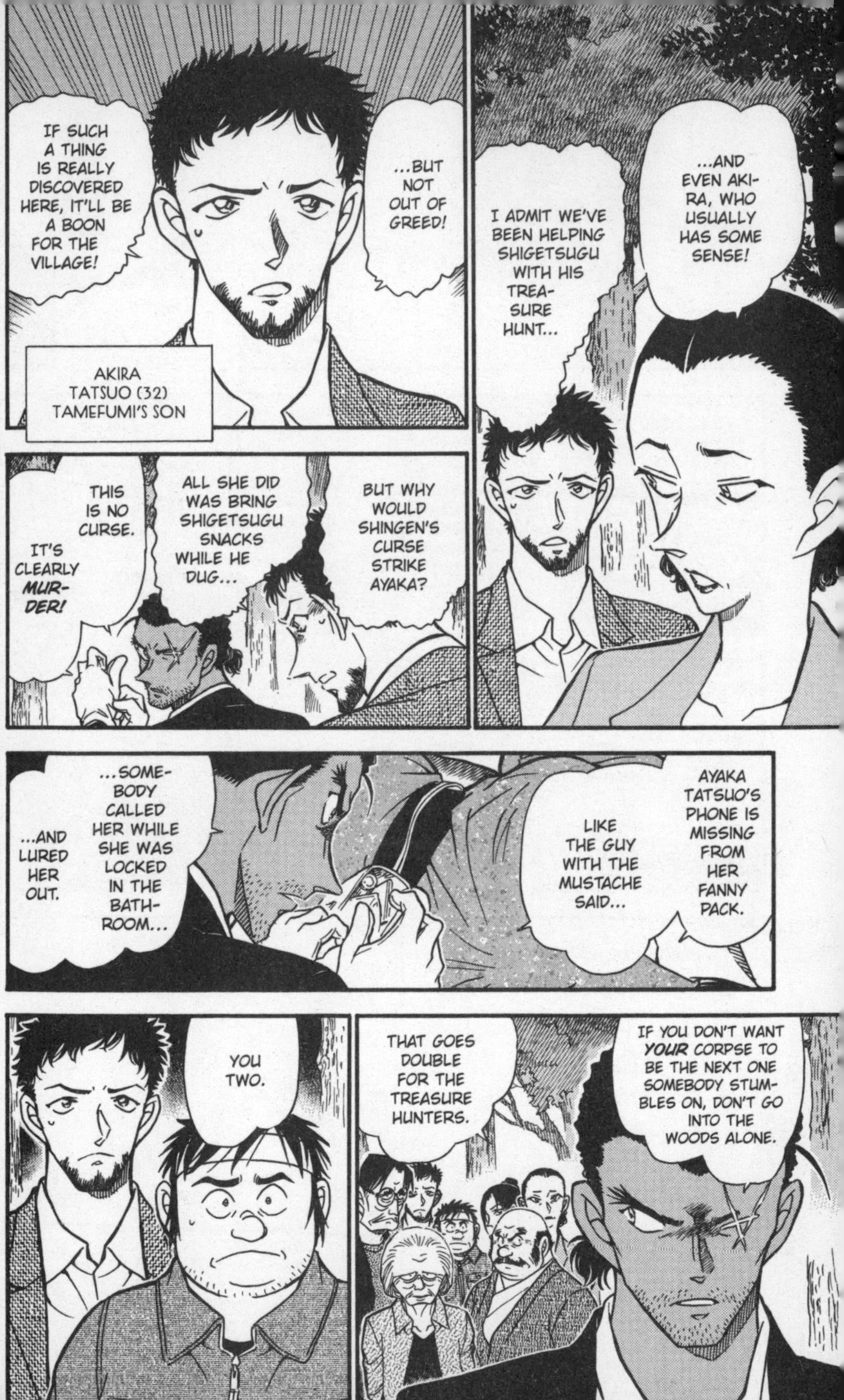
I ADMIT WE'VE BEEN HELPING SHIGETSUGU WITH HIS TREASURE HUNT...
...AND EVEN AKIRA, WHO USUALLY HAS SOME SENSE!
IF SUCH A THING IS REALLY DISCOVERED HERE, IT'LL BE A BOON FOR THE VILLAGE!
...BUT NOT OUT OF GREED!
AKIRA TATSUO (32) TAMEFUMI'S SON
BUT WHY WOULD SHINGEN'S CURSE STRIKE AYAKA?
ALL SHE DID WAS BRING SHIGETSUGU SNACKS WHILE HE DUG...
THIS IS NO CURSE.
IT'S CLEARLY ***MURDER!***
AYAKA TATSUO'S PHONE IS MISSING FROM HER FANNY PACK.
LIKE THE GUY WITH THE MUSTACHE SAID...
...SOMEBODY CALLED HER WHILE SHE WAS LOCKED IN THE BATHROOM...
...AND LURED HER OUT.
IF YOU DON'T WANT ***YOUR*** CORPSE TO BE THE NEXT ONE SOMEBODY STUMBLES ON, DON'T GO INTO THE WOODS ALONE.
THAT GOES DOUBLE FOR THE TREASURE HUNTERS.
YOU TWO.

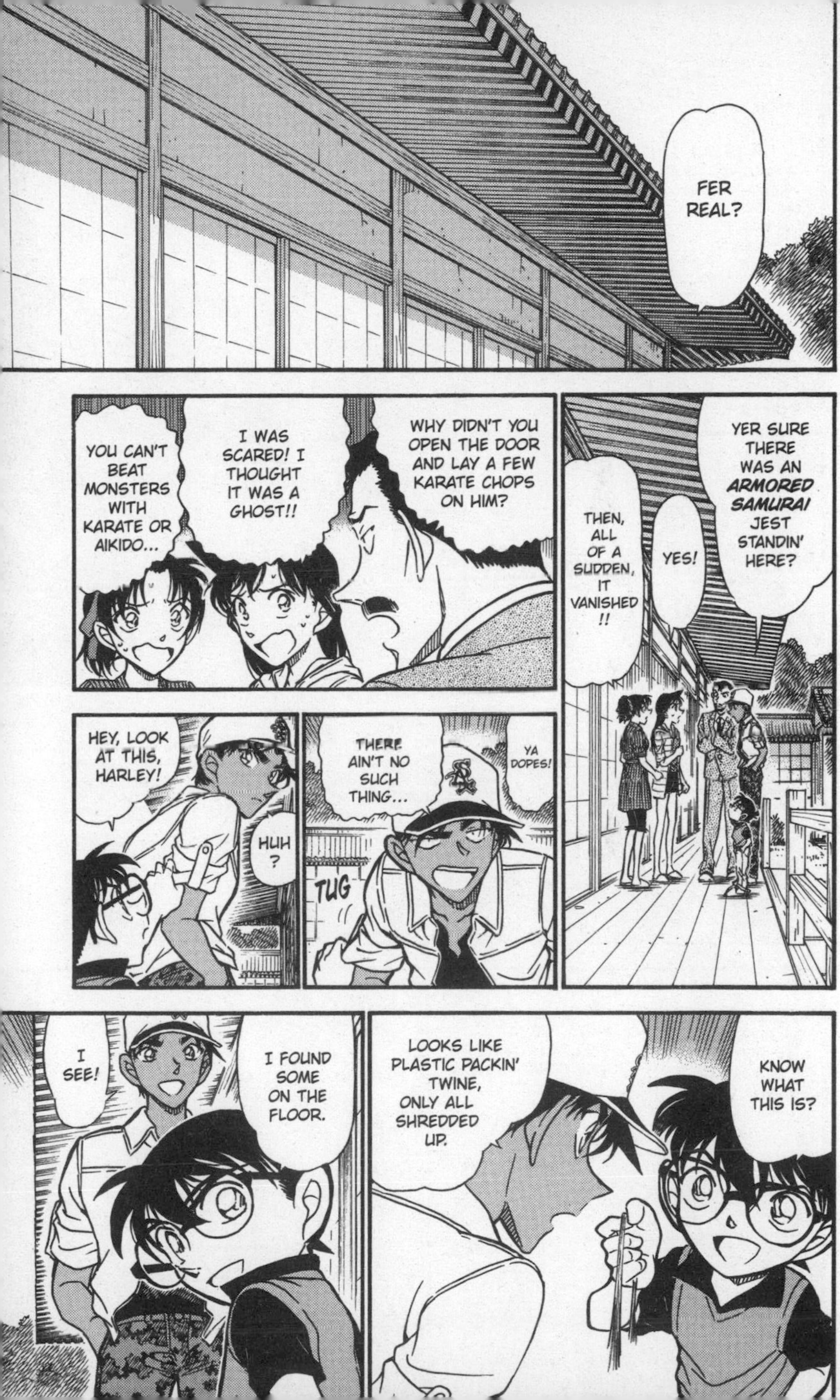
FER REAL?
YER SURE THERE WAS AN ARMORED SAMURAI JEST STANDIN' HERE?
YES!
THEN, ALL OF A SUDDEN, IT VANISHED!!
WHY DIDN'T YOU OPEN THE DOOR AND LAY A FEW KARATE CHOPS ON HIM?
I WAS SCARED! I THOUGHT IT WAS A GHOST!!
YOU CAN'T BEAT MONSTERS WITH KARATE OR AIKIDO...
THERE AIN'T NO SUCH THING...
YA DOPES!
TUG
HEY, LOOK AT THIS, HARLEY!
HUH?
KNOW WHAT THIS IS?
LOOKS LIKE PLASTIC PACKIN' TWINE, ONLY ALL SHREDDED UP.
I FOUND SOME ON THE FLOOR.
I SEE!

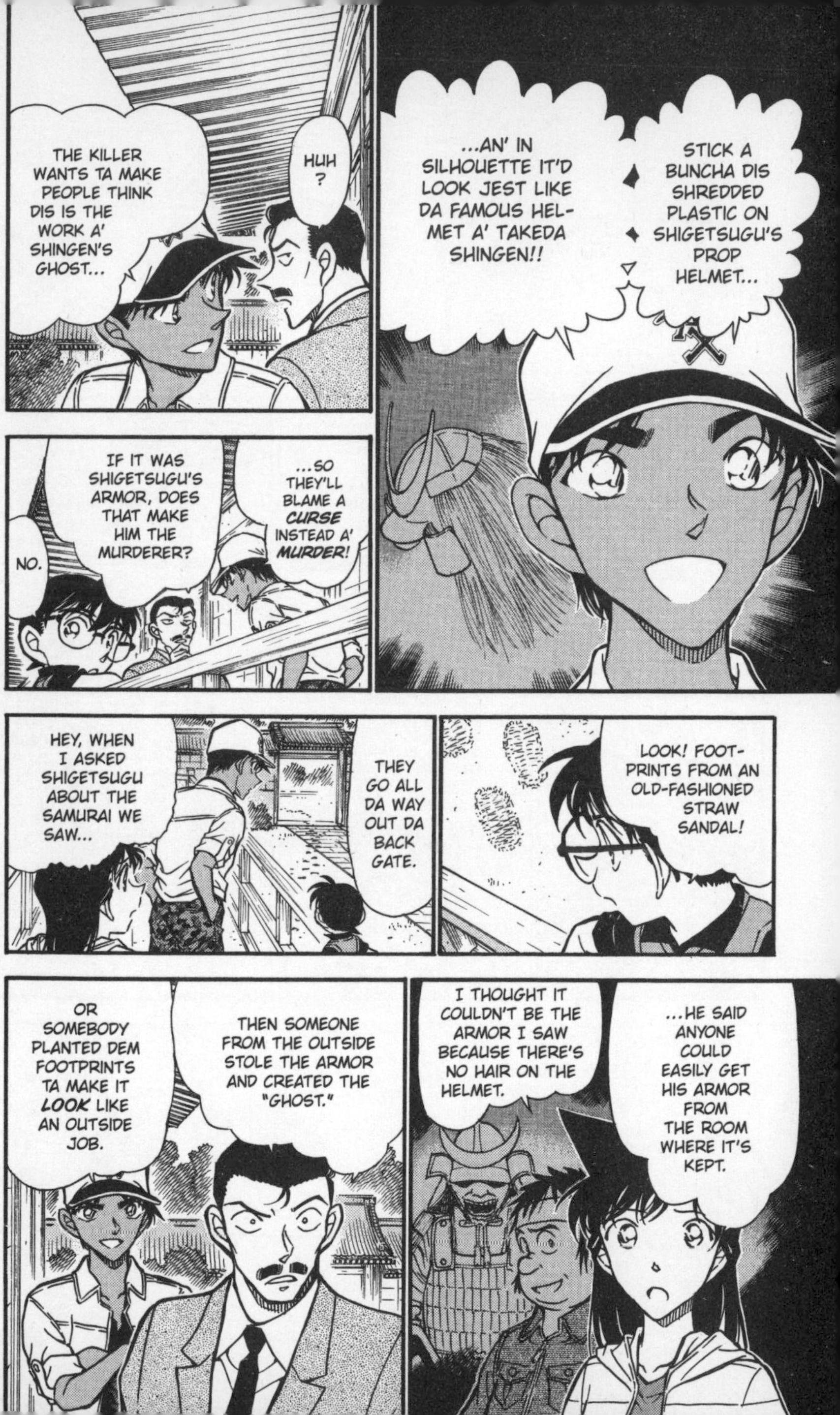

STICK A BUNCHA DIS SHREDDED PLASTIC ON SHIGETSUGU'S PROP HELMET...
...AN' IN SILHOUETTE IT'D LOOK JEST LIKE DA FAMOUS HEL-MET A' TAKEDA SHINGEN!!
HUH?
THE KILLER WANTS TA MAKE PEOPLE THINK DIS IS THE WORK A' SHINGEN'S GHOST...
...SO THEY'LL BLAME A CURSE INSTEAD A' MURDER!
IF IT WAS SHIGETSUGU'S ARMOR, DOES THAT MAKE HIM THE MURDERER?
NO.
LOOK! FOOT-PRINTS FROM AN OLD-FASHIONED STRAW SANDAL!
THEY GO ALL DA WAY OUT DA BACK GATE.
HEY, WHEN I ASKED SHIGETSUGU ABOUT THE SAMURAI WE SAW...
...HE SAID ANYONE COULD EASILY GET HIS ARMOR FROM THE ROOM WHERE IT'S KEPT.
I THOUGHT IT COULDN'T BE THE ARMOR I SAW BECAUSE THERE'S NO HAIR ON THE HELMET.
THEN SOMEONE FROM THE OUTSIDE STOLE THE ARMOR AND CREATED THE "GHOST."
OR SOMEBODY PLANTED DEM FOOTPRINTS TA MAKE IT LOOK LIKE AN OUTSIDE JOB.

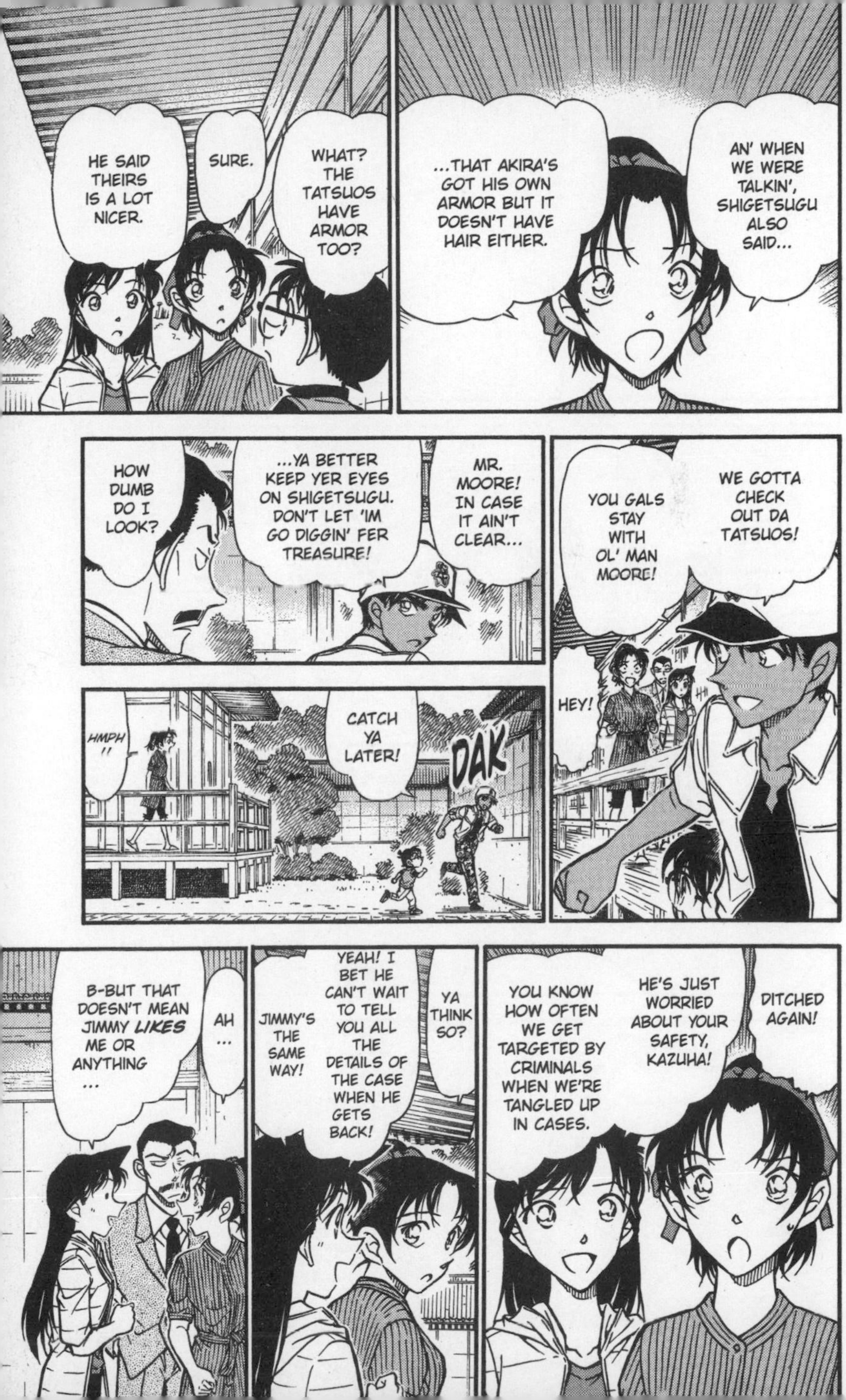
AN' WHEN WE WERE TALKIN', SHIGETSUGU ALSO SAID...
...THAT AKIRA'S GOT HIS OWN ARMOR BUT IT DOESN'T HAVE HAIR EITHER.
WHAT? THE TATSUOS HAVE ARMOR TOO?
SURE.
HE SAID THEIRS IS A LOT NICER.
WE GOTTA CHECK OUT DA TATSUOS!
YOU GALS STAY WITH OL' MAN MOORE!
HEY!
MR. MOORE! IN CASE IT AIN'T CLEAR...
...YA BETTER KEEP YER EYES ON SHIGETSUGU. DON'T LET 'IM GO DIGGIN' FER TREASURE!
HOW DUMB DO I LOOK?
CATCH YA LATER!
DAK
HMPH !!
DITCHED AGAIN!
HE'S JUST WORRIED ABOUT YOUR SAFETY, KAZUHA!
YOU KNOW HOW OFTEN WE GET TARGETED BY CRIMINALS WHEN WE'RE TANGLED UP IN CASES.
YA THINK SO?
YEAH! I BET HE CAN'T WAIT TO TELL YOU ALL THE DETAILS OF THE CASE WHEN HE GETS BACK!
JIMMY'S THE SAME WAY!
AH ...
B-BUT THAT DOESN'T MEAN JIMMY *LIKES* ME OR ANYTHING ...

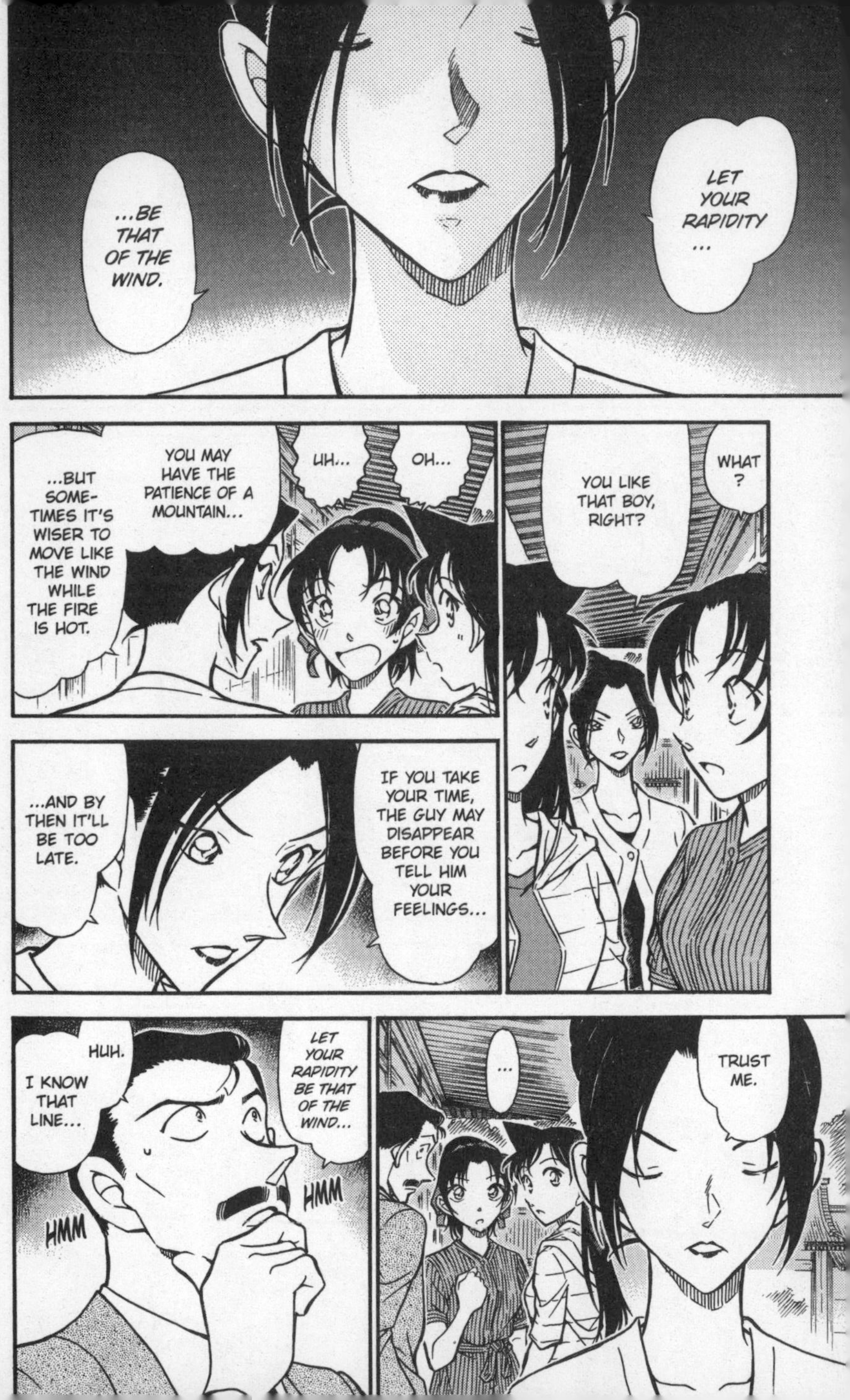
LET YOUR RAPIDITY...
...BE THAT OF THE WIND.
WHAT?
YOU LIKE THAT BOY, RIGHT?
OH...
UH...
YOU MAY HAVE THE PATIENCE OF A MOUNTAIN...
...BUT SOMETIMES IT'S WISER TO MOVE LIKE THE WIND WHILE THE FIRE IS HOT.
IF YOU TAKE YOUR TIME, THE GUY MAY DISAPPEAR BEFORE YOU TELL HIM YOUR FEELINGS...
...AND BY THEN IT'LL BE TOO LATE.
TRUST ME.
...
LET YOUR RAPIDITY BE THAT OF THE WIND...
HUH.
I KNOW THAT LINE...
HMM
HMM

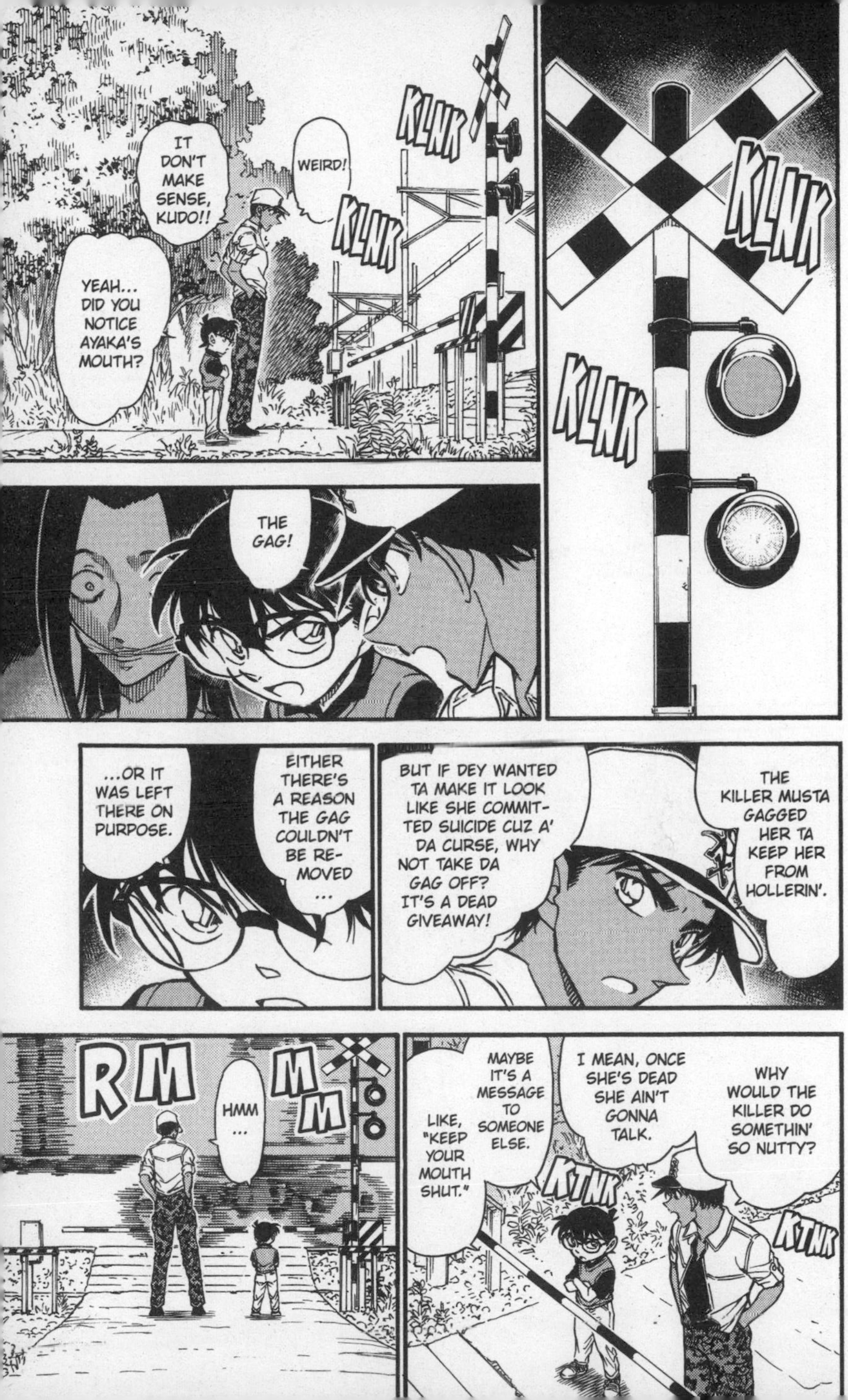
KLNK
KLNK
KLNK
WEIRD!
KLNK
IT DON'T MAKE SENSE, KUDO!!
YEAH... DID YOU NOTICE AYAKA'S MOUTH?
THE GAG!
THE KILLER MUSTA GAGGED HER TA KEEP HER FROM HOLLERIN'.
BUT IF DEY WANTED TA MAKE IT LOOK LIKE SHE COMMIT-TED SUICIDE CUZ A' DA CURSE, WHY NOT TAKE DA GAG OFF? IT'S A DEAD GIVEAWAY!
EITHER THERE'S A REASON THE GAG COULDN'T BE RE-MOVED ...
...OR IT WAS LEFT THERE ON PURPOSE.
WHY WOULD THE KILLER DO SOMETHIN' SO NUTTY?
I MEAN, ONCE SHE'S DEAD SHE AIN'T GONNA TALK.
MAYBE IT'S A MESSAGE TO SOMEONE ELSE.
LIKE, "KEEP YOUR MOUTH SHUT."
KTNK
KTNK
RMMMM
HMM ...

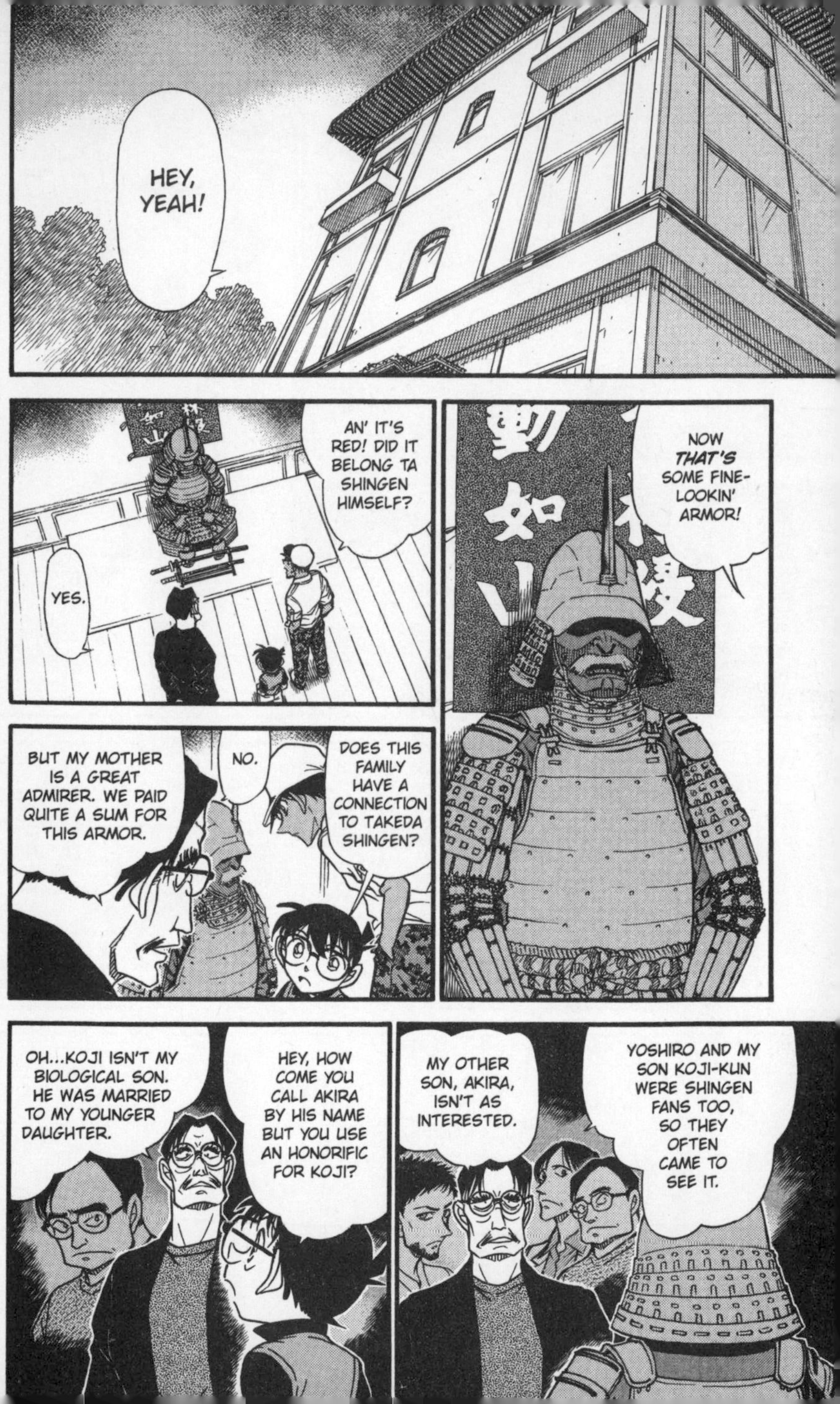
HEY, YEAH!
NOW *THAT'S* SOME FINE-LOOKIN' ARMOR!
AN' IT'S RED! DID IT BELONG TA SHINGEN HIMSELF?
YES.
DOES THIS FAMILY HAVE A CONNECTION TO TAKEDA SHINGEN?
NO.
BUT MY MOTHER IS A GREAT ADMIRER. WE PAID QUITE A SUM FOR THIS ARMOR.
YOSHIRO AND MY SON KOJI-KUN WERE SHINGEN FANS TOO, SO THEY OFTEN CAME TO SEE IT.
MY OTHER SON, AKIRA, ISN'T AS INTERESTED.
HEY, HOW COME YOU CALL AKIRA BY HIS NAME BUT YOU USE AN HONORIFIC FOR KOJI?
OH...KOJI ISN'T MY BIOLOGICAL SON. HE WAS MARRIED TO MY YOUNGER DAUGHTER.

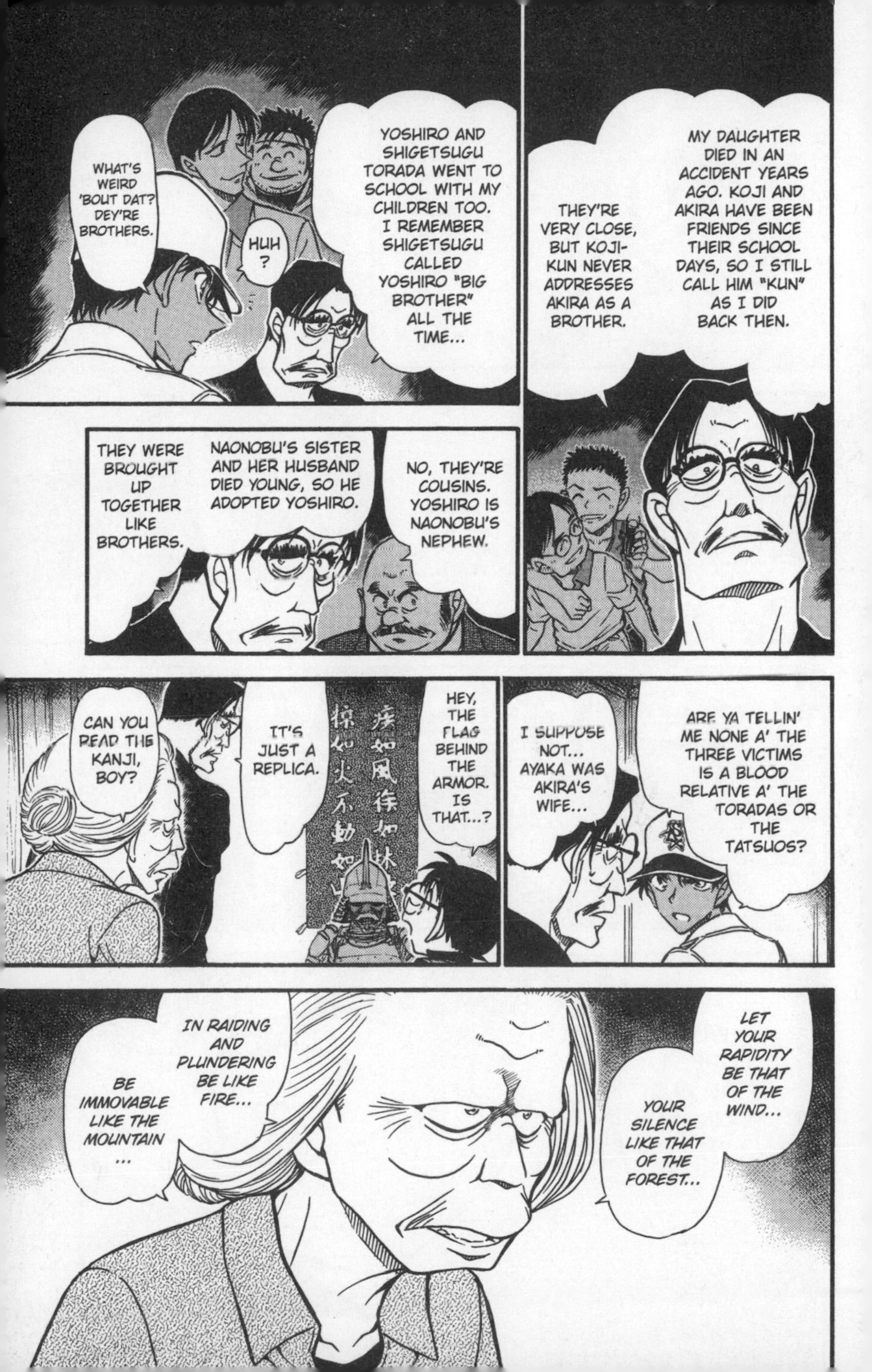
MY DAUGHTER DIED IN AN ACCIDENT YEARS AGO. KOJI AND AKIRA HAVE BEEN FRIENDS SINCE THEIR SCHOOL DAYS, SO I STILL CALL HIM "KUN" AS I DID BACK THEN.
THEY'RE VERY CLOSE, BUT KOJI-KUN NEVER ADDRESSES AKIRA AS A BROTHER.
YOSHIRO AND SHIGETSUGU TORADA WENT TO SCHOOL WITH MY CHILDREN TOO. I REMEMBER SHIGETSUGU CALLED YOSHIRO "BIG BROTHER" ALL THE TIME...
HUH?
WHAT'S WEIRD 'BOUT DAT? DEY'RE BROTHERS.
NO, THEY'RE COUSINS. YOSHIRO IS NAONOBU'S NEPHEW.
NAONOBU'S SISTER AND HER HUSBAND DIED YOUNG, SO HE ADOPTED YOSHIRO.
THEY WERE BROUGHT UP TOGETHER LIKE BROTHERS.
ARE YA TELLIN' ME NONE A' THE THREE VICTIMS IS A BLOOD RELATIVE A' THE TORADAS OR THE TATSUOS?
I SUPPOSE NOT... AYAKA WAS AKIRA'S WIFE...
HEY, THE FLAG BEHIND THE ARMOR. IS THAT...?
IT'S JUST A REPLICA.
CAN YOU READ THE KANJI, BOY?
LET YOUR RAPIDITY BE THAT OF THE WIND...
YOUR SILENCE LIKE THAT OF THE FOREST...
IN RAIDING AND PLUNDERING BE LIKE FIRE...
BE IMMOVABLE LIKE THE MOUNTAIN...

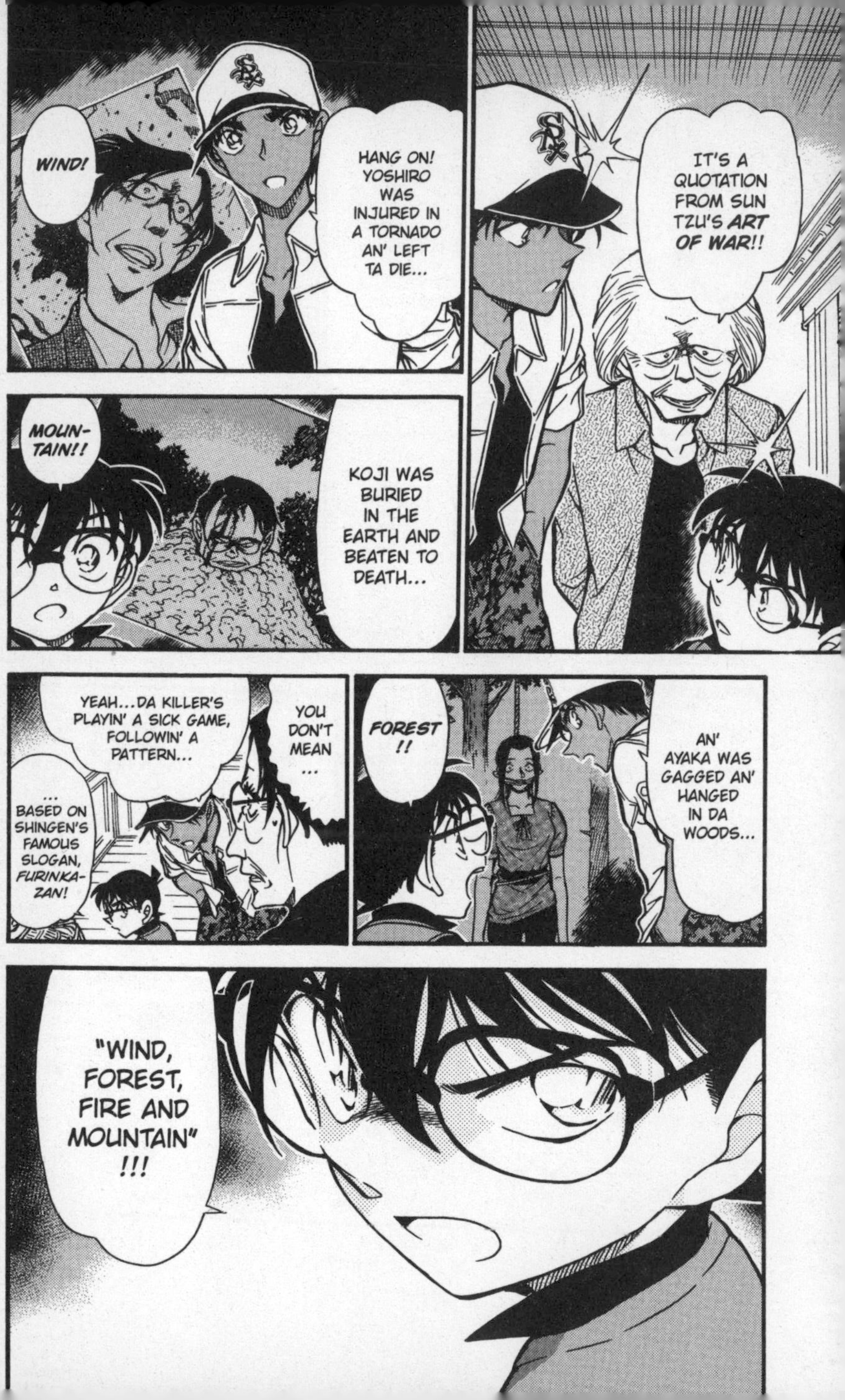
IT'S A QUOTATION FROM SUN TZU'S ART OF WAR!!
HANG ON! YOSHIRO WAS INJURED IN A TORNADO AN' LEFT TA DIE...
WIND!
KOJI WAS BURIED IN THE EARTH AND BEATEN TO DEATH...
MOUN-TAIN!!
AN' AYAKA WAS GAGGED AN' HANGED IN DA WOODS...
FOREST !!
YOU DON'T MEAN ...
YEAH...DA KILLER'S PLAYIN' A SICK GAME, FOLLOWIN' A PATTERN...
... BASED ON SHINGEN'S FAMOUS SLOGAN, FURINKA-ZAN!
"WIND, FOREST, FIRE AND MOUNTAIN" !!!

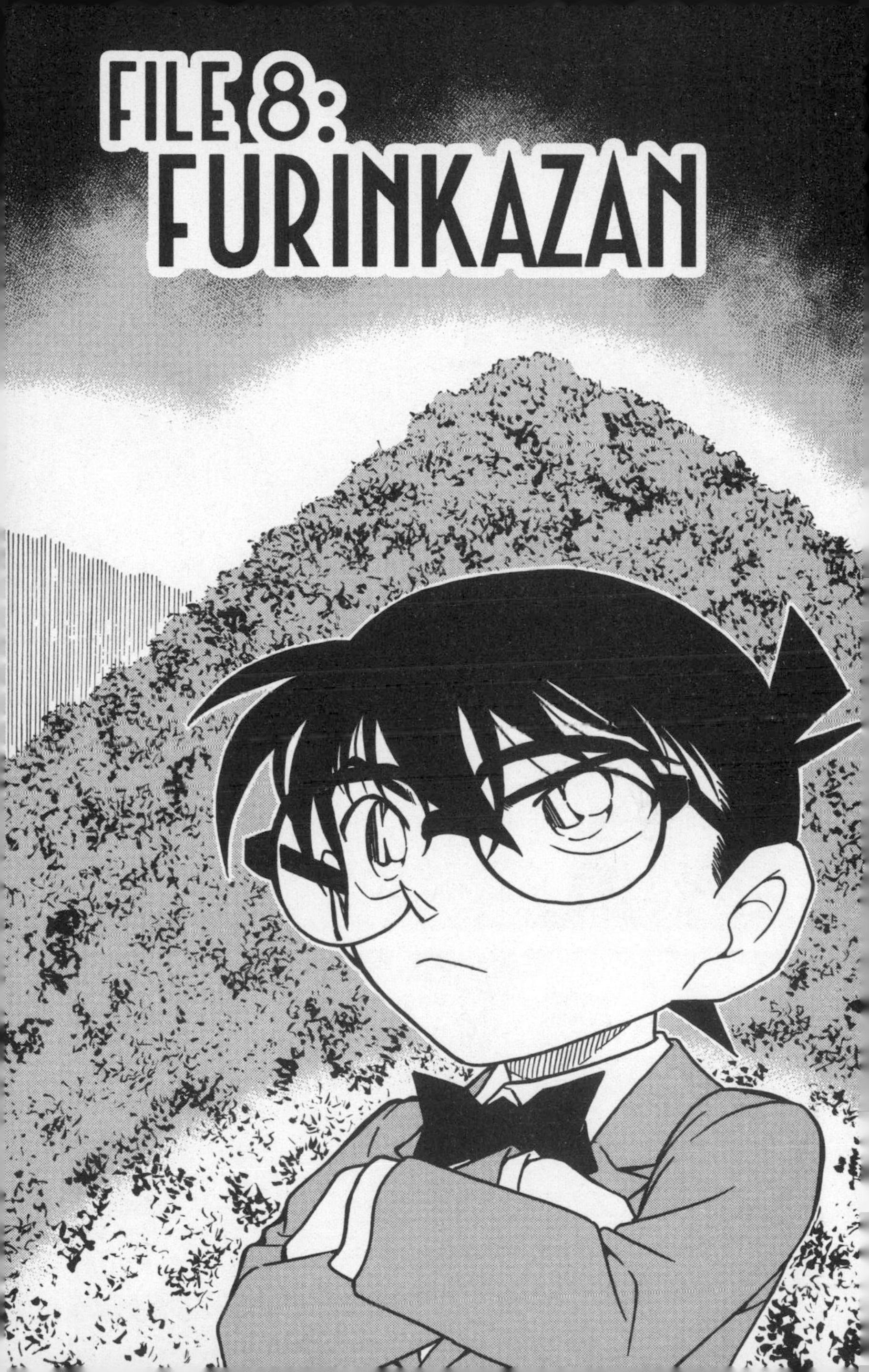
FILE 8:
FURINKAZAN

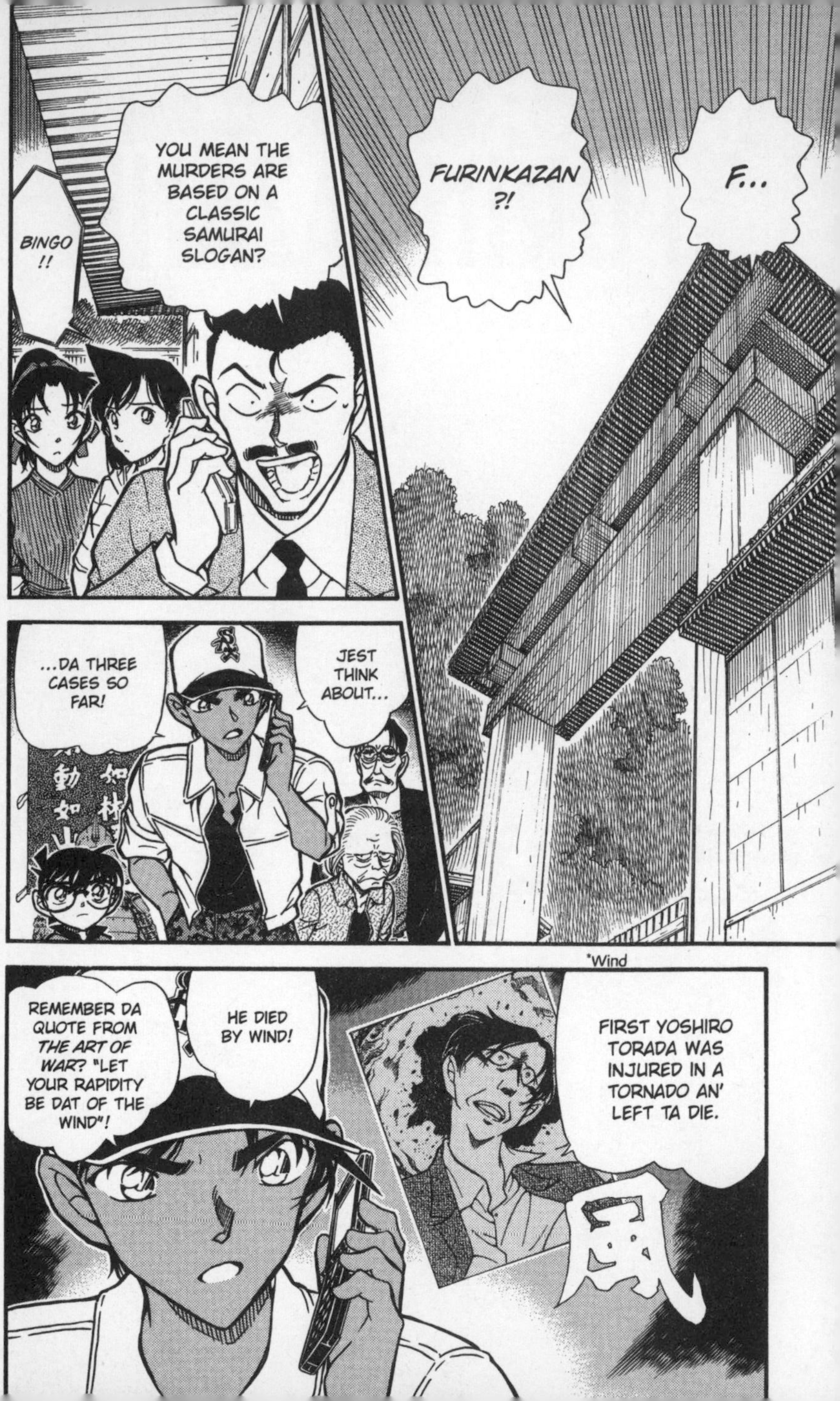
F...
FURINKAZAN ?!
YOU MEAN THE MURDERS ARE BASED ON A CLASSIC SAMURAI SLOGAN?
BINGO !!
JEST THINK ABOUT...
...DA THREE CASES SO FAR!
FIRST YOSHIRO TORADA WAS INJURED IN A TORNADO AN' LEFT TA DIE.
風
HE DIED BY WIND!
REMEMBER DA QUOTE FROM *THE ART OF WAR*? "LET YOUR RAPIDITY BE DAT OF THE WIND"!
*Wind

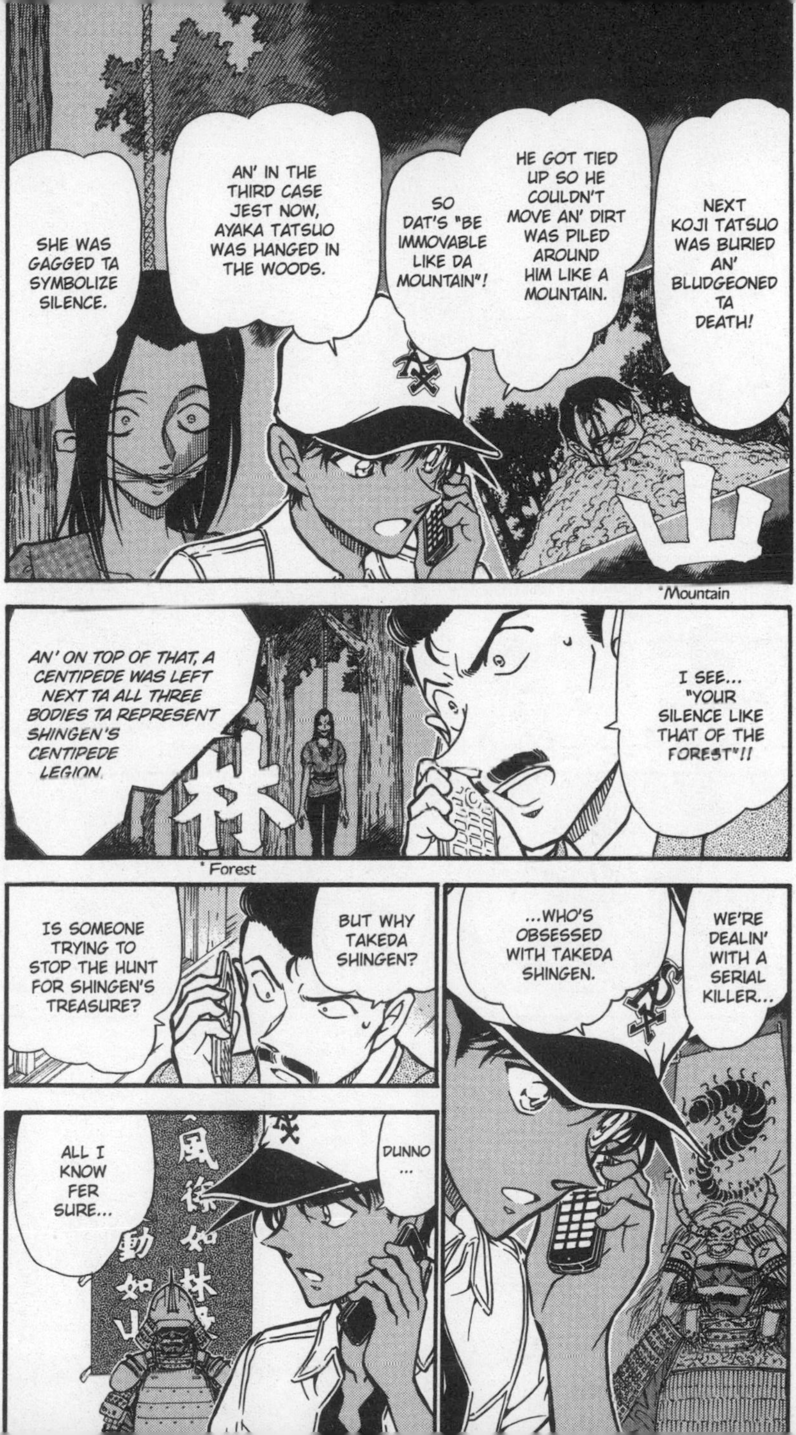
NEXT KOJI TATSUO WAS BURIED AN' BLUDGEONED TA DEATH!
HE GOT TIED UP SO HE COULDN'T MOVE AN' DIRT WAS PILED AROUND HIM LIKE A MOUNTAIN.
SO DAT'S "BE IMMOVABLE LIKE DA MOUNTAIN"!
AN' IN THE THIRD CASE JEST NOW, AYAKA TATSUO WAS HANGED IN THE WOODS.
SHE WAS GAGGED TA SYMBOLIZE SILENCE.
山
*Mountain
I SEE... "YOUR SILENCE LIKE THAT OF THE FOREST"!!
AN' ON TOP OF THAT, A CENTIPEDE WAS LEFT NEXT TA ALL THREE BODIES TA REPRESENT SHINGEN'S CENTIPEDE LEGION.
林
*Forest
BUT WHY TAKEDA SHINGEN?
IS SOMEONE TRYING TO STOP THE HUNT FOR SHINGEN'S TREASURE?
DUNNO ...
ALL I KNOW FER SURE...
WE'RE DEALIN' WITH A SERIAL KILLER...
...WHO'S OBSESSED WITH TAKEDA SHINGEN.

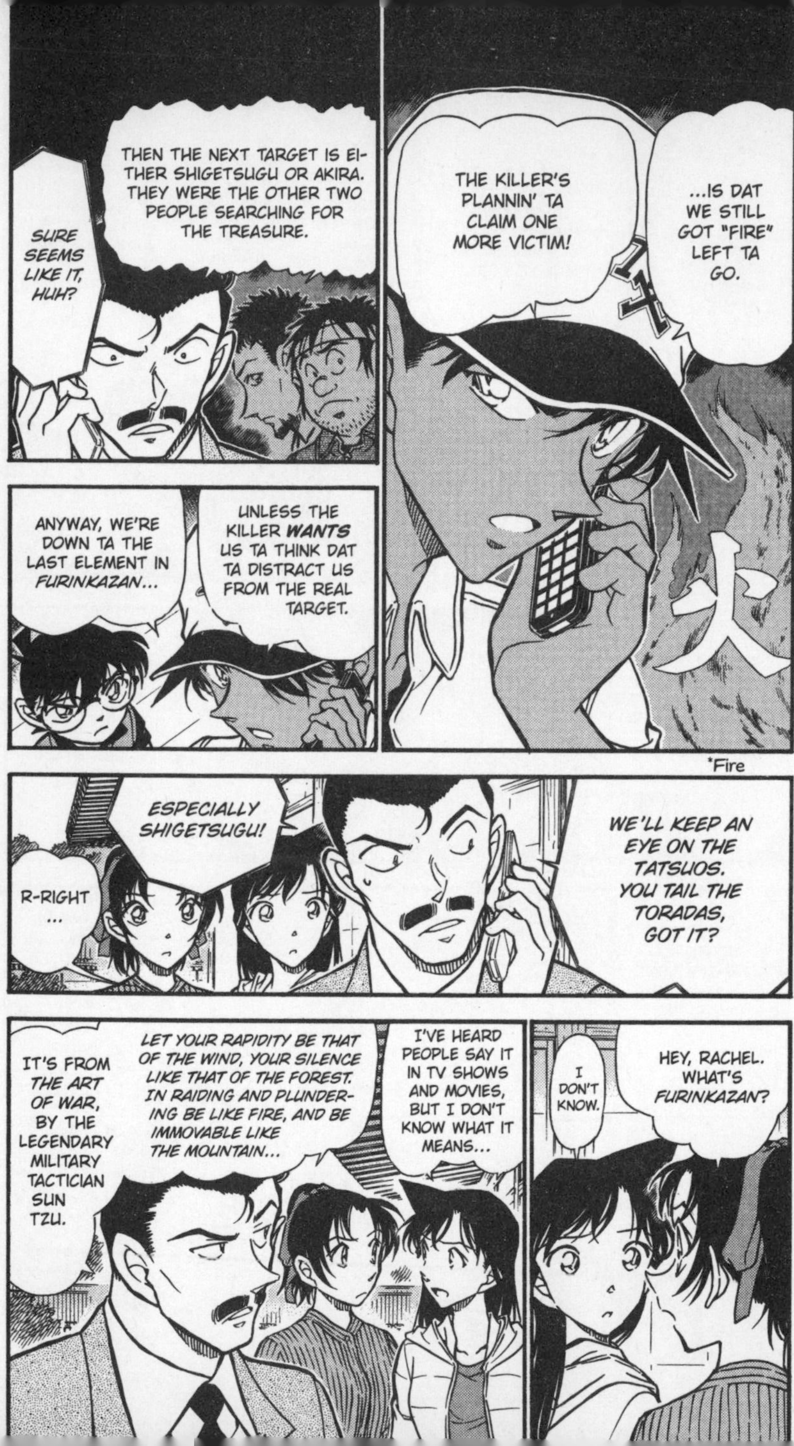
...IS DAT WE STILL GOT "FIRE" LEFT TA GO.
THE KILLER'S PLANNIN' TA CLAIM ONE MORE VICTIM!
火
THEN THE NEXT TARGET IS EI-THER SHIGETSUGU OR AKIRA. THEY WERE THE OTHER TWO PEOPLE SEARCHING FOR THE TREASURE.
SURE SEEMS LIKE IT, HUH?
UNLESS THE KILLER WANTS US TA THINK DAT TA DISTRACT US FROM THE REAL TARGET.
ANYWAY, WE'RE DOWN TA THE LAST ELEMENT IN FURINKAZAN...
*Fire
WE'LL KEEP AN EYE ON THE TATSUOS. YOU TAIL THE TORADAS, GOT IT?
ESPECIALLY SHIGETSUGU!
R-RIGHT ...
HEY, RACHEL. WHAT'S FURINKAZAN?
I DON'T KNOW.
I'VE HEARD PEOPLE SAY IT IN TV SHOWS AND MOVIES, BUT I DON'T KNOW WHAT IT MEANS...
LET YOUR RAPIDITY BE THAT OF THE WIND, YOUR SILENCE LIKE THAT OF THE FOREST. IN RAIDING AND PLUNDER-ING BE LIKE FIRE, AND BE IMMOVABLE LIKE THE MOUNTAIN...
IT'S FROM THE ART OF WAR, BY THE LEGENDARY MILITARY TACTICIAN SUN TZU.

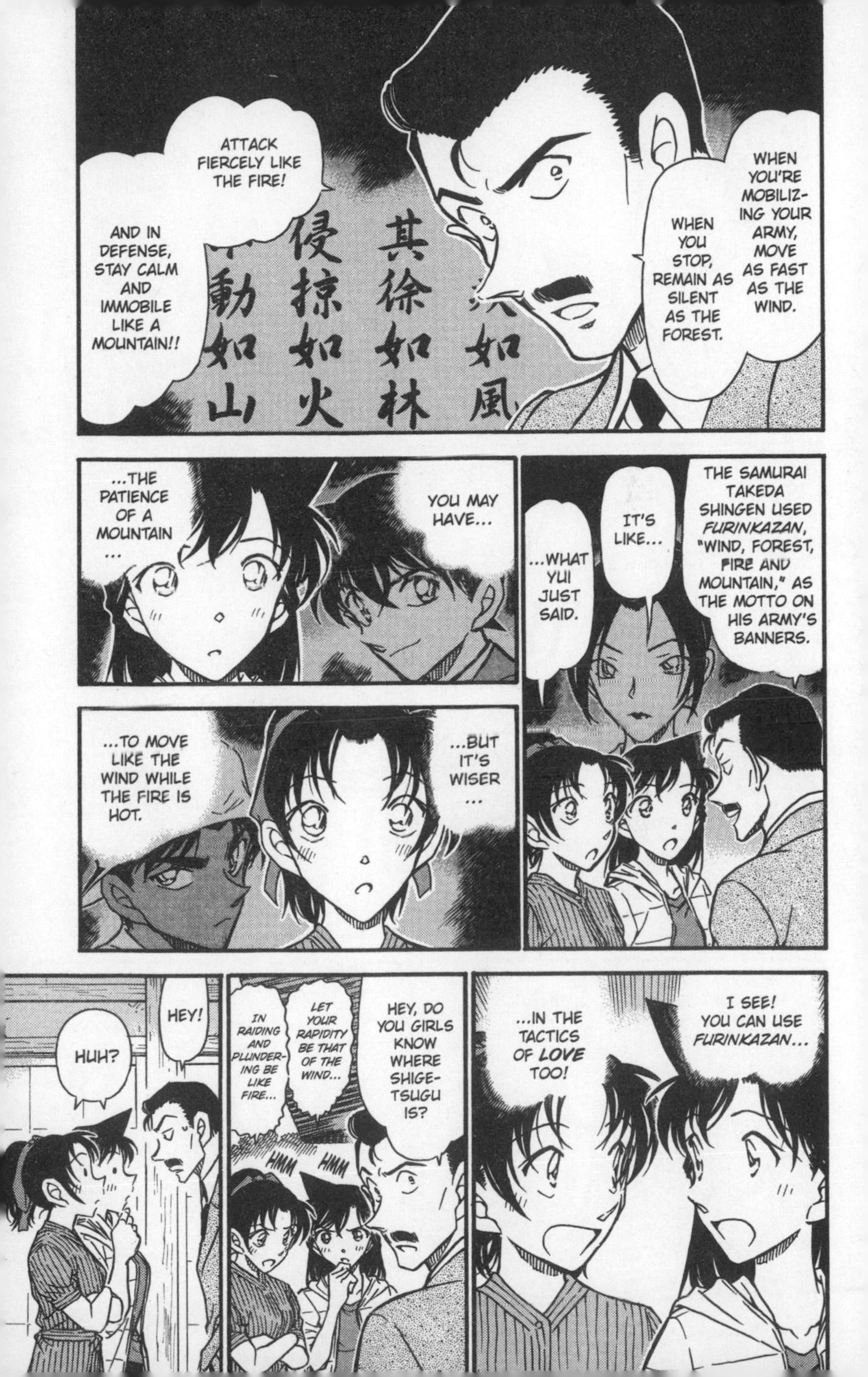
WHEN YOU'RE MOBILIZ-ING YOUR ARMY, MOVE AS FAST AS THE WIND.
WHEN YOU STOP, REMAIN AS SILENT AS THE FOREST.
如風
其徐如林
侵掠如火
動如山
ATTACK FIERCELY LIKE THE FIRE!
AND IN DEFENSE, STAY CALM AND IMMOBILE LIKE A MOUNTAIN!!
THE SAMURAI TAKEDA SHINGEN USED *FURINKAZAN*, "WIND, FOREST, FIRE AND MOUNTAIN," AS THE MOTTO ON HIS ARMY'S BANNERS.
IT'S LIKE...
...WHAT YUI JUST SAID.
YOU MAY HAVE...
...THE PATIENCE OF A MOUNTAIN...
...BUT IT'S WISER...
...TO MOVE LIKE THE WIND WHILE THE FIRE IS HOT.
I SEE! YOU CAN USE *FURINKAZAN*...
...IN THE TACTICS OF **LOVE** TOO!
HEY, DO YOU GIRLS KNOW WHERE SHIGE-TSUGU IS?
LET YOUR RAPIDITY BE THAT OF THE WIND...
IN RAIDING AND PLUNDER-ING BE LIKE FIRE...
HMM
HMM
HEY!
HUH?

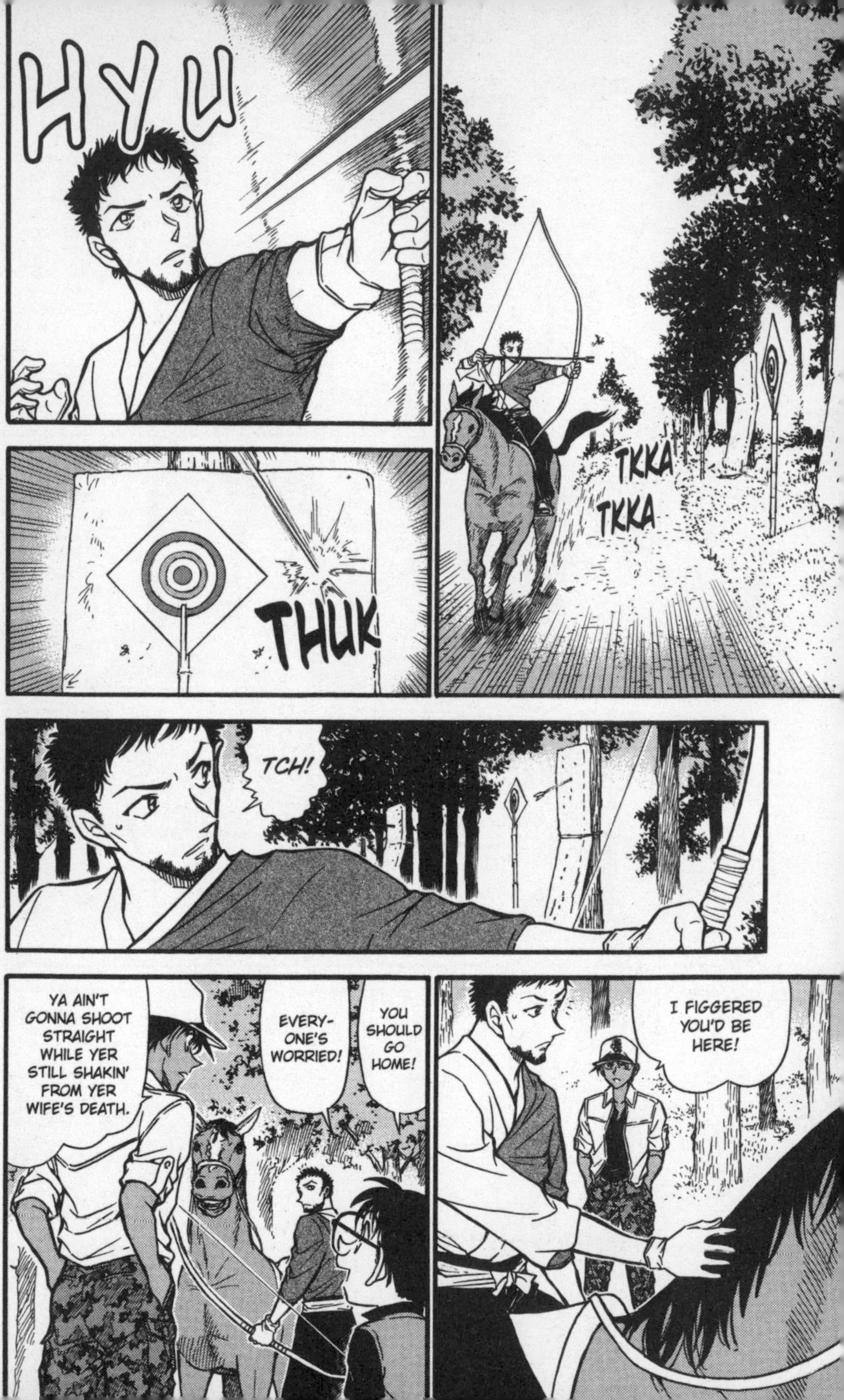
TKKA
TKKA
HYU
THUK
TCH!
I FIGGERED YOU'D BE HERE!
YOU SHOULD GO HOME!
EVERY-ONE'S WORRIED!
YA AIN'T GONNA SHOOT STRAIGHT WHILE YER STILL SHAKIN' FROM YER WIFE'S DEATH.

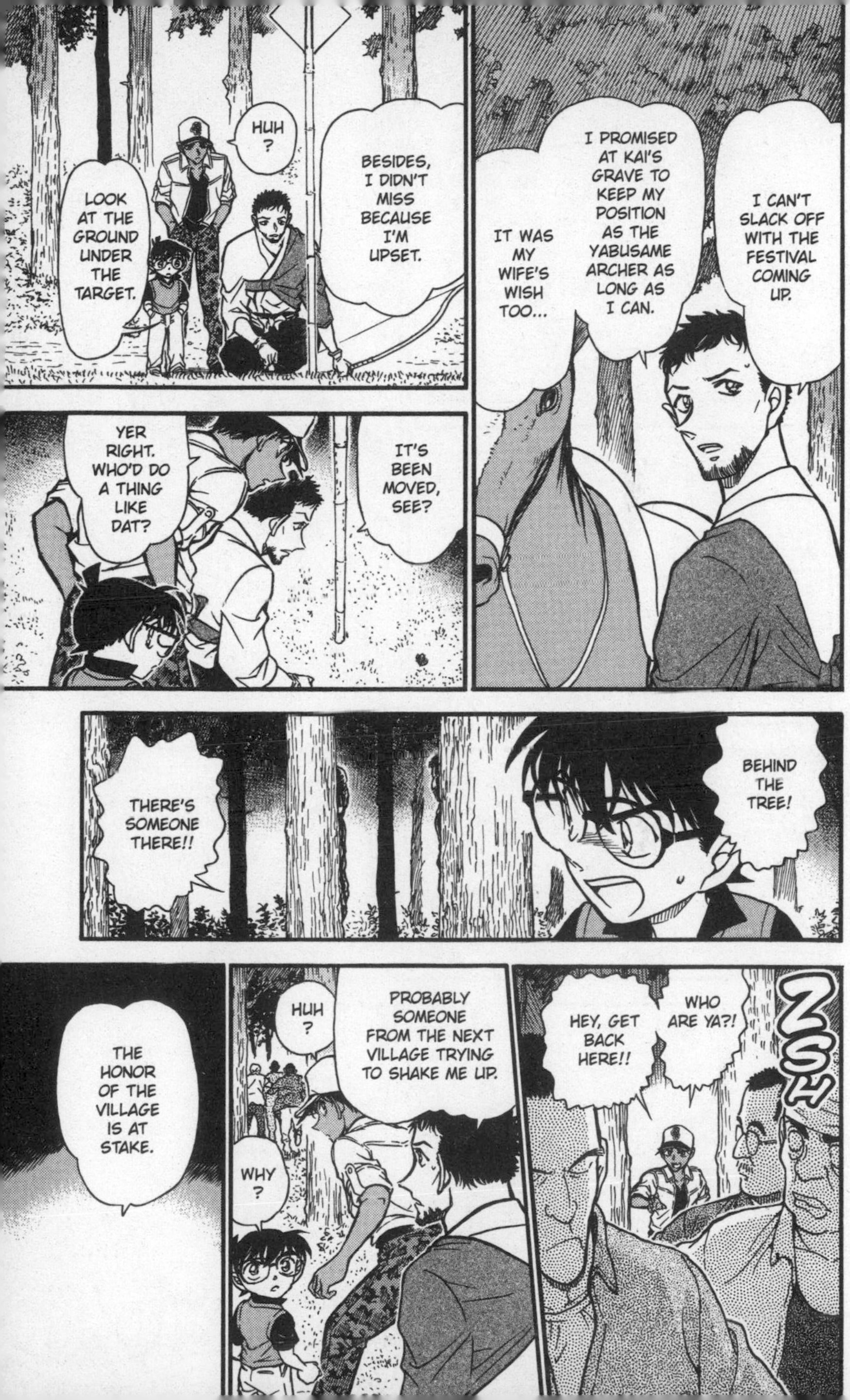
I CAN'T SLACK OFF WITH THE FESTIVAL COMING UP.
I PROMISED AT KAI'S GRAVE TO KEEP MY POSITION AS THE YABUSAME ARCHER AS LONG AS I CAN.
IT WAS MY WIFE'S WISH TOO...
BESIDES, I DIDN'T MISS BECAUSE I'M UPSET.
HUH?
LOOK AT THE GROUND UNDER THE TARGET.
IT'S BEEN MOVED, SEE?
YER RIGHT. WHO'D DO A THING LIKE DAT?
BEHIND THE TREE!
THERE'S SOMEONE THERE!!
ZSH
WHO ARE YA?!
HEY, GET BACK HERE!!
PROBABLY SOMEONE FROM THE NEXT VILLAGE TRYING TO SHAKE ME UP.
HUH?
WHY?
THE HONOR OF THE VILLAGE IS AT STAKE.

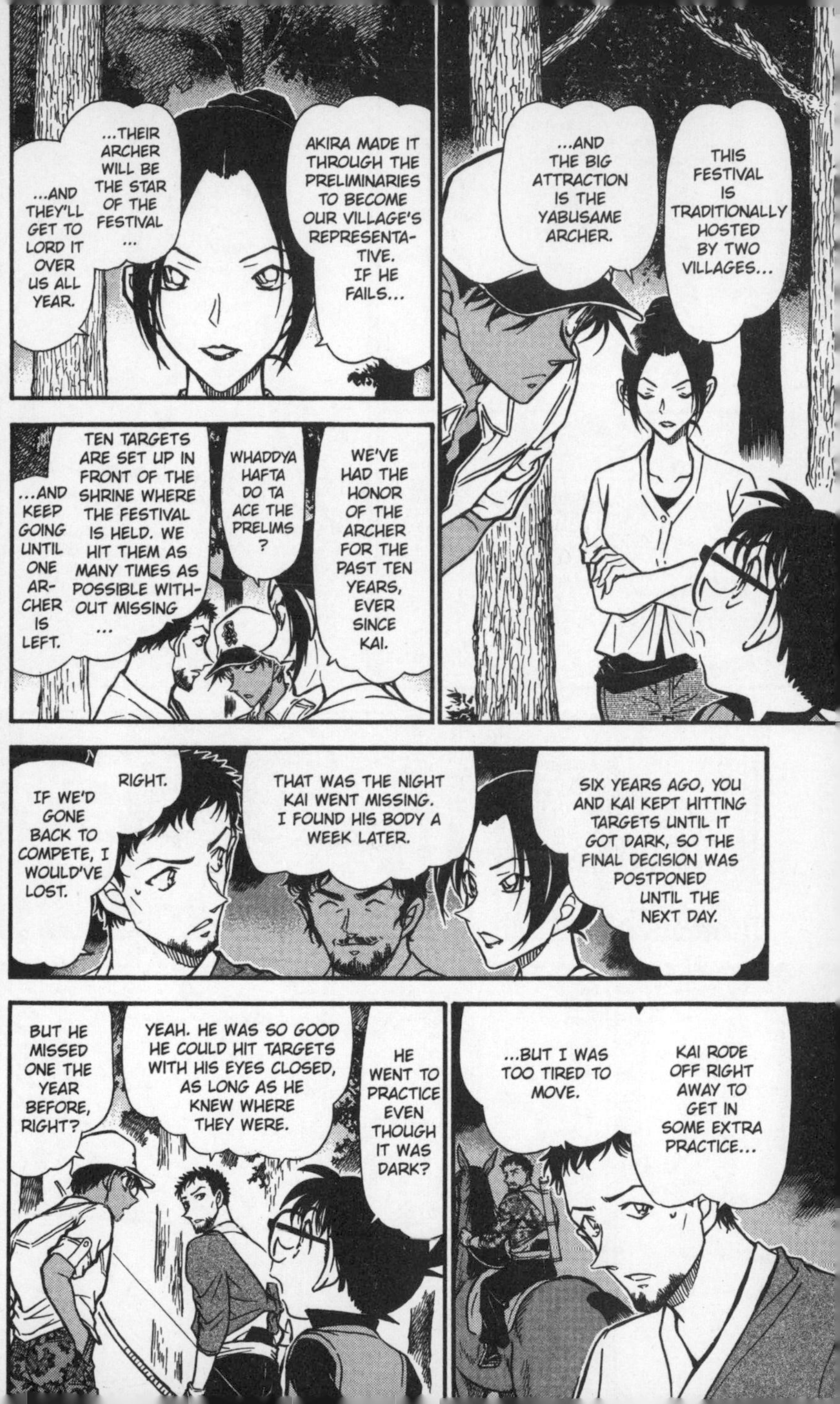
THIS FESTIVAL IS TRADITIONALLY HOSTED BY TWO VILLAGES...
...AND THE BIG ATTRACTION IS THE YABUSAME ARCHER.
AKIRA MADE IT THROUGH THE PRELIMINARIES TO BECOME OUR VILLAGE'S REPRESENTATIVE. IF HE FAILS...
...THEIR ARCHER WILL BE THE STAR OF THE FESTIVAL ...
...AND THEY'LL GET TO LORD IT OVER US ALL YEAR.
WE'VE HAD THE HONOR OF THE ARCHER FOR THE PAST TEN YEARS, EVER SINCE KAI.
WHADDYA HAFTA DO TA ACE THE PRELIMS?
TEN TARGETS ARE SET UP IN FRONT OF THE SHRINE WHERE THE FESTIVAL IS HELD. WE HIT THEM AS MANY TIMES AS POSSIBLE WITHOUT MISSING ...
...AND KEEP GOING UNTIL ONE ARCHER IS LEFT.
SIX YEARS AGO, YOU AND KAI KEPT HITTING TARGETS UNTIL IT GOT DARK, SO THE FINAL DECISION WAS POSTPONED UNTIL THE NEXT DAY.
THAT WAS THE NIGHT KAI WENT MISSING. I FOUND HIS BODY A WEEK LATER.
RIGHT.
IF WE'D GONE BACK TO COMPETE, I WOULD'VE LOST.
KAI RODE OFF RIGHT AWAY TO GET IN SOME EXTRA PRACTICE...
...BUT I WAS TOO TIRED TO MOVE.
HE WENT TO PRACTICE EVEN THOUGH IT WAS DARK?
YEAH. HE WAS SO GOOD HE COULD HIT TARGETS WITH HIS EYES CLOSED, AS LONG AS HE KNEW WHERE THEY WERE.
BUT HE MISSED ONE THE YEAR BEFORE, RIGHT?

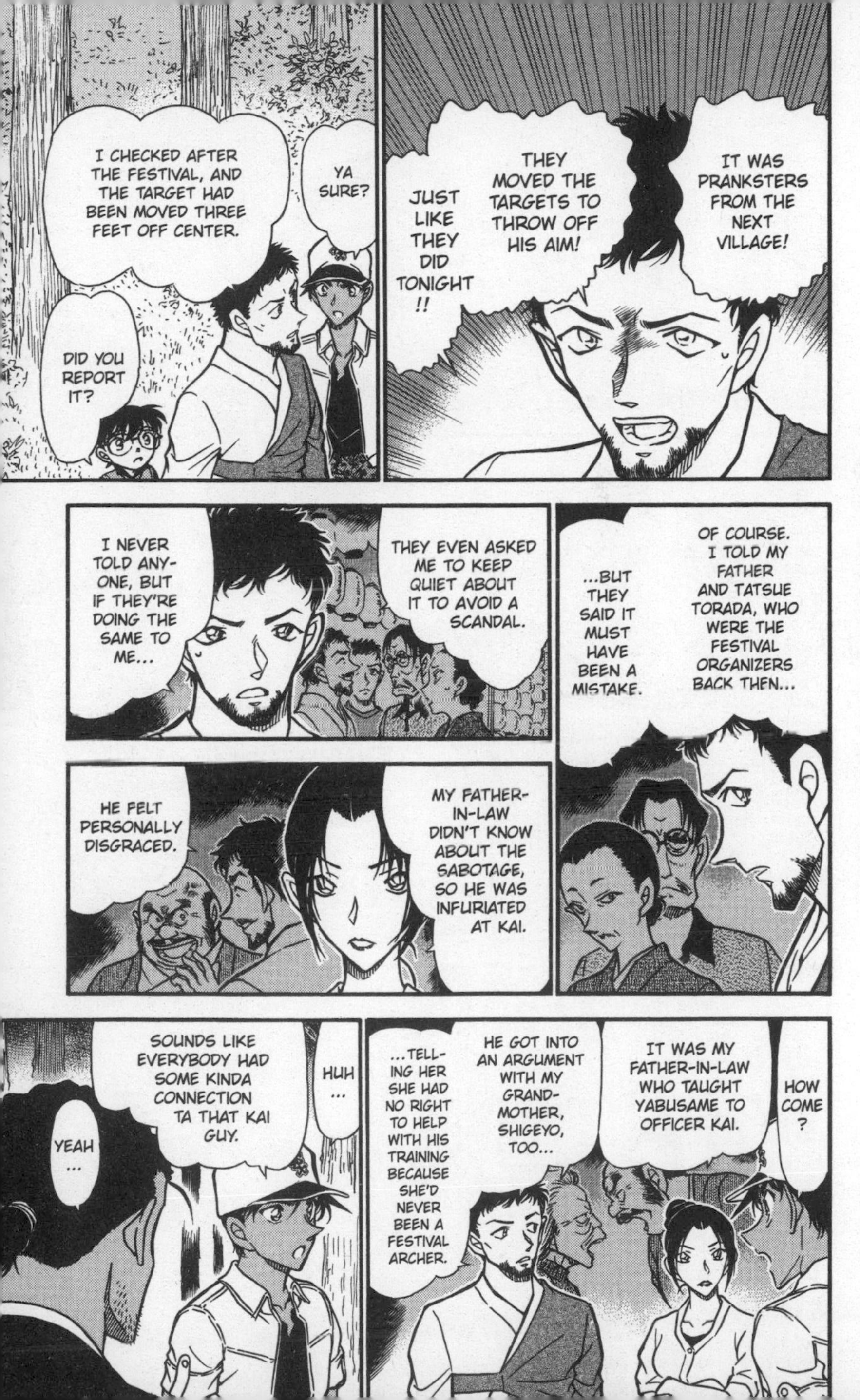
IT WAS PRANKSTERS FROM THE NEXT VILLAGE!
THEY MOVED THE TARGETS TO THROW OFF HIS AIM!
JUST LIKE THEY DID TONIGHT!!
YA SURE?
I CHECKED AFTER THE FESTIVAL, AND THE TARGET HAD BEEN MOVED THREE FEET OFF CENTER.
DID YOU REPORT IT?
OF COURSE. I TOLD MY FATHER AND TATSUE TORADA, WHO WERE THE FESTIVAL ORGANIZERS BACK THEN...
...BUT THEY SAID IT MUST HAVE BEEN A MISTAKE.
THEY EVEN ASKED ME TO KEEP QUIET ABOUT IT TO AVOID A SCANDAL.
I NEVER TOLD ANYONE, BUT IF THEY'RE DOING THE SAME TO ME...
MY FATHER-IN-LAW DIDN'T KNOW ABOUT THE SABOTAGE, SO HE WAS INFURIATED AT KAI.
HE FELT PERSONALLY DISGRACED.
HOW COME?
IT WAS MY FATHER-IN-LAW WHO TAUGHT YABUSAME TO OFFICER KAI.
HE GOT INTO AN ARGUMENT WITH MY GRANDMOTHER, SHIGEYO, TOO...
...TELLING HER SHE HAD NO RIGHT TO HELP WITH HIS TRAINING BECAUSE SHE'D NEVER BEEN A FESTIVAL ARCHER.
HUH...
SOUNDS LIKE EVERYBODY HAD SOME KINDA CONNECTION TA THAT KAI GUY.
YEAH...

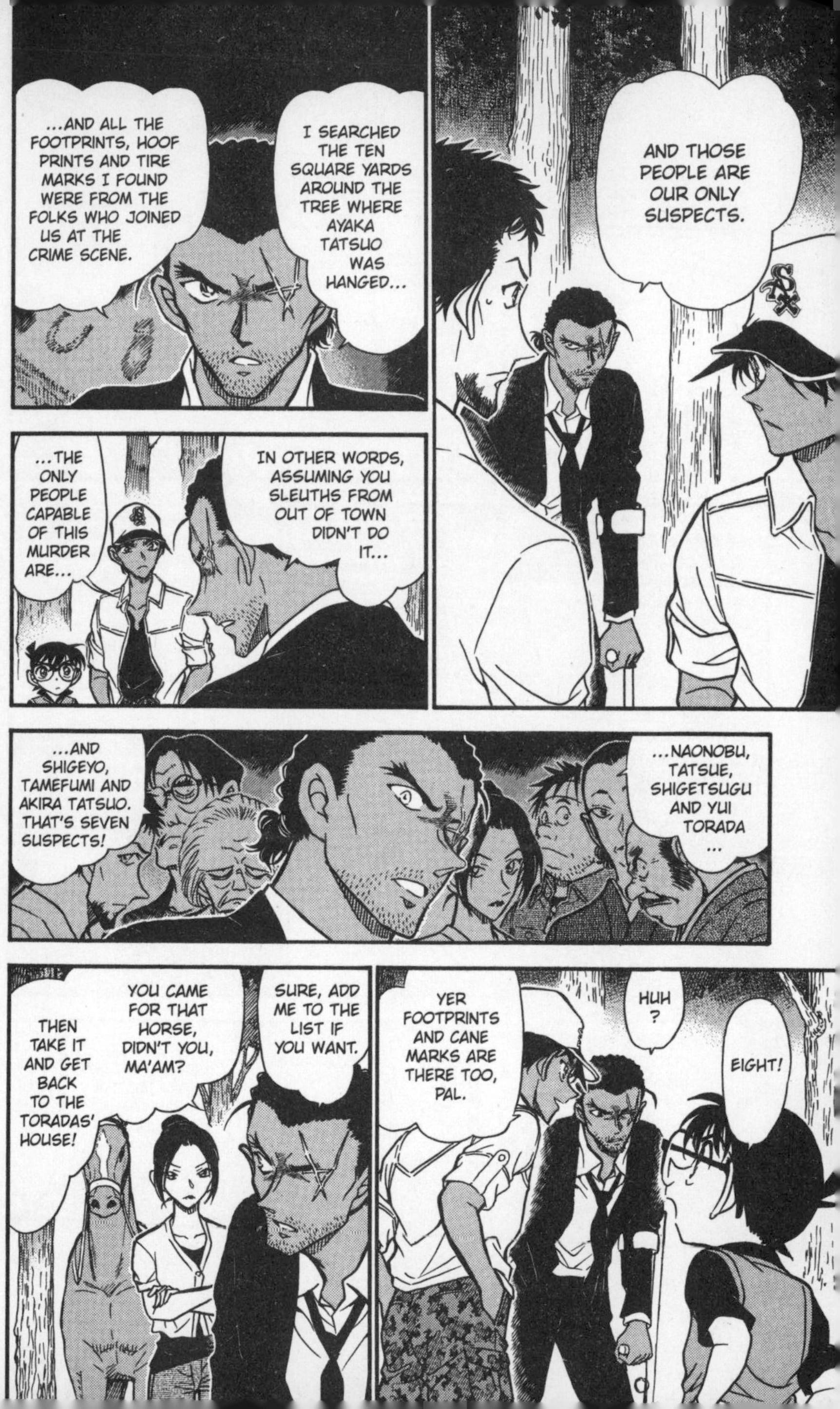
I SEARCHED THE TEN SQUARE YARDS AROUND THE TREE WHERE AYAKA TATSUO WAS HANGED...
...AND ALL THE FOOTPRINTS, HOOF PRINTS AND TIRE MARKS I FOUND WERE FROM THE FOLKS WHO JOINED US AT THE CRIME SCENE.
AND THOSE PEOPLE ARE OUR ONLY SUSPECTS.
IN OTHER WORDS, ASSUMING YOU SLEUTHS FROM OUT OF TOWN DIDN'T DO IT...
...THE ONLY PEOPLE CAPABLE OF THIS MURDER ARE...
...NAONOBU, TATSUE, SHIGETSUGU AND YUI TORADA ...
...AND SHIGEYO, TAMEFUMI AND AKIRA TATSUO. THAT'S SEVEN SUSPECTS!
EIGHT!
HUH ?
YER FOOTPRINTS AND CANE MARKS ARE THERE TOO, PAL.
SURE, ADD ME TO THE LIST IF YOU WANT.
YOU CAME FOR THAT HORSE, DIDN'T YOU, MA'AM?
THEN TAKE IT AND GET BACK TO THE TORADAS' HOUSE!

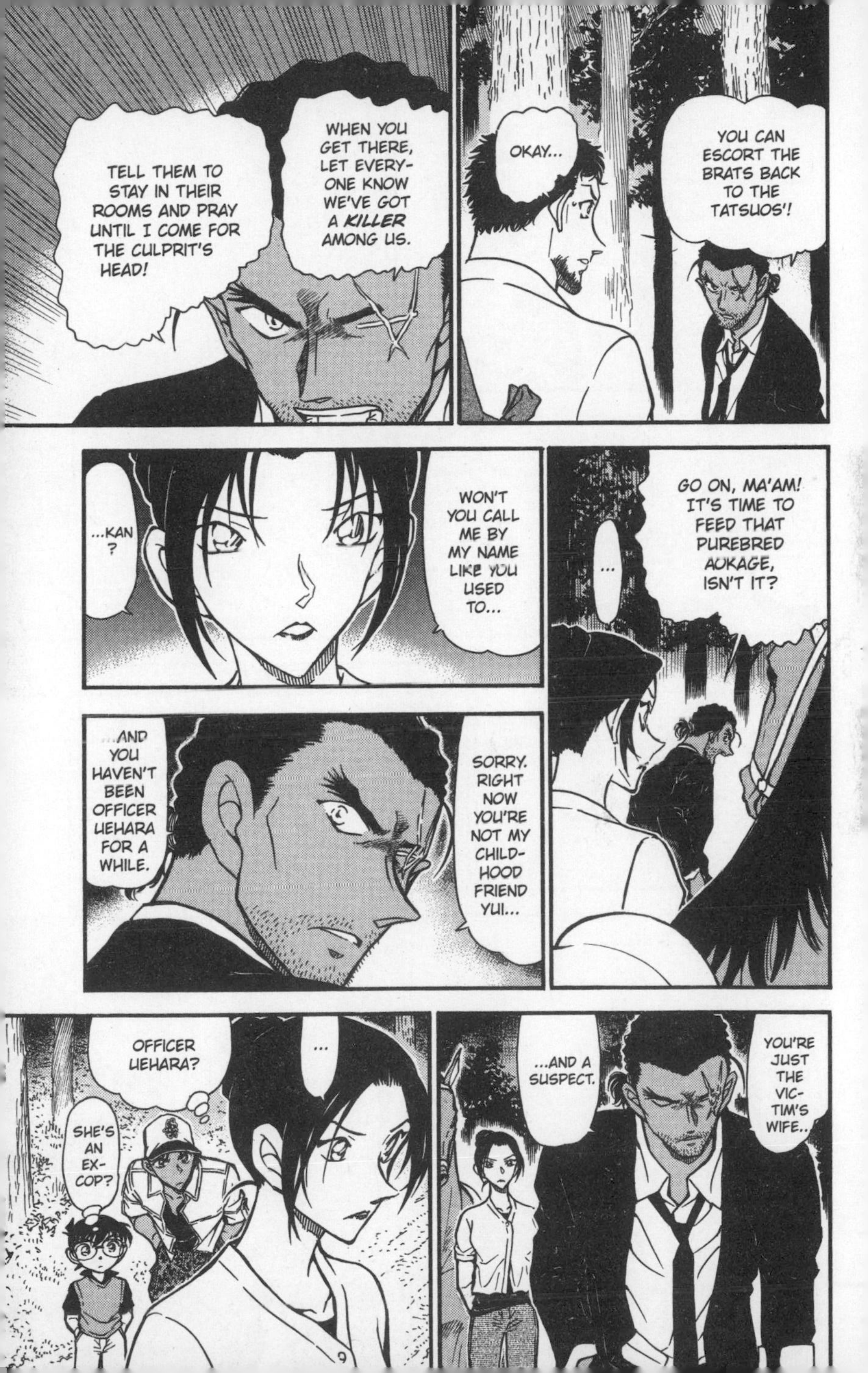
YOU CAN ESCORT THE BRATS BACK TO THE TATSUOS'!
OKAY...
WHEN YOU GET THERE, LET EVERYONE KNOW WE'VE GOT A *KILLER* AMONG US.
TELL THEM TO STAY IN THEIR ROOMS AND PRAY UNTIL I COME FOR THE CULPRIT'S HEAD!
GO ON, MA'AM! IT'S TIME TO FEED THAT PUREBRED AOKAGE, ISN'T IT?
...
WON'T YOU CALL ME BY MY NAME LIKE YOU USED TO...
...KAN?
SORRY. RIGHT NOW YOU'RE NOT MY CHILDHOOD FRIEND YUI...
...AND YOU HAVEN'T BEEN OFFICER UEHARA FOR A WHILE.
YOU'RE JUST THE VICTIM'S WIFE..
...AND A SUSPECT.
...
OFFICER UEHARA?
SHE'S AN EX-COP?

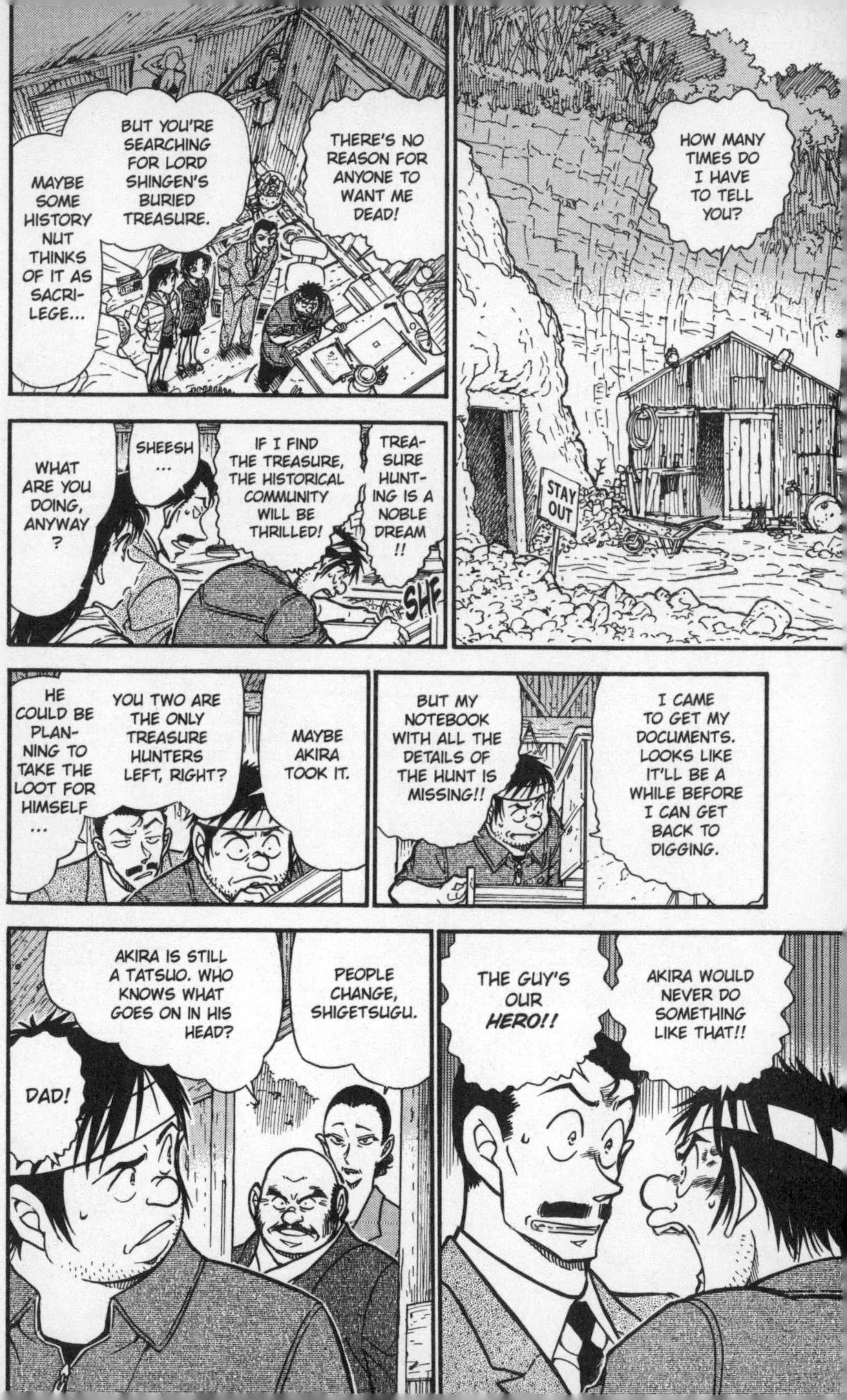
HOW MANY TIMES DO I HAVE TO TELL YOU?
STAY OUT
THERE'S NO REASON FOR ANYONE TO WANT ME DEAD!
BUT YOU'RE SEARCHING FOR LORD SHINGEN'S BURIED TREASURE.
MAYBE SOME HISTORY NUT THINKS OF IT AS SACRI-LEGE...
TREA-SURE HUNT-ING IS A NOBLE DREAM!!
SHF
IF I FIND THE TREASURE, THE HISTORICAL COMMUNITY WILL BE THRILLED!
SHEESH...
WHAT ARE YOU DOING, ANYWAY?
I CAME TO GET MY DOCUMENTS. LOOKS LIKE IT'LL BE A WHILE BEFORE I CAN GET BACK TO DIGGING.
BUT MY NOTEBOOK WITH ALL THE DETAILS OF THE HUNT IS MISSING!!
MAYBE AKIRA TOOK IT.
YOU TWO ARE THE ONLY TREASURE HUNTERS LEFT, RIGHT?
HE COULD BE PLAN-NING TO TAKE THE LOOT FOR HIMSELF...
AKIRA WOULD NEVER DO SOMETHING LIKE THAT!!
THE GUY'S OUR HERO!!
PEOPLE CHANGE, SHIGETSUGU.
AKIRA IS STILL A TATSUO. WHO KNOWS WHAT GOES ON IN HIS HEAD?
DAD!

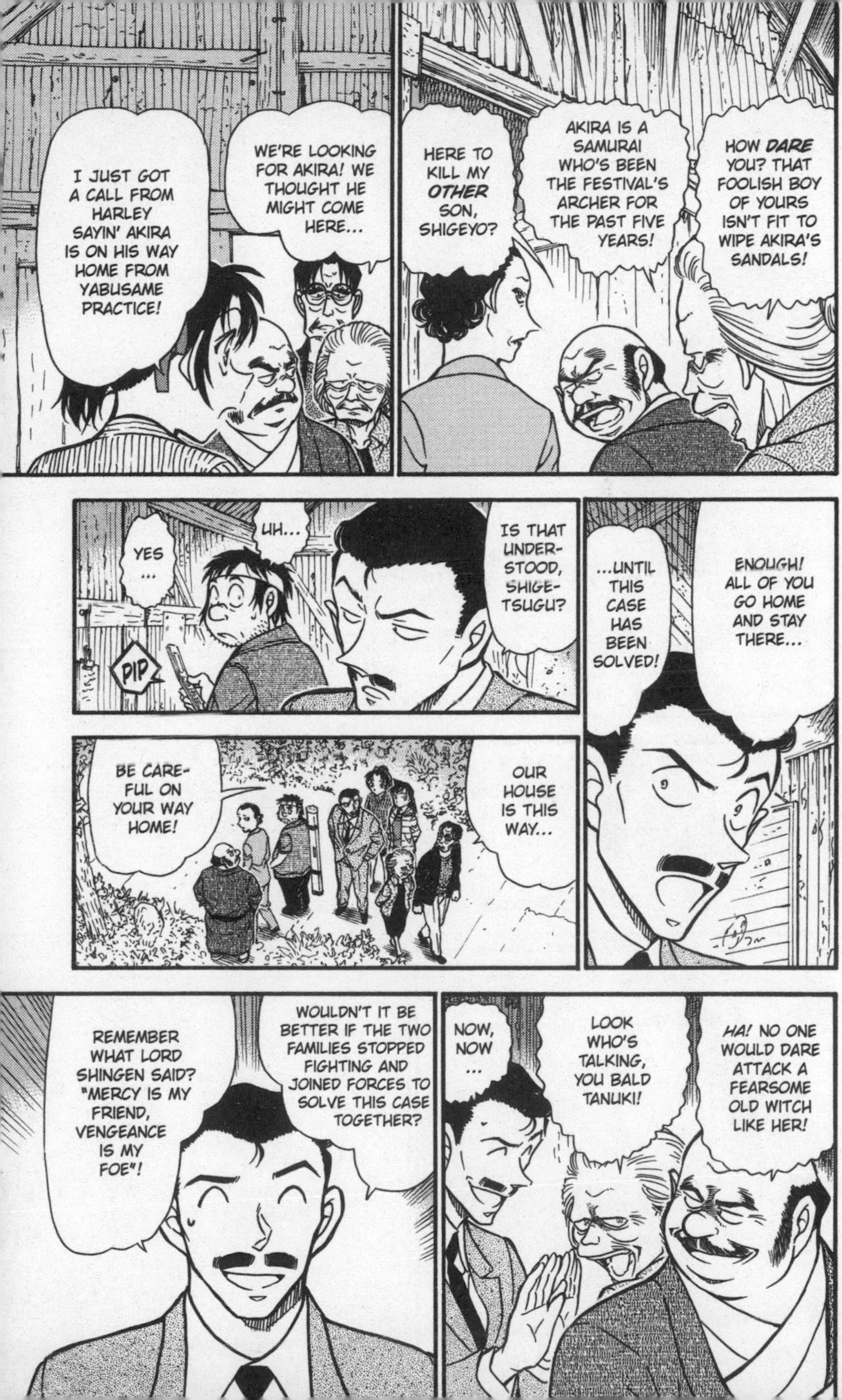
HOW DARE YOU? THAT FOOLISH BOY OF YOURS ISN'T FIT TO WIPE AKIRA'S SANDALS!
AKIRA IS A SAMURAI WHO'S BEEN THE FESTIVAL'S ARCHER FOR THE PAST FIVE YEARS!
HERE TO KILL MY OTHER SON, SHIGEYO?
WE'RE LOOKING FOR AKIRA! WE THOUGHT HE MIGHT COME HERE...
I JUST GOT A CALL FROM HARLEY SAYIN' AKIRA IS ON HIS WAY HOME FROM YABUSAME PRACTICE!
ENOUGH! ALL OF YOU GO HOME AND STAY THERE...
...UNTIL THIS CASE HAS BEEN SOLVED!
IS THAT UNDER-STOOD, SHIGE-TSUGU?
UH...
YES ...
PIP
OUR HOUSE IS THIS WAY...
BE CARE-FUL ON YOUR WAY HOME!
HA! NO ONE WOULD DARE ATTACK A FEARSOME OLD WITCH LIKE HER!
LOOK WHO'S TALKING, YOU BALD TANUKI!
NOW, NOW ...
WOULDN'T IT BE BETTER IF THE TWO FAMILIES STOPPED FIGHTING AND JOINED FORCES TO SOLVE THIS CASE TOGETHER?
REMEMBER WHAT LORD SHINGEN SAID? "MERCY IS MY FRIEND, VENGEANCE IS MY FOE"!

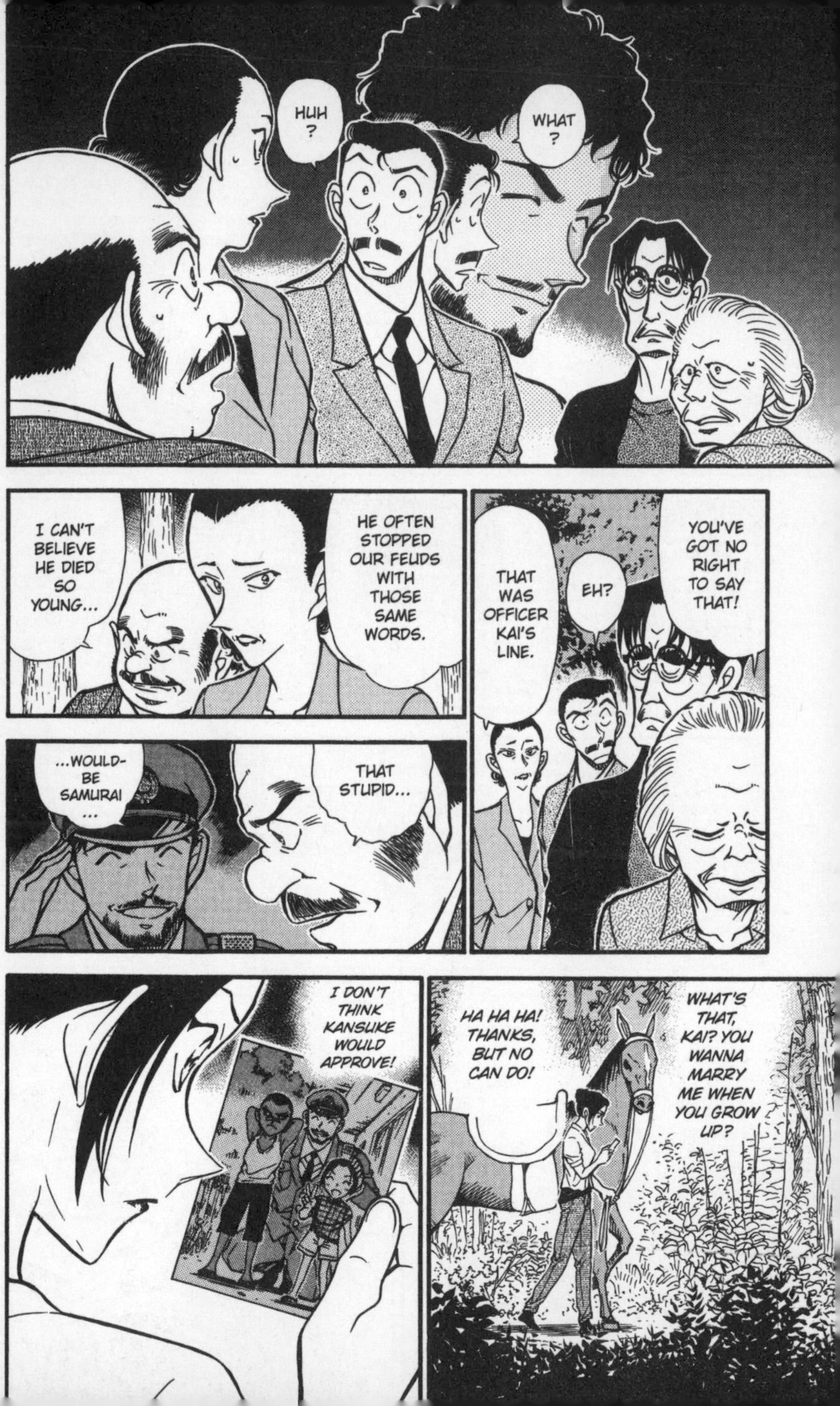
WHAT?
HUH?
YOU'VE GOT NO RIGHT TO SAY THAT!
EH?
THAT WAS OFFICER KAI'S LINE.
HE OFTEN STOPPED OUR FEUDS WITH THOSE SAME WORDS.
I CAN'T BELIEVE HE DIED SO YOUNG...
THAT STUPID...
...WOULD-BE SAMURAI...
WHAT'S THAT, KAI? YOU WANNA MARRY ME WHEN YOU GROW UP?
HA HA HA! THANKS, BUT NO CAN DO!
I DON'T THINK KANSUKE WOULD APPROVE!

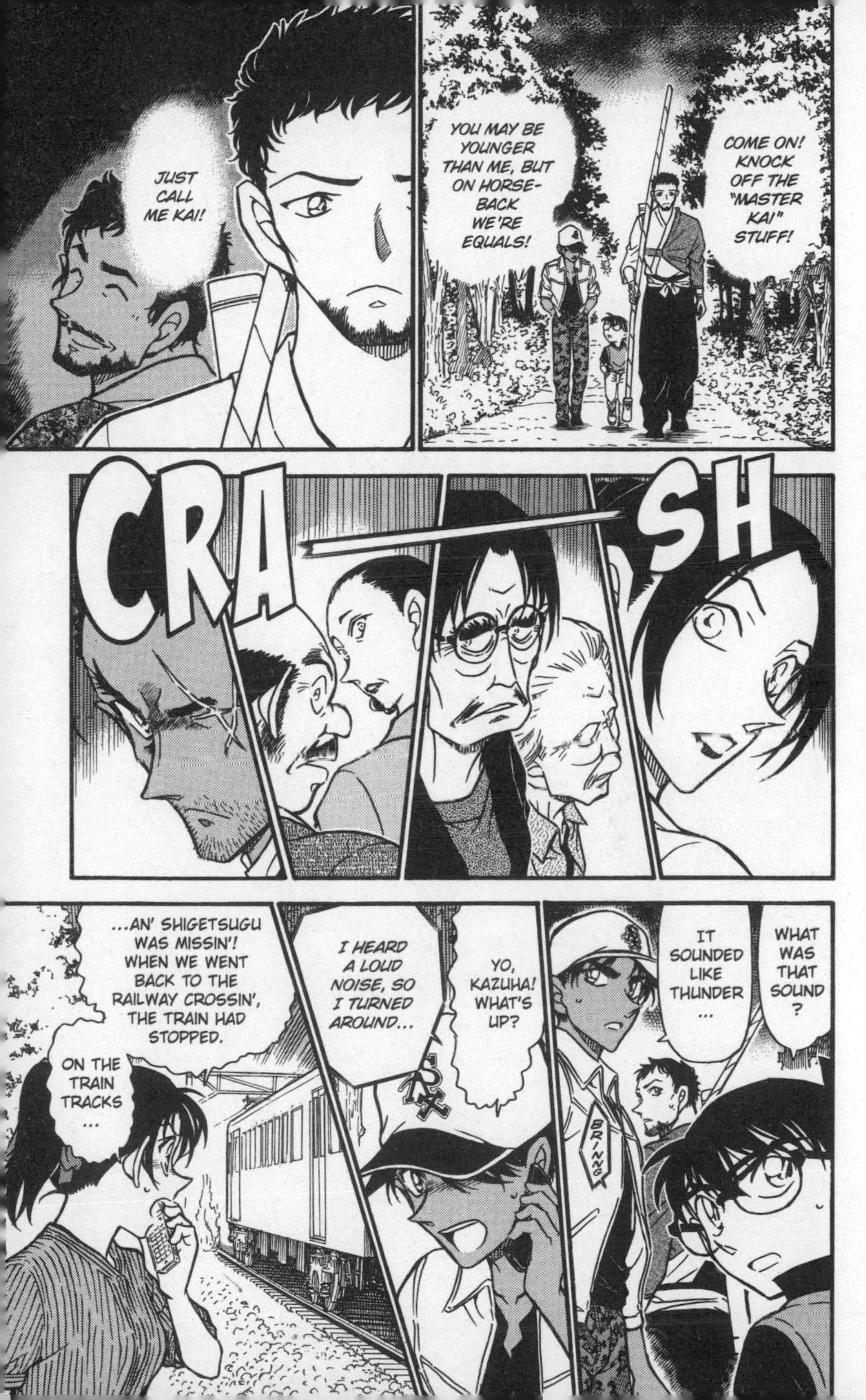
COME ON! KNOCK OFF THE "MASTER KAI" STUFF!
YOU MAY BE YOUNGER THAN ME, BUT ON HORSE-BACK WE'RE EQUALS!
JUST CALL ME KAI!
CRASH
WHAT WAS THAT SOUND?
IT SOUNDED LIKE THUNDER...
BRINNG
YO, KAZUHA! WHAT'S UP?
I HEARD A LOUD NOISE, SO I TURNED AROUND...
...AN' SHIGETSUGU WAS MISSIN'! WHEN WE WENT BACK TO THE RAILWAY CROSSIN', THE TRAIN HAD STOPPED.
ON THE TRAIN TRACKS...

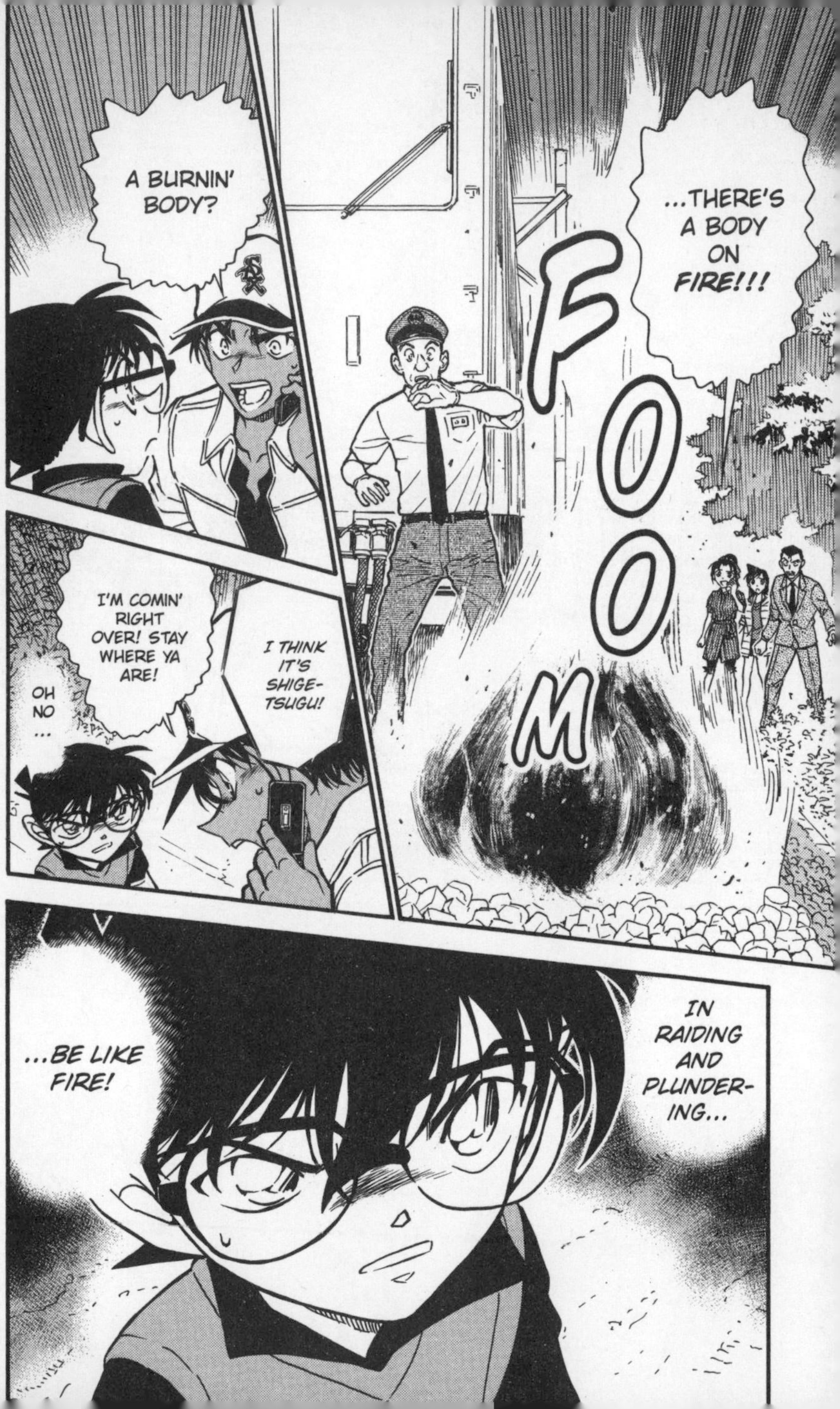
...THERE'S A BODY ON FIRE!!!
FOOM
A BURNIN' BODY?
I THINK IT'S SHIGE-TSUGU!
I'M COMIN' RIGHT OVER! STAY WHERE YA ARE!
OH NO ...
IN RAIDING AND PLUNDER-ING...
...BE LIKE FIRE!

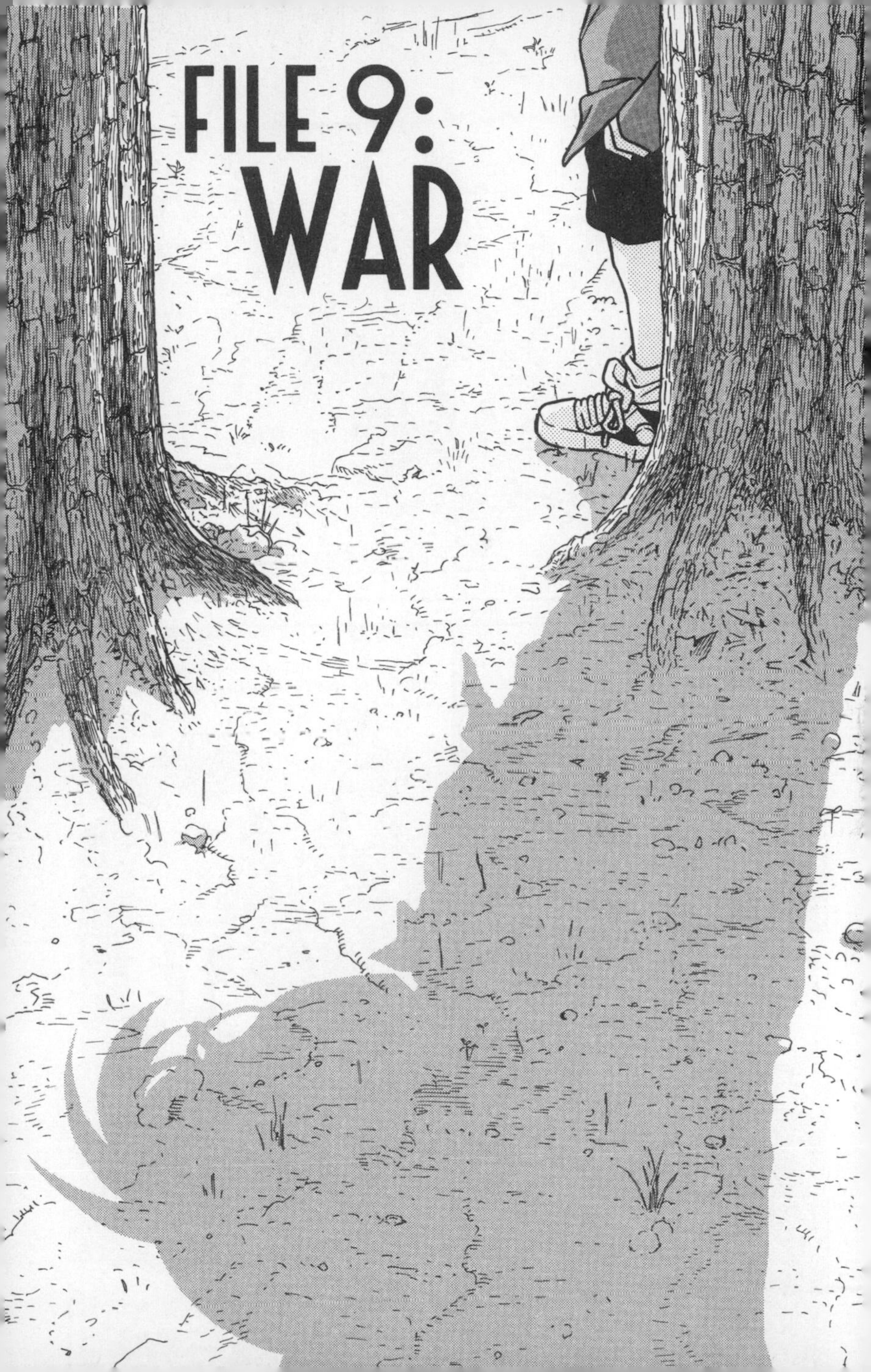
FILE 9:
WAR

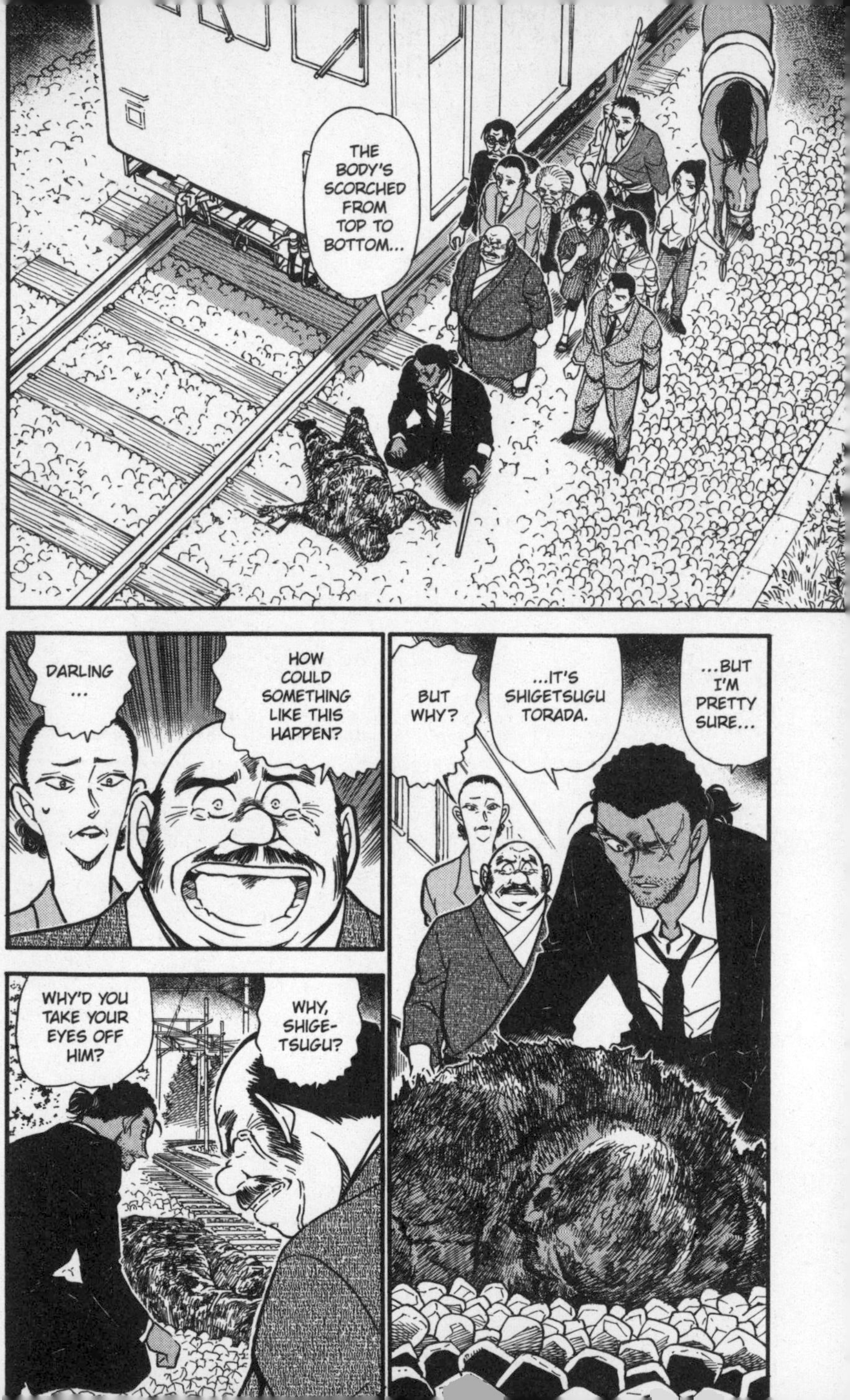
THE BODY'S SCORCHED FROM TOP TO BOTTOM...
...BUT I'M PRETTY SURE...
...IT'S SHIGETSUGU TORADA.
BUT WHY?
HOW COULD SOMETHING LIKE THIS HAPPEN?
DARLING ...
WHY, SHIGE-TSUGU?
WHY'D YOU TAKE YOUR EYES OFF HIM?

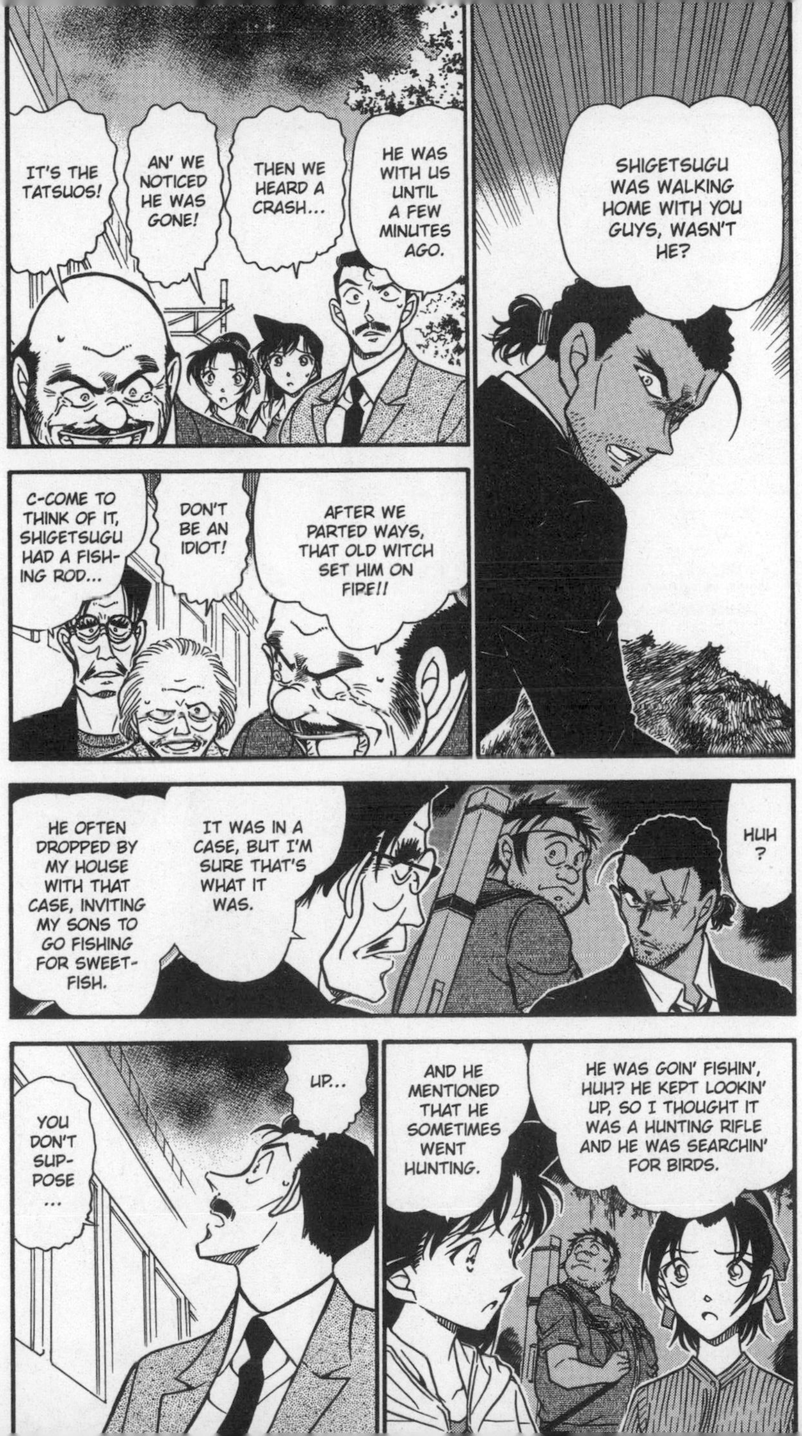
SHIGETSUGU WAS WALKING HOME WITH YOU GUYS, WASN'T HE?
HE WAS WITH US UNTIL A FEW MINUTES AGO.
THEN WE HEARD A CRASH...
AN' WE NOTICED HE WAS GONE!
IT'S THE TATSUOS!
AFTER WE PARTED WAYS, THAT OLD WITCH SET HIM ON FIRE!!
DON'T BE AN IDIOT!
C-COME TO THINK OF IT, SHIGETSUGU HAD A FISHING ROD...
HUH?
IT WAS IN A CASE, BUT I'M SURE THAT'S WHAT IT WAS.
HE OFTEN DROPPED BY MY HOUSE WITH THAT CASE, INVITING MY SONS TO GO FISHING FOR SWEETFISH.
HE WAS GOIN' FISHIN', HUH? HE KEPT LOOKIN' UP, SO I THOUGHT IT WAS A HUNTING RIFLE AND HE WAS SEARCHIN' FOR BIRDS.
AND HE MENTIONED THAT HE SOMETIMES WENT HUNTING.
UP...
YOU DON'T SUPPOSE...

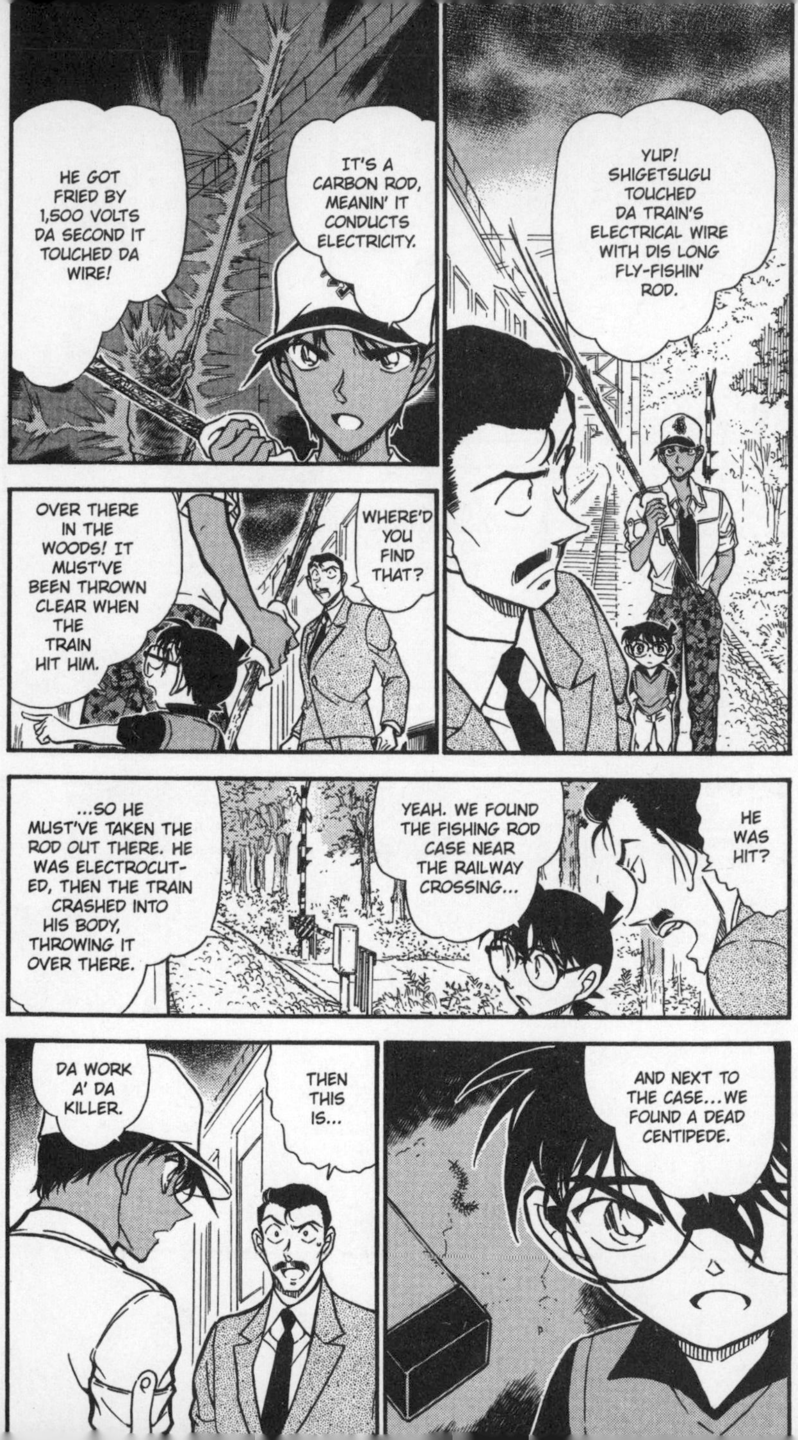
YUP! SHIGETSUGU TOUCHED DA TRAIN'S ELECTRICAL WIRE WITH DIS LONG FLY-FISHIN' ROD.
IT'S A CARBON ROD, MEANIN' IT CONDUCTS ELECTRICITY.
HE GOT FRIED BY 1,500 VOLTS DA SECOND IT TOUCHED DA WIRE!
WHERE'D YOU FIND THAT?
OVER THERE IN THE WOODS! IT MUST'VE BEEN THROWN CLEAR WHEN THE TRAIN HIT HIM.
HE WAS HIT?
YEAH. WE FOUND THE FISHING ROD CASE NEAR THE RAILWAY CROSSING...
...SO HE MUST'VE TAKEN THE ROD OUT THERE. HE WAS ELECTROCUT-ED, THEN THE TRAIN CRASHED INTO HIS BODY, THROWING IT OVER THERE.
AND NEXT TO THE CASE...WE FOUND A DEAD CENTIPEDE.
THEN THIS IS...
DA WORK A' DA KILLER.

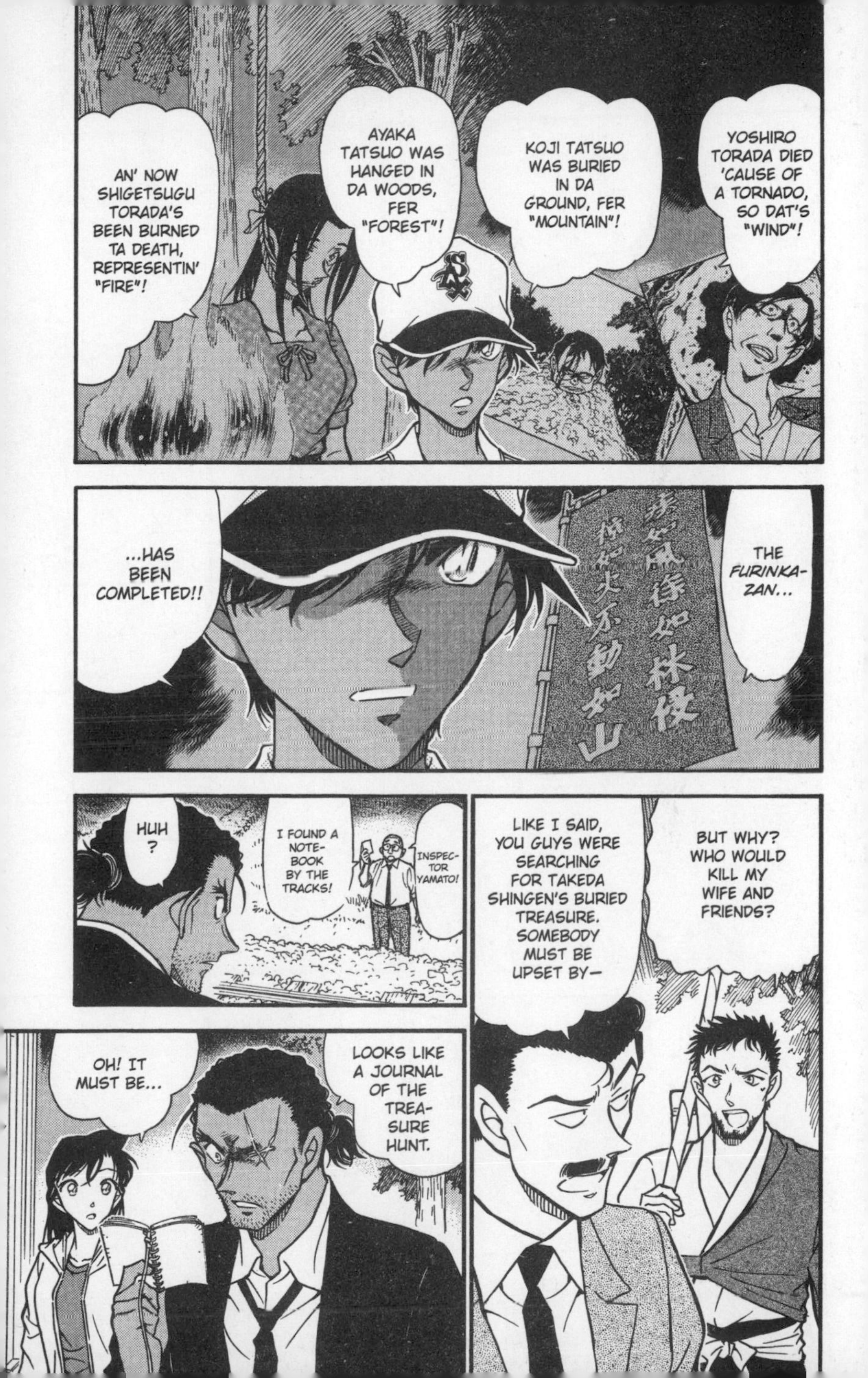
YOSHIRO TORADA DIED 'CAUSE OF A TORNADO, SO DAT'S "WIND"!
KOJI TATSUO WAS BURIED IN DA GROUND, FER "MOUNTAIN"!
AYAKA TATSUO WAS HANGED IN DA WOODS, FER "FOREST"!
AN' NOW SHIGETSUGU TORADA'S BEEN BURNED TA DEATH, REPRESENTIN' "FIRE"!
THE *FURINKAZAN*...
...HAS BEEN COMPLETED!!
BUT WHY? WHO WOULD KILL MY WIFE AND FRIENDS?
LIKE I SAID, YOU GUYS WERE SEARCHING FOR TAKEDA SHINGEN'S BURIED TREASURE. SOMEBODY MUST BE UPSET BY—
INSPECTOR YAMATO!
I FOUND A NOTEBOOK BY THE TRACKS!
HUH?
LOOKS LIKE A JOURNAL OF THE TREASURE HUNT.
OH! IT MUST BE...

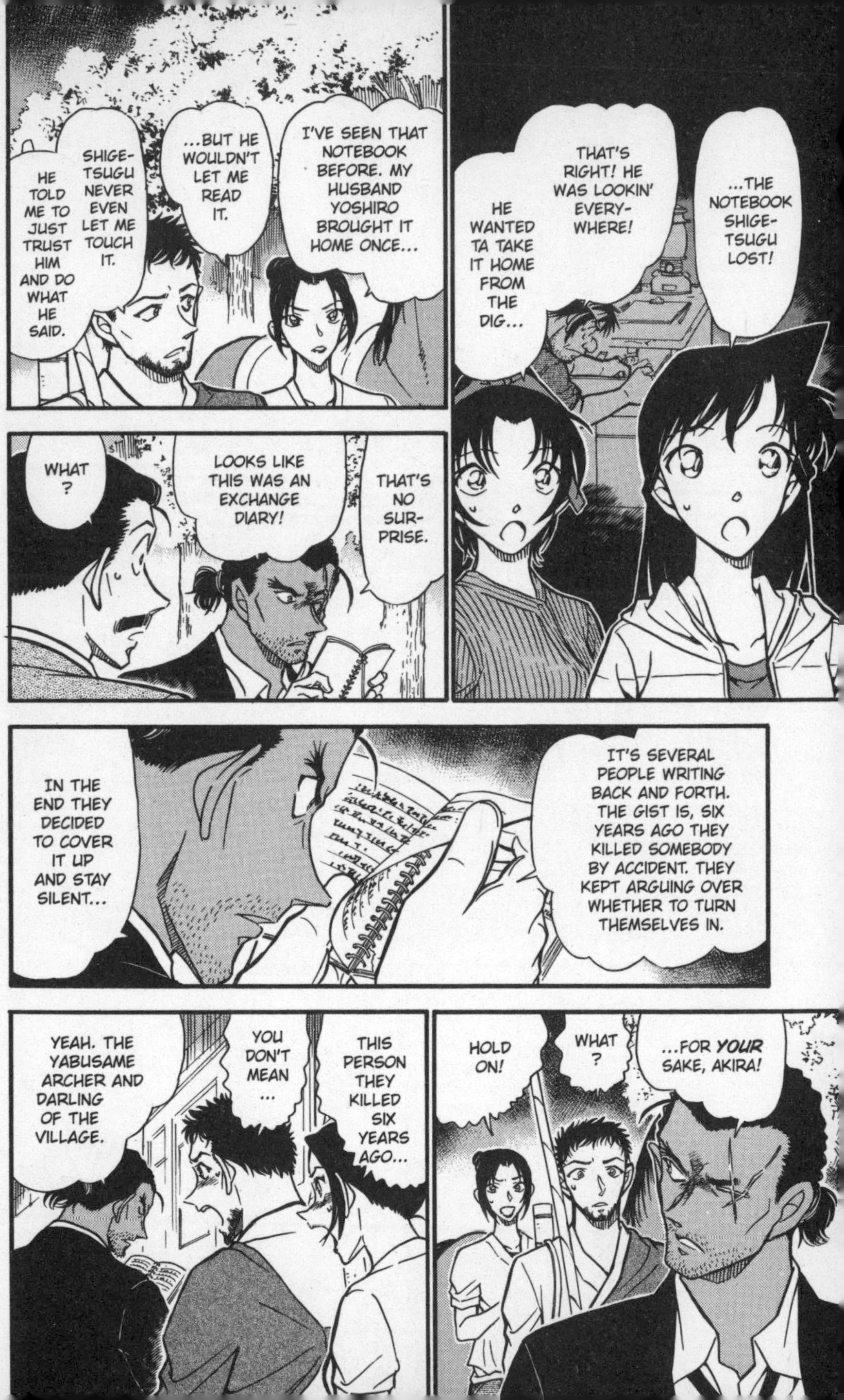
...THE NOTEBOOK SHIGE-TSUGU LOST!
THAT'S RIGHT! HE WAS LOOKIN' EVERY-WHERE!
HE WANTED TA TAKE IT HOME FROM THE DIG...
I'VE SEEN THAT NOTEBOOK BEFORE. MY HUSBAND YOSHIRO BROUGHT IT HOME ONCE...
...BUT HE WOULDN'T LET ME READ IT.
SHIGE-TSUGU NEVER EVEN LET ME TOUCH IT.
HE TOLD ME TO JUST TRUST HIM AND DO WHAT HE SAID.
THAT'S NO SUR-PRISE.
LOOKS LIKE THIS WAS AN EXCHANGE DIARY!
WHAT?
IT'S SEVERAL PEOPLE WRITING BACK AND FORTH. THE GIST IS, SIX YEARS AGO THEY KILLED SOMEBODY BY ACCIDENT. THEY KEPT ARGUING OVER WHETHER TO TURN THEMSELVES IN.
IN THE END THEY DECIDED TO COVER IT UP AND STAY SILENT...
...FOR ***YOUR*** SAKE, AKIRA!
WHAT?
HOLD ON!
THIS PERSON THEY KILLED SIX YEARS AGO...
YOU DON'T MEAN...
YEAH. THE YABUSAME ARCHER AND DARLING OF THE VILLAGE.

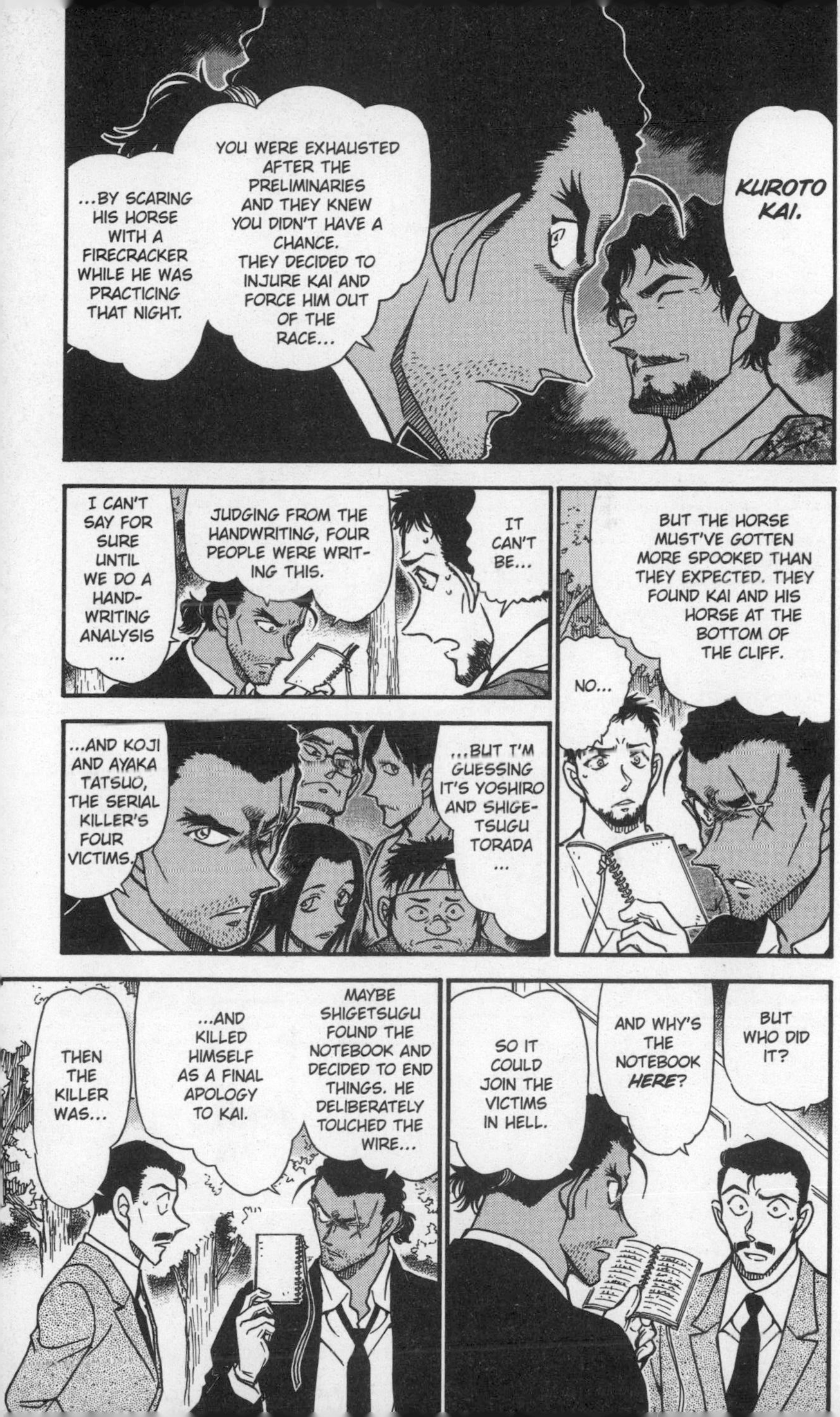
KUROTO KAI.
YOU WERE EXHAUSTED AFTER THE PRELIMINARIES AND THEY KNEW YOU DIDN'T HAVE A CHANCE. THEY DECIDED TO INJURE KAI AND FORCE HIM OUT OF THE RACE...
...BY SCARING HIS HORSE WITH A FIRECRACKER WHILE HE WAS PRACTICING THAT NIGHT.
BUT THE HORSE MUST'VE GOTTEN MORE SPOOKED THAN THEY EXPECTED. THEY FOUND KAI AND HIS HORSE AT THE BOTTOM OF THE CLIFF.
NO...
IT CAN'T BE...
JUDGING FROM THE HANDWRITING, FOUR PEOPLE WERE WRIT-ING THIS.
I CAN'T SAY FOR SURE UNTIL WE DO A HAND-WRITING ANALYSIS ...
...BUT I'M GUESSING IT'S YOSHIRO AND SHIGE-TSUGU TORADA ...
...AND KOJI AND AYAKA TATSUO, THE SERIAL KILLER'S FOUR VICTIMS.
BUT WHO DID IT?
AND WHY'S THE NOTEBOOK HERE?
SO IT COULD JOIN THE VICTIMS IN HELL.
MAYBE SHIGETSUGU FOUND THE NOTEBOOK AND DECIDED TO END THINGS. HE DELIBERATELY TOUCHED THE WIRE...
...AND KILLED HIMSELF AS A FINAL APOLOGY TO KAI.
THEN THE KILLER WAS...

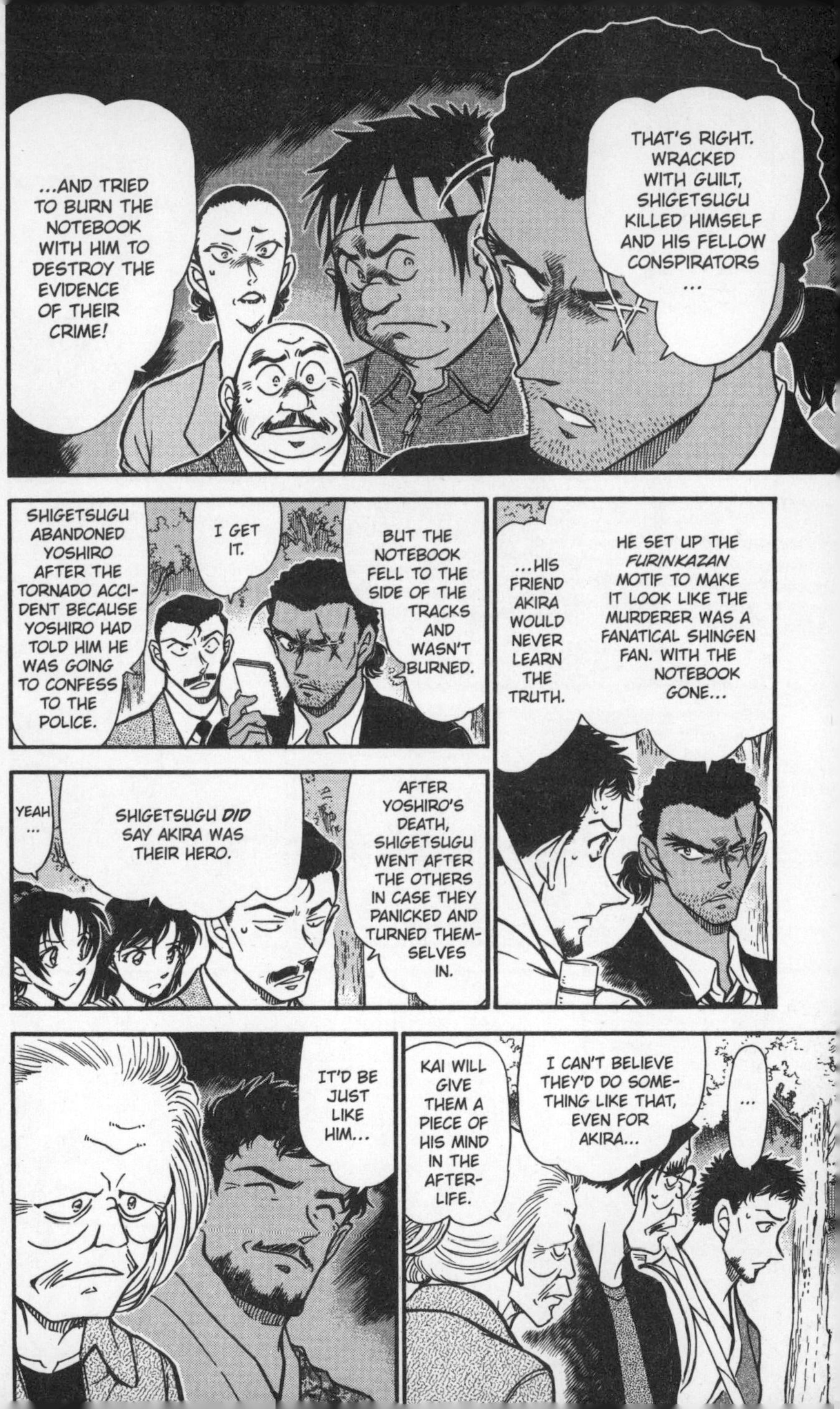
THAT'S RIGHT. WRACKED WITH GUILT, SHIGETSUGU KILLED HIMSELF AND HIS FELLOW CONSPIRATORS ...
...AND TRIED TO BURN THE NOTEBOOK WITH HIM TO DESTROY THE EVIDENCE OF THEIR CRIME!
HE SET UP THE *FURINKAZAN* MOTIF TO MAKE IT LOOK LIKE THE MURDERER WAS A FANATICAL SHINGEN FAN. WITH THE NOTEBOOK GONE...
...HIS FRIEND AKIRA WOULD NEVER LEARN THE TRUTH.
BUT THE NOTEBOOK FELL TO THE SIDE OF THE TRACKS AND WASN'T BURNED.
I GET IT.
SHIGETSUGU ABANDONED YOSHIRO AFTER THE TORNADO ACCIDENT BECAUSE YOSHIRO HAD TOLD HIM HE WAS GOING TO CONFESS TO THE POLICE.
AFTER YOSHIRO'S DEATH, SHIGETSUGU WENT AFTER THE OTHERS IN CASE THEY PANICKED AND TURNED THEMSELVES IN.
SHIGETSUGU *DID* SAY AKIRA WAS THEIR HERO.
YEAH ...
...
I CAN'T BELIEVE THEY'D DO SOMETHING LIKE THAT, EVEN FOR AKIRA...
KAI WILL GIVE THEM A PIECE OF HIS MIND IN THE AFTERLIFE.
IT'D BE JUST LIKE HIM...

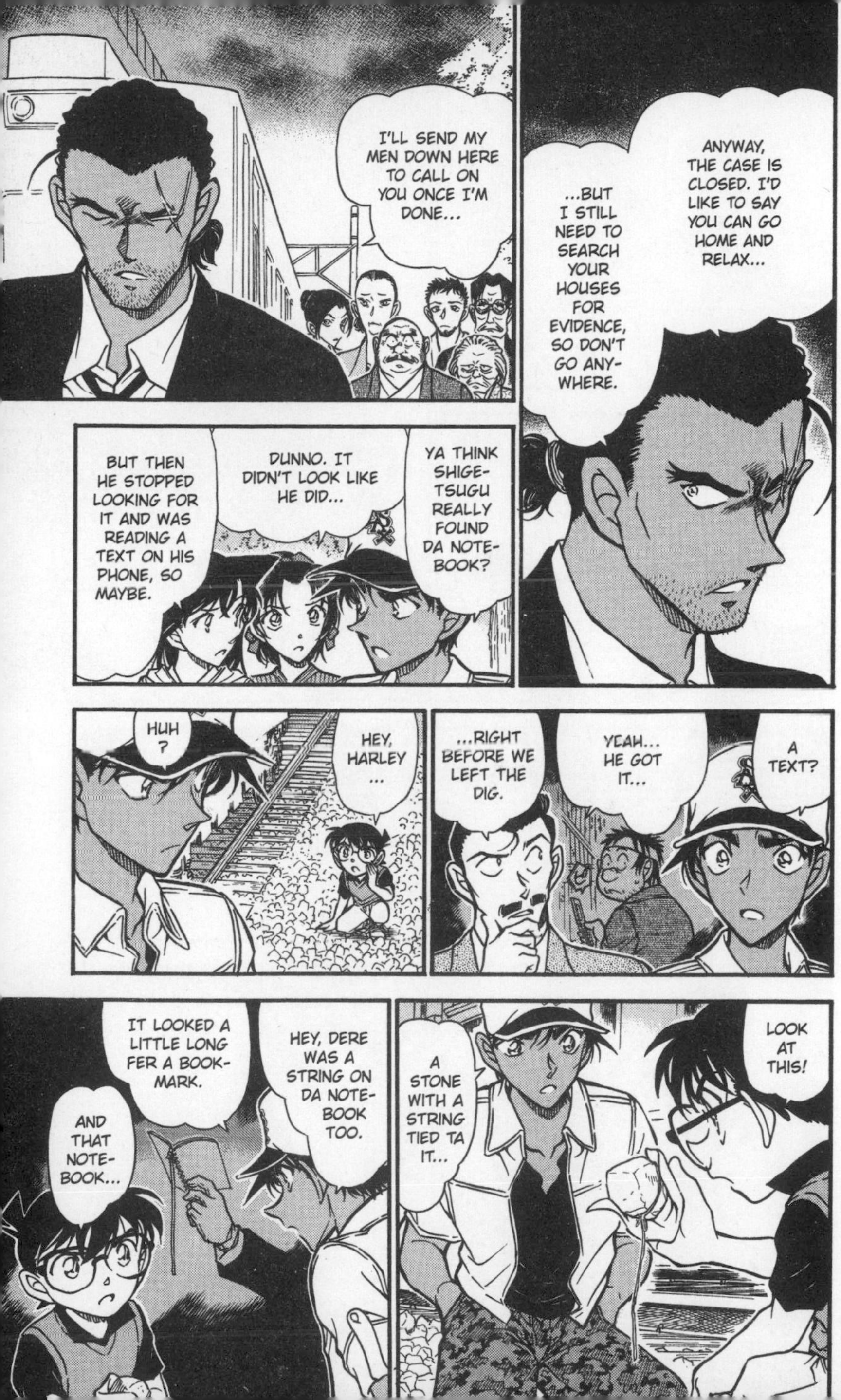
ANYWAY, THE CASE IS CLOSED. I'D LIKE TO SAY YOU CAN GO HOME AND RELAX...
...BUT I STILL NEED TO SEARCH YOUR HOUSES FOR EVIDENCE, SO DON'T GO ANY-WHERE.
I'LL SEND MY MEN DOWN HERE TO CALL ON YOU ONCE I'M DONE...
YA THINK SHIGE-TSUGU REALLY FOUND DA NOTE-BOOK?
DUNNO. IT DIDN'T LOOK LIKE HE DID...
BUT THEN HE STOPPED LOOKING FOR IT AND WAS READING A TEXT ON HIS PHONE, SO MAYBE.
A TEXT?
YEAH... HE GOT IT...
...RIGHT BEFORE WE LEFT THE DIG.
HEY, HARLEY ...
HUH ?
LOOK AT THIS!
A STONE WITH A STRING TIED TA IT...
HEY, DERE WAS A STRING ON DA NOTE-BOOK TOO.
IT LOOKED A LITTLE LONG FER A BOOK-MARK.
AND THAT NOTE-BOOK...

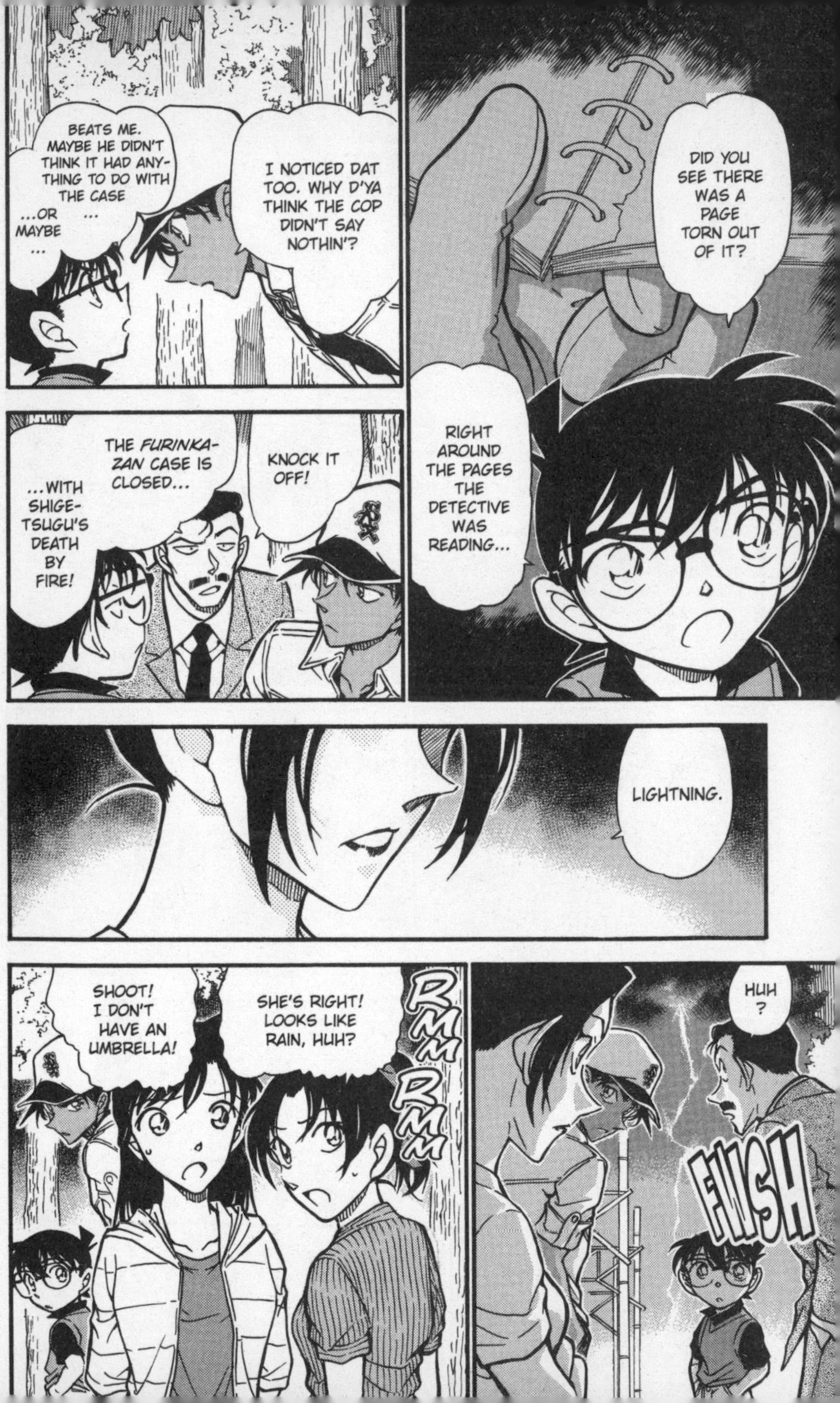
DID YOU SEE THERE WAS A PAGE TORN OUT OF IT?
RIGHT AROUND THE PAGES THE DETECTIVE WAS READING...
I NOTICED DAT TOO. WHY D'YA THINK THE COP DIDN'T SAY NOTHIN'?
BEATS ME. MAYBE HE DIDN'T THINK IT HAD ANY-THING TO DO WITH THE CASE ...
...OR MAYBE ...
KNOCK IT OFF!
THE *FURINKA-ZAN* CASE IS CLOSED...
...WITH SHIGE-TSUGU'S DEATH BY FIRE!
LIGHTNING.
HUH ?
FWSH
RMM RMM
SHE'S RIGHT! LOOKS LIKE RAIN, HUH?
SHOOT! I DON'T HAVE AN UMBRELLA!

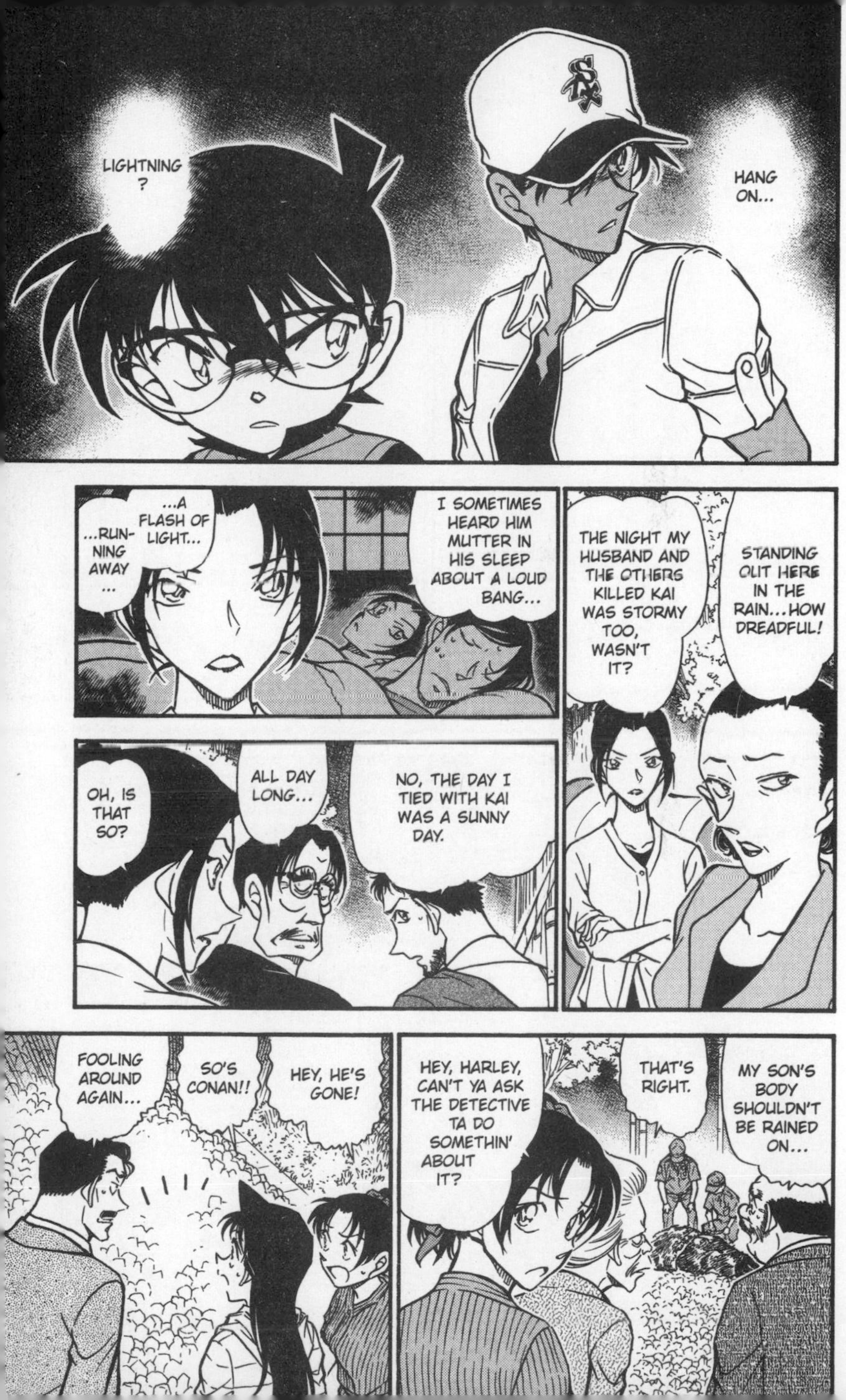
HANG ON...
LIGHTNING ?
STANDING OUT HERE IN THE RAIN...HOW DREADFUL!
THE NIGHT MY HUSBAND AND THE OTHERS KILLED KAI WAS STORMY TOO, WASN'T IT?
I SOMETIMES HEARD HIM MUTTER IN HIS SLEEP ABOUT A LOUD BANG...
...A FLASH OF LIGHT...
...RUNNING AWAY...
NO, THE DAY I TIED WITH KAI WAS A SUNNY DAY.
ALL DAY LONG...
OH, IS THAT SO?
MY SON'S BODY SHOULDN'T BE RAINED ON...
THAT'S RIGHT.
HEY, HARLEY, CAN'T YA ASK THE DETECTIVE TA DO SOMETHIN' ABOUT IT?
HEY, HE'S GONE!
SO'S CONAN!!
FOOLING AROUND AGAIN...

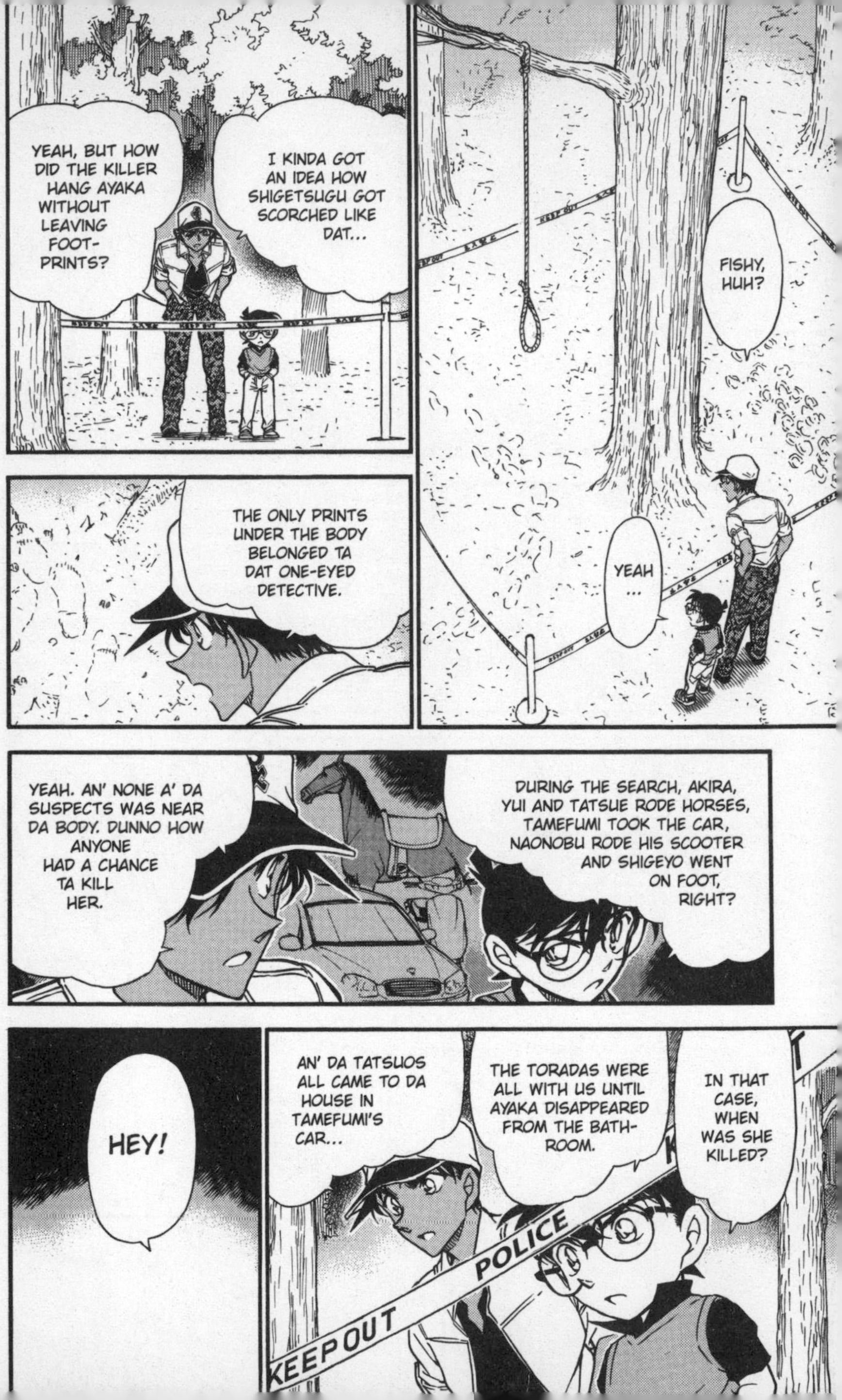
FISHY, HUH?
YEAH ...
I KINDA GOT AN IDEA HOW SHIGETSUGU GOT SCORCHED LIKE DAT...
YEAH, BUT HOW DID THE KILLER HANG AYAKA WITHOUT LEAVING FOOT-PRINTS?
THE ONLY PRINTS UNDER THE BODY BELONGED TA DAT ONE-EYED DETECTIVE.
DURING THE SEARCH, AKIRA, YUI AND TATSUE RODE HORSES, TAMEFUMI TOOK THE CAR, NAONOBU RODE HIS SCOOTER AND SHIGEYO WENT ON FOOT, RIGHT?
YEAH. AN' NONE A' DA SUSPECTS WAS NEAR DA BODY. DUNNO HOW ANYONE HAD A CHANCE TA KILL HER.
IN THAT CASE, WHEN WAS SHE KILLED?
THE TORADAS WERE ALL WITH US UNTIL AYAKA DISAPPEARED FROM THE BATH-ROOM.
AN' DA TATSUOS ALL CAME TO DA HOUSE IN TAMEFUMI'S CAR...
POLICE
KEEPOUT
HEY!

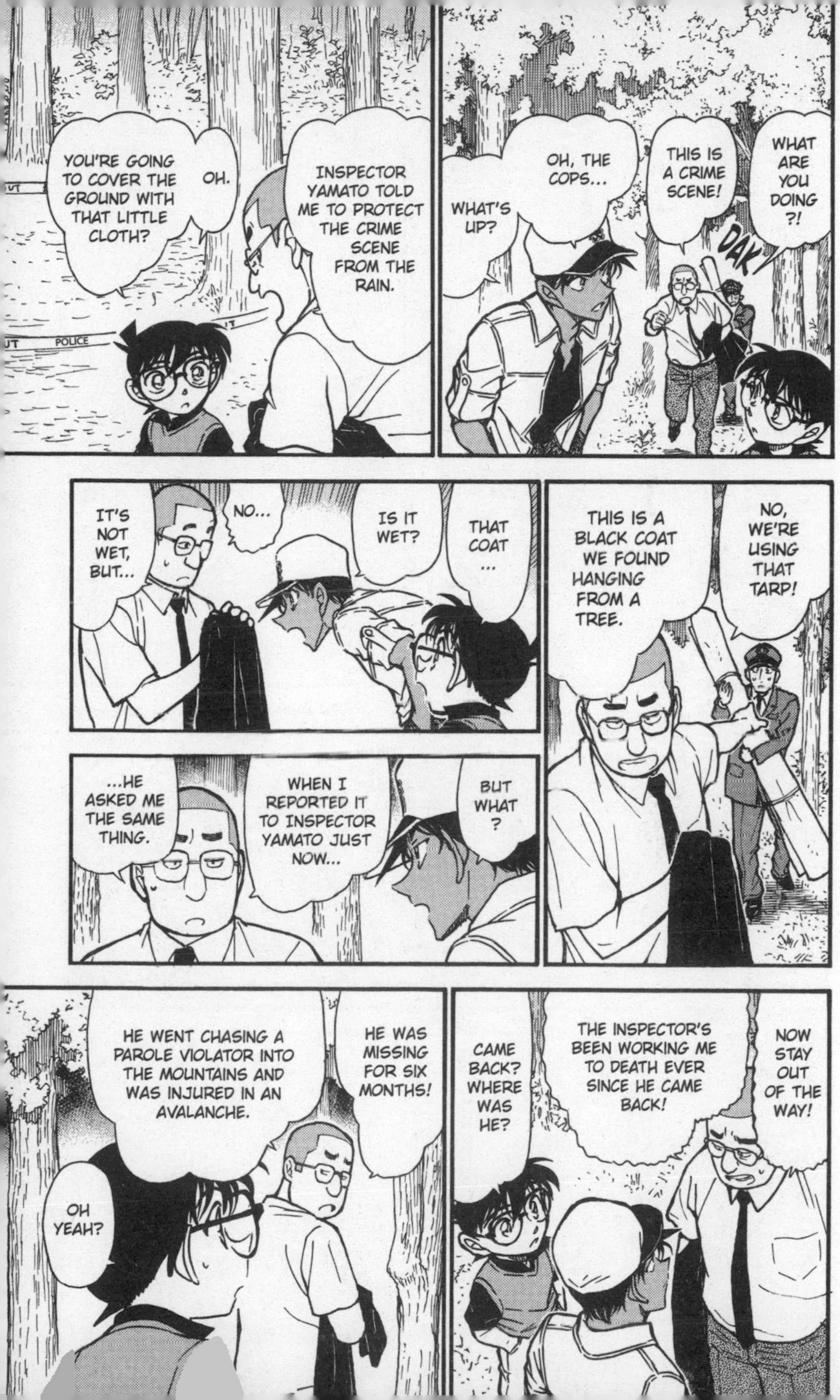
WHAT ARE YOU DOING ?!
DAK!
THIS IS A CRIME SCENE!
OH, THE COPS...
WHAT'S UP?
INSPECTOR YAMATO TOLD ME TO PROTECT THE CRIME SCENE FROM THE RAIN.
OH.
YOU'RE GOING TO COVER THE GROUND WITH THAT LITTLE CLOTH?
POLICE
NO, WE'RE USING THAT TARP!
THIS IS A BLACK COAT WE FOUND HANGING FROM A TREE.
THAT COAT ...
IS IT WET?
NO...
IT'S NOT WET, BUT...
BUT WHAT ?
WHEN I REPORTED IT TO INSPECTOR YAMATO JUST NOW...
...HE ASKED ME THE SAME THING.
NOW STAY OUT OF THE WAY!
THE INSPECTOR'S BEEN WORKING ME TO DEATH EVER SINCE HE CAME BACK!
CAME BACK? WHERE WAS HE?
HE WAS MISSING FOR SIX MONTHS!
HE WENT CHASING A PAROLE VIOLATOR INTO THE MOUNTAINS AND WAS INJURED IN AN AVALANCHE.
OH YEAH?

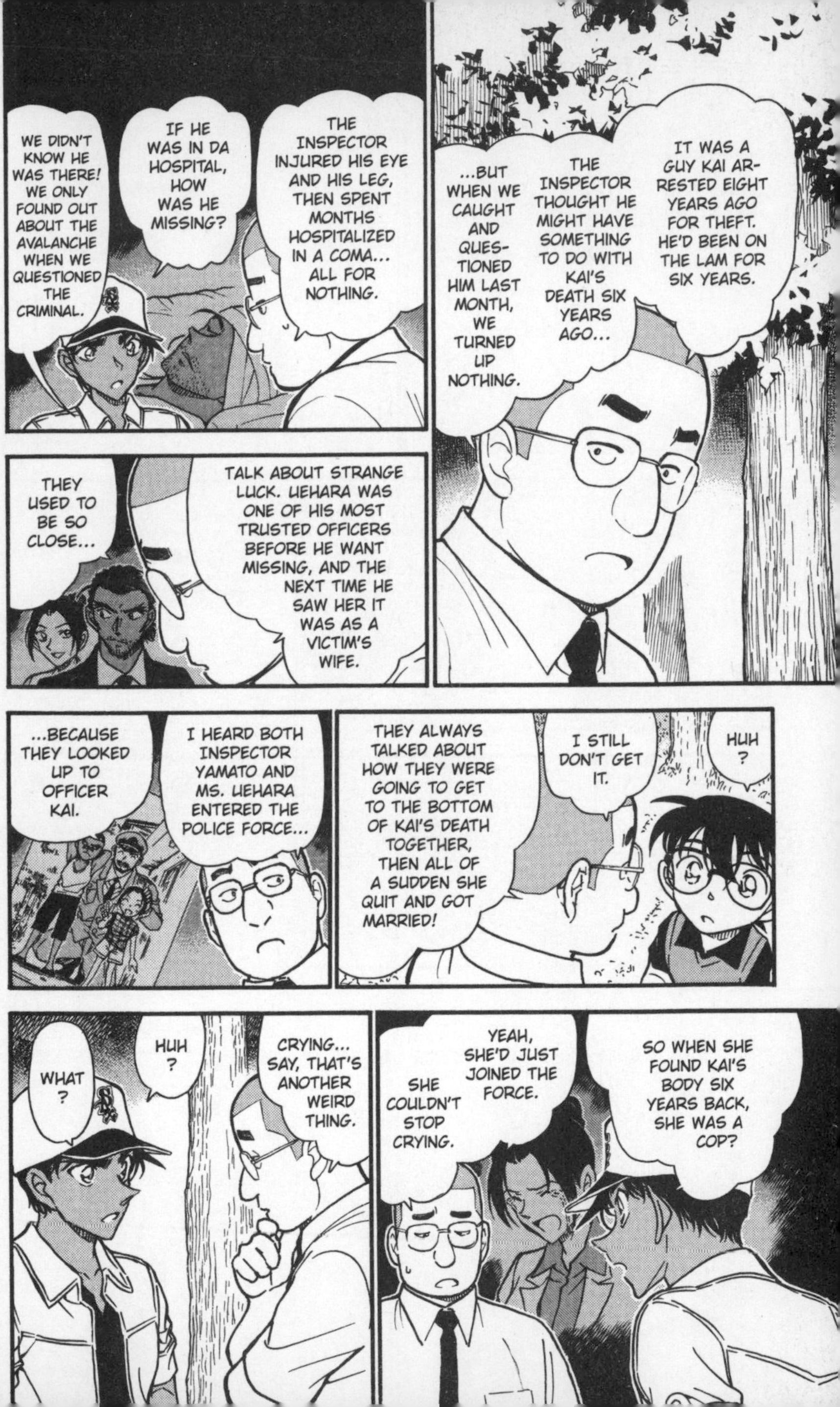
IT WAS A GUY KAI ARRESTED EIGHT YEARS AGO FOR THEFT. HE'D BEEN ON THE LAM FOR SIX YEARS.
THE INSPECTOR THOUGHT HE MIGHT HAVE SOMETHING TO DO WITH KAI'S DEATH SIX YEARS AGO...
...BUT WHEN WE CAUGHT AND QUESTIONED HIM LAST MONTH, WE TURNED UP NOTHING.
THE INSPECTOR INJURED HIS EYE AND HIS LEG, THEN SPENT MONTHS HOSPITALIZED IN A COMA... ALL FOR NOTHING.
IF HE WAS IN DA HOSPITAL, HOW WAS HE MISSING?
WE DIDN'T KNOW HE WAS THERE! WE ONLY FOUND OUT ABOUT THE AVALANCHE WHEN WE QUESTIONED THE CRIMINAL.
TALK ABOUT STRANGE LUCK. UEHARA WAS ONE OF HIS MOST TRUSTED OFFICERS BEFORE HE WANT MISSING, AND THE NEXT TIME HE SAW HER IT WAS AS A VICTIM'S WIFE.
THEY USED TO BE SO CLOSE...
HUH?
I STILL DON'T GET IT.
THEY ALWAYS TALKED ABOUT HOW THEY WERE GOING TO GET TO THE BOTTOM OF KAI'S DEATH TOGETHER, THEN ALL OF A SUDDEN SHE QUIT AND GOT MARRIED!
I HEARD BOTH INSPECTOR YAMATO AND MS. UEHARA ENTERED THE POLICE FORCE...
...BECAUSE THEY LOOKED UP TO OFFICER KAI.
SO WHEN SHE FOUND KAI'S BODY SIX YEARS BACK, SHE WAS A COP?
YEAH, SHE'D JUST JOINED THE FORCE.
SHE COULDN'T STOP CRYING.
CRYING... SAY, THAT'S ANOTHER WEIRD THING.
HUH?
WHAT?

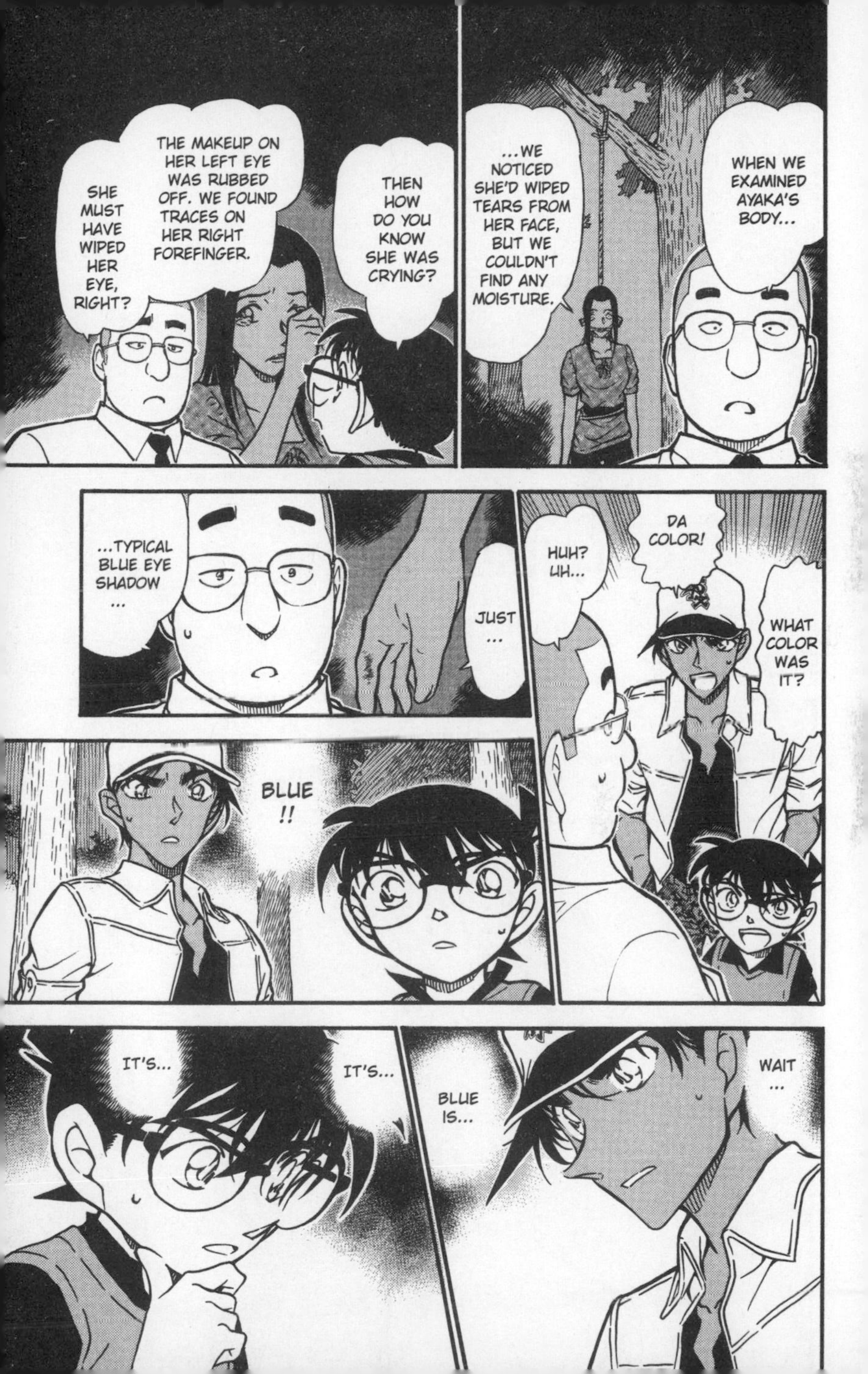
WHEN WE EXAMINED AYAKA'S BODY...
...WE NOTICED SHE'D WIPED TEARS FROM HER FACE, BUT WE COULDN'T FIND ANY MOISTURE.
THEN HOW DO YOU KNOW SHE WAS CRYING?
THE MAKEUP ON HER LEFT EYE WAS RUBBED OFF. WE FOUND TRACES ON HER RIGHT FOREFINGER.
SHE MUST HAVE WIPED HER EYE, RIGHT?
WHAT COLOR WAS IT?
DA COLOR!
HUH? UH...
JUST ...
...TYPICAL BLUE EYE SHADOW ...
BLUE !!
WAIT ...
BLUE IS...
IT'S...
IT'S...

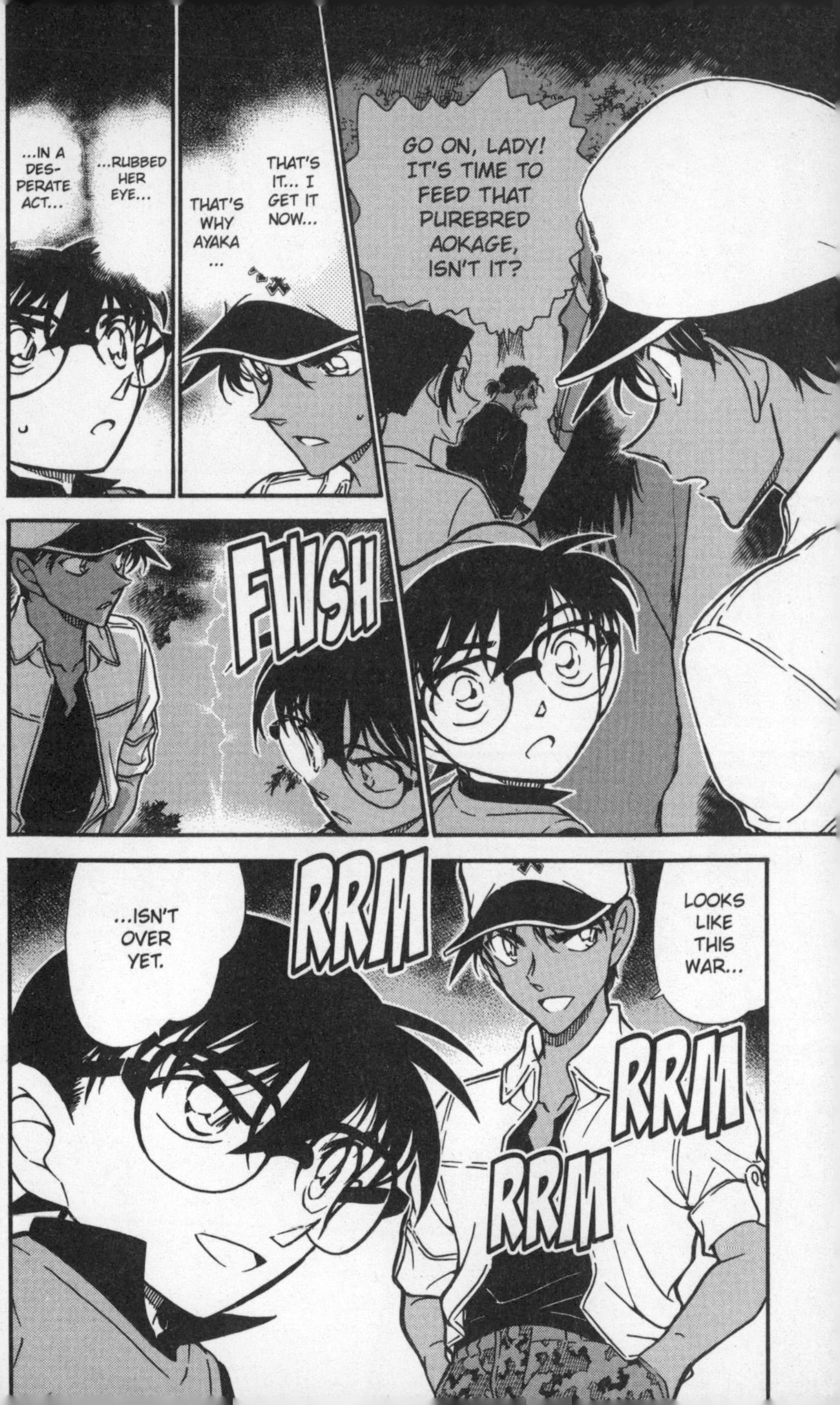
GO ON, LADY! IT'S TIME TO FEED THAT PUREBRED AOKAGE, ISN'T IT?
THAT'S IT... I GET IT NOW...
THAT'S WHY AYAKA ...
...RUBBED HER EYE...
...IN A DES-PERATE ACT...
F.WSH
LOOKS LIKE THIS WAR...
RRM
RRM
RRM
...ISN'T OVER YET.

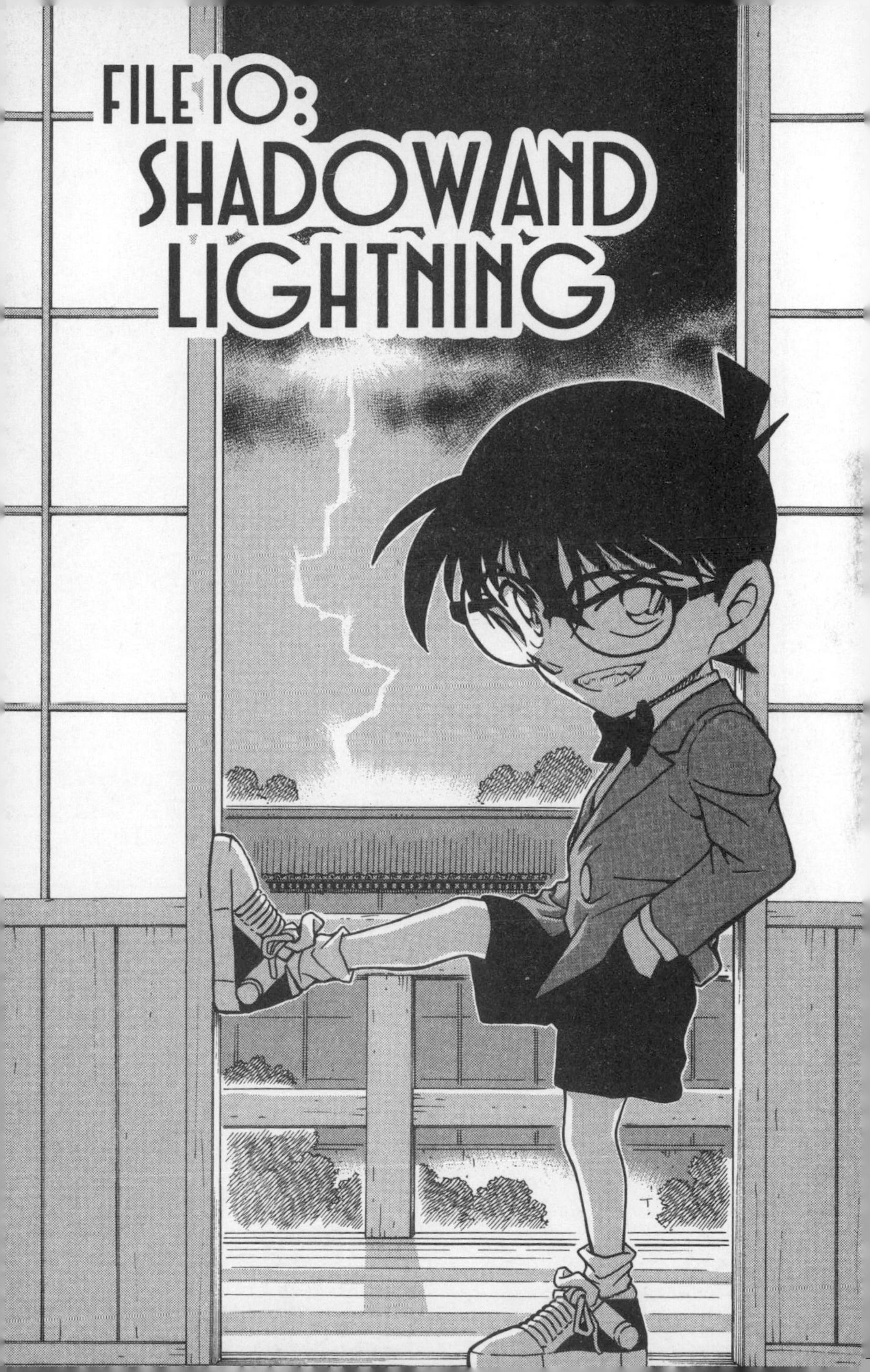
FILE 10:
SHADOW AND LIGHTNING

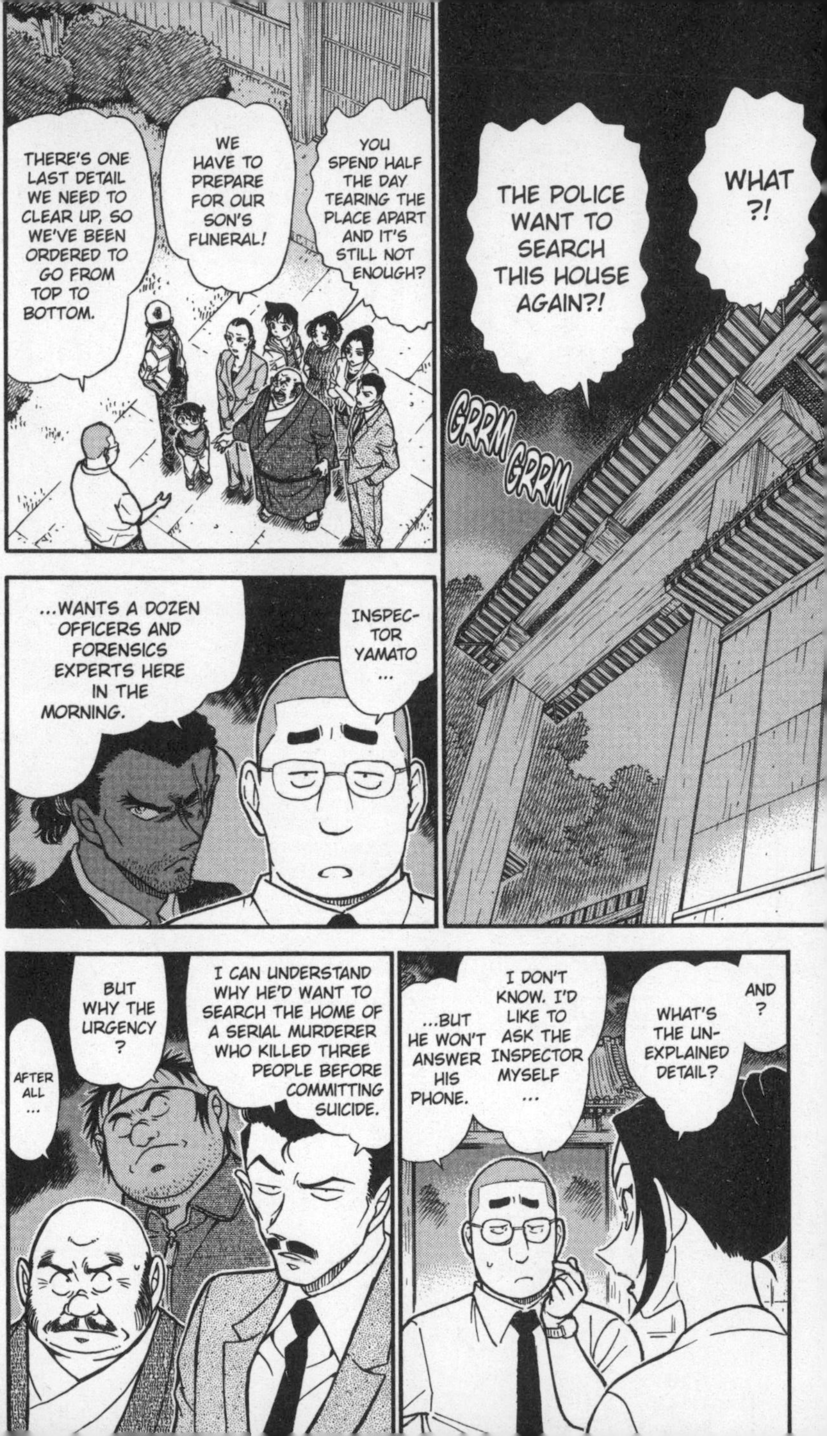
WHAT?!
THE POLICE WANT TO SEARCH THIS HOUSE AGAIN?!
GRRM GRRM
YOU SPEND HALF THE DAY TEARING THE PLACE APART AND IT'S STILL NOT ENOUGH?
WE HAVE TO PREPARE FOR OUR SON'S FUNERAL!
THERE'S ONE LAST DETAIL WE NEED TO CLEAR UP, SO WE'VE BEEN ORDERED TO GO FROM TOP TO BOTTOM.
INSPECTOR YAMATO ...
...WANTS A DOZEN OFFICERS AND FORENSICS EXPERTS HERE IN THE MORNING.
AND ?
WHAT'S THE UNEXPLAINED DETAIL?
I DON'T KNOW. I'D LIKE TO ASK THE INSPECTOR MYSELF ...
...BUT HE WON'T ANSWER HIS PHONE.
I CAN UNDERSTAND WHY HE'D WANT TO SEARCH THE HOME OF A SERIAL MURDERER WHO KILLED THREE PEOPLE BEFORE COMMITTING SUICIDE.
BUT WHY THE URGENCY ?
AFTER ALL ...

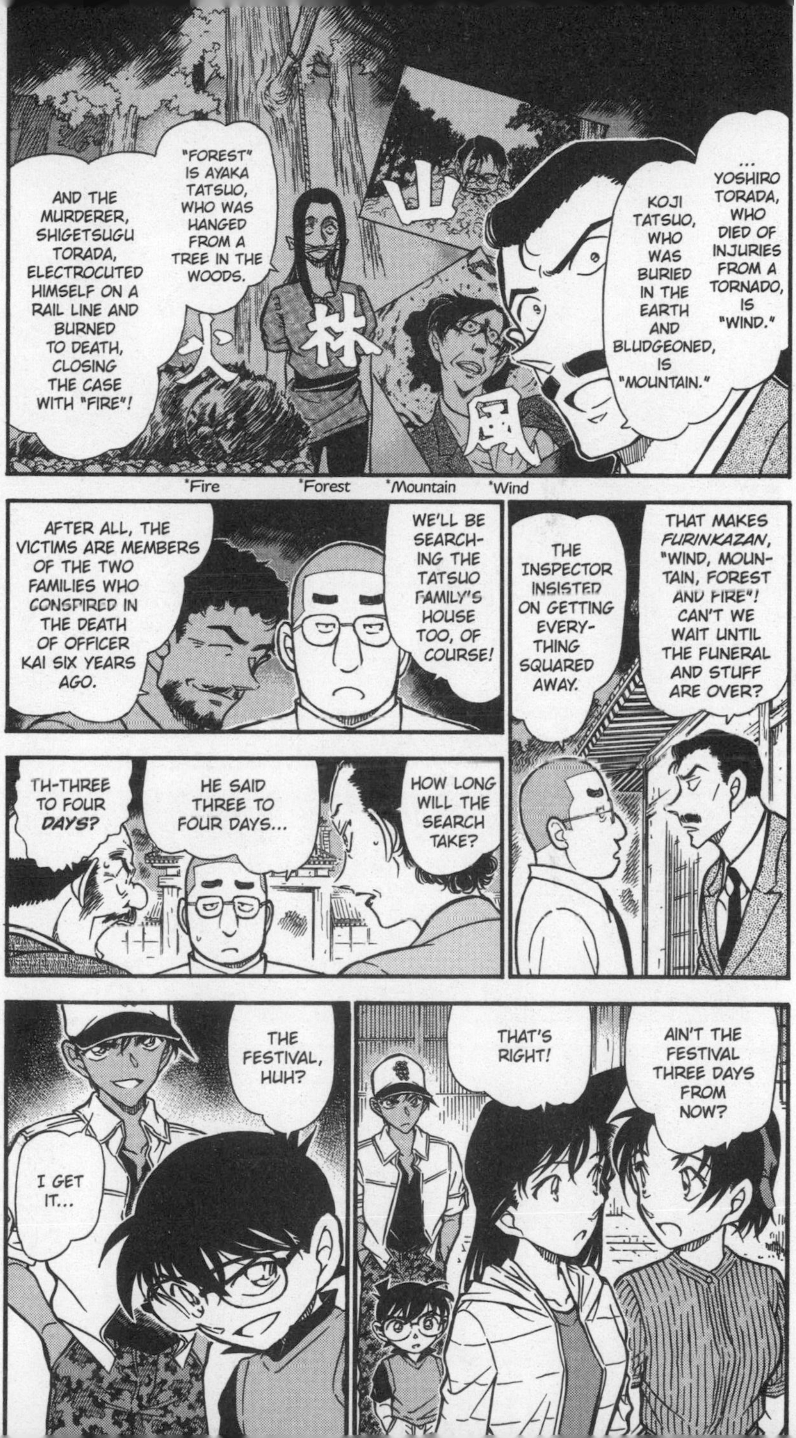
... YOSHIRO TORADA, WHO DIED OF INJURIES FROM A TORNADO, IS "WIND."
KOJI TATSUO, WHO WAS BURIED IN THE EARTH AND BLUDGEONED, IS "MOUNTAIN."
風
山
"FOREST" IS AYAKA TATSUO, WHO WAS HANGED FROM A TREE IN THE WOODS.
林
AND THE MURDERER, SHIGETSUGU TORADA, ELECTROCUTED HIMSELF ON A RAIL LINE AND BURNED TO DEATH, CLOSING THE CASE WITH "FIRE"!
火
*Fire *Forest *Mountain *Wind
THAT MAKES *FURINKAZAN*, "WIND, MOUNTAIN, FOREST AND FIRE"! CAN'T WE WAIT UNTIL THE FUNERAL AND STUFF ARE OVER?
THE INSPECTOR INSISTED ON GETTING EVERYTHING SQUARED AWAY.
WE'LL BE SEARCHING THE TATSUO FAMILY'S HOUSE TOO, OF COURSE!
AFTER ALL, THE VICTIMS ARE MEMBERS OF THE TWO FAMILIES WHO CONSPIRED IN THE DEATH OF OFFICER KAI SIX YEARS AGO.
HOW LONG WILL THE SEARCH TAKE?
HE SAID THREE TO FOUR DAYS...
TH-THREE TO FOUR *DAYS*?
AIN'T THE FESTIVAL THREE DAYS FROM NOW?
THAT'S RIGHT!
THE FESTIVAL, HUH?
I GET IT...

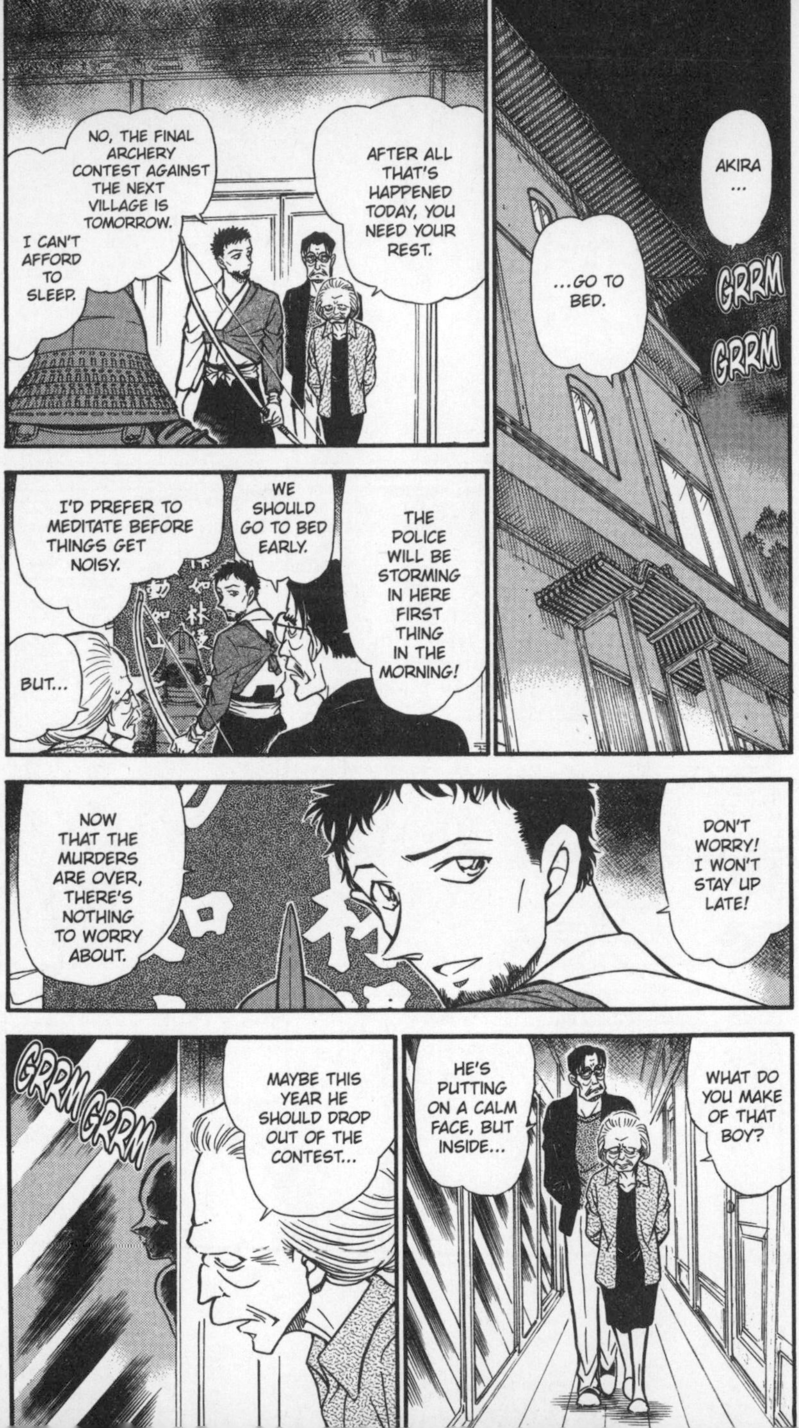
AKIRA ...
...GO TO BED.
GRRM
GRRM
AFTER ALL THAT'S HAPPENED TODAY, YOU NEED YOUR REST.
NO, THE FINAL ARCHERY CONTEST AGAINST THE NEXT VILLAGE IS TOMORROW.
I CAN'T AFFORD TO SLEEP.
THE POLICE WILL BE STORMING IN HERE FIRST THING IN THE MORNING!
WE SHOULD GO TO BED EARLY.
I'D PREFER TO MEDITATE BEFORE THINGS GET NOISY.
BUT...
DON'T WORRY! I WON'T STAY UP LATE!
NOW THAT THE MURDERS ARE OVER, THERE'S NOTHING TO WORRY ABOUT.
WHAT DO YOU MAKE OF THAT BOY?
HE'S PUTTING ON A CALM FACE, BUT INSIDE...
MAYBE THIS YEAR HE SHOULD DROP OUT OF THE CONTEST...
GRRM GRRM

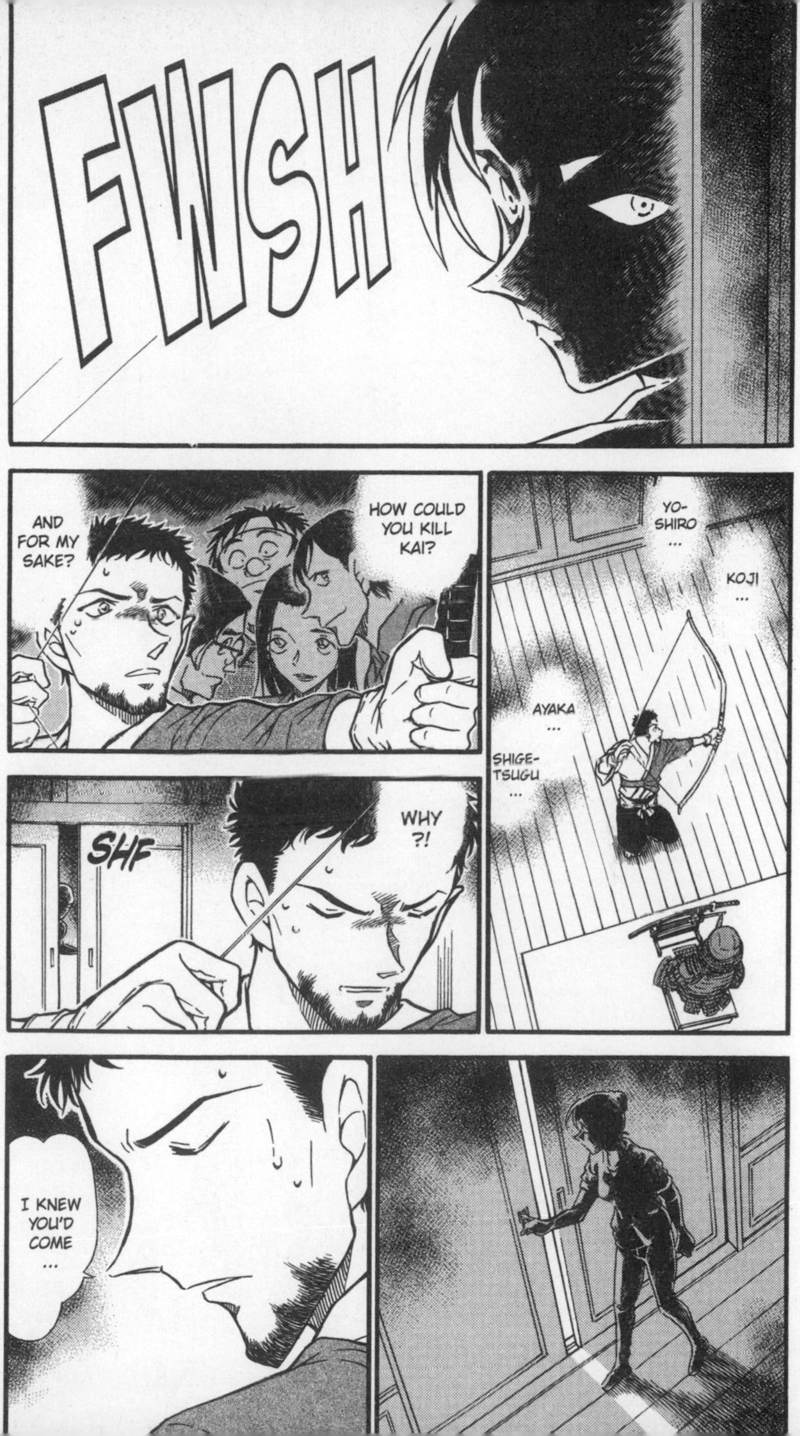
FWSH
YO-SHIRO...
KOJI...
AYAKA...
SHIGE-TSUGU...
HOW COULD YOU KILL KAI?
AND FOR MY SAKE?
WHY?!
SHF
I KNEW YOU'D COME...

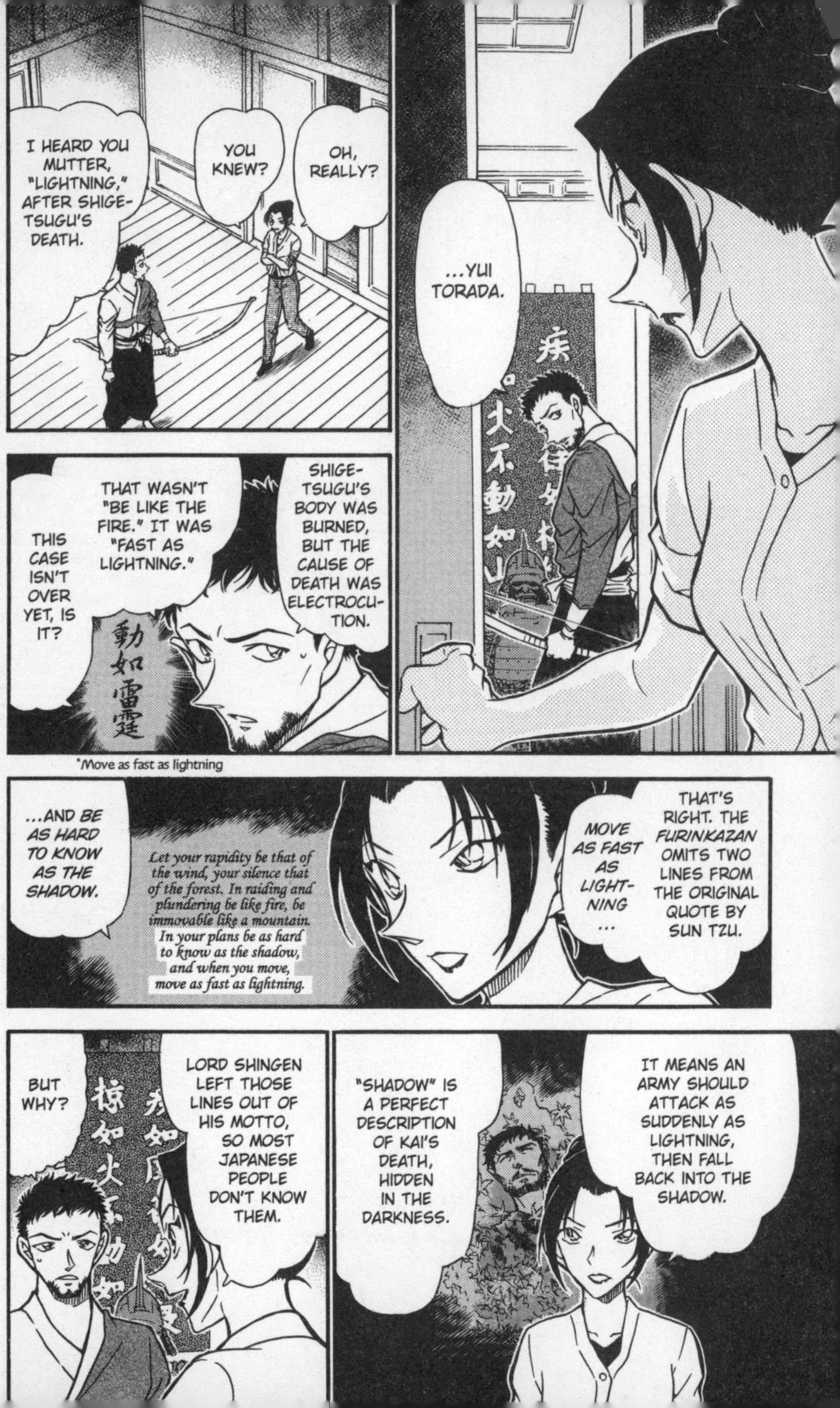
...YUI TORADA.
OH, REALLY?
YOU KNEW?
I HEARD YOU MUTTER, "LIGHTNING," AFTER SHIGE-TSUGU'S DEATH.
SHIGE-TSUGU'S BODY WAS BURNED, BUT THE CAUSE OF DEATH WAS ELECTROCU-TION.
THAT WASN'T "BE LIKE THE FIRE." IT WAS "FAST AS LIGHTNING."
THIS CASE ISN'T OVER YET, IS IT?
動如雷霆
THAT'S RIGHT. THE *FURINKAZAN* OMITS TWO LINES FROM THE ORIGINAL QUOTE BY SUN TZU.
MOVE AS FAST AS LIGHTNING...
Let your rapidity be that of the wind, your silence that of the forest. In raiding and plundering be like fire, be immovable like a mountain. In your plans be as hard to know as the shadow, and when you move, move as fast as lightning.
...AND *BE AS HARD TO KNOW AS THE SHADOW.*
IT MEANS AN ARMY SHOULD ATTACK AS SUDDENLY AS LIGHTNING, THEN FALL BACK INTO THE SHADOW.
"SHADOW" IS A PERFECT DESCRIPTION OF KAI'S DEATH, HIDDEN IN THE DARKNESS.
LORD SHINGEN LEFT THOSE LINES OUT OF HIS MOTTO, SO MOST JAPANESE PEOPLE DON'T KNOW THEM.
BUT WHY?
*Move as fast as lightning

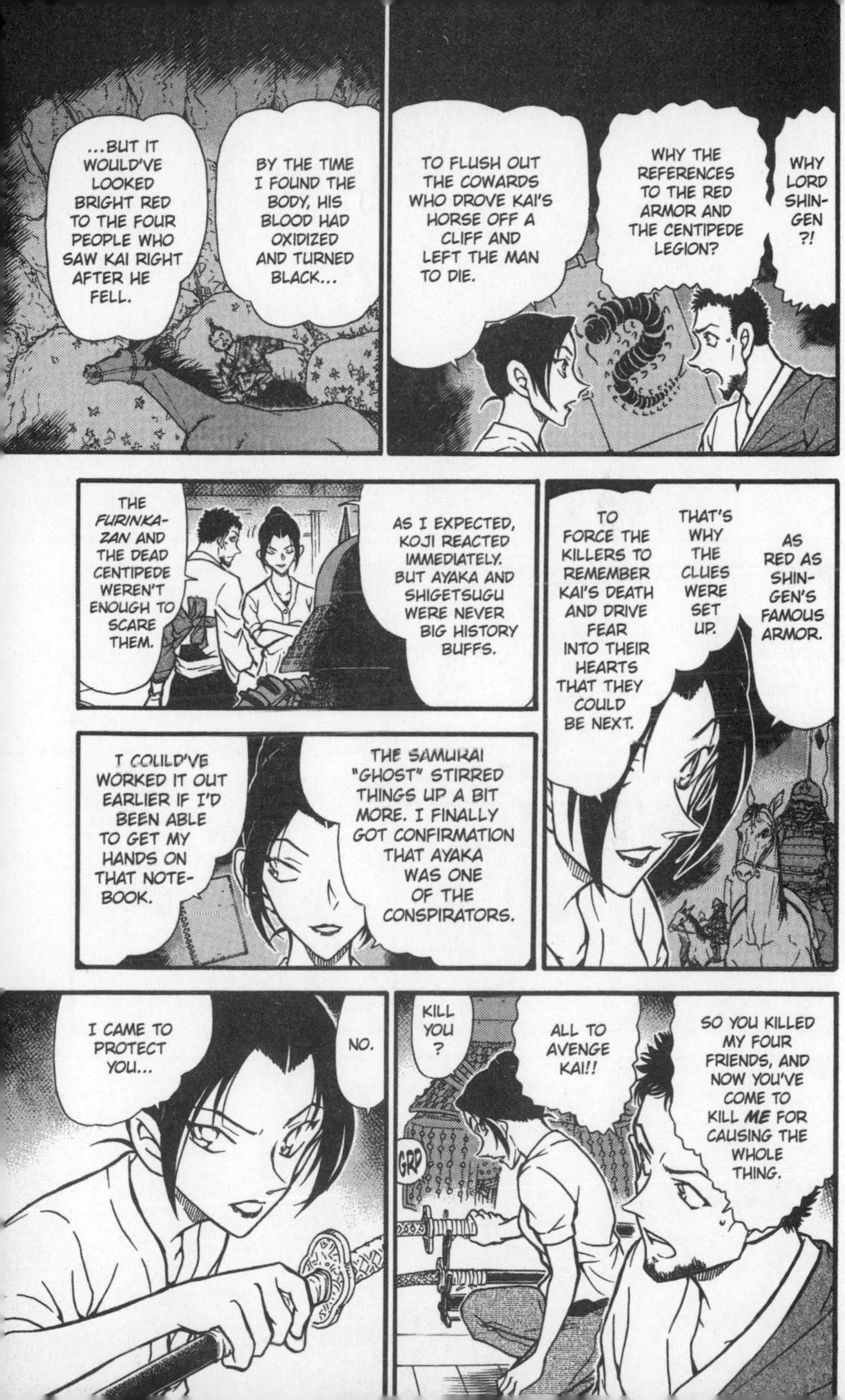
WHY LORD SHIN-GEN?!
WHY THE REFERENCES TO THE RED ARMOR AND THE CENTIPEDE LEGION?
TO FLUSH OUT THE COWARDS WHO DROVE KAI'S HORSE OFF A CLIFF AND LEFT THE MAN TO DIE.
BY THE TIME I FOUND THE BODY, HIS BLOOD HAD OXIDIZED AND TURNED BLACK...
...BUT IT WOULD'VE LOOKED BRIGHT RED TO THE FOUR PEOPLE WHO SAW KAI RIGHT AFTER HE FELL.
AS RED AS SHIN-GEN'S FAMOUS ARMOR.
THAT'S WHY THE CLUES WERE SET UP.
TO FORCE THE KILLERS TO REMEMBER KAI'S DEATH AND DRIVE FEAR INTO THEIR HEARTS THAT THEY COULD BE NEXT.
AS I EXPECTED, KOJI REACTED IMMEDIATELY. BUT AYAKA AND SHIGETSUGU WERE NEVER BIG HISTORY BUFFS.
THE *FURINKA-ZAN* AND THE DEAD CENTIPEDE WEREN'T ENOUGH TO SCARE THEM.
THE SAMURAI "GHOST" STIRRED THINGS UP A BIT MORE. I FINALLY GOT CONFIRMATION THAT AYAKA WAS ONE OF THE CONSPIRATORS.
I COULD'VE WORKED IT OUT EARLIER IF I'D BEEN ABLE TO GET MY HANDS ON THAT NOTE-BOOK.
SO YOU KILLED MY FOUR FRIENDS, AND NOW YOU'VE COME TO KILL *ME* FOR CAUSING THE WHOLE THING.
ALL TO AVENGE KAI!!
KILL YOU?
GRP
NO.
I CAME TO PROTECT YOU...

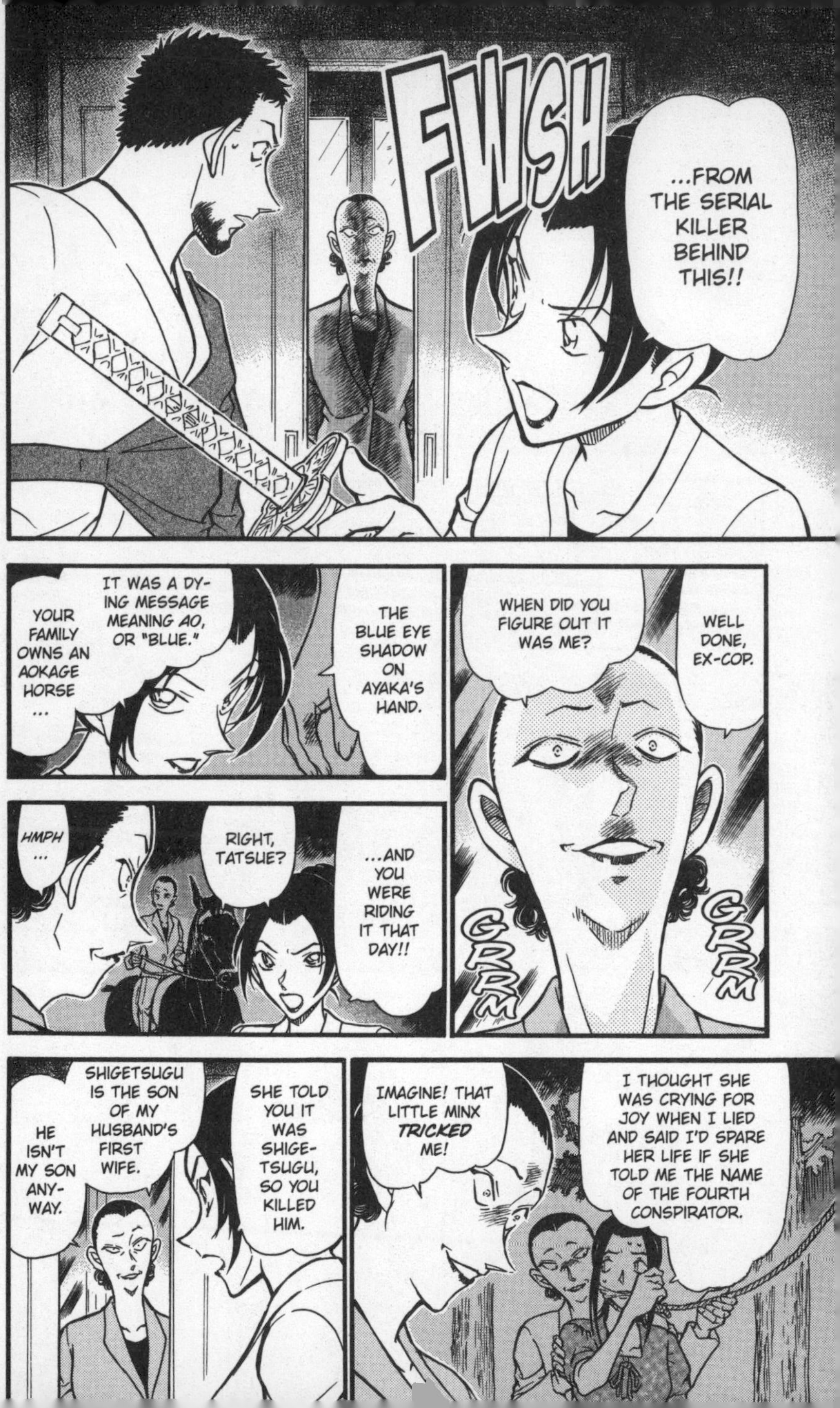
FWSH
...FROM THE SERIAL KILLER BEHIND THIS!!
WELL DONE, EX-COP.
WHEN DID YOU FIGURE OUT IT WAS ME?
GRRM
GRRM
THE BLUE EYE SHADOW ON AYAKA'S HAND.
IT WAS A DYING MESSAGE MEANING *AO*, OR "BLUE."
YOUR FAMILY OWNS AN AOKAGE HORSE ...
...AND YOU WERE RIDING IT THAT DAY!!
RIGHT, TATSUE?
HMPH ...
I THOUGHT SHE WAS CRYING FOR JOY WHEN I LIED AND SAID I'D SPARE HER LIFE IF SHE TOLD ME THE NAME OF THE FOURTH CONSPIRATOR.
IMAGINE! THAT LITTLE MINX ***TRICKED*** ME!
SHE TOLD YOU IT WAS SHIGE-TSUGU, SO YOU KILLED HIM.
SHIGETSUGU IS THE SON OF MY HUSBAND'S FIRST WIFE.
HE ISN'T MY SON ANY-WAY.

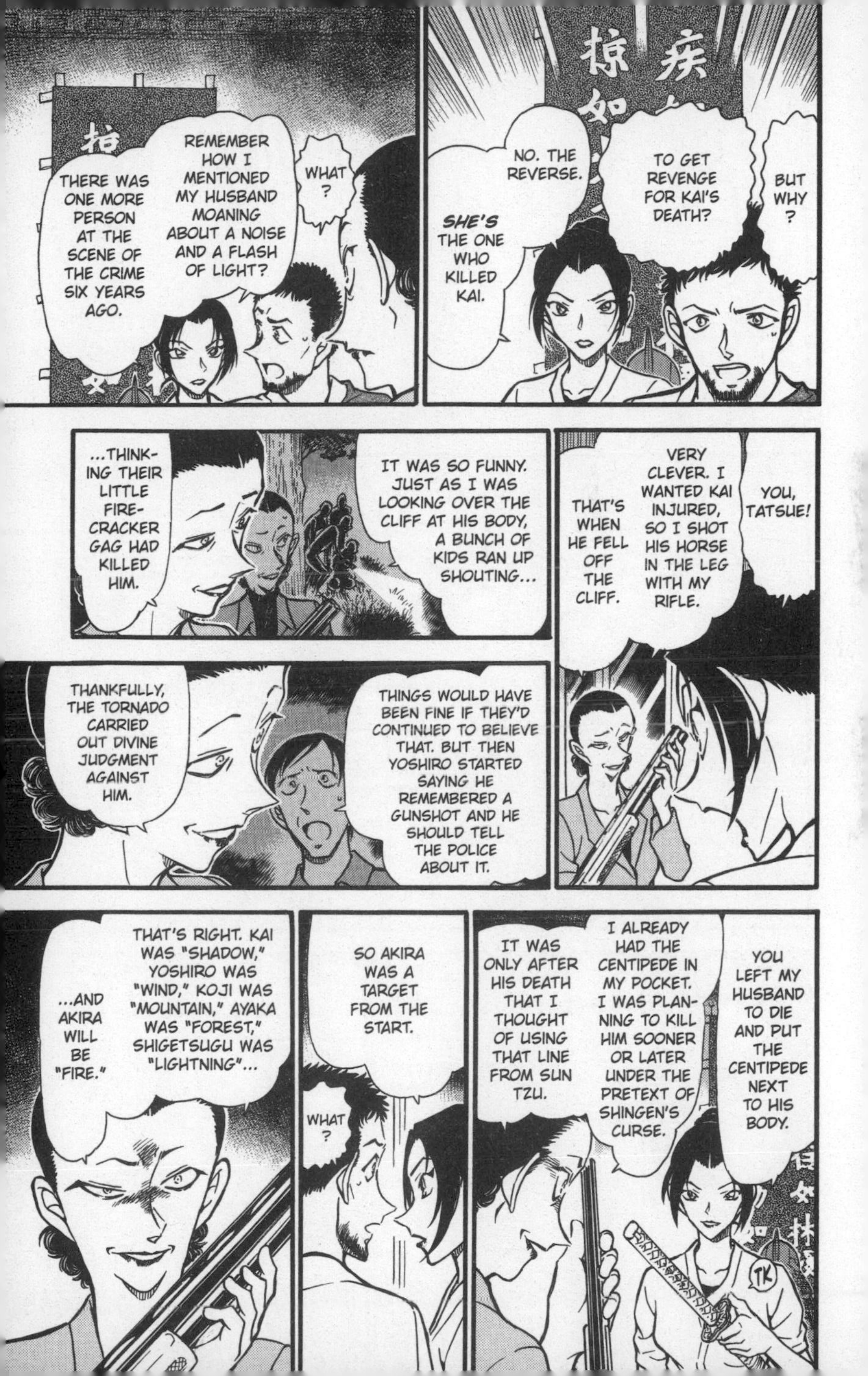
BUT WHY?
TO GET REVENGE FOR KAI'S DEATH?
NO. THE REVERSE.
SHE'S THE ONE WHO KILLED KAI.
WHAT?
REMEMBER HOW I MENTIONED MY HUSBAND MOANING ABOUT A NOISE AND A FLASH OF LIGHT?
THERE WAS ONE MORE PERSON AT THE SCENE OF THE CRIME SIX YEARS AGO.
YOU, TATSUE!
VERY CLEVER. I WANTED KAI INJURED, SO I SHOT HIS HORSE IN THE LEG WITH MY RIFLE.
THAT'S WHEN HE FELL OFF THE CLIFF.
IT WAS SO FUNNY. JUST AS I WAS LOOKING OVER THE CLIFF AT HIS BODY, A BUNCH OF KIDS RAN UP SHOUTING...
...THINKING THEIR LITTLE FIRE-CRACKER GAG HAD KILLED HIM.
THINGS WOULD HAVE BEEN FINE IF THEY'D CONTINUED TO BELIEVE THAT. BUT THEN YOSHIRO STARTED SAYING HE REMEMBERED A GUNSHOT AND HE SHOULD TELL THE POLICE ABOUT IT.
THANKFULLY, THE TORNADO CARRIED OUT DIVINE JUDGMENT AGAINST HIM.
YOU LEFT MY HUSBAND TO DIE AND PUT THE CENTIPEDE NEXT TO HIS BODY.
I ALREADY HAD THE CENTIPEDE IN MY POCKET. I WAS PLAN-NING TO KILL HIM SOONER OR LATER UNDER THE PRETEXT OF SHINGEN'S CURSE.
IT WAS ONLY AFTER HIS DEATH THAT I THOUGHT OF USING THAT LINE FROM SUN TZU.
TK
SO AKIRA WAS A TARGET FROM THE START.
WHAT?
THAT'S RIGHT. KAI WAS "SHADOW," YOSHIRO WAS "WIND," KOJI WAS "MOUNTAIN," AYAKA WAS "FOREST," SHIGETSUGU WAS "LIGHTNING"...
...AND AKIRA WILL BE "FIRE."

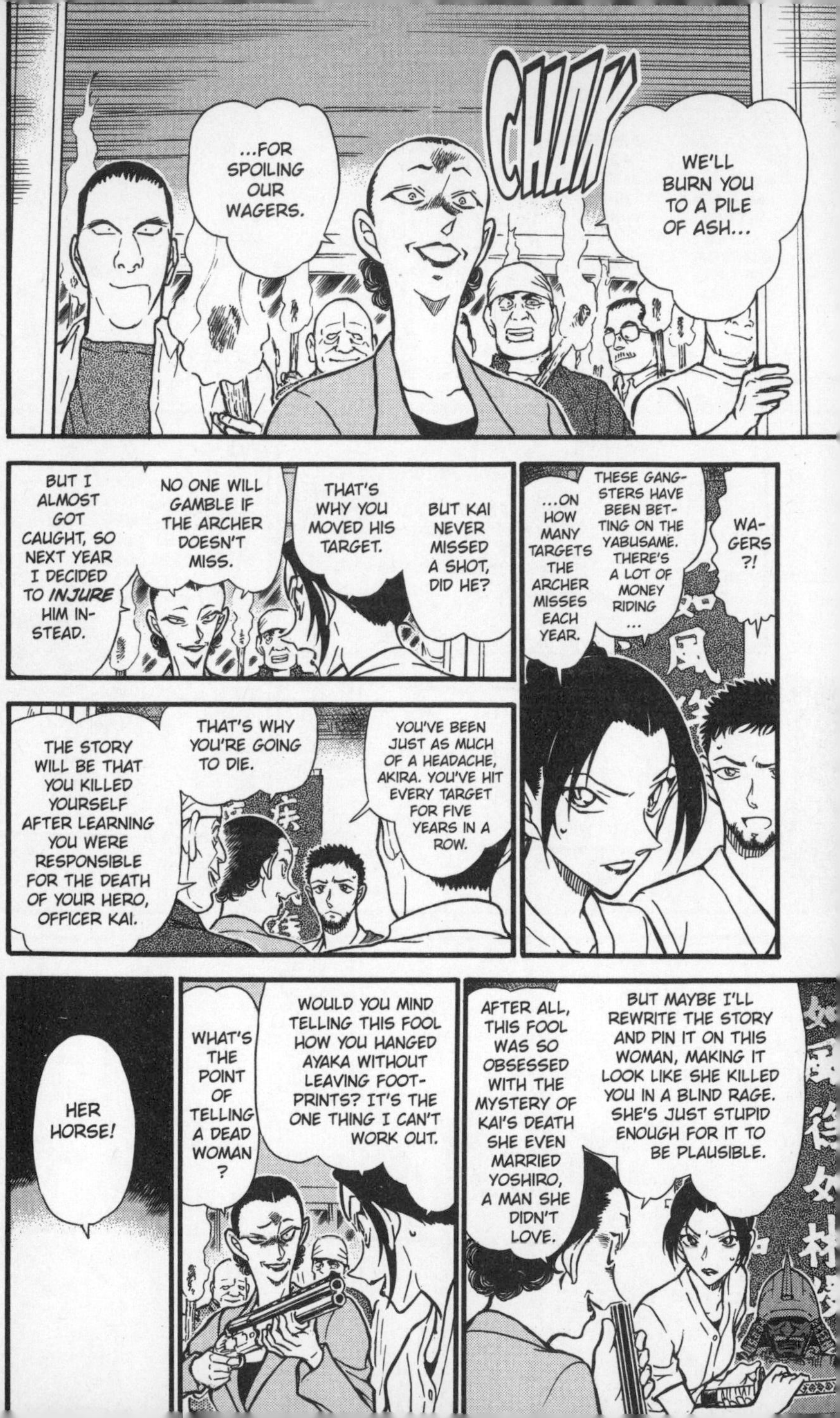
CHAK
WE'LL BURN YOU TO A PILE OF ASH...
...FOR SPOILING OUR WAGERS.
WAGERS?!
THESE GANGSTERS HAVE BEEN BETTING ON THE YABUSAME. THERE'S A LOT OF MONEY RIDING...
...ON HOW MANY TARGETS THE ARCHER MISSES EACH YEAR.
BUT KAI NEVER MISSED A SHOT, DID HE?
THAT'S WHY YOU MOVED HIS TARGET.
NO ONE WILL GAMBLE IF THE ARCHER DOESN'T MISS.
BUT I ALMOST GOT CAUGHT, SO NEXT YEAR I DECIDED TO *INJURE* HIM INSTEAD.
YOU'VE BEEN JUST AS MUCH OF A HEADACHE, AKIRA. YOU'VE HIT EVERY TARGET FOR FIVE YEARS IN A ROW.
THAT'S WHY YOU'RE GOING TO DIE.
THE STORY WILL BE THAT YOU KILLED YOURSELF AFTER LEARNING YOU WERE RESPONSIBLE FOR THE DEATH OF YOUR HERO, OFFICER KAI.
BUT MAYBE I'LL REWRITE THE STORY AND PIN IT ON THIS WOMAN, MAKING IT LOOK LIKE SHE KILLED YOU IN A BLIND RAGE. SHE'S JUST STUPID ENOUGH FOR IT TO BE PLAUSIBLE.
AFTER ALL, THIS FOOL WAS SO OBSESSED WITH THE MYSTERY OF KAI'S DEATH SHE EVEN MARRIED YOSHIRO, A MAN SHE DIDN'T LOVE.
WOULD YOU MIND TELLING THIS FOOL HOW YOU HANGED AYAKA WITHOUT LEAVING FOOT-PRINTS? IT'S THE ONE THING I CAN'T WORK OUT.
WHAT'S THE POINT OF TELLING A DEAD WOMAN?
HER HORSE!

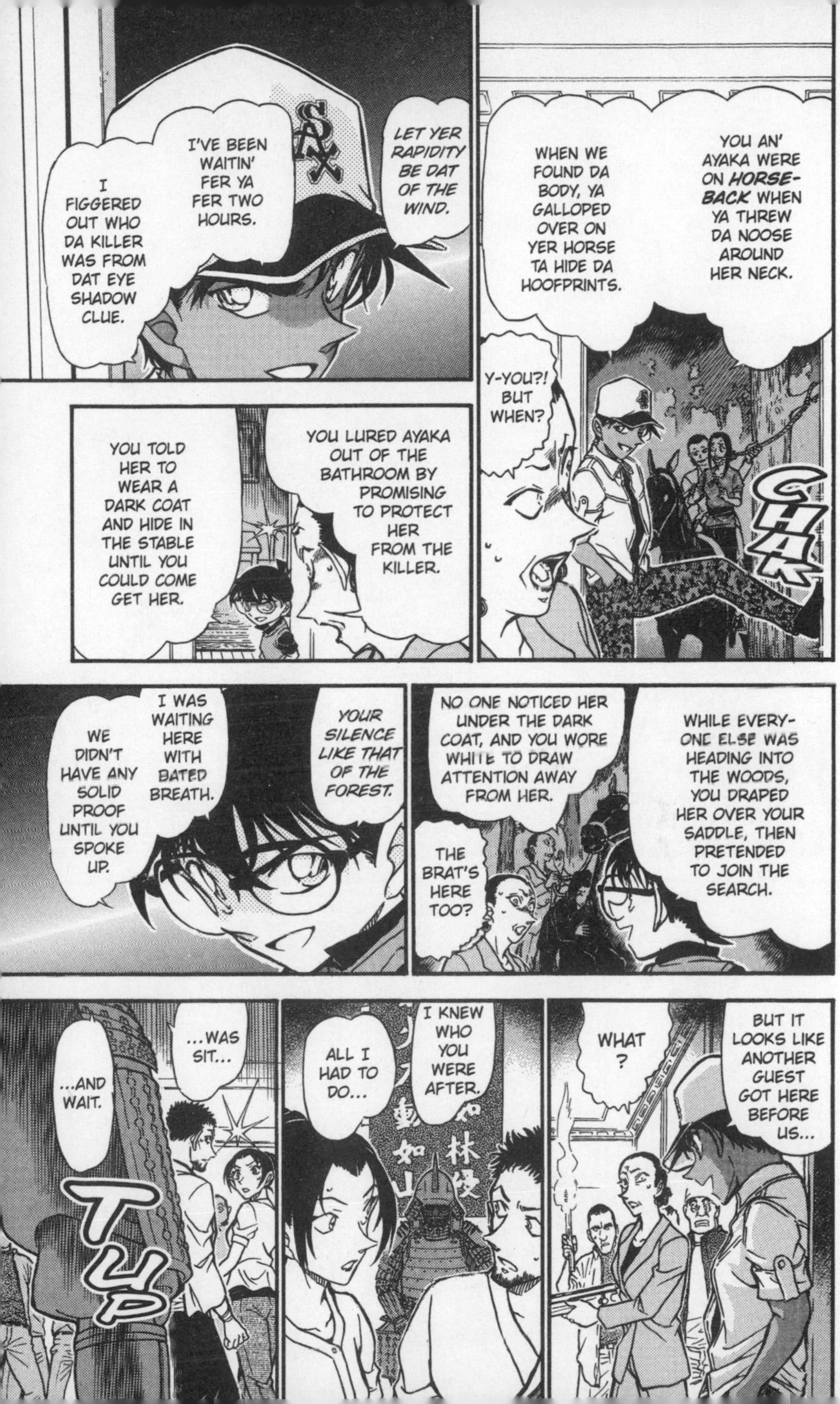
YOU AN' AYAKA WERE ON ***HORSE-BACK*** WHEN YA THREW DA NOOSE AROUND HER NECK.
WHEN WE FOUND DA BODY, YA GALLOPED OVER ON YER HORSE TA HIDE DA HOOFPRINTS.
Y-YOU?! BUT WHEN?
CHAK
LET YER RAPIDITY BE DAT OF THE WIND.
I'VE BEEN WAITIN' FER YA FER TWO HOURS.
I FIGGERED OUT WHO DA KILLER WAS FROM DAT EYE SHADOW CLUE.
YOU LURED AYAKA OUT OF THE BATHROOM BY PROMISING TO PROTECT HER FROM THE KILLER.
YOU TOLD HER TO WEAR A DARK COAT AND HIDE IN THE STABLE UNTIL YOU COULD COME GET HER.
WHILE EVERY-ONE ELSE WAS HEADING INTO THE WOODS, YOU DRAPED HER OVER YOUR SADDLE, THEN PRETENDED TO JOIN THE SEARCH.
NO ONE NOTICED HER UNDER THE DARK COAT, AND YOU WORE WHITE TO DRAW ATTENTION AWAY FROM HER.
THE BRAT'S HERE TOO?
YOUR SILENCE LIKE THAT OF THE FOREST.
I WAS WAITING HERE WITH BATED BREATH.
WE DIDN'T HAVE ANY SOLID PROOF UNTIL YOU SPOKE UP.
BUT IT LOOKS LIKE ANOTHER GUEST GOT HERE BEFORE US...
WHAT?
I KNEW WHO YOU WERE AFTER.
ALL I HAD TO DO...
...WAS SIT...
...AND WAIT.
TUP

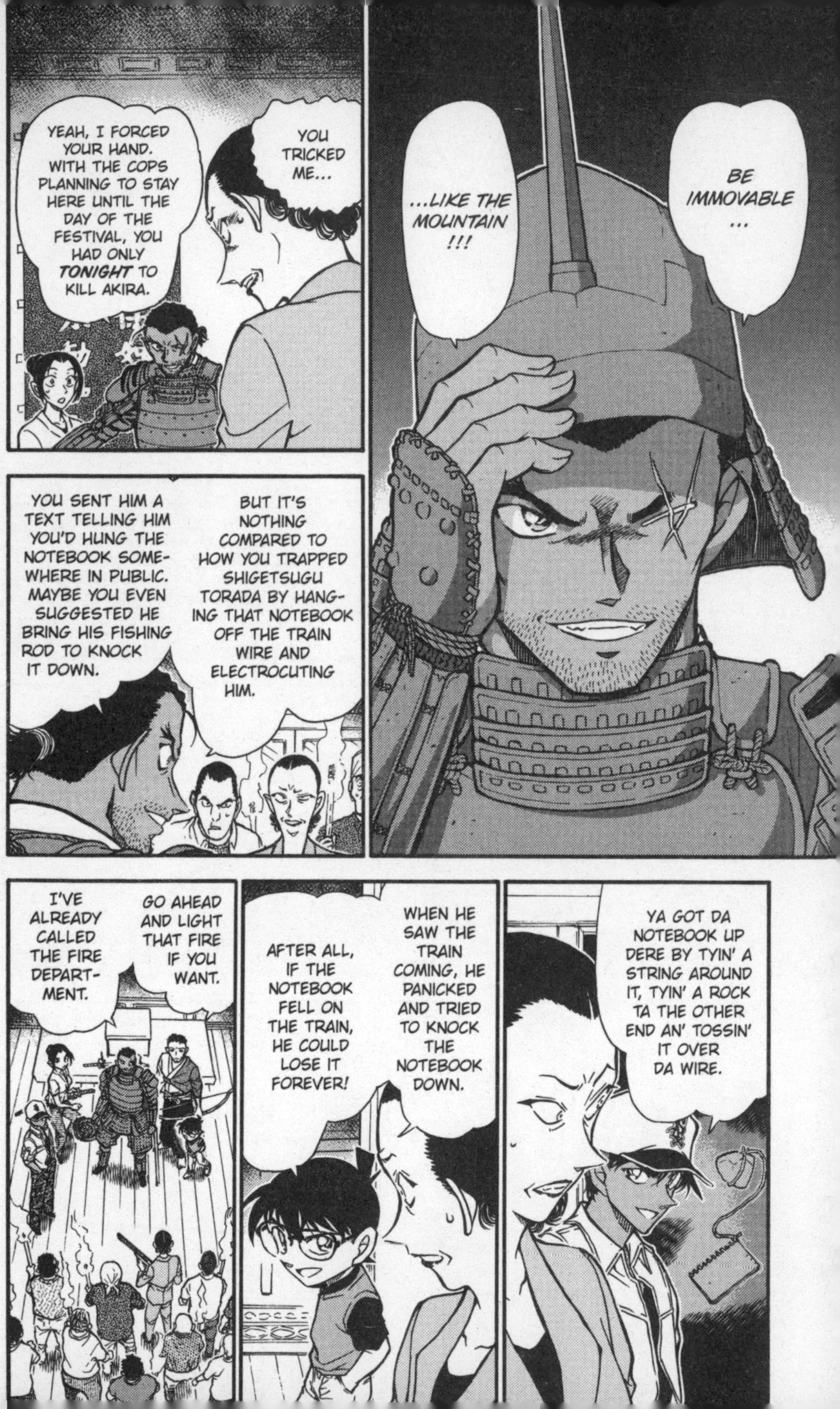
BE IMMOVABLE ...
...LIKE THE MOUNTAIN !!!
YOU TRICKED ME...
YEAH, I FORCED YOUR HAND. WITH THE COPS PLANNING TO STAY HERE UNTIL THE DAY OF THE FESTIVAL, YOU HAD ONLY *TONIGHT* TO KILL AKIRA.
YOU SENT HIM A TEXT TELLING HIM YOU'D HUNG THE NOTEBOOK SOME-WHERE IN PUBLIC. MAYBE YOU EVEN SUGGESTED HE BRING HIS FISHING ROD TO KNOCK IT DOWN.
BUT IT'S NOTHING COMPARED TO HOW YOU TRAPPED SHIGETSUGU TORADA BY HANG-ING THAT NOTEBOOK OFF THE TRAIN WIRE AND ELECTROCUTING HIM.
YA GOT DA NOTEBOOK UP DERE BY TYIN' A STRING AROUND IT, TYIN' A ROCK TA THE OTHER END AN' TOSSIN' IT OVER DA WIRE.
WHEN HE SAW THE TRAIN COMING, HE PANICKED AND TRIED TO KNOCK THE NOTEBOOK DOWN.
AFTER ALL, IF THE NOTEBOOK FELL ON THE TRAIN, HE COULD LOSE IT FOREVER!
GO AHEAD AND LIGHT THAT FIRE IF YOU WANT.
I'VE ALREADY CALLED THE FIRE DEPART-MENT.

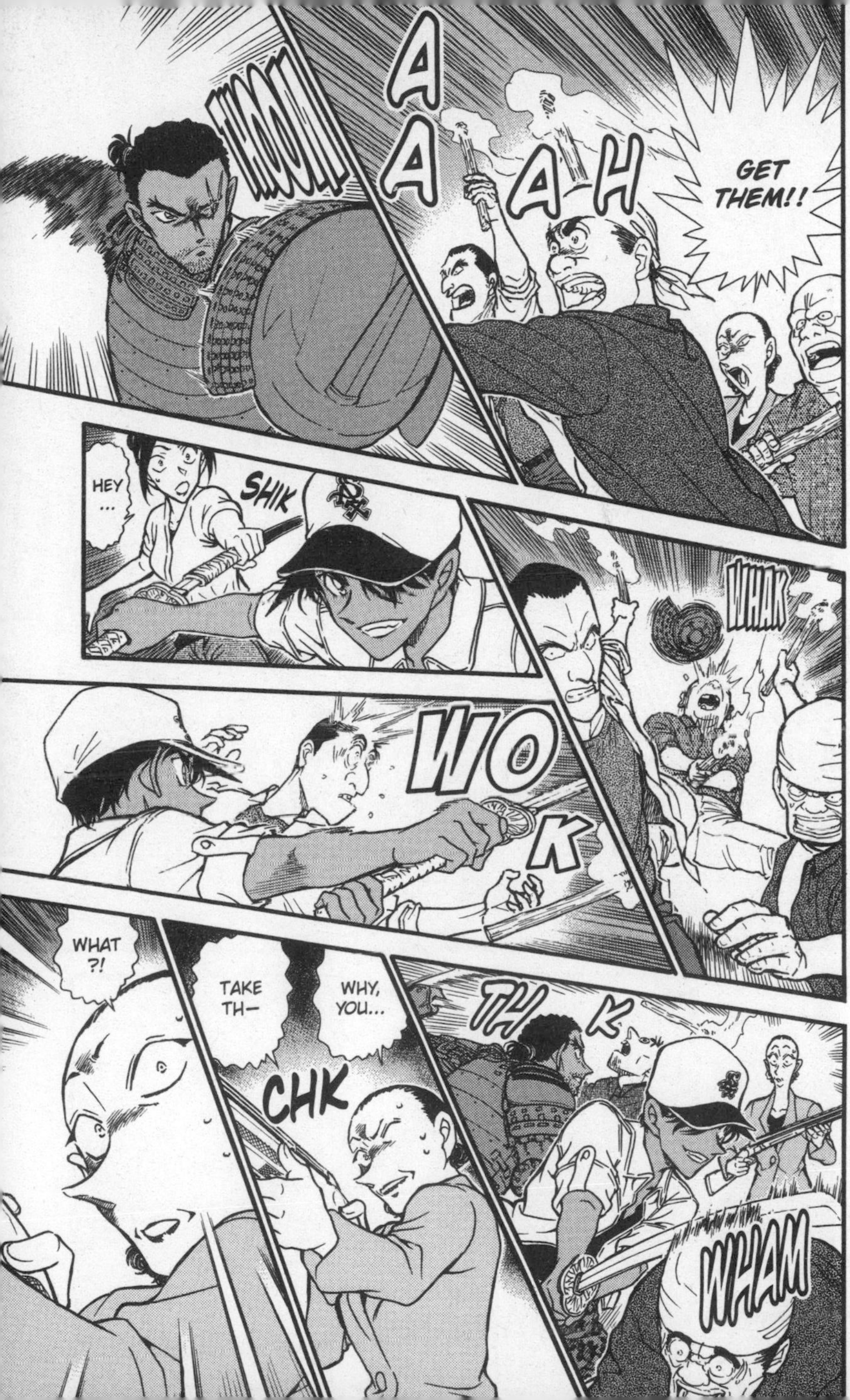
GET THEM!!
AAAH
THOOM
WHAK
HEY ...
SHIK
WOK
TH K
WHAM
WHY, YOU...
TAKE TH—
CHK
WHAT ?!

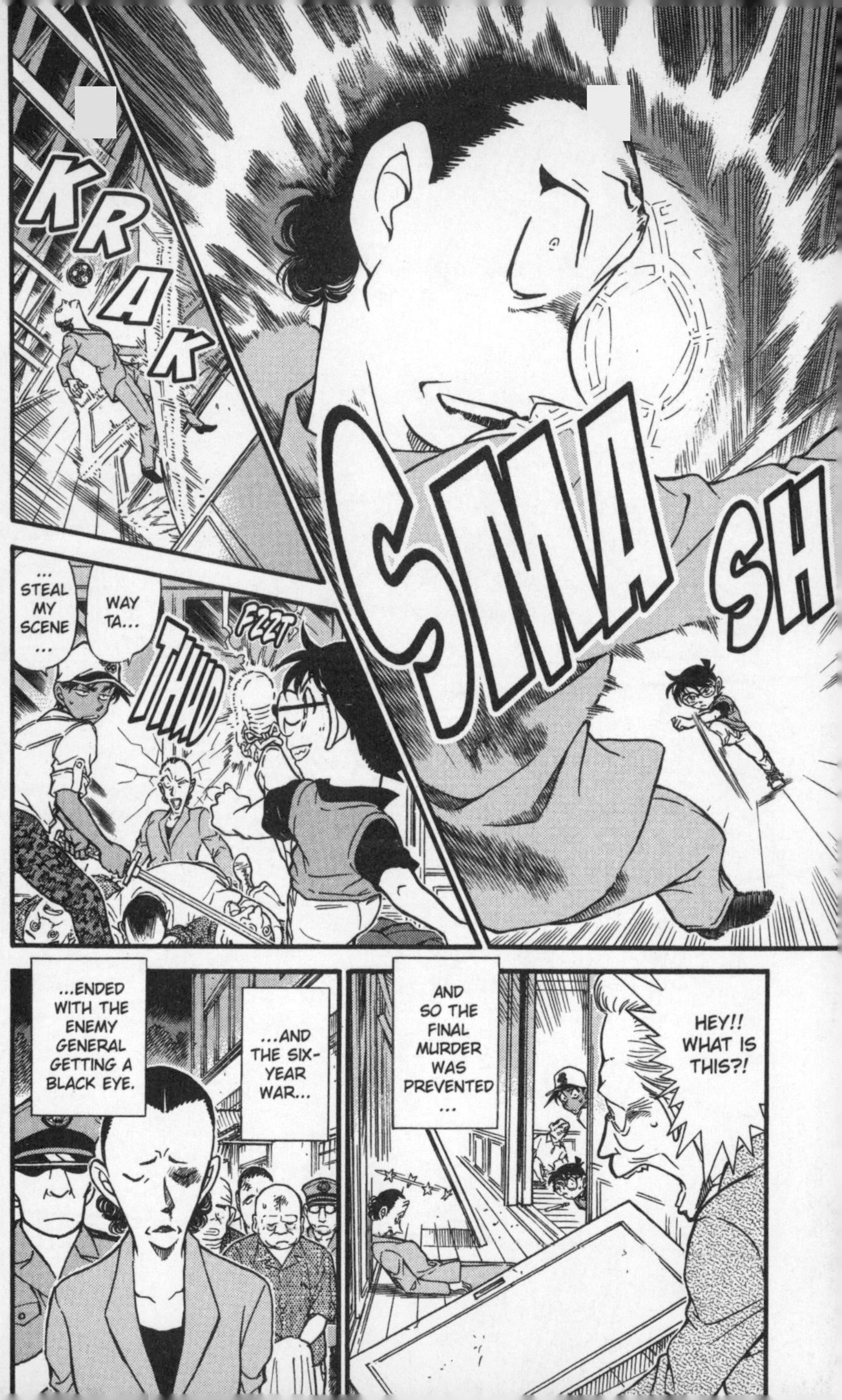
SMASH
KRAK
WAY TA...
...STEAL MY SCENE...
THUD
FZZT
AND SO THE FINAL MURDER WAS PREVENTED...
HEY!! WHAT IS THIS?!
...AND THE SIX-YEAR WAR...
...ENDED WITH THE ENEMY GENERAL GETTING A BLACK EYE.

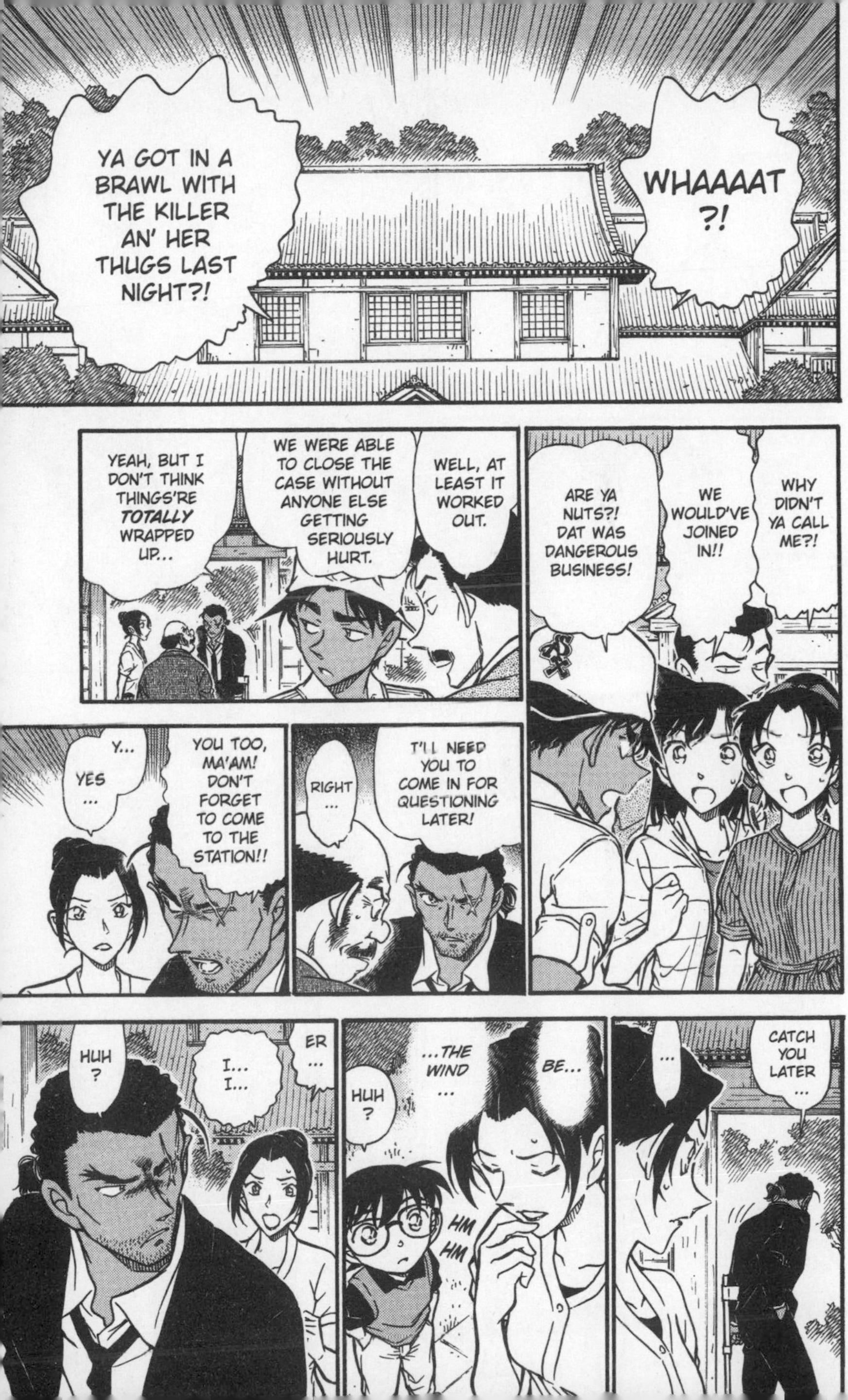
WHAAAAT ?!
YA GOT IN A BRAWL WITH THE KILLER AN' HER THUGS LAST NIGHT?!
WHY DIDN'T YA CALL ME?!
WE WOULD'VE JOINED IN!!
ARE YA NUTS?! DAT WAS DANGEROUS BUSINESS!
WELL, AT LEAST IT WORKED OUT.
WE WERE ABLE TO CLOSE THE CASE WITHOUT ANYONE ELSE GETTING SERIOUSLY HURT.
YEAH, BUT I DON'T THINK THINGS'RE *TOTALLY* WRAPPED UP...
I'LL NEED YOU TO COME IN FOR QUESTIONING LATER!
RIGHT ...
YOU TOO, MA'AM! DON'T FORGET TO COME TO THE STATION!!
Y... YES ...
CATCH YOU LATER ...
...
BE...
...THE WIND ...
HUH ?
HM HM
ER ...
I... I...
HUH ?

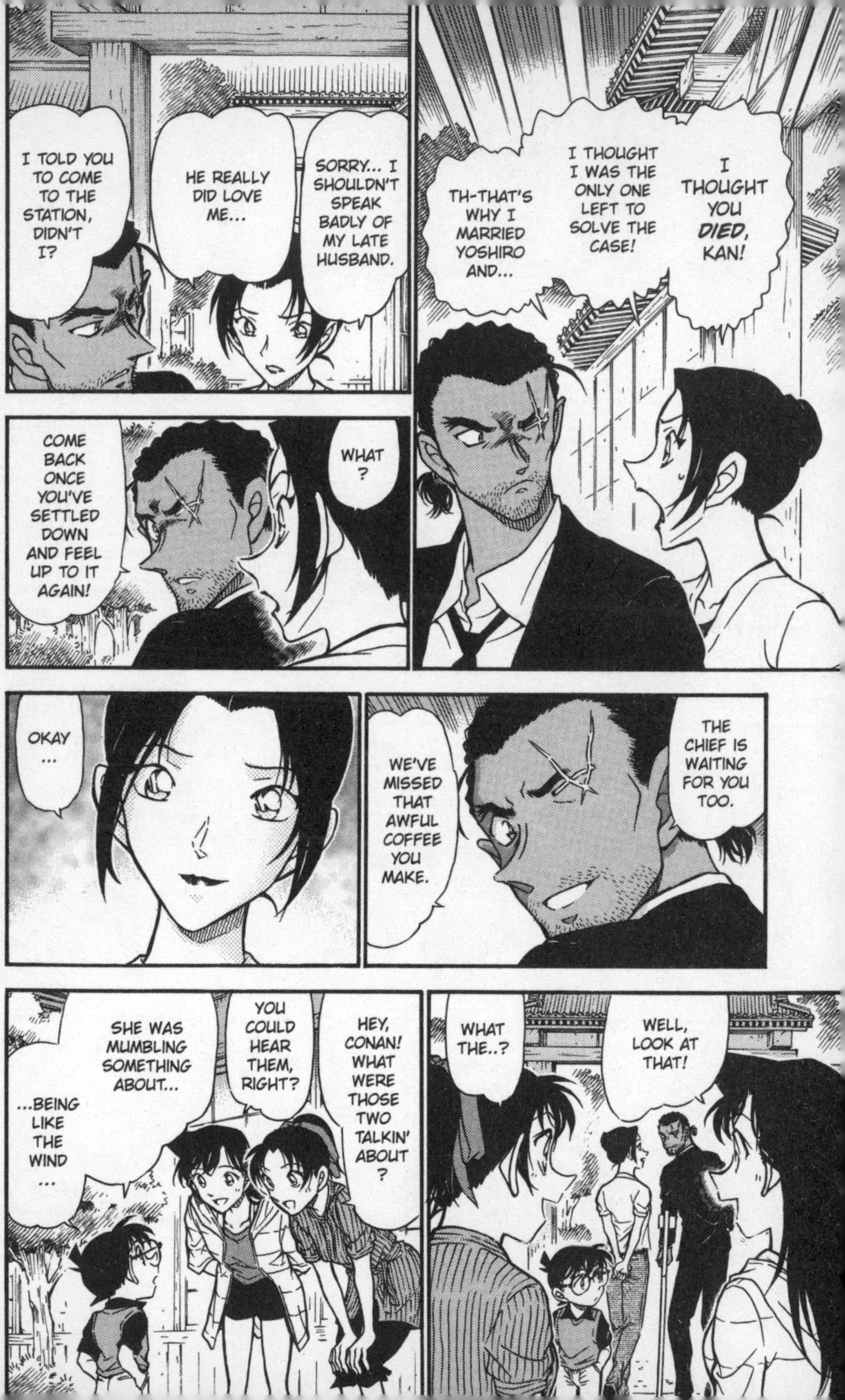
I THOUGHT YOU *DIED*, KAN!
I THOUGHT I WAS THE ONLY ONE LEFT TO SOLVE THE CASE!
TH-THAT'S WHY I MARRIED YOSHIRO AND...
SORRY... I SHOULDN'T SPEAK BADLY OF MY LATE HUSBAND.
HE REALLY DID LOVE ME...
I TOLD YOU TO COME TO THE STATION, DIDN'T I?
WHAT?
COME BACK ONCE YOU'VE SETTLED DOWN AND FEEL UP TO IT AGAIN!
THE CHIEF IS WAITING FOR YOU TOO.
WE'VE MISSED THAT AWFUL COFFEE YOU MAKE.
OKAY...
WELL, LOOK AT THAT!
WHAT THE..?
HEY, CONAN! WHAT WERE THOSE TWO TALKIN' ABOUT?
YOU COULD HEAR THEM, RIGHT?
SHE WAS MUMBLING SOMETHING ABOUT...
...BEING LIKE THE WIND...

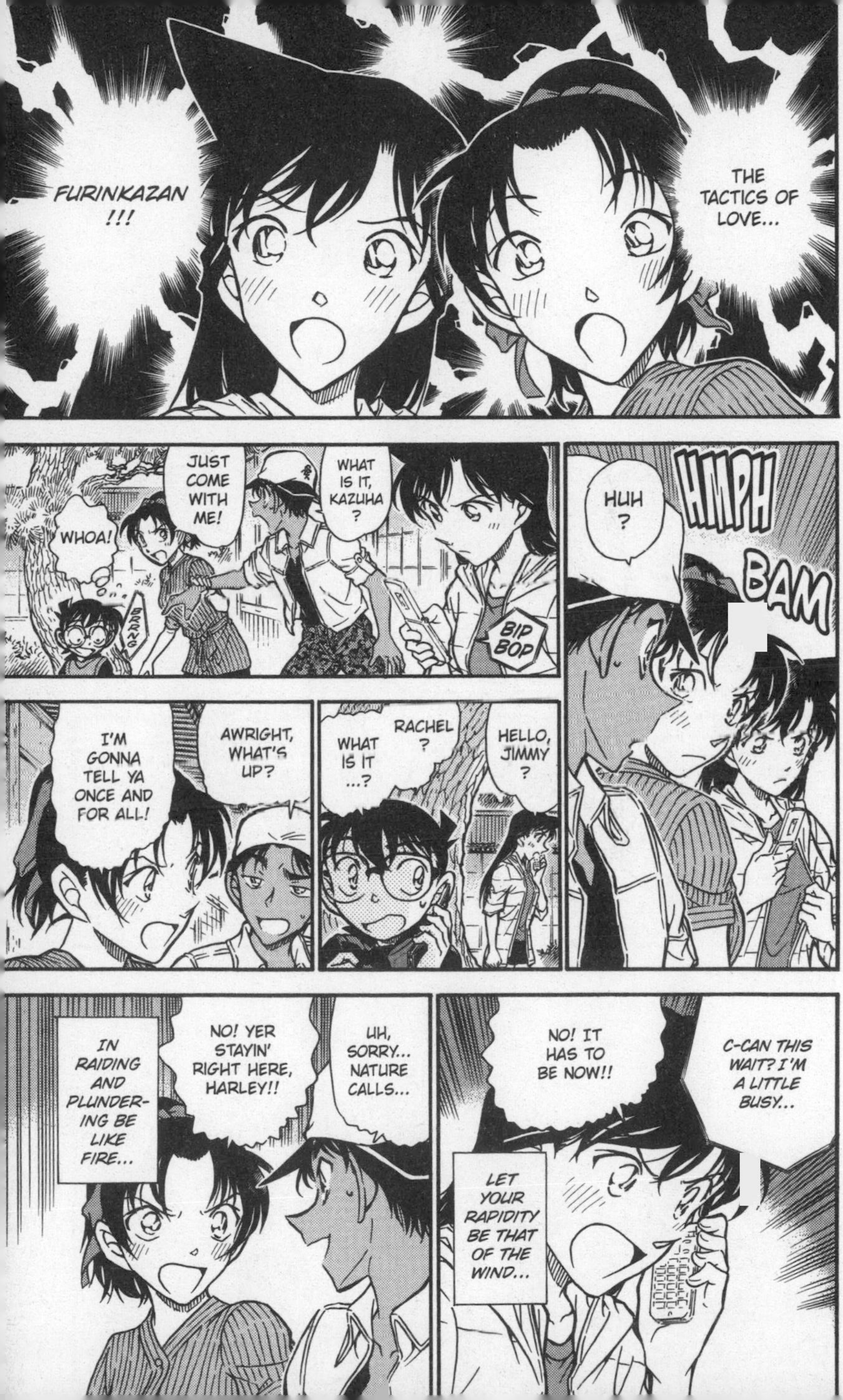
THE TACTICS OF LOVE...
FURINKAZAN !!!
HUH?
HMPH
BAM
BIP BOP
WHAT IS IT, KAZUHA?
JUST COME WITH ME!
WHOA!
BRRNG
HELLO, JIMMY?
RACHEL?
WHAT IS IT ...?
AWRIGHT, WHAT'S UP?
I'M GONNA TELL YA ONCE AND FOR ALL!
C-CAN THIS WAIT? I'M A LITTLE BUSY...
NO! IT HAS TO BE NOW!!
LET YOUR RAPIDITY BE THAT OF THE WIND...
UH, SORRY... NATURE CALLS...
NO! YER STAYIN' RIGHT HERE, HARLEY!!
IN RAIDING AND PLUNDER-ING BE LIKE FIRE...

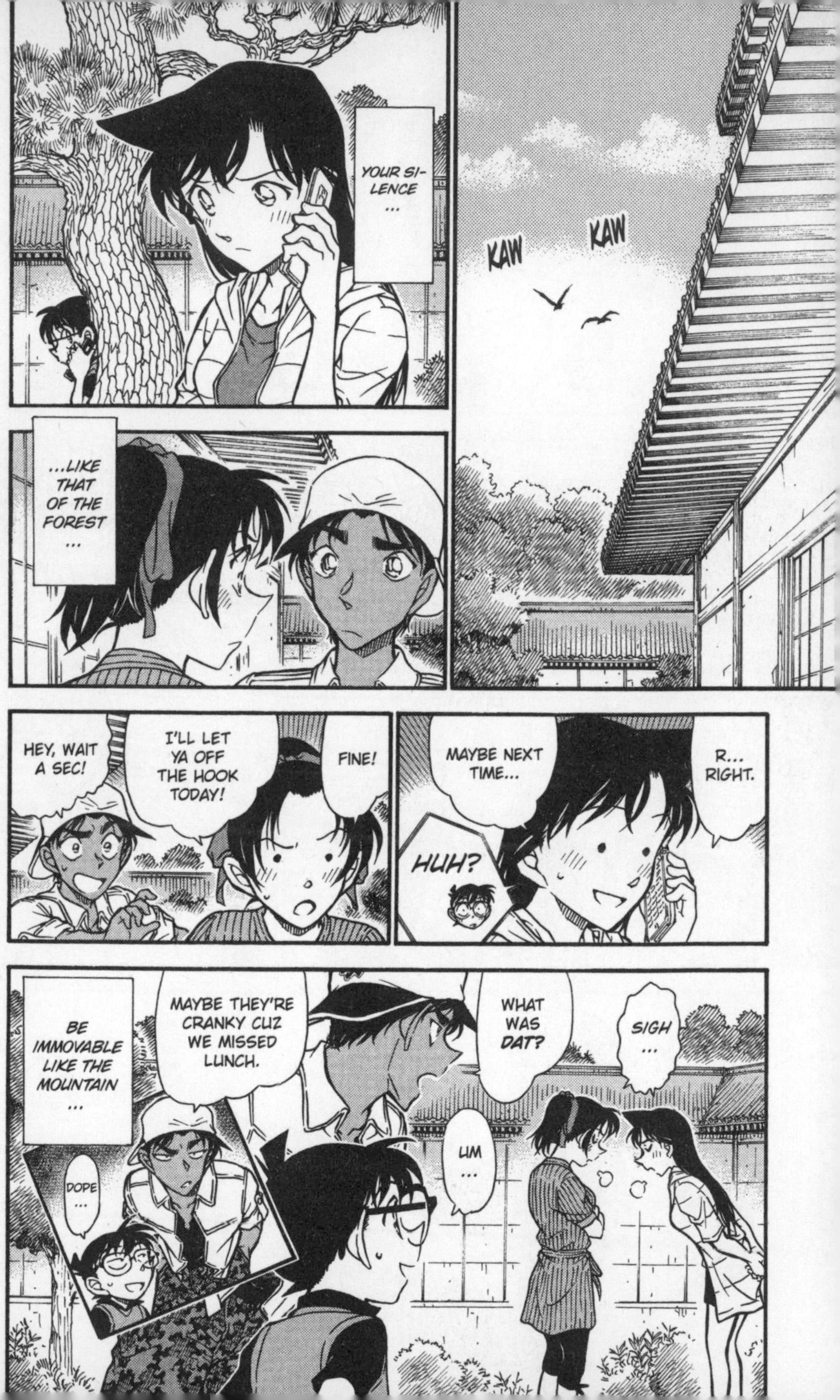
KAW
KAW
YOUR SI-LENCE...
...LIKE THAT OF THE FOREST...
R... RIGHT.
MAYBE NEXT TIME...
HUH?
FINE!
I'LL LET YA OFF THE HOOK TODAY!
HEY, WAIT A SEC!
SIGH...
WHAT WAS DAT?
MAYBE THEY'RE CRANKY CUZ WE MISSED LUNCH.
BE IMMOVABLE LIKE THE MOUNTAIN...
UM...
DOPE...

FILE 11: EISUKE ACCUSED

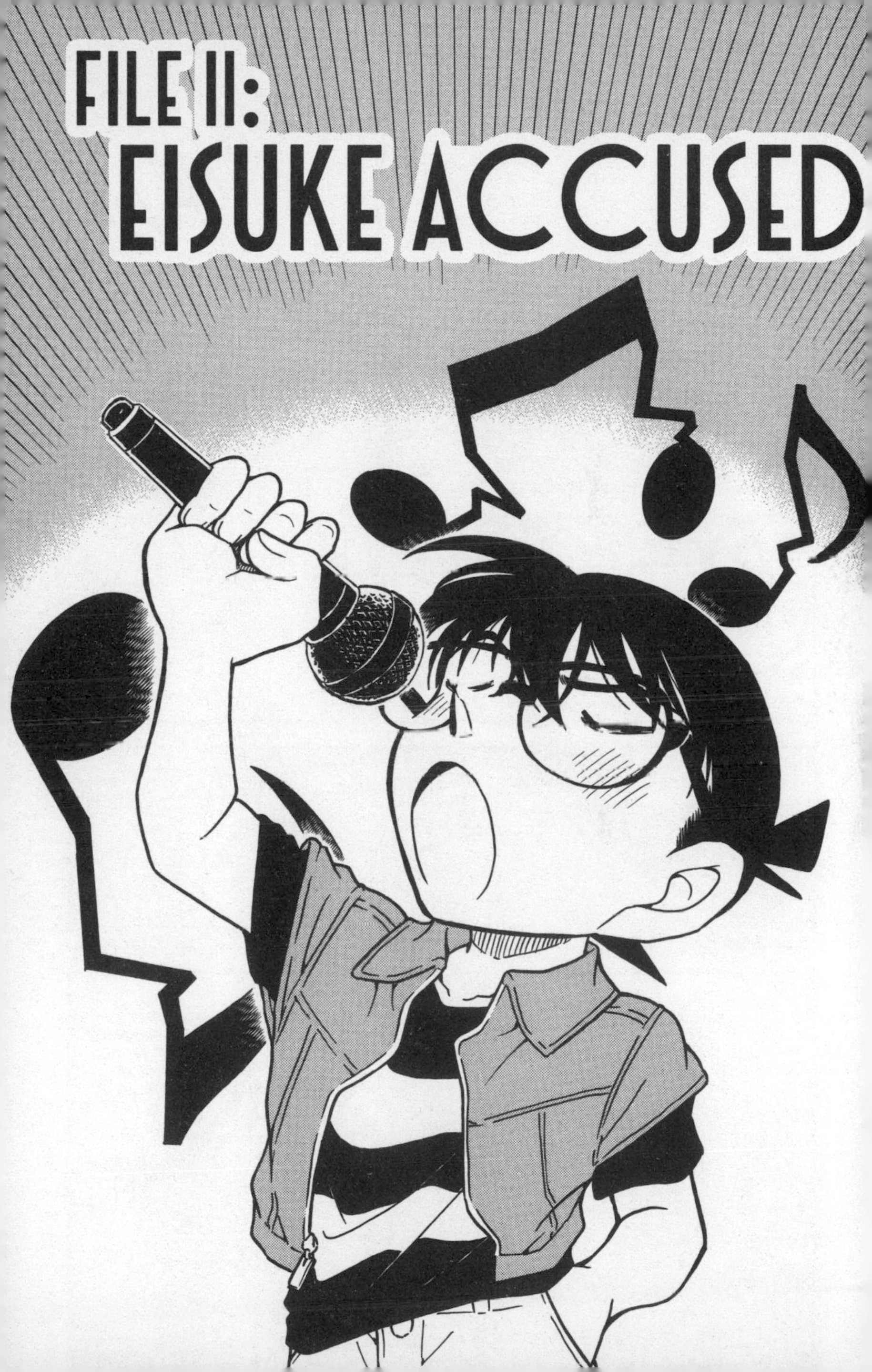

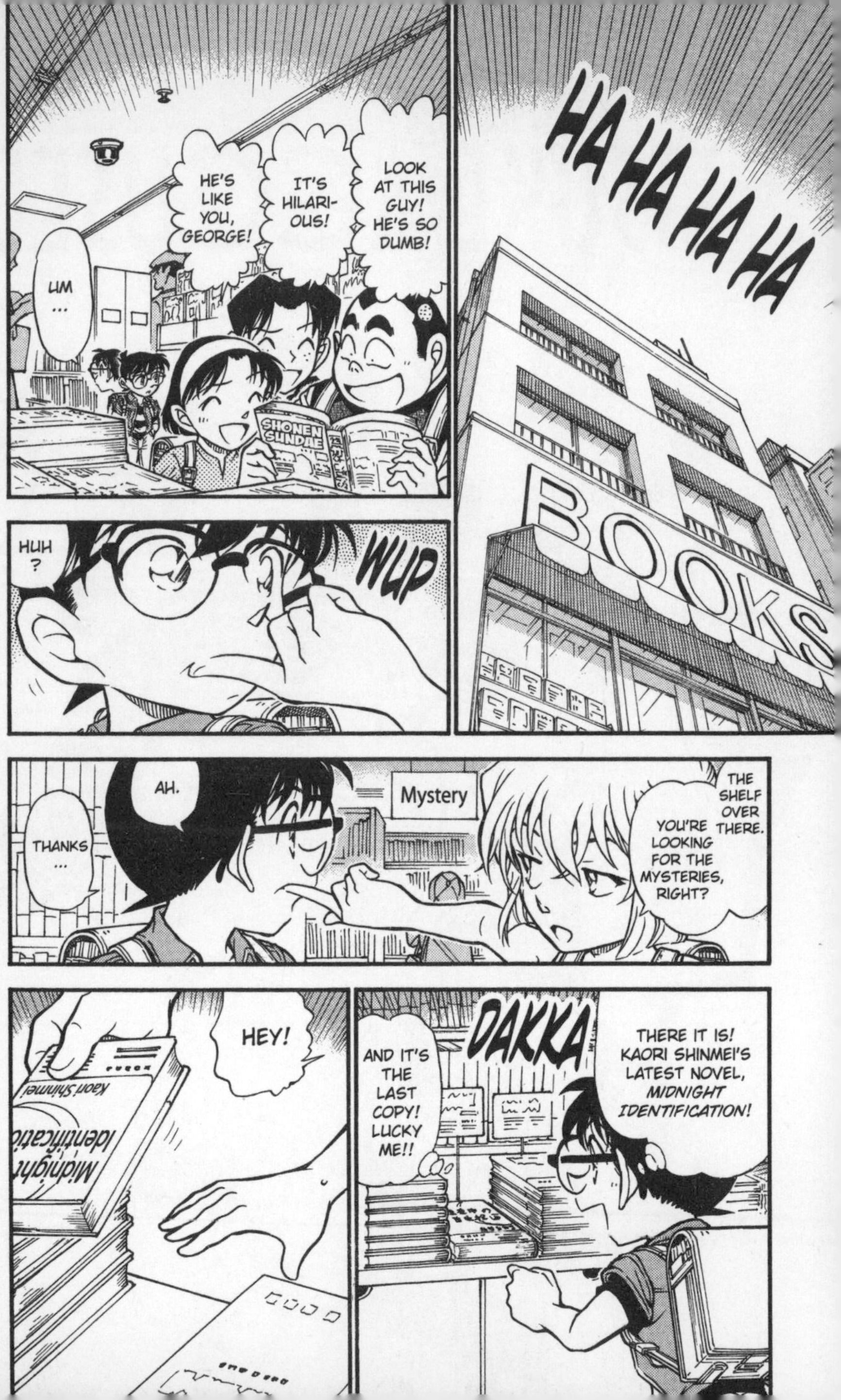
HA HA HA HA HA
BOOKS
LOOK AT THIS GUY! HE'S SO DUMB!
IT'S HILARI-OUS!
HE'S LIKE YOU, GEORGE!
SHONEN SUNDAE
UM ...
WUP
HUH ?
THE SHELF OVER THERE.
YOU'RE LOOKING FOR THE MYSTERIES, RIGHT?
Mystery
AH.
THANKS ...
THERE IT IS! KAORI SHINMEI'S LATEST NOVEL, *MIDNIGHT IDENTIFICATION*!
DAKKA
AND IT'S THE LAST COPY! LUCKY ME!!
HEY!
Kaori Shinmei

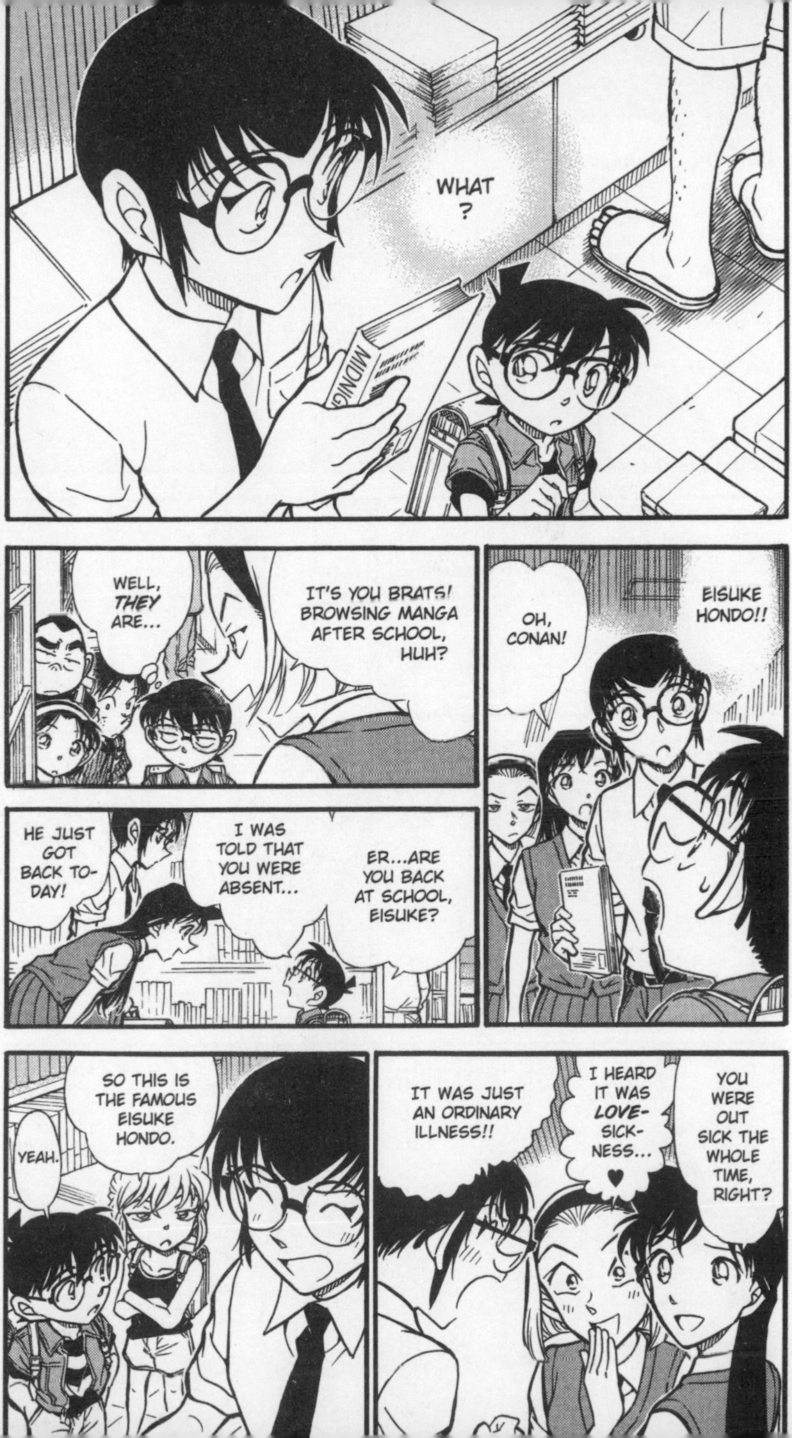
WHAT ?
EISUKE HONDO!!
OH, CONAN!
IT'S YOU BRATS! BROWSING MANGA AFTER SCHOOL, HUH?
WELL, THEY ARE...
ER...ARE YOU BACK AT SCHOOL, EISUKE?
I WAS TOLD THAT YOU WERE ABSENT...
HE JUST GOT BACK TO-DAY!
YOU WERE OUT SICK THE WHOLE TIME, RIGHT?
I HEARD IT WAS LOVE-SICKNESS... ♥
IT WAS JUST AN ORDINARY ILLNESS!!
SO THIS IS THE FAMOUS EISUKE HONDO.
YEAH.

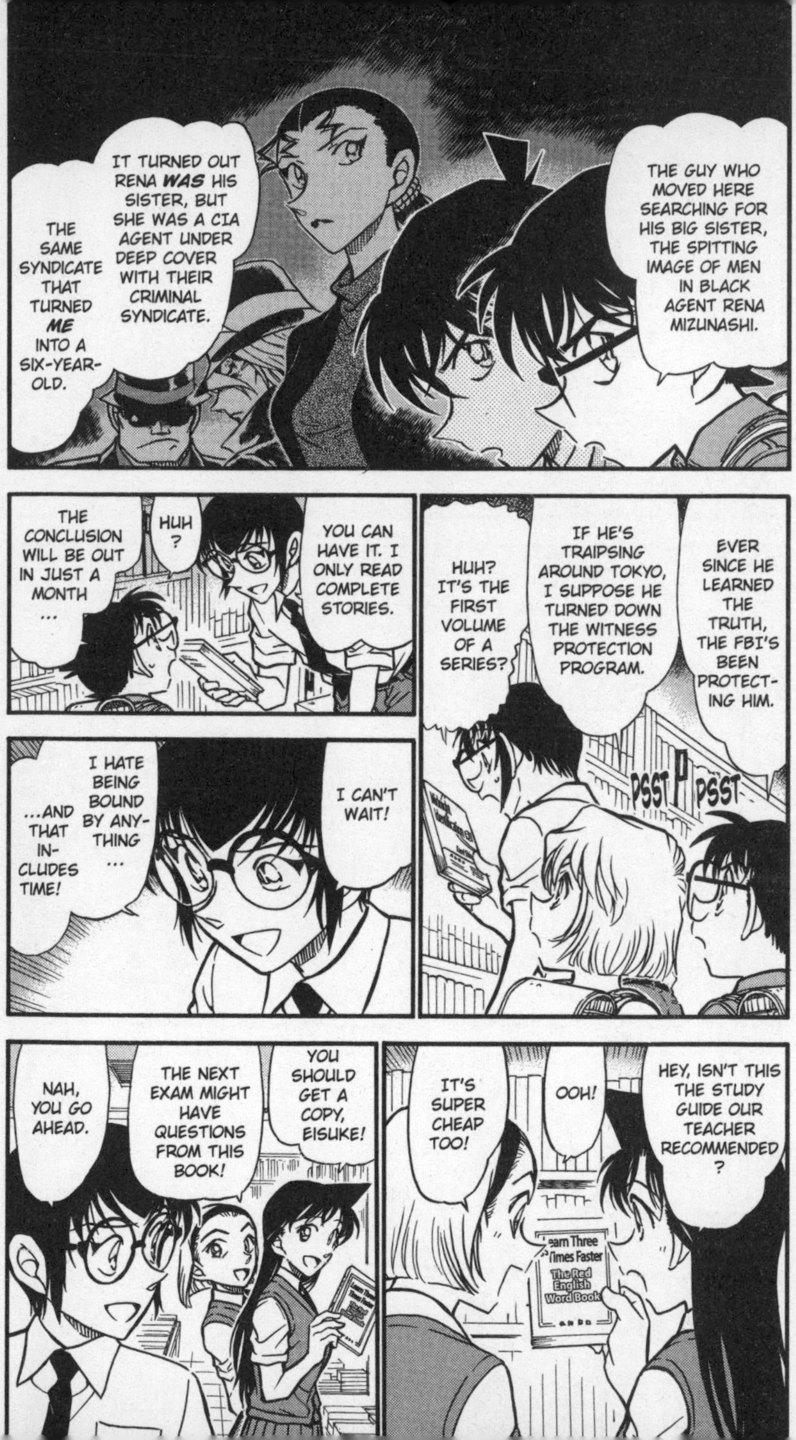
THE GUY WHO MOVED HERE SEARCHING FOR HIS BIG SISTER, THE SPITTING IMAGE OF MEN IN BLACK AGENT RENA MIZUNASHI.
IT TURNED OUT RENA ***WAS*** HIS SISTER, BUT SHE WAS A CIA AGENT UNDER DEEP COVER WITH THEIR CRIMINAL SYNDICATE.
THE SAME SYNDICATE THAT TURNED ***ME*** INTO A SIX-YEAR-OLD.
EVER SINCE HE LEARNED THE TRUTH, THE FBI'S BEEN PROTECTING HIM.
IF HE'S TRAIPSING AROUND TOKYO, I SUPPOSE HE TURNED DOWN THE WITNESS PROTECTION PROGRAM.
HUH? IT'S THE FIRST VOLUME OF A SERIES?
PSST P PSST
YOU CAN HAVE IT. I ONLY READ COMPLETE STORIES.
HUH?
THE CONCLUSION WILL BE OUT IN JUST A MONTH...
I CAN'T WAIT!
I HATE BEING BOUND BY ANYTHING...
...AND THAT INCLUDES TIME!
HEY, ISN'T THIS THE STUDY GUIDE OUR TEACHER RECOMMENDED?
OOH!
IT'S SUPER CHEAP TOO!
Learn Three Times Faster
The Red English Word Book
YOU SHOULD GET A COPY, EISUKE!
THE NEXT EXAM MIGHT HAVE QUESTIONS FROM THIS BOOK!
NAH, YOU GO AHEAD.

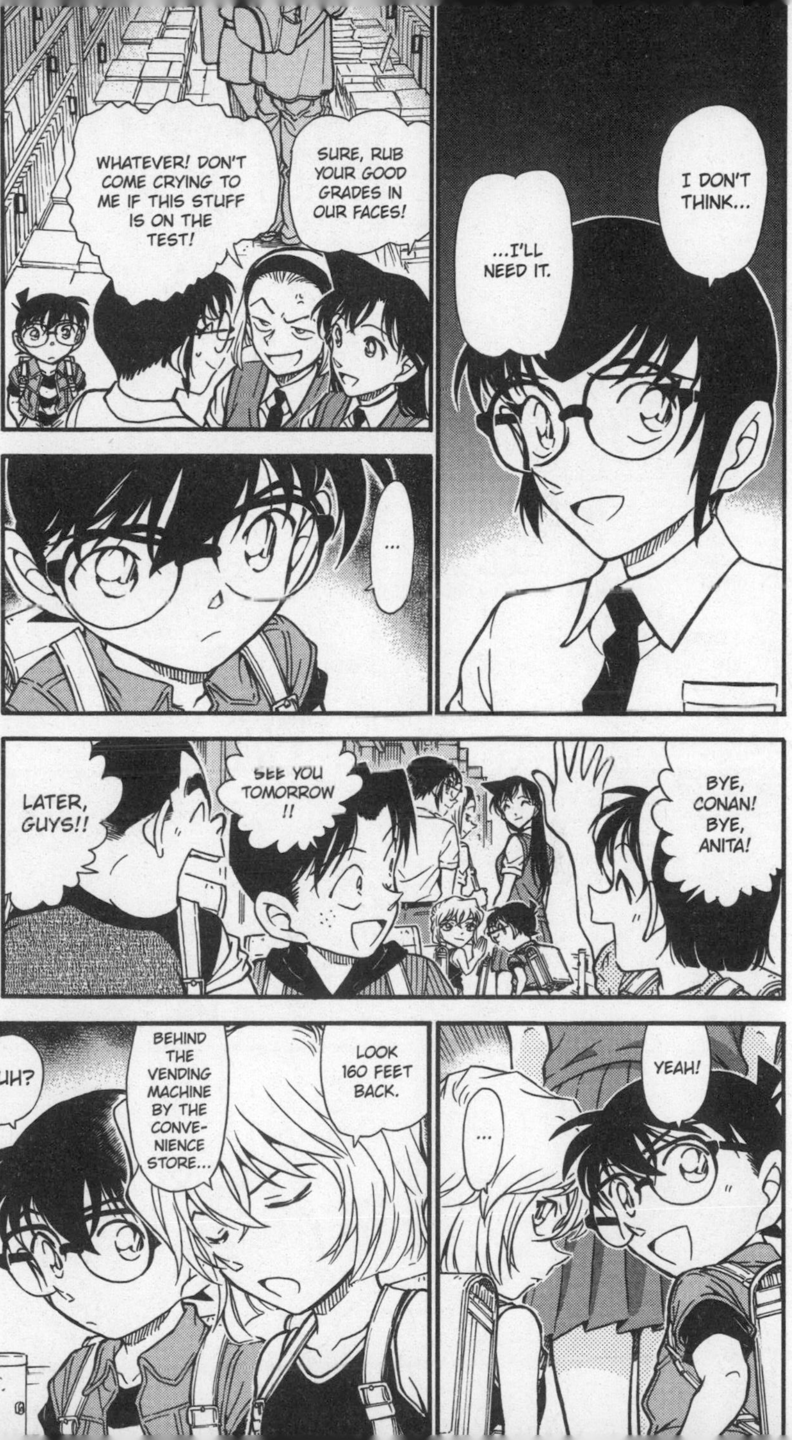
I DON'T THINK...
...I'LL NEED IT.
SURE, RUB YOUR GOOD GRADES IN OUR FACES!
WHATEVER! DON'T COME CRYING TO ME IF THIS STUFF IS ON THE TEST!
...
BYE, CONAN! BYE, ANITA!
SEE YOU TOMORROW !!
LATER, GUYS!!
YEAH!
...
LOOK 160 FEET BACK.
BEHIND THE VENDING MACHINE BY THE CONVE- NIENCE STORE...
HUH?

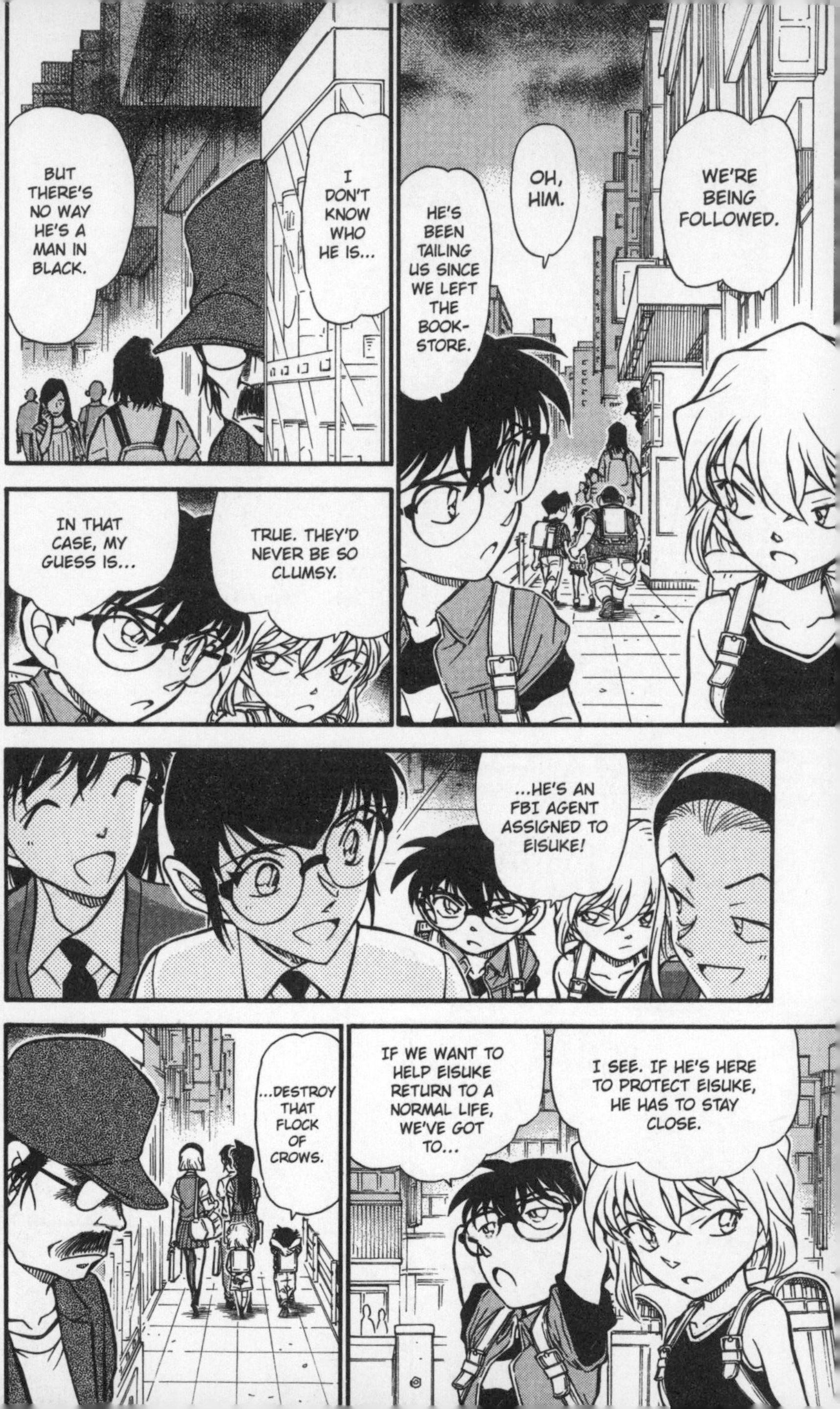
WE'RE BEING FOLLOWED.
OH, HIM.
HE'S BEEN TAILING US SINCE WE LEFT THE BOOK-STORE.
I DON'T KNOW WHO HE IS...
BUT THERE'S NO WAY HE'S A MAN IN BLACK.
TRUE. THEY'D NEVER BE SO CLUMSY.
IN THAT CASE, MY GUESS IS...
...HE'S AN FBI AGENT ASSIGNED TO EISUKE!
I SEE. IF HE'S HERE TO PROTECT EISUKE, HE HAS TO STAY CLOSE.
IF WE WANT TO HELP EISUKE RETURN TO A NORMAL LIFE, WE'VE GOT TO...
...DESTROY THAT FLOCK OF CROWS.

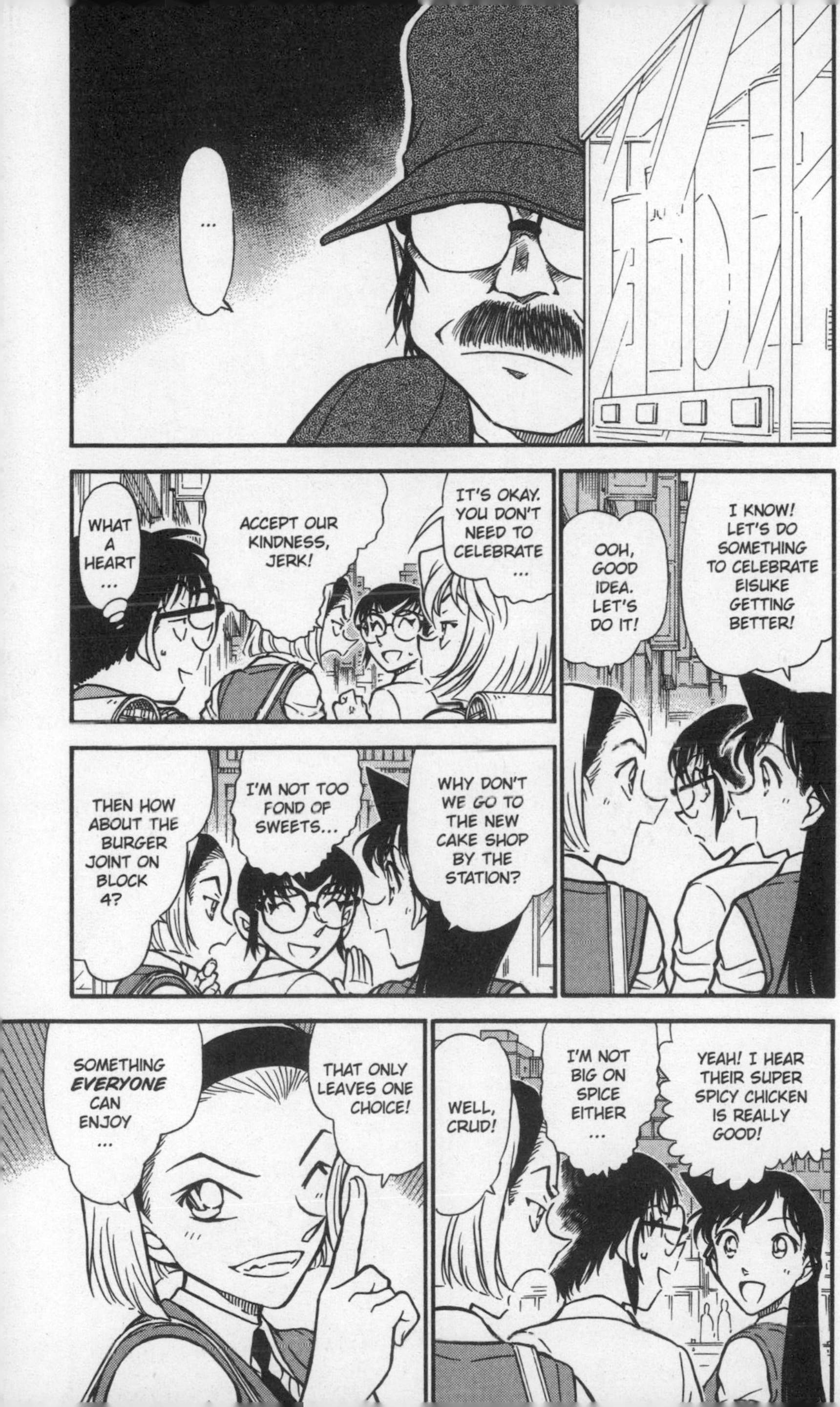
...
I KNOW! LET'S DO SOMETHING TO CELEBRATE EISUKE GETTING BETTER!
OOH, GOOD IDEA. LET'S DO IT!
IT'S OKAY. YOU DON'T NEED TO CELEBRATE...
ACCEPT OUR KINDNESS, JERK!
WHAT A HEART...
WHY DON'T WE GO TO THE NEW CAKE SHOP BY THE STATION?
I'M NOT TOO FOND OF SWEETS...
THEN HOW ABOUT THE BURGER JOINT ON BLOCK 4?
YEAH! I HEAR THEIR SUPER SPICY CHICKEN IS REALLY GOOD!
I'M NOT BIG ON SPICE EITHER...
WELL, CRUD!
THAT ONLY LEAVES ONE CHOICE!
SOMETHING *EVERYONE* CAN ENJOY...

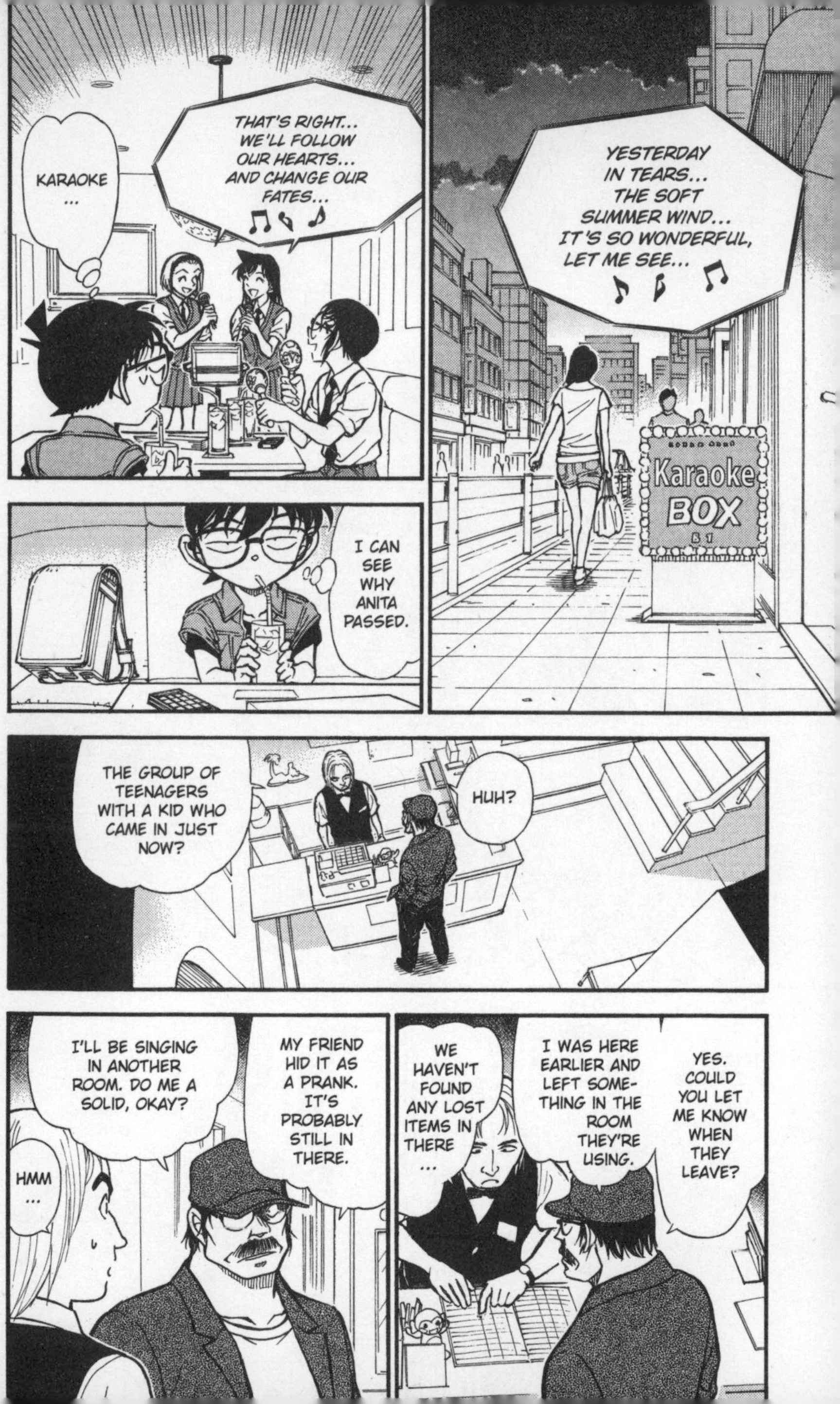
YESTERDAY IN TEARS... THE SOFT SUMMER WIND... IT'S SO WONDERFUL, LET ME SEE...
Karaoke BOX
THAT'S RIGHT... WE'LL FOLLOW OUR HEARTS... AND CHANGE OUR FATES...
KARAOKE ...
I CAN SEE WHY ANITA PASSED.
HUH?
THE GROUP OF TEENAGERS WITH A KID WHO CAME IN JUST NOW?
YES. COULD YOU LET ME KNOW WHEN THEY LEAVE?
I WAS HERE EARLIER AND LEFT SOME-THING IN THE ROOM THEY'RE USING.
WE HAVEN'T FOUND ANY LOST ITEMS IN THERE ...
MY FRIEND HID IT AS A PRANK. IT'S PROBABLY STILL IN THERE.
I'LL BE SINGING IN ANOTHER ROOM. DO ME A SOLID, OKAY?
HMM ...

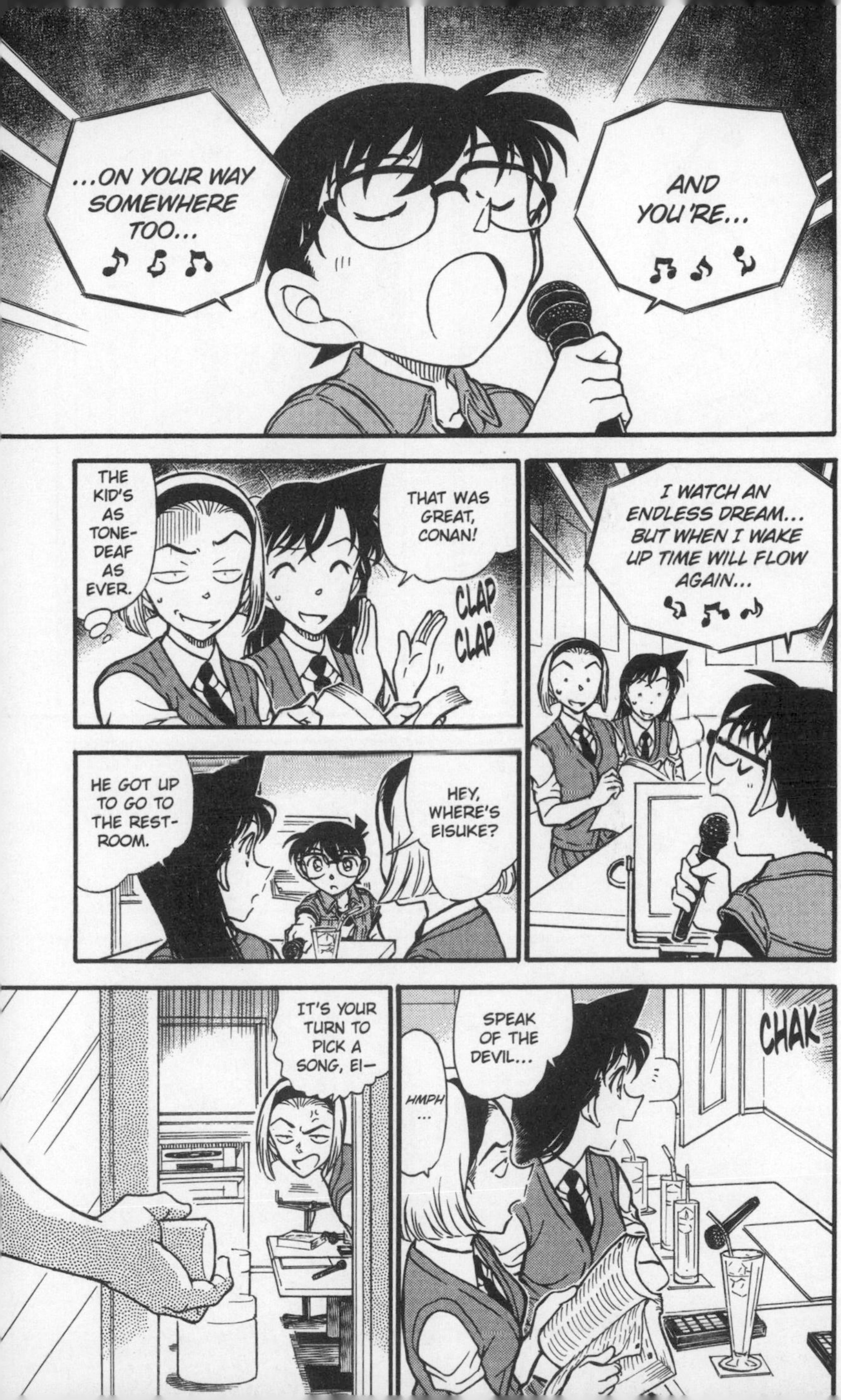
AND YOU'RE... ♫ ♪ ♪
...ON YOUR WAY SOMEWHERE TOO... ♪ ♫ ♫
I WATCH AN ENDLESS DREAM... BUT WHEN I WAKE UP TIME WILL FLOW AGAIN... ♪ ♫ ♪
THAT WAS GREAT, CONAN!
CLAP CLAP
THE KID'S AS TONE-DEAF AS EVER.
HEY, WHERE'S EISUKE?
HE GOT UP TO GO TO THE REST-ROOM.
CHAK
SPEAK OF THE DEVIL...
HMPH...
IT'S YOUR TURN TO PICK A SONG, EI—

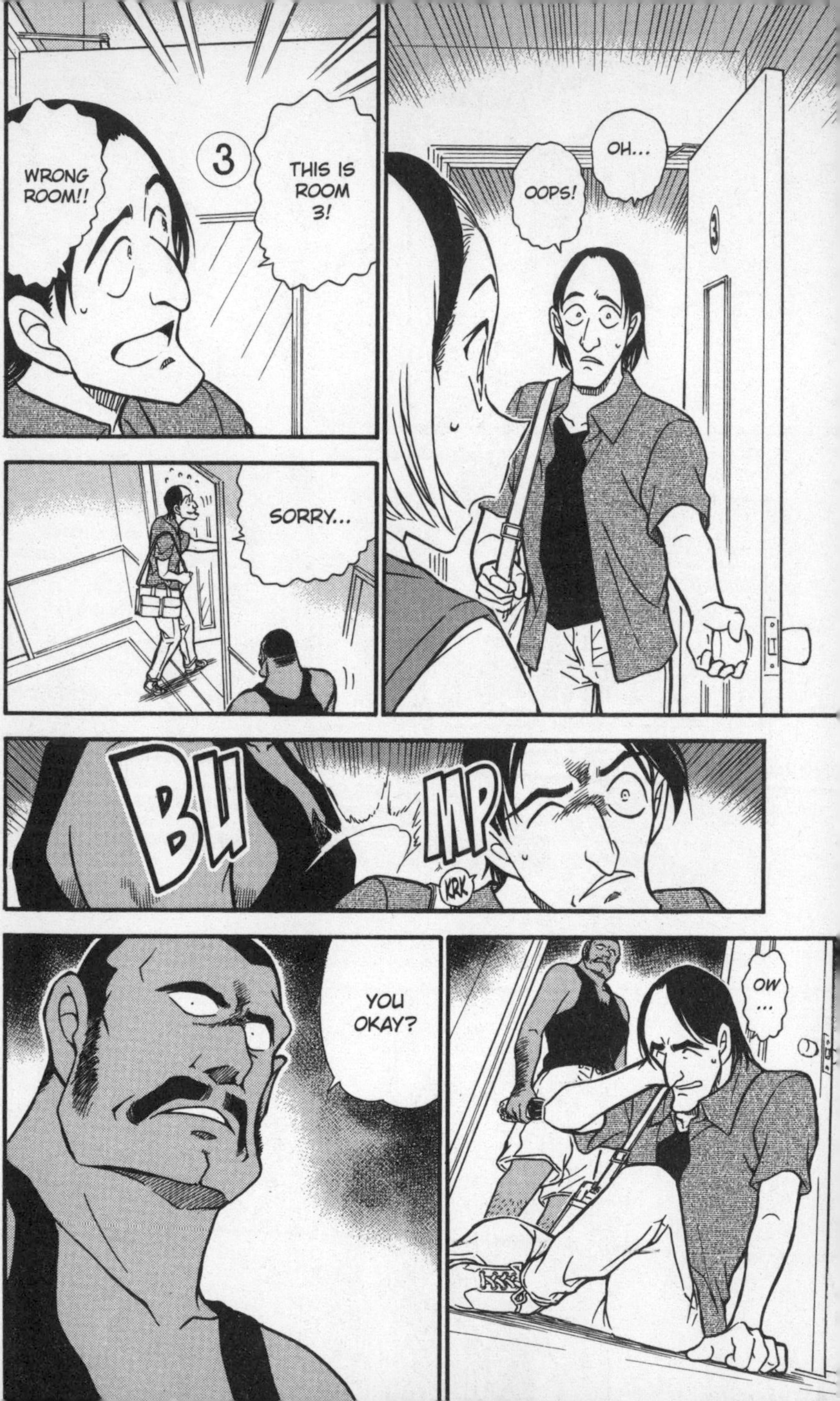
OH...
OOPS!
3
THIS IS ROOM 3!
WRONG ROOM!!
SORRY...
BUMP
KRK
OW ...
YOU OKAY?

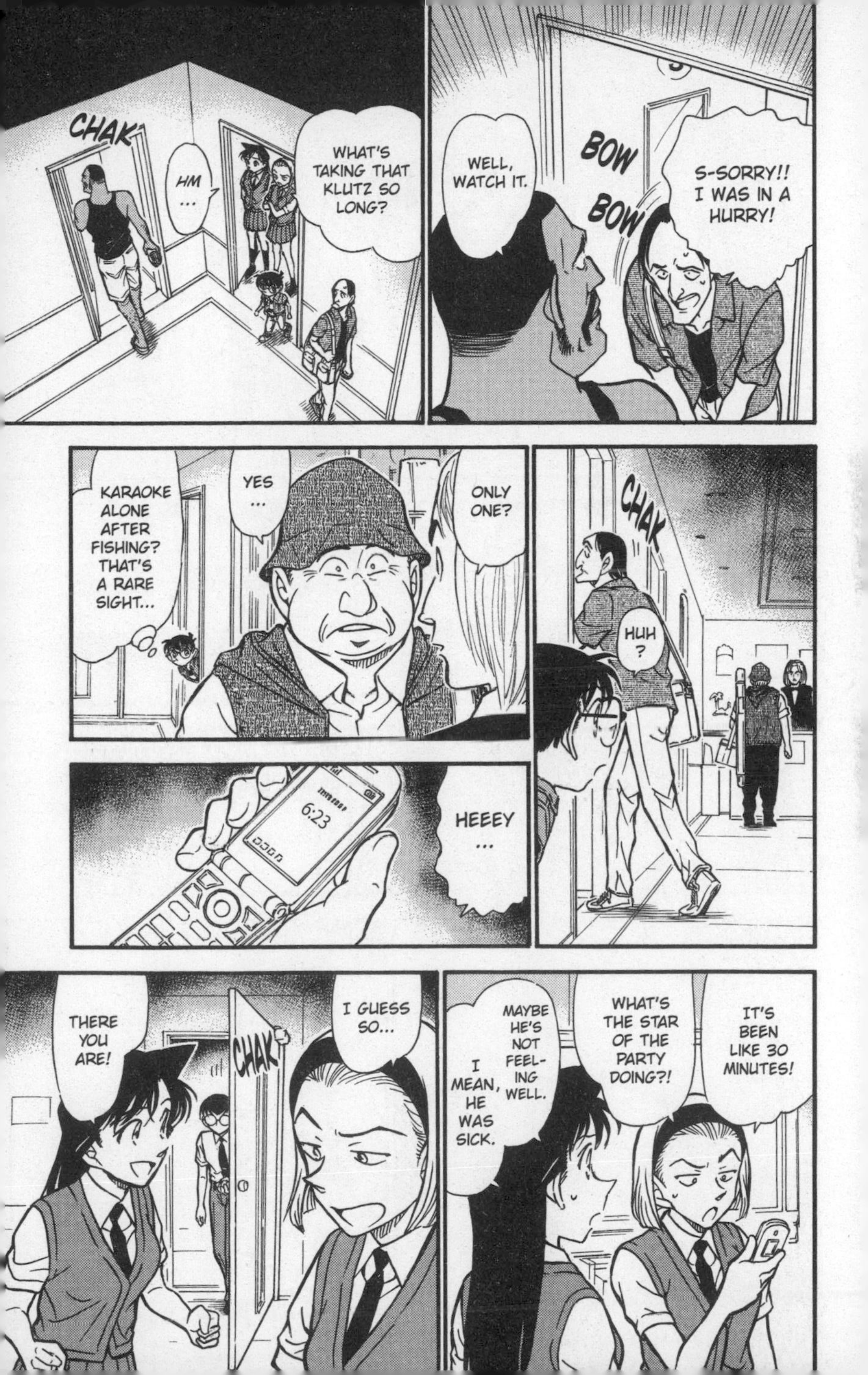
S-SORRY!! I WAS IN A HURRY!
BOW BOW
WELL, WATCH IT.
WHAT'S TAKING THAT KLUTZ SO LONG?
HM ...
CHAK
CHAK
HUH ?
ONLY ONE?
YES ...
KARAOKE ALONE AFTER FISHING? THAT'S A RARE SIGHT...
6:23
HEEEY ...
IT'S BEEN LIKE 30 MINUTES!
WHAT'S THE STAR OF THE PARTY DOING?!
MAYBE HE'S NOT FEEL-ING WELL.
I MEAN, HE WAS SICK.
I GUESS SO...
CHAK
THERE YOU ARE!

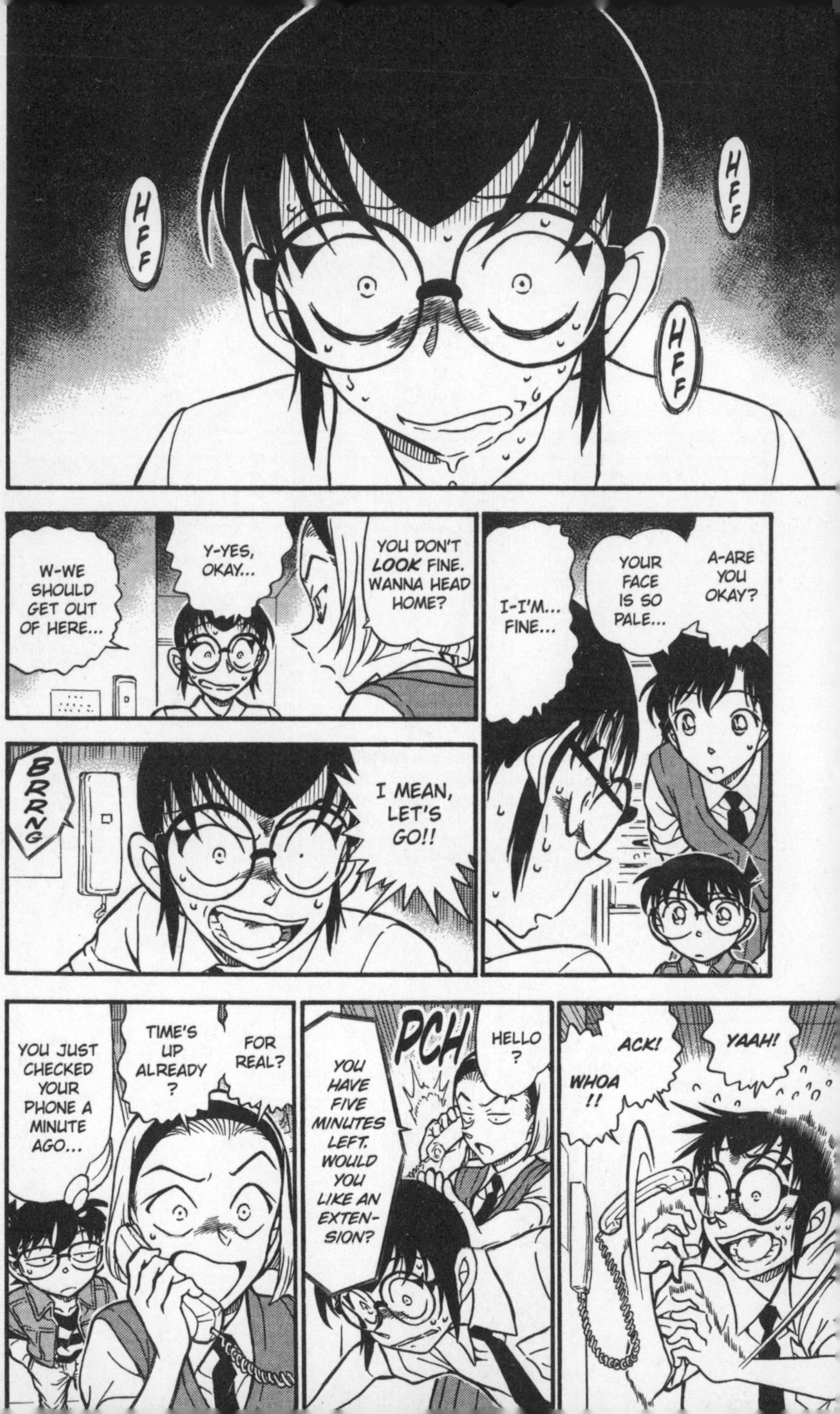
HFF
HFF
HFF
A-ARE YOU OKAY?
YOUR FACE IS SO PALE...
I-I'M... FINE...
YOU DON'T LOOK FINE. WANNA HEAD HOME?
Y-YES, OKAY...
W-WE SHOULD GET OUT OF HERE...
I MEAN, LET'S GO!!
BRRNG
YAAH!
ACK!
WHOA!!
HELLO?
PCH
YOU HAVE FIVE MINUTES LEFT. WOULD YOU LIKE AN EXTENSION?
FOR REAL?
TIME'S UP ALREADY?
YOU JUST CHECKED YOUR PHONE A MINUTE AGO...

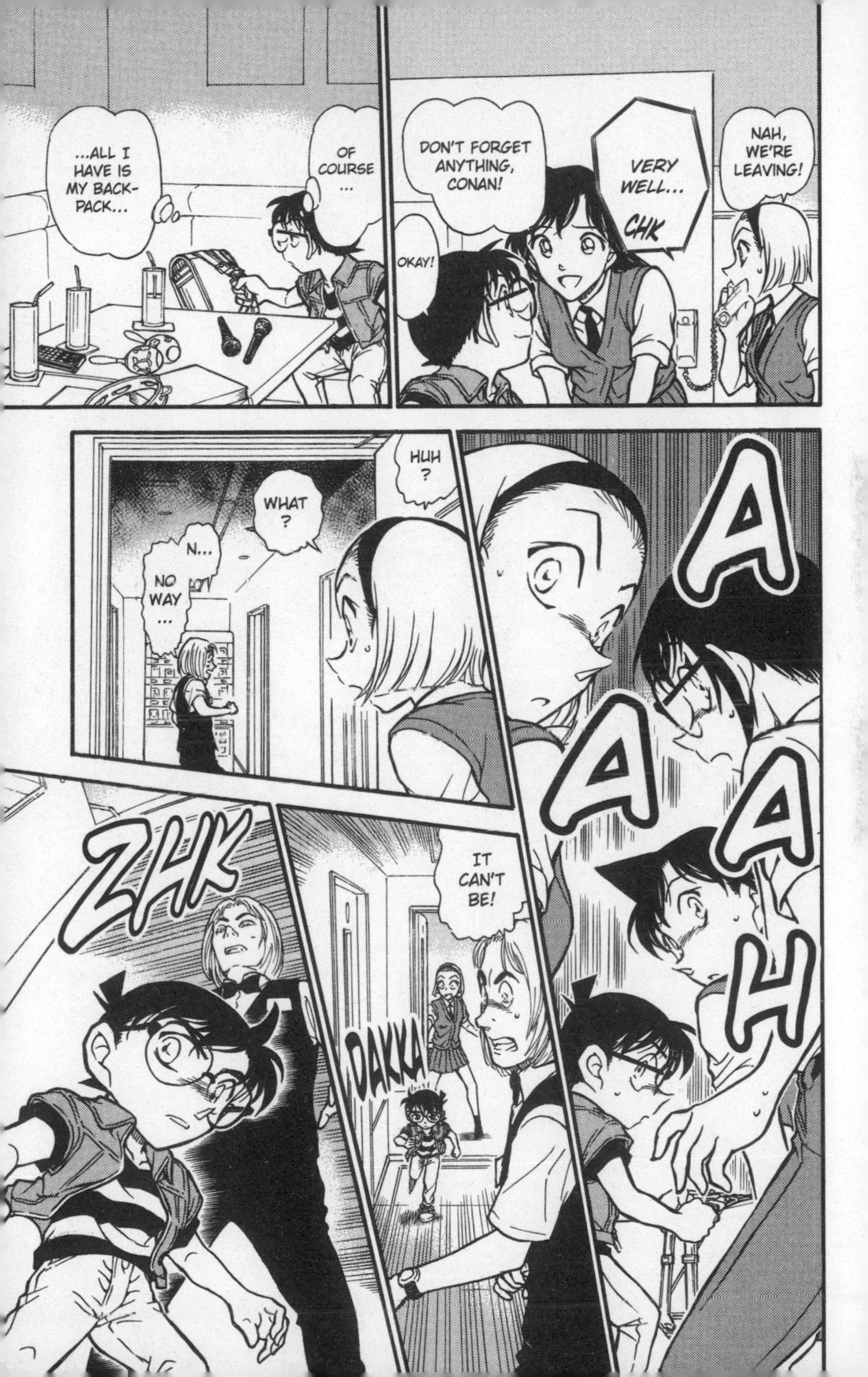
NAH, WE'RE LEAVING!
VERY WELL...
CHK
DON'T FORGET ANYTHING, CONAN!
OKAY!
OF COURSE ...
...ALL I HAVE IS MY BACK-PACK...
AAAH
HUH ?
WHAT ?
N...
NO WAY ...
IT CAN'T BE!
DAKKA
ZHK

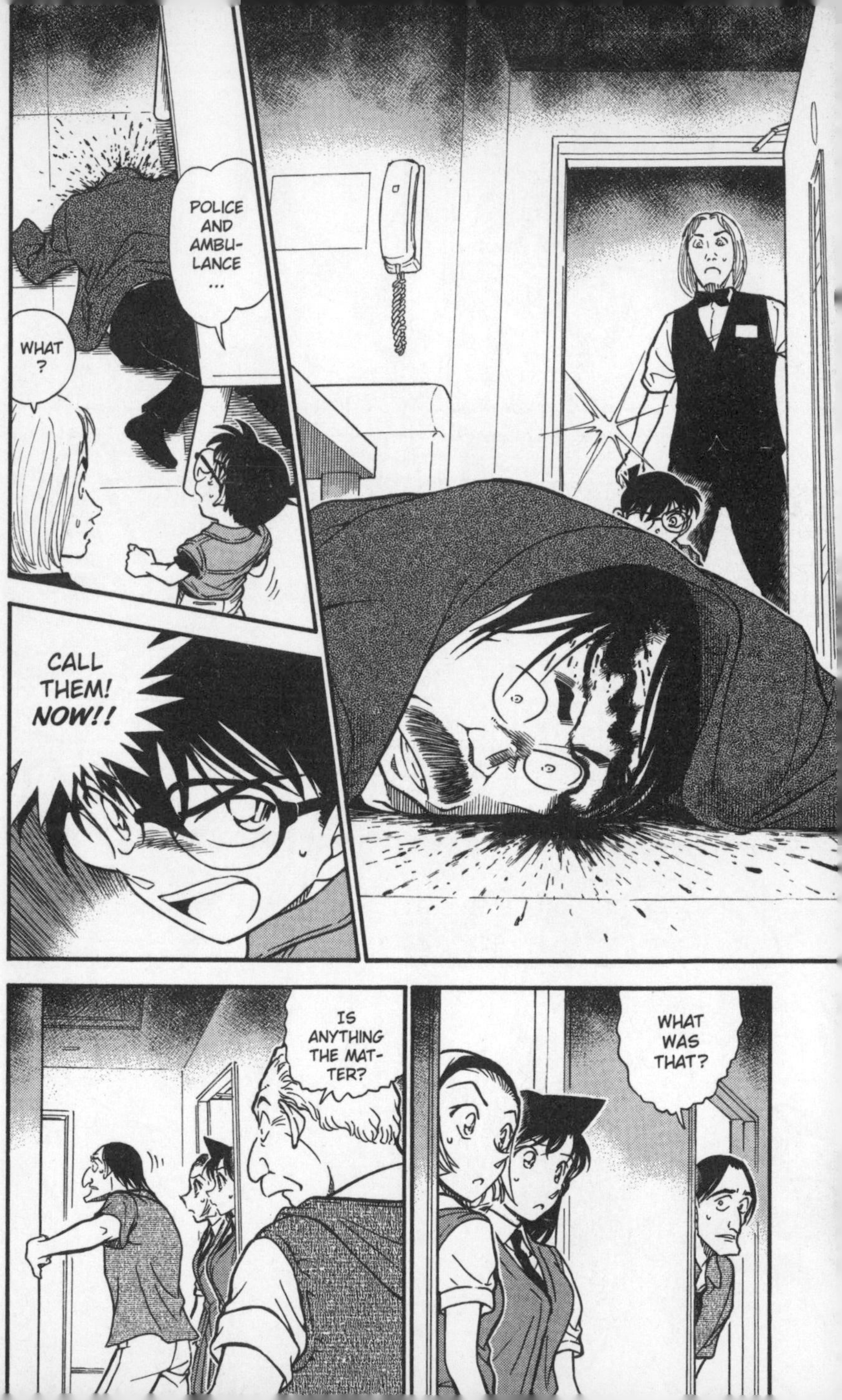
POLICE AND AMBULANCE ...
WHAT?
CALL THEM! *NOW!!*
WHAT WAS THAT?
IS ANYTHING THE MATTER?

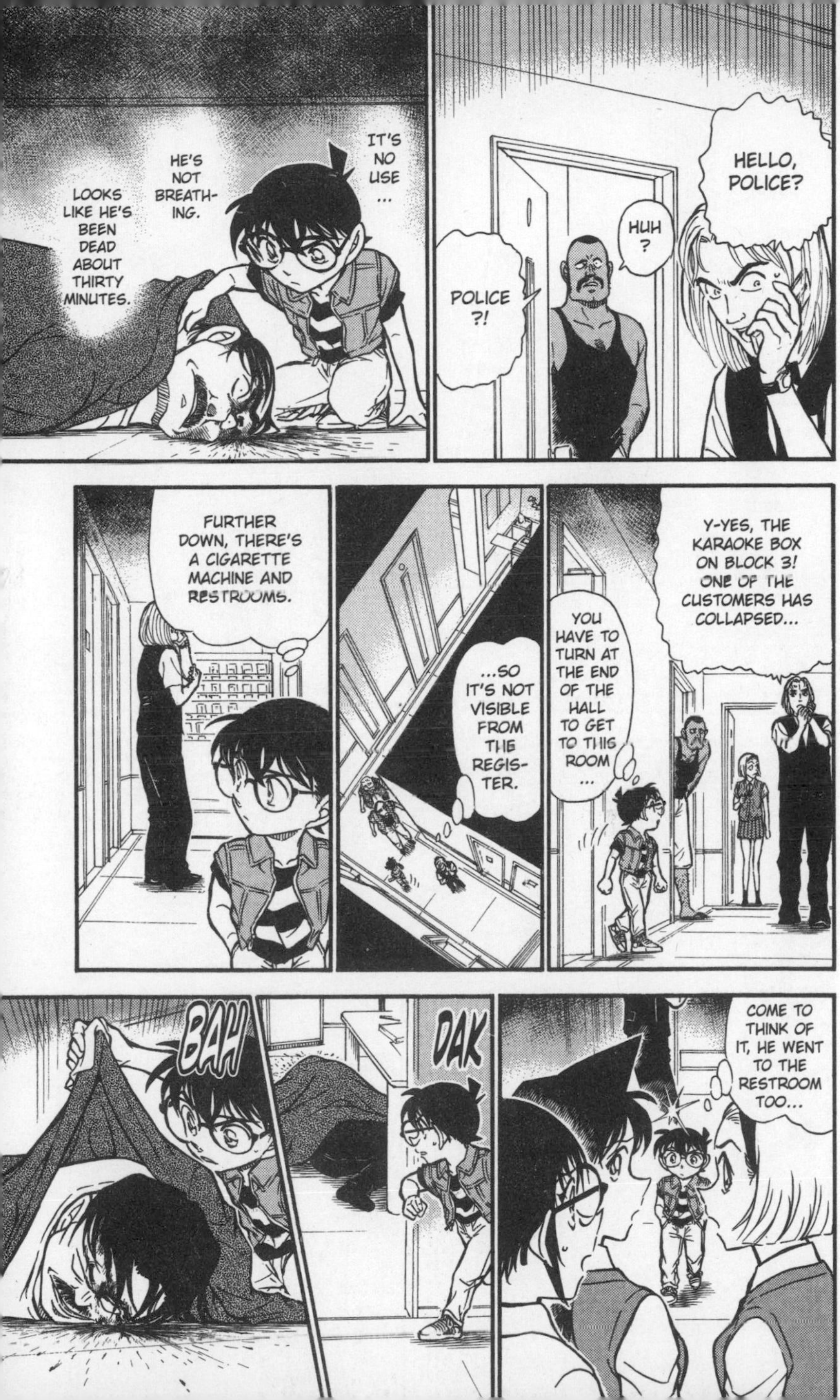
HELLO, POLICE?
HUH ?
POLICE ?!
IT'S NO USE ...
HE'S NOT BREATHING.
LOOKS LIKE HE'S BEEN DEAD ABOUT THIRTY MINUTES.
Y-YES, THE KARAOKE BOX ON BLOCK 3! ONE OF THE CUSTOMERS HAS COLLAPSED...
YOU HAVE TO TURN AT THE END OF THE HALL TO GET TO THIS ROOM ...
...SO IT'S NOT VISIBLE FROM THE REGISTER.
FURTHER DOWN, THERE'S A CIGARETTE MACHINE AND RESTROOMS.
COME TO THINK OF IT, HE WENT TO THE RESTROOM TOO...
DAK
BAH

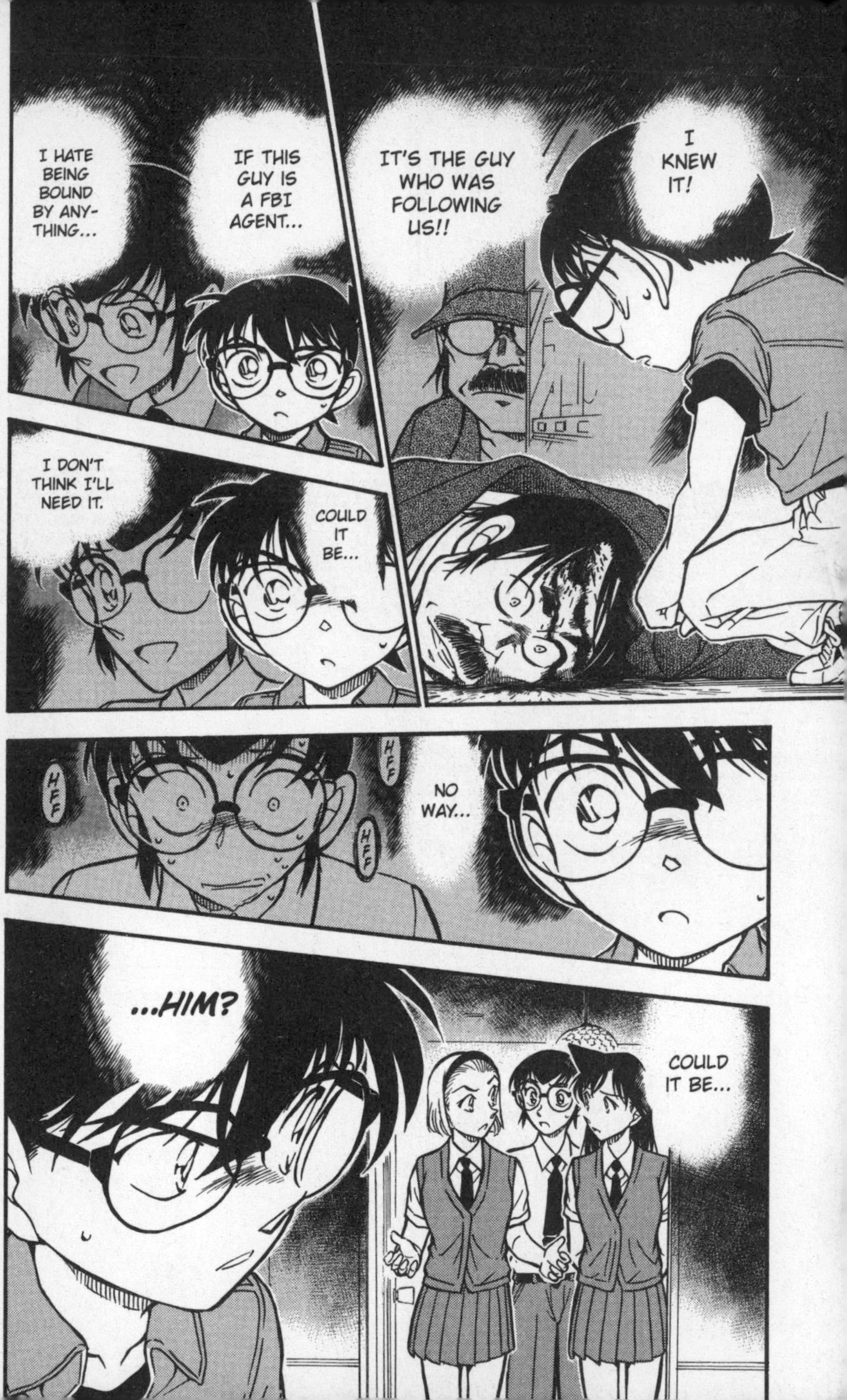
I KNEW IT!
IT'S THE GUY WHO WAS FOLLOWING US!!
IF THIS GUY IS A FBI AGENT...
I HATE BEING BOUND BY ANY-THING...
COULD IT BE...
I DON'T THINK I'LL NEED IT.
NO WAY...
HFF
HFF
HFF
COULD IT BE...
...HIM?

Hello, Aoyama here.

Another live-action *Case Closed* TV drama* is in the works for this winter! And it's going to be a battle against the Men in Black! I put all my effort into brainstorming ideas and we came up with a really fascinating story. Heh. I'd like to thank Watanabe, the screenwriter. ♪

*Originally aired in 2007.

SCYA

Gosho Aoyama's Mystery Library

59

M O M

She may not have a detective office, but she's a sleuth in her own home. She's the detective known simply as "Mom," created by James Yaffe! Every Friday, her son David from the homicide department visits her house in the Bronx, but not just to eat her home cooking. She's capable of solving the most baffling cases simply by hearing the details! According to her, sniffing out a murderer is child's play. She uses her common sense and sharp insight, traits she developed while dealing with the sly local shopkeepers.

I hear the Bronx is a dangerous place, but I'd willingly go there to eat her cooking too. And, of course, to pick up ideas for *Case Closed*...heh.

I recommend *Mom Knows Best*.